Whither College Sports

Whither College Sports

Amateurism, Athlete Safety, and Academic Integrity

Andrew Zimbalist

RUTGERS UNIVERSITY PRESS
NEW BRUNSWICK, CAMDEN, AND NEWARK, NEW JERSEY, AND LONDON

Library of Congress Cataloging-in-Publication Data
Names: Zimbalist, Andrew S., author.
Title: Whither college sports : amateurism, athlete safety, and academic integrity / Andrew Zimbalist.
Description: New Brunswick : Rutgers University Press, [2021] | Includes bibliographical references and index.
Identifiers: LCCN 2021009983 | ISBN 9781978828131 (paperback) | ISBN 9781978828148 (cloth) | ISBN 9781978828155 (epub) | ISBN 9781978828162 (pdf)
Subjects: LCSH: College sports—Corrupt practices—United States. | College sports—Moral and ethical aspects—United States. | College sports—United States—Management. | College athletes—United States. | College sports—Economic aspects—United States.
Classification: LCC GV351 .Z57 2021 | DDC 796.04/30973—dc23
LC record available at https://lccn.loc.gov/2021009983

A British Cataloging-in-Publication record for this book is available from the British Library.

This collection copyright © 2021 by Rutgers, The State University of New Jersey
For sources to previously published material please see first page of each essay.
All rights reserved
No part of this book may be reproduced or utilized in any form or by any means, electronic or mechanical, or by any information storage and retrieval system, without written permission from the publisher. Please contact Rutgers University Press, 106 Somerset Street, New Brunswick, NJ 08901. The only exception to this prohibition is "fair use" as defined by U.S. copyright law.

∞ The paper used in this publication meets the requirements of the American National Standard for Information Sciences—Permanence of Paper for Printed Library Materials, ANSI Z39.48-1992.

www.rutgersuniversitypress.org

Manufactured in the United States of America

Contents

Introduction 1

PART I
Academic Papers

1 Taxation of College Sports: Policies and Controversies 25
Andrew Zimbalist

2 Reforming College Sports: The Case for a Limited and Conditional Antitrust Exemption 39
Jayma Meyer and Andrew Zimbalist

3 A Win-Win: College Athletes Get Paid for Their Names, Images, and Likenesses and Colleges Maintain the Primacy of Academics 93
Jayma Meyer and Andrew Zimbalist

4 The Impact of College Athletic Success on Donations and Applicant Quality 154
Benjamin Baumer and Andrew Zimbalist

PART II
Position Papers by The Drake Group

5 The "Big Five" Power Grab: The Real Threat to College Sports 191
Brian Porto, Gerald Gurney, Donna Lopiano, David Ridpath, Allen Sack, Mary Willingham, and Andrew Zimbalist

6 Why the NCAA Academic Progress Rate (APR) and the Graduation Success Rate (GSR) Should Be Abandoned and Replaced with More Effective Academic Metrics 195
Gerald Gurney, Donna Lopiano, Mary Willingham, Jayma Meyer, Brian Porto, David Ridpath, Allen Sack, and Andrew Zimbalist

7 Fixing the Dysfunctional NCAA Enforcement System 228
Brian Porto, Gerald Gurney, Donna Lopiano, David Ridpath, Allen Sack, Mary Willingham, and Andrew Zimbalist

8 College Athlete Health and Protection from Physical and Psychological Harm 239
Donna Lopiano, Janet Blade, Gerald Gurney, Sheila Hudson, Brian Porto, Allen Sack, David Ridpath and Andrew Zimbalist

9 Compensation of College Athletes Including Revenues Earned from Commercial Use of Their Names, Images, and Likenesses and Outside Employment 281
Brian Porto, Gerald Gurney, Donna Lopiano, David Ridpath, Allen Sack, Julie Sommer, Mary Willingham, and Andrew Zimbalist

PART III
Op-Eds

10 Unionizing Is Proof That College Athletics Need to Be Reformed 307
Andrew Zimbalist

11 College Coaches' Salaries and Higher Education 309
Andrew Zimbalist

12 Time for a Presidential Panel to Investigate College Sports 312
Andrew Zimbalist

13 Paying College Athletes: Take Two 316
Andrew Zimbalist

14 Antitrust Exemption May Aid College Sports' Untenable Situation 321
Andrew Zimbalist

15 The NCAA's Women Problem 325
Andrew Zimbalist

16 Big-Time College Basketball in the Crosshairs 328
Andrew Zimbalist

17 In the End, Commission's Reform Suggestions Only Provide a Smokescreen of Legitimacy for the NCAA 332
Andrew Zimbalist

18 One-and-Done: Take Two 338
Andrew Zimbalist

19 How Financial Pressures Can Lead to Athletic Scandals 341
Andrew Zimbalist

20 Female Athletes Are Undervalued, in Both Money and Media Terms 345
Carrie N. Baker, Emma Seymour, and Andrew Zimbalist

21 The Collegiate Sports Model Is Broken: It Needs Help 348
Andrew Zimbalist

22 Sports Being on Hiatus Gives the NCAA an Opportunity to Rethink the Structure of College Sports 351
Andrew Zimbalist, Gerry Gurney, and Donna Lopiano

23 Has Higher Education Lost Its Mind? 355
Donna Lopiano and Andrew Zimbalist

24 Theater of the Absurd and the Immoral: College Football 2020 358
Donna Lopiano and Andrew Zimbalist

25 Rutgers' Athletics Deficit Reveals the Hidden Caste in the College Sports Hierarchy 363
Andrew Zimbalist

Index 367

Whither College Sports

Introduction

Andrew Zimbalist

The winds of change have been howling around college sports since the first intercollegiate athletic match between the Harvard and Yale boat clubs in 1852. From rowing to football, college presidents saw in sport contests an opportunity to promote their schools in an era of rapid expansion of land-grant institutions and excess supply of university beds. When football became too violent and dozens of deaths ensued at the turn of the twentieth century, President Teddy Roosevelt threatened to close down the sport if new rules were not imposed. This executive big stick led to the formation of the National Collegiate Athletic Association (NCAA) in December 1905.

New rules minimized deaths, but college presidents realized that the best publicity came from winning teams. Pledges of amateurism and education first notwithstanding, rogue players and payments under the table abounded, and cries for reform grew louder. A 1929 report by the Carnegie Foundation revealed that three-quarters of the 112 universities in its study violated the NCAA's code and principles of amateurism. Two years later, Robert Hutchins, president of the University of Chicago, wrote, "College is not a great athletic association and social club in which provision is made, merely incidentally, for intellectual activity on the part of the physically and socially unfit. College is an association of scholars in which provision is made for the development of traits and powers which must be cultivated, in addition to which are purely intellectual, if one is to become a well-balanced and useful member of any community."[1] The University of Chicago dropped football in 1939.

As television and corporate sponsorship money emerged and then multiplied, the contradictions between education and amateurism, on the one hand, and commercialism, athlete exploitation, and private inurement, on the other, became more pronounced. The modern economic system of big-time intercollegiate athletics gradually crystallized with its inherent characteristics:

1. Stylized amateurism wherein college athletes are not allowed to receive a cash income (though they sometimes do anyway)
2. With income suppressed, recruitment allurements based on coaches' notoriety, fancy facilities, first-class travel and dining, academic shortcuts, and so on
3. Money transfers from football and men's basketball (with 49 percent and 55 percent Black players in NCAA Division I Football Bowl Subdivision [FBS], respectively) to a dozen or two "nonrevenue" or "Olympic" sports (played mostly by higher income, white students)[2]
4. A caste system of divisions and subdivisions wherein only a select few athletics departments generate an annual surplus with substantial losses elsewhere (more shortly)
5. Centrifugal forces impelling the sixty-five universities in the Power Five conferences of the FBS to periodically threaten that unless granted greater autonomy, they will exit the NCAA with their money and reduce the association to a skeleton of its historical self[3]
6. The introduction and quasi-enforcement of Title IX, which mandates that women receive equal sports participation opportunities and resources as men in higher-education institutions—institutions that benefit from $130 billion plus annually in federal aid

Let us take a closer look at the financial results of commercialized college sports and the forces that drive them. The NCAA consists of three divisions: Division I, with 351 schools; Division II, with 308 schools; and

Division III, with 433 schools. Division I is the sole division that receives significant money from commercialization and itself is split into three subdivisions: FBS, with 130 schools; NCAA Division I Football Championship Subdivision (FCS), with 127 schools; and Division I without football, with 94 schools. FBS is the most heavily commercialized subdivision and the only one in which the most successful schools occasionally turn an operating surplus in their athletics departments.[4]

The financial results for Division I schools in fiscal year 2019 are presented in table I.1.[5]

The revenue disparity between FBS and FCS is sharp, as are the net generated revenue outcomes. No athletics department in FCS or Division I without football operated with a budget surplus. Although the median athletics department in FBS ran a budget deficit of $18.8 million, there were twenty-five departments that reported a surplus, with the largest surplus being $43.7 million. There is an important caveat to these reported figures: the actual budgetary results are considerably worse than reported for most schools. This is because there tends to be an incomplete accounting of capital costs, which results from facilities being financed often with state- or university-issued bonds. The annual debt service on these bonds can run into the tens of millions of dollars and frequently will not be recorded in the athletics department budget. There are also a variety of indirect costs

TABLE I.1

DIVISION I FINANCIAL RESULTS, FY 2019 (MILLIONS $)

	FBS	*FCS*	*Division I without football*
Generated revenues			
Median	61.99	4.74	3.57
Range	5.5 to 223.9	1.4 to 40.1	0.88 to 24.7
Net generated revenues			
Median	−18.8	−14.3	−14.4
Range	−65.3 to 43.7	−42.1 to −2.2	−42.5 to −3.6

TABLE I.2

FBS FINANCIAL RESULTS, FY 2019 (MILLIONS $)

	Power Five	*Group of Five*
Generated revenues		
Median	109.8	14.2
Range	58.1 to 223.9	5.7 to 62.0
Net generated revenues		
Median	−6.97	−23
Range	−45.2 to 43.7	−65.3 to 6.0

which will not appear in the department's budget.[6] Further, the median FBS athletics department receives 23 percent of its revenue from donations. To the extent that some of these donations may have flowed instead to the school's education budget, there is an additional cost to the institution from its athletics program.[7]

Table I.2 shows that there is another sharp disparity within FBS between the so-called Power Five (or Autonomous) conferences and the Group of Five (or Non-Autonomous) conferences. The median revenue among the sixty-five Power Five schools' athletics departments is $109.8 million, or 7.7 times the median for the Group of Five schools ($14.2 million), while the median deficit for the Group of Five is 3.3 times as large as that of the Power Five.

Finally, as indicated in Table I.3 by considering the results for the top quartile of FBS schools (thirty-two teams) and the second quartile (thirty-two teams), there is also an acute inequality within the Power Five institutions. Not only is median generated revenue 60.4 percent higher in quartile 1, but the median school reported a departmental operating surplus of $2.2 million in quartile 1, while no school in quartile 2 had a surplus and the median deficit for this group was $11.2 million. It is appropriate to observe that most of the twenty-five departments reporting a surplus (albeit with a modest median value of only $2.2 million) do not have a real surplus because, as discussed earlier, many of their costs are not included in their accounting.

The foregoing is a snapshot of where the big-time college athletics programs found themselves prior to COVID-19. The overall financial results are hardly robust and are characterized by glaring inequalities.[8]

How is it possible that well-known, extremely popular university athletics departments run multimillion-dollar deficits year after year? The answer is not that these schools have a revenue problem. Indeed, revenues have been growing by leaps and bounds: the median FBS athletics department's generated revenue grew from $22.86 million in fiscal year 2004 to $61.99 million in fiscal year 2019, or by 2.7 times. Rather, they have a shopping problem. Without stockholders pressuring for profitability, these programs instead have stakeholders (boosters, alumni, state legislators, students) pressuring for victories. Whenever an athletics director sees a new revenue stream arriving, he or she finds a way to spend the money in the pursuit of a championship team. Since schools are unable to attract the best high school athletes by offering them more income (at least not over-the-table income), they instead attempt to attract these athletes by offering them famous coaches; top-notch training facilities; first-class lodging, meals, and transportation; modern stadiums and arenas with premium seating and oversized high-definition scoreboards; and so on. Without meaningful market discipline, the costs explode as schools chase one another to provide better indirect allurements.

Of course, the impact of COVID-19 took a difficult financial situation and made it a lot worse. Power Five programs found their revenues reduced by tens of millions of dollars, but severe financial hits also affected the rest of Division I and, to a lesser degree, Divisions II and III.[9] How did they respond? According to press reports, as of October 2020, fewer than thirty athletics departments nationwide chose to eliminate some of the

TABLE I.3

FBS FINANCIAL RESULTS, FY 2019, BY QUARTILE (MILLIONS $)

	Quartile 1	*Quartile 2*	*Quartile 3*	*Quartile 4*
Generated revenues	142.3	88.7	26.7	11.9
Net generated revenues	2.1	−11.2	−25.5	−20.9

individual sports they sponsored.[10] A few that did announce cuts of sport teams later retracted, following vocal protests from students, parents, and alumni or the threat of Title IX lawsuits. The more sensible strategy was to take advantage of the crisis and reexamine spending policies. Not surprisingly, massive excess and waste were discovered, and substantial (mostly short-run) savings ensued for many schools. Many departments also made recourse to reserve funds and/or accessed the credit market.

As COVID-19 recedes, intercollege athletics will continue to face preexisting and emerging financial challenges. The tax act of 2018 eliminated the 80 percent deduction for seat purchases at school games and imposed a 21 percent excise tax on salaries over $1 million to the top-five paid employees.[11] The 80 percent deduction, in essence, enabled boosters to get a federal subsidy for buying choice seats to college football and basketball games. The removal of this deduction may reduce donations to athletics programs, which constitute almost one-quarter of the average Power Five school's athletic budget. The levy of the 21 percent tax on high salaries will also impose an additional cost, but much of the potential incremental cost here probably will be avoided by having sneaker companies and other corporate sponsors pay the coaches directly, rather than indirectly through payments to the athletics department.

Meanwhile, developments in the media market have created considerable uncertainty about the future of television or streaming rights fees. Since the 1980s, sports rights fees have been buoyed by the cable and regional sports network (RSN) structure that enabled cable companies to pass along rights fees to all households in an area, whether or not the households had an interest in watching sports events. With the fragmentation of media markets, the proliferation of video entertainment options, and the ascendance of direct-to-consumer contracting, it is unclear whether the continual growth of media contracts over recent decades will continue.

Another financial challenge is presented by the recent NIL (names, images, and likenesses) and athlete compensation lawsuits that brought about increased medical expenses (by mandating new coverage) for Power Five programs, as well as several million dollars of annual expense from cost-of-attendance (COA) stipends and growing athletic and academic awards. As I write in early December 2020, thirty-nine states have introduced legislation to allow college athletes to receive income for use of their NILs, and six of those states have already passed this legislation. Starting as early as mid-2021, in two states, these bills will allow athletes to sell their NILs. Some companies will find it more useful to promote their products by aligning directly with star student athletes rather than with athletics departments. To what extent this occurs and thereby reduces athletics department revenues will depend on the details of state, or prospective federal, legislation as well as on the evolution of corporate promotional strategy.

Unfortunately, there is considerable variation in what these thirty-nine state bills provide. It would be unworkable for colleges in the same conference but in different states to have different provisions regarding in what ways, in what quantities, and under what conditions athletes can earn income. Accordingly, a uniform law commission is trying to reconcile the differences, and Congress is getting in on the act in search of national legislation.

Not surprisingly, there is as much division in the Congress as there is among the states.

One line of congressional reform proposals calls for college athletes to receive a share of the revenue generated by their athletics departments in addition to NIL income.[12] That is, on top of earning publicity rights income from third parties outside the institution, these proposals would have athletes paid a share of athletics department revenues. If implemented, paying athletes cash income, not tethered to education, would be a game changer, with several undesirable consequences.

First, according to NCAA data, on an operating basis, only 44 to 52 percent of the FBS football and men's basketball teams generate a reported surplus. These data, however, are misleading, as noted earlier, because for many schools, it excludes a large share of capital costs (which are often financed by debt issued and serviced by the institution or the state) as well as a variety of indirect expenses. If nothing else changes, paying the star athletes a cash income will necessitate larger subsidies from the institution or the state and/or motivate the cutting of Olympic and women's sports. Of course, eventually, coaches' salaries will begin to adjust downward as will other expenses, offsetting most of the cost increase—but this will take time. Many coaches have long-term contracts, and debt service on facilities may be around for decades.

Second, if a law is passed that mandates cash payments to athletes, there emerges a thorny problem: Which athletes should be paid, and how much? Title IX would appear to mandate that women share equally in the payouts. Beyond that, does the college remunerate all 120 athletes on the football team or just the 85 scholarship athletes? What if some walk-ons are starters and some scholarship athletes do not play? And what is done with the athletes on the baseball or volleyball teams? (Keep in mind that the athletes who arguably generate a significant surplus are the stars on the football and men's basketball teams and are most likely to earn significant NIL income while still enrolled and, in a year or two, will be earning millions of dollars annually in the NFL or NBA.) What impact will the pay-for-play plan that emerges have on the recruitment of high school athletes? What impact will it have on the educational culture at the university?

Unless something is done to the underlying incentive system, the introduction of NILs and cash payments will only drive athletics programs to develop more and more revenue-generating projects, accelerating the arms race and deficits for the vast majority of schools. This dynamic will amplify the existing pattern of special admissions to academically underprepared basketball and football players, steering them to take less demanding courses and majors, watching them graduate at lower rates than athletes in other sports, and leaving them without the education to succeed after college. Only about 1.6 percent of college football players ever play a game in the NFL, and only 1.2 percent of college basketball players make it to the NBA. Thus, what 98 to 99 percent of college football and men's basketball players need more than anything else is a solid education.[13]

The introduction of cash payments will give the coaches still more power over the players, further diminishing the emphasis the school places on actually educating its athletes in big-time sports and further leaving the educationally earnest athlete without the opportunity and the time to pursue a proper course of study.

Third, reinforcing the underemphasis on actually educating athletes, cash payments will promote an employer-employee relationship between the school and the athlete, further displacing the educator-student relationship. While all of the legal angles will undoubtedly take time to work their way through the judicial system, there is a likelihood that the athletes will have to pay income taxes on their cash payments and possibly on their scholarships and that the university will have to contribute payroll taxes, unemployment insurance, and workers' compensation benefits. It is also possible that certain tax privileges enjoyed by college athletics departments will be challenged.

Fourth, we do college athletes a disservice if we do not insist that they be treated like other students. Other students, such as the singer, the musician, or the dancer who participate in campus theater or symphony performances, do not receive a share of the revenues they generate in extracurricular activities.[14] They can, however, take their talent and earn income by performing outside school. Allowing college athletes to do the same is the basic premise of the state and federal NIL legislative initiatives.

Of the thirty-nine states that have proposed or passed NIL legislation, only four contemplate revenue sharing with the athletes. The rest simply give the athlete the right to monetize his or her NIL or engage in other employment outside the institution.

Nonathlete students and professors are well aware of the special treatment of athletes—they have their own tutors, their own computer labs and study facilities, their own lounges, their own training table (totally unnecessary given today's 24/7 student food courts), their own more lavish dormitories or off-campus apartments, their own sport and strength training facilities that are not open to other students. All of this on top of the fact that significant nonathlete tuition dollars and mandatory student activity fees are subsidizing the athletic enterprise, increasing student debt and backstopped by $130 billion in federal student loans and Pell Grants.

Fifth, there is a clear and identifiable priority need to attend to the short- and long-term medical needs of all college athletes before we even begin to think of using new or existing athletics resources to provide cash payments to athletes. Athletics programs should be responsible for full insurance and medical cost coverage for athletic injuries. The NFL has a $1 billion fund to deal with the latter among former professional football players who ten to twenty years following retirement suffer from dementia, Alzheimer's, Parkinson's, and CTE. Neither the NCAA nor its member institutions have any dollars set aside or plans to confront this issue.

Finally, no one knows what will happen to the fan base of college sports if they professionalize. Will they come to be perceived much as minor league baseball? The successful branding of intercollegiate athletics should not be taken for granted.

Into this muddled and problematic picture steps the legalization of sports betting. Thus far, over twenty states have legalized sports betting, and in most cases, the legalization extends to college sports. Billions of dollars on the black market were bet on college sports before 2018, when New Jersey became the first state after Nevada to legalize sports betting. One major difference between black-market and legalized betting is that in the latter, the regulation of bets is possible and the teams (or athletics departments) and leagues (or conferences) have a greater chance of earning some of the betting handle. The teams and leagues can receive revenue by charging for the use of their data, especially for prop or in-game bets, by partnering with sportsbooks or media companies and by setting up sportsbooks in their facilities. The NCAA has been cautious in promoting this new source of revenue, but its posture appears to have become more accommodating.[15]

So, whither college sports? It is clear that the original and proclaimed purpose of college sports as an extracurricular activity that complements the primary educational role of the university has been subverted. There are two fundamental paths of reform: (a) toward marketization and professionalism or (b) toward educationally centered athletics and amateurism. The first path is embodied in the current Jenkins/Alston case filed in the Ninth Circuit. It argues that the NCAA functions as a cartel that artificially and injuriously colludes to preclude the development of a labor market for college athletes and to prevent them from receiving fair compensation given their revenue contribution to the school. In December 2019, the trial courts found partially in favor of the plaintiffs, ruling that the NCAA's limits on athlete compensation unreasonably restrain trade. The matter first was appealed to the US Ninth Circuit Court of Appeals and then to the US Supreme Court, where a summer 2021 decision is expected. If successful, the Jenkins/Alston suit would lead toward a marketization of labor markets in intercollegiate athletics. While this suit has much economic logic to commend it, it only makes sense in my judgment if it is accompanied by a separation of big-time intercollegiate sports from the university. Such a schism, in turn, would have serious consequences for the maintenance of college sports as we know them and would encounter the pay-for-play problems discussed earlier. While the marketization path is filled with deficiencies, I view it as preferable to the dysfunctional, hypocritical, and exploitative path that college athletics is on.

But I also believe that there is a far preferable alternative. The second path is to reinforce the educationally centered, extracurricular model of college athletics. A major factor that facilitated, accelerated, and deepened the commercialization of college sports was the 1984 Supreme Court decision in *NCAA v. Board of Regents of the University of Oklahoma*. The majority of justices in that case ruled that the commercial activities of the NCAA were subject to antitrust law and that the NCAA's existing national television contract with ABC, CBS, and TBS was an illegal restraint of trade. The ruling set the stage for subsequent conference contracts with the television networks, a mergers-and-acquisitions phase of conference growth that redrew geographical conference lines to maximize the value of media deals and heightened incentives to compromise academic integrity in pursuit of athletic glory.

One logical way to confront this tendency toward the subordination of academics to athletics is to revisit the major source of the post-1984 commercialization juggernaut: the antitrust treatment of college sports. By legislating a partial and conditional antitrust exemption for the governing body of college sports, it would be possible not only to blunt the incentives that are corroding academic integrity but also to arrest the runaway expenses that are burning a deep hole in the pockets of athletics programs and, therefore, also of university budgets.

The limited antitrust exemption should be conditioned on the governing body enacting certain reforms to promote academic integrity and the fair treatment of athletes, including short- and long-term medical coverage. Because the Sherman Antitrust Act was designed to focus only on commercial decisions, it is very difficult to apply it to activities that are a hybrid, with both commercial and noncommercial effects, as is the case with many NCAA policies. Most of the former and current antitrust lawsuits filed against the NCAA fall in this hybrid, gray space, where the key question is whether the rules such as controlling compensation to athletes, the value of athletic scholarships, and so on are necessary in order to protect the separation between college and professional sport. There are no clear-cut balancing tests or other mechanisms to make these policy judgments cleanly. The answers end up depending on the judgment of the particular court and not on any straightforward objective standards.

This pattern is illustrated clearly in the September 2015 ruling of the Ninth Circuit of Appeals in *O'Bannon*. The NCAA appealed the district-court decision by Judge Claudia Wilken, who had ruled that there were two less restrictive ways that the NCAA could still maintain amateurism and yet improve the compensation of athletes: first, by allowing member schools to offer scholarships that included a COA allowance and, second, by allowing member schools to offer a deferred payment to athletes of up to $5,000 annually for use of their NILs. Judges Jay Bybee, Gordon Quist, and Sidney Thomas heard the NCAA's appeal and ruled that the NCAA did not have to allow a deferred NIL payment to athletes because it would amount to pay for a noneducational function and would violate the norms of amateurism. To arrive at this conclusion, Judges Bybee and Quist opined that consumers of college sports would lose interest in the product if athletes received NIL payments, even on a deferred basis (payment not made until after they left college). Curiously, they made this judgment without any solid empirical evidence whatsoever.[16] Applying the same logic, the judges would have concluded that if college sports had been based on a system of slavery and if the consumers found this appealing, slavery would have been legal as far as the antitrust laws are concerned. They compounded their error by never engaging in a balancing test regarding the anti- and pro-competitive aspects of the NCAA's prohibition on NIL payments to athletes.[17]

A limited antitrust exemption in the hybrid space between professionalism and amateurism would seek to define clearly those actions of the NCAA that could not be questioned under the Sherman Antitrust Act on the grounds that they are controls necessary to achieve the priority purposes of higher education in the conduct of intercollegiate athletics as an extracurricular activity.

According to the NCAA, a fundamental function of the association is to maintain a clear line of demarcation between college sports as an extracurricular activity secondary to the academic responsibilities of students, on the one hand, and professional sports, which require priority on athletics excellence and revenue production that are inappropriate for a nonprofit educational institution, on the other. Actions that should be considered the legitimate functions of a nonprofit national intercollegiate athletics governance association typically include, among others, those that (1) control the cost of athletics (athletics programs are heavily subsidized by student fees and general funds) so the support of athletics programs does not damage the ability of the institution to support its primary academic programs, (2) prevent the operation of varsity sport programs from conflicting with student academic responsibilities (e.g., control of sport schedules so they do not conflict with class attendance, restriction of athletic participation for students who are not performing academically, limiting time spent on sport activities in order to allow sufficient time for study, etc.), and (3) protect the health and welfare of college athletes (e.g., provision of insurance and protections related to return to play following injury).

Some of these actions also have commercial implications and will be the target of antitrust lawsuits. A limited antitrust exemption that applies only to these legitimate categories of controls will enable higher-education institutions to collectively enact needed reforms without fear of legal liability and is both justifiable and necessary. Such antitrust lawsuits represent huge costs for legal representation, participation in court cases, and payment of damages. These funds would otherwise be available to advance the NCAA's and its member institutions' purported nonprofit educational purposes.

In what follows, I first elaborate on what areas might be granted an antitrust exemption and then on the conditions the governing body must follow to qualify for the partial exemption.

Potentially Exempt Areas

First, the NCAA would be exempt from imposing limits on the salaries paid to football and men's basketball coaches, which often exceed the salaries of the universities' presidents by a factor of five to ten.[18] In 2019, there were 176 college football and men's basketball coaches who received salaries exceeding $1 million, 71 coaches exceeded $3 million, and 38 exceeded $4 million. The highest paid coach was Dabo Swinney at Clemson, with a guaranteed salary of $9.3 million plus bonuses of $1.1 million and a potential buyout clause worth $50 million. Swinney's assistant coaches pulled in a total pay of $6.8 million, raising the total for all football coaches to $17.2 million, without considering their handsome perquisites and possible outside income.

Perquisites generally include free use of cars, housing subsidies, country-club memberships, private jet service, exceptionally generous severance packages, and more.[19] The coaches also have attractive opportunities to earn outside income via apparel or sneaker endorsements, the lecture circuit, summer camps, and book contracts. In forty states, the head football or basketball coach on a college team makes more than the governor.[20]

Back in 1924, Centenary College in Shreveport, Louisiana, the nation's first liberal-arts college west of the Mississippi, was denied accreditation by the Southern Association of Colleges and Schools because the school placed an "undue emphasis on athletics." The primary evidence of Centenary's misplaced priorities by the Southern Association was that the college paid its football coach more than it paid its college president. The next year, the football coach was fired, and the college gained accreditation.[21]

In more recent times, Bear Bryant, the legendary head football coach at the University of Alabama (1958–82), adhered to a firm policy of always keeping his salary one dollar below that of the school president. Bryant believed that it was symbolically important for the university president to be paid more than the head football coach.[22]

Defenders of multimillion-dollar salaries for head coaches are wont to repeat the mantra, "Coaches' compensation packages are driven by market forces." Fair enough, but what drives the market forces? It is clear that the market for coaches is sustained by several artificial factors: (a) no compensation is paid to the athletes, (b) intercollegiate sports benefit from substantial tax privileges, (c) no shareholders demand dividend distributions or higher profits to bolster stock prices at the end of every quarter, (d) athletics departments are nourished by university and statewide financial support, and (e) coaches' salaries are negotiated by athletic directors whose own worth rises with the salaries of their employees.

In a normal competitive market, college football and basketball coaches would not be getting compensated almost at the same level as NFL and NBA coaches. Average NFL team revenues are roughly four to eight times the revenue of the top thirty-two college football teams' revenues, and average NBA team revenues are approximately seven to ten times the revenues of the top thirty teams in college basketball. Yet the compensation packages of college and professional coaches in football and basketball are strikingly similar.

What is wrong with this picture? Basically, it is that the coaches are being paid the value created by the players they recruit. Much recruiting is done by assistant coaches, and much of the allure of the recruitment effort has to do with the school's history and brand and its facilities. Moreover, the coaches' bloated compensation packages are almost all economic rent. That is, they are being paid way beyond what they would have to be paid to induce them to offer their labor in the college coaching market. If the Nick Sabans and John Caliparis of the college coaching world did not coach in an FBS program, their next best alternative employment opportunity probably would be coaching at FCS or Division II or III or high school. Thus, if the NCAA placed, say, a $400,000 limit on coaches' compensation packages, it would not affect the quality of coaching or the level of intercollegiate competition one iota. Stated differently, it would not affect the allocation of coaching resources or diminish the entertainment value of college sports. Further, it would address the Bear Bryant concern of sending a twisted signal to undergraduate students about the importance of the college president or the professoriate relative to the head football or basketball coach.[23]

A second exempt policy would be the size of FBS football teams. FBS football teams are allowed 85 scholarships; 60 (or fewer) would do fine.[24] NFL teams have a maximum active roster of 48, plus a maximum practice squad of 12 additional players.[25] The average FBS team has 36 walk-ons plus 85 scholarship players—121 players in all![26] If football scholarships were cut to 60, the average college would probably save close to $1.25 million annually[27]—easily enough to finance an average FBS soccer team plus an average FBS golf team, or an FBS tennis team plus gymnastics team, and have several hundred thousand dollars left over.[28] Even assuming that the number of walk-ons would not increase with the lower scholarship limit, the average squad size would still be over 90. Is there a rational coach who would dare to argue that 90-plus players on a football team is inadequate?

A third exempt policy would be restrictions on the payment of salary to athletes for the performance in their sport. Athletes could continue to receive full scholarships for participating on their team, along with a cost-of-living allowance and other elements, but they could not be paid directly for what they do on the football field or basketball court. This is basically the concept of amateurism (i.e., no compensation for *playing* a sport) that is applied by the Amateur Athletic Union (AAU) and other amateur sports organizations in the United States.

Relatedly, a fourth area of exemption would be the establishment of guardrails to accompany the introduction of NIL income for college athletes. These guardrails are necessary to prevent NIL income from opening up a back door to full marketization of the college sports labor market. Once the needed guardrails are set, the body that implements them will probably need an antitrust exemption. The legal and economic issues surrounding NIL income to athletes are discussed in chapter 3.

Other areas of exemption that lean more toward the academic-integrity end of the spectrum include restrictions on weeknight football and basketball games, the length of competitive seasons, the number of in-season and out-of-season practice and game hours per week, and academic eligibility standards, inter alia.[29]

Conditions for Granting Partial Exemption

One can imagine a variety of conditionality stipulations geared toward ensuring that athletes are treated fairly and that academic fraud is, if not extirpated, minimized. For the NCAA or an alternative governing body to be granted a partial antitrust exemption, the association would have to enact and implement certain pro-educational reforms. A suggested, non-inclusive list follows.

Initial eligibility standards need to be strengthened. Since the 2003 sliding scale was introduced, it is possible for athletes to gain full initial eligibility and still receive a zero score on standardized tests by raising their grade point average to a 2.5.[30] If, however, the high school rigs the athlete's classes and teachers to achieve this grade point average (GPA), then the initial eligibility standard is a mockery. Similar issues apply to the continuing eligibility standards and to the Academic Progress Rate (APR) metric.

New, more meaningful standards need to be set and become conditions for the antitrust exemption. Such standards and metrics are discussed in the essays of the Drake Group in part 2.[31]

Athletes' rights must be fortified. The governing body should also be required to put in place appropriate due process procedures for all schools, administrators, and athletes who are accused of transgressions prior to penalizing them.

Health and safety protections as well as broader injury insurance coverage should be instituted. Athletes should be given wide margin to earn NIL or publicity rights income, and athletes should have the right to work with counsel or an agent regarding NIL activity and career choices prior to entering a professional draft or participating in a sports league combine. All academic-support programs for athletes should be removed from the athletics department and put entirely under academic control. Transfer athletes should not lose a year of eligibility.

The national championship football playoff system, inaugurated in 2014–15, generates almost $500 million in television revenue, over 80 percent of which is distributed to the Power Five conferences. This skewed distribution, at once, enhances the financial incentives toward victory at any cost and, importantly, diminishes funding for Olympic sports and women's sports throughout the NCAA's three divisions. All national championships except the FBS football playoff are controlled by the NCAA. A condition for receiving a partial antitrust exemption should be to bring the football playoff into the fold.

Other conditionality reforms might include whistle-blower protection, Title IX compliance, and defined controls over game scheduling. The chapters in parts 2 and 3 contain an extensive discussion of needed reforms on which the limited antitrust exemption should be conditioned.

I have participated either as the sole, co-, or joint author of all the chapters in this collection. The essays in part 2 are all by individuals belonging to a working collective of the Drake Group. The Drake Group is a national organization of faculty and others whose mission is to defend academic integrity in higher education from the corrosive aspects of commercialized college sports.[32] The group was formed at a conference at Drake University in 1999.

I put this volume together during 2020 under the severe conditions of the COVID-19 pandemic. During this year, together with Donna Lopiano, president of the Drake Group, and some other members, I have been actively involved in consulting with members of the US Congress and their staffs to offer legislation that addresses NIL income and other structural reforms concerning college sport.

College sport is clearly at a crossroads, and major change is coming. The traditional cry of members of Congress that they do not want to get the government involved in micromanaging college sports makes little sense. A panoply of tax preferences, financing privileges, and over $130 billion of annual federal aid to higher education make it abundantly clear that government is already involved. Leaving college sports up to the NCAA and to the heterogeneous and frequently poorly informed court system is both expensive and potentially perilous. The role of college sports in the university and in our society is a matter for public policy. I am hopeful that the essays herein will help orient and instruct the discussions about the most effective reform path.

NOTES

1. Murray Sperber, *Onward to Victory* (New York: Henry Holt, 1998), 42.

2. Two caveats here. First, note that many traditional white sports, such as tennis and golf, now have increasing numbers of Black participants. Assistant and head coaches need to alter their recruiting circuits to reach the inner cities and to begin connecting with students of color in these sports. Second, according to NCAA figures, in FBS only 52 percent of football programs and 44 percent of men's basketball programs generated an operating surplus in FY 2019. This means that in roughly half the schools, this transfer mechanism from "revenue" to "nonrevenue" sports was not operative.

3. Historically, while the leading football schools have been ready to make this threat, they have settled for concessions (such as the greater financial autonomy granted them in 2015). Full separation from the NCAA could undermine many advantages they currently experience, such as amateur/education branding, favorable Unrelated Business Income Tax (UBIT) and payroll-tax treatment, issuance of tax-exempt bonds, among others. Needless to point out, threats notwithstanding, thus far the leading programs have not found it in their interest to exit the NCAA.

4. As I write in December 2020, the Knight Commission has called for FBS football

to be governed by a new national association, separate from the NCAA. While it is unclear where this proposal will go, it does underscore how different FBS football is from the rest of intercollegiate athletics.

5. The source for the data in this and subsequent tables is the NCAA annual report *Revenues and Expenses of Division I Intercollegiate Athletics Programs Report.*

6. For example, if a university president spends, say, 10 percent of his or her time on athletics, the athletics department will not apportion 10 percent of the president's compensation to its budget. Nor will it allocate a portion on the president's staff or impute a rent on the president's office.

7. Note that there is a factor that tends to bias the reported deficit in the opposite direction. Namely, although the practice varies significantly from school to school, many athletics departments attribute the full out-of-state sticker price of tuition, room, board, and fees to their budget because they are required to reimburse the central budget for this amount, at least in an accounting sense. Since the typical school does not receive the full sticker price from the average student (the share is closer to 50 percent), the opportunity cost to the school of a full athletic scholarship is below the full retail price. When adjustments are made for cost-of-attendance stipends and some other factors, it would probably be reasonable to assume that only half the sticker price should be counted as a cost. Even with such an adjustment (approximately $6.5 million), however, the factors pushing the reported deficit to be too small (incomplete accounting of capital cost, indirect cost, and donations) have a larger effect. More generally, a variety of accounting practices are not standardized, and balance sheets are not publicly available, making interpretation of the true financial picture of an athletics department rather challenging. For schools with empty beds, the computation becomes more complicated but still resolves the same way.

8. Whether or not athletics departments create a deficit that depletes university finances in the short run, many people argue that big-time college sports programs provide positive publicity for schools and thereby promote increased student applications, enabling more selectivity and an improved student body, as well as increased donations to the general fund or appropriations from the state legislature. While there is some evidence that athletic success in prominent sports increases student applications, the effect here is modest and does not result in improved standardized-testing or class-rank statistics of the student body. It appears that those students who are motivated to apply to a school that has athletic success are at the bottom of the academic qualifications hierarchy. The evidence on athletic success increasing donations to a school's general fund is more ambiguous. See chapter 4, by Baumer and Zimbalist, in part 1.

9. Below Division I, the main impact on athletics department budgets was through reduced appropriations from the school's central fund, which was depleted by reduced enrollment and increased health-safety expenses.

10. Matt Marshall, Daniel Arkin, and Kanwal Syed, "College Sports Cuts in the Wake of Covid-19 Are Clouding the Future of Olympics Participation," NBC News, October 17, 2020, https://www.nbcnews.com/news/sports/college-sports-cuts-wake-covid-19-are-clouding-future-certain-n1243803.

11. The deduction for seat purchases was actually for a "donation," but the donation was required in order to be able to purchase choice seats at the football stadium or basketball arena.

12. Perhaps the most prominent of these initiatives is the so-called "College Athletes Bill of Rights," introduced in December 2020 by Senators Cory Booker and Richard Blumenthal. In addition to legislating important athlete rights related to short- and long-term health care, recruitment practices, NIL income, transfer freedoms, and edu-

cational guarantees, inter alia, the bill calls for athletes in subdivisions where the sport generates more revenue than it pays out in scholarships to receive 50 percent of all generated revenue (including scholarships, which account for roughly 13 percent of revenue at FBS schools). According to the formula in the bill, based on 2018–19 NCAA figures, this revenue sharing would provide $157,000 yearly to every FBS football player on scholarship and $272,000 yearly to every FBS men's basketball player on scholarship. Men's FBS hockey players would receive $17,000. These numbers are in addition to their scholarships. No other players on men's or women's teams would receive a distribution. Hence, the revenue-sharing distribution algorithm in the bill would constitute a glaring violation of the equal treatment provision in Title IX.

13. Just considering Division I, 3.8 percent of eligible football players were drafted by the NFL in 2019, and 4.2 percent of eligible basketball players were drafted by the NBA. Of course, not all drafted players make it to the active rosters. Further, the NCAA's methodology to derive these estimates ignores the fact that basketball players can enter the draft after one year in college and football players can enter the draft three years after the graduation of their high school class. Thus, the percentages cited will tend to overestimate the odds for a Division I player to actually play in the NBA or NFL. It is also notable that over three-quarters of college basketball players believe that they will play professionally. NCAA, "Estimated Probability of Competing in Professional Athletics," accessed November 21, 2020, http://www.ncaa.org/about/resources/research/estimated-probability-competing-professional-athletics.

14. Some schools do provide a modest stipend to student thespians, dancers, or musicians, but these are not linked to the generated revenue. The payments are more akin to the stipends paid to work-study students.

15. The prospect of legalized betting on college sports is foreboding. Unlike the pros, college athletes are not paid and increasingly feel materially exploited. They are prime targets for gamblers looking to control the outcome of contests.

16. To be sure, I believe that the contrary evidence is also unpersuasive. While the general popularity of big-time college football and basketball has been maintained over the past ten years as athletic scholarships and backdoor payments have grown (though television ratings for college sports have been in a gradual descent since 2015), it is far from apparent that the general perception of amateurism in college sports has changed.

17. The ruling further overlooked the fact that the AAU, the USGA (United States Golfers Association), and other amateur sport organizations have considerably looser rules to define amateurism. These rules essentially proscribe compensation for playing the sport, not for activity such as endorsements off the playing field.

18. In a sample of forty-five Division I public universities, the Duke economist Charles Clotfelter found that between 1986 and 2007, the average compensation of full professors rose 30 percent, while that of university presidents grew 100 percent, that of head basketball coaches jumped 400 percent, and that of head football coaches increased 500 percent. Clotfelter, *Big-Time Sports in American Universities* (New York: Cambridge University Press, 2011). (Clotfelter had full data on basketball salaries for twenty-two schools and on football salaries for forty-five.)

19. One eye-popping severance clause appeared in the contract of Mike Sherman, Texas A&M's football coach, who, if terminated, would have been paid $150,000 a month for the remainder of his contract, which would have amounted to a $7.8 million golden handshake.

20. In a forty-first state, New Hampshire, the head ice hockey coach earns more than the governor.

21. James Johnson, "The Suicide Season," *Shreveport Times*, September 4, 2008.

22. Allen Barra, *The Last Coach: A Life of Paul "Bear" Bryant* (New York: Norton, 2005).

23. Some people might object that Saban or Calipari could coach in the pros. Indeed, they could, and they both have, though the skill sets for coaching in the pro and college ranks are appreciably different. Further, if they go to the pros, then they replace pro coaches, who become available to the college ranks. The quantity of coaching talent available to college teams stays the same.

24. College coaches have protested that college football teams cannot be properly compared to professional teams. The latter, they say, can always call up reserves when players get injured, but college teams must have players on their rosters to replace the injured. First, NFL teams have a maximum of 12 players on reserve and practice squads to complement their 48-man active rosters. Second, the NCAA Injury Surveillance System Summary reports that for the 2000–2001 season, the serious-injury rate during games in football was 14.1 per 1,000 exposures, while the rate in football practices was 1.6 per 1,000. If we assume that 60 players enter a game and the team plays thirteen games during the year (that is, including a postseason game), then the average total number of serious injuries (in which a player is out seven or more days) from games is eleven per year. If on average each such player misses two games, then the average number of game-injured players is 1.69 per game. Performing a similar calculation for practice-injured players yields 1.48 per game, for a combined average of 3.17 injured players per game. This hardly constitutes a justification for carrying 85 scholarship and 117 total players on an FBS team.

25. Teams are also allowed to carry up to twelve additional players on their practice squads.

26. NCAA, *Gender Equity Report, 2005–06* (October 2008), 27.

27. This number is based on twenty-five men's scholarships at $50,000 each, plus the possibility of savings on women's scholarships and the probable reduction in athletic support staff and equipment.

28. NCAA, *NCAA Revenues and Expenses: Division I Intercollegiate Athletics Programs Report, 2004–08* (October 2009), 37.

29. Of course, it may be argued that many of these policies are not commercial and, hence, would not be subject to the antitrust laws. Nonetheless, it would be desirable to stipulate that they are permissible to avoid lengthy and costly litigations.

30. This sliding scale eligibility was introduced after a two-decade struggle with the Black Coaches Association, which claimed that a hard cutoff on standardized tests was arbitrary and discriminatory toward minority athletes. It is interesting to note that the growth in the participation of African American athletes in college sports actually was more rapid prior to 2003 than it was after.

31. Concerns about the discrimination against minority and low-income students in today's standardized testing are valid. Statistical adjustments on test scores should be made to level the playing field.

32. The Drake Group's goals include (1) to ensure that universities provide accountability of trustees, administrators, and faculty by publicly disclosing information about the quality of education that college athletes receive, (2) to advance proposals that ensure quality education for students who participate in intercollegiate athletics, (3) to support faculty and staff whose job security and professional standing are threatened when they defend academic standards in intercollegiate sports, (4) to influence public discourse on current issues and controversies in sports and higher education, and (5) to coordinate local and national reform efforts with other groups that share its mission and goals. Other essays by and activities of the Drake Group can be found at its website: http://thedrakegroup.org.

PART I

Academic Papers

CHAPTER 1

Taxation of College Sports

POLICIES AND CONTROVERSIES

Andrew Zimbalist

On October 2, 2006, US House Ways and Means Committee Chairman Bill Thomas sent then National Collegiate Athletic Association (NCAA) President Myles Brand a long letter questioning why the NCAA and intercollegiate athletics should be able to retain their plethora of tax privileges. Thomas pointedly inquired how the hypercommercialized activities of Division I athletics supported the tax-exempt educational mission of US colleges and universities. This essay seeks to understand this issue, both from the perspective of tax law and from that of public policy.

Before one can meaningfully answer the question of why intercollegiate athletics should have tax privileges, it is necessary to understand what those privileges are as well as the legal basis for them. There are two principal areas of tax privileges for college sports:

1. The ability of college sports programs to issue facility bonds, the interest on which is tax exempt to their holders
2. The ability to avoid taxation on activities that are unrelated to the purpose of the tax exemption held by US colleges and universities[1]

These tax privileges are based on a broader tax exemption that is afforded US colleges and universities. The exemption, in turn, is based (a) for public

---

Most of the material in this essay originally appeared in Eddie Comeaux, ed., *Introduction to Intercollegiate Athletics*, 123–34. © 2015 Johns Hopkins University Press. Reprinted with permission of Johns Hopkins University Press.

universities on the assumption that the state is providing a service that may otherwise have to be produced by the federal government and (b) for private universities on the assumption that education is a public good whose development promotes the general welfare and functioning of our democratic government. Public universities, as state enterprises, are automatically exempt, while private universities fall under the 501(c)(3) category, which provides exemption for charitable, nonprofit organizations. In 1976, the US Congress passed an amendment to 501(c)(3) that explicitly classified the promotion of amateur sports as a charitable activity. Hence, the NCAA was able to obtain 501(c)(3) status and therefore is covered by the tax exemption, as are private universities and colleges. According to Internal Revenue Service (IRS) code, however, both public and private nonprofit universities are explicitly made subject to the Unrelated Business Income Tax (UBIT); and, as we shall see, some key questions in connection to the UBIT arise about the relationship of intercollegiate athletics to the educational mission of universities, questions that form the basis for the frequently heard call for college sports to be taxed.

Issuance of Tax-Exempt Bonds for Facility Construction

Athletics departments in either public or nonprofit, private universities are able, through their schools, to finance facility construction or renovation through the issuance of bonds, the interest on which is tax exempt to their holders. Bond buyers are generally high-income individuals. Consider the following example. If a bond buyer, in the highest 39.6 percent tax bracket, buys a nonexempt corporate bond, with, say, a 7 percent interest rate, the net (after tax) interest rate is 4.23 percent. For a tax-exempt bond to be competitive with this corporate bond, the interest would only have to be 4.23 percent (or lower, given that there may also be an exemption from state income tax). In this example, a bond to finance the construction or renovation of a college football stadium would save 2.72 percent, which on a $200 million bond amounts to a $5.44 million annual saving on the bond's debt service, or a yearly federal subsidy to the stadium of $5.44 million.

Since 1995, US universities have spent over $35 billion on sports facilities. Many observers believe that there is an arms race among schools, wherein the forces of competition push these expenditures on modernized structures, replete with luxury boxes, club seating, signage boards, restaurants, and more. The federal subsidy encourages this lavish spending.

Given that a university's tax-exempt status is meant to underwrite its central purpose of education, there is a legitimate question of whether the hypercommercialized business of big-time intercollegiate athletics is sufficiently related to this central purpose to justify extending the exemption to the construction of sports stadiums, arenas, training facilities, and tutoring buildings for athletes.

NCAA President Myles Brand wrote in his 2006 letter to the US Congress, "Athletics facilities, state-of-the-art or otherwise, are necessary for the support of the activity for which there is a tax exemption. These facilities, often paid for through bonds or charitable contributions, also generate revenue that offsets the operational cost of athletics that might not otherwise be provided through institutional funds." If, however, these facilities generate sufficient funds to justify the investment in them, then there is no reason for the federal government to subsidize them. In the end, the modern stadiums and arenas raise the revenue level of big-time college sports. Since there are no stockholders to profit from successful sports programs and athletes are not remunerated beyond the basic grant-in-aid plus cost-of-attendance (COA) stipend, a substantial part of the additional revenue flows to the coaches and administrators of the system. Thus, critics ask, Why should the taxpayer be called on to support fancy facilities for college sports?

Avoidance of UBIT Levies

When a public or nonprofit institution sets up its own commercial enterprise, the net income of this operation may be subject to taxation. This principle was established by the UBIT legislation passed by the US Congress in 1950. Prior to 1950, and dating back to a Supreme Court decision in 1924, charitable entities were permitted to run a commercial business and not have to pay taxes on its profits if the profits were used to support the entities' charitable activities. In 1950, however, out of concern (a) that such businesses would have an unfair competitive advantage over independent businesses producing the same product or service and (b) that the policy reduced government tax revenues, Congress enacted the Unrelated Business Income Tax (UBIT). UBIT was prompted by the Mueller Pasta Company, which was owned by the School of Law of New York University (NYU). In 2004, the government collected over $192 million in UBIT revenue from 501(3)(c) entities. This collection was based on reported gross income of $5.5 billion, constituting a tax rate of only 3.5 percent. The low rate is a product of the 501(c)(3) entities' ability to shift revenues and costs to lower the taxable income of their unrelated entities.[2]

Understanding how UBIT applies to big-time intercollegiate athletics is not a simple matter and, like much of the law, is subject to interpretation. The basic criterion is whether the commercial entity's output is functionally related to and in furtherance of the basic mission of the charity (in this case, either education or the provision of amateur sports), and IRS interpretation of this criterion over the years has tended to be narrow. For instance, in 1968, the IRS ruled that a hospital's charitable purpose was providing health care to the patients in the hospital; accordingly, a pharmacy within the hospital that provided drugs to patients in the hospital was functionally related to the charitable purpose, but the sale of drugs to the general public by such a pharmacy was not. In 1973, the IRS ruled that the sale of science books in an art museum bookstore was subject to UBIT, but the sale of reproductions or postcards was not. In the context of the university, a Treasury Department regulation stipulates that "the presentation of . . . drama and music events contributes importantly to the overall educational and cultural function of the university" and, hence, is not subject to UBIT.[3] Following this logic, a case can be made to the Treasury to apply the same reasoning to intercollegiate athletics.

The IRS briefly contemplated taxing television revenues in intercollegiate sports back in 1977 but reversed itself and in 1980 ruled that TV revenues were not subject to UBIT.[4] In 1991, the IRS ruled that corporate advertising/sponsorship revenue in college sports was subject to UBIT, but in 1997, Congress voted to exempt such income from UBIT provided that it was not comparative and promotional in nature.[5] Thus, Coca-Cola could have a sign at the Camp Randall Stadium in Madison, Wisconsin, that simply stated "Coke" or "Coca-Cola Supports Badgers' Football," but it could not have a tax-exempt sign that stated "Coke Is No. 1" or "Nothing Beats Coke for a Satisfying Refreshment."[6] Similarly, buying naming rights to a facility does not involve explicit promotion and is exempt from UBIT taxation.

Current law also excludes all passive income from UBIT, such as royalty or licensing income from the sale of logos, images or game highlights, and the like. In 2005, licensing and royalty revenue in college sports was estimated at $203 million.[7] In 2018, this figure had risen to over $800 million.[8]

For an entity to retain its 501(c)(3) status and, hence, its eligibility to remain tax exempt, it must also meet certain limitations. One such limitation is that there can be no "private inurement," or siphoning of surplus to the benefit of an employee of the entity. In order to meet this standard, it is required that employees be paid a fair, market-based compensation for their services. The question has been raised about the high salaries of head coaches of Division I football and men's basketball teams and whether these constitute private inurement, which is addressed later in this chapter.

Another limitation is that there can be no "private benefit," which refers to an outsider to a 501(c)(3) organization gaining excessively from its relationship with the charitable entity, whether or not the payment is at a market rate. Consider how the NFL and the NBA gain excessively from the development and promotion of players in college sports. In baseball, the average major league team spends roughly $25 million on player development within its minor league system, while the NBA's development league expenses are diminutive and the NFL has no minor league or development system. In this way, college sports serve as a minor league and development system for the NBA and NFL, with the added bonus that Division I teams get enough media coverage for the players who come to the pros with substantial public résumés and notoriety.

Finally, it is appropriate to inquire whether applying UBIT to college sports would make a difference. If college sports departments can shift costs and benefits among various college departments (e.g., buildings and grounds, dance, music, dining services, general administration) and thereby avoid showing any net income, or if there is truly no net income in the vast majority of programs anyway, would it matter if college sports were subject to an income tax? The short answer is that UBIT law also contains a fragmentation principle that allows the IRS to view the separate parts of a 501(c)(3) entity independently. Thus, in theory at least, the IRS could consider net income from football, from basketball, or from corporate sponsorships, even though the entire athletics department did not generate a surplus. We turn now to consider the debate around this aforementioned question.

Joining the Debate

Both at a technical level regarding the details of tax policy and at a political/philosophical level, a fundamental question is whether commercialized intercollegiate athletics is functionally related to the educational mission of US colleges and universities. On the one hand, it can be argued that engagement in college sports by students provides a salutary balancing of an otherwise largely cerebral and sedentary lifestyle. Participation in intercollegiate athletics also can help student athletes develop constructive personality traits, including the development of leadership skills, teamwork, tenacity, good time management, and positive self-esteem, among others. These qualities of college sports appear to be functionally related to the educational mission of colleges and universities and, indeed, to provide an important complement to help create a well-rounded and healthy college experience.

On the other hand, it can be retorted that these positive attributes apply to college sports in intramural form, in club sports form, or in the less commercialized form of intercollegiate athletics of Divisions II and III. But at the highly commercialized level of Division I, and particularly Football Bowl Subdivision (FBS), the time demands on the student athletes, the intrusive, television-driven scheduling of games, the frequent and increasingly distant travel, the lowering of admissions and classroom standards, the transformation of college culture, the incentives to transgress NCAA rules, and the outsized payments to the football and men's basketball head and assistant coaches all detract from the central charitable and educational purpose of the university.

The US Congress's Congressional Budget Office (CBO) conducted a study in May 2009 that considered this question, finding that 82.3 percent of the revenues for FBS college sports came from commercial sources. This share fell to 28.8 percent in Football Championship Subdivision (FCS) and to 27.9 percent in Division I without football. For universities as a whole, this share was only 10.9 percent, excluding hospitals and athletics.[9] The implication of the CBO finding is that big-time college sports operates in a distinct fashion from higher education generally and, thus, could logically be given a different tax status.

The NCAA has justified the commercial growth of FBS football and Division I basketball, in part, on the grounds that the surplus generated by these sports helps to fund dozens of nonrevenue sports for both men and women. After all, in 1976, Congress explicitly denominated the promotion of amateur sports to be a charitable activity, and the revenue from big-time sports appears to be helping to fund these amateur teams.

Critics point to several problems with this argument. First, according to NCAA data, fewer than one-fifth of the football and men's basketball teams in Division I generate an operating surplus. During the academic year 2018–19, 67 of 129 FBS football teams and 57 basketball teams reported an operating surplus.[10] Only a handful of FCS football and basketball teams generated an operating surplus. Hence, in the vast majority of Division I schools, the big-time sports actually detract from the funds available for the promotion of the nonrevenue sports.

Second, even in those programs where there is an operating surplus in football or men's basketball, the actual financial picture is less sanguine. When all athletically related capital expenses (e.g., debt service on football stadiums, basketball arenas, tutoring buildings, or training facilities) and administrative overhead (e.g., a pro rata charge for the school president's time spent on football) are included, the actual surplus generated is either diminished greatly or nonexistent. In a study for the NCAA, Jonathan and Peter Orszag estimated that the average FBS program had yearly capital expenses of over $20 million.[11] Since over 20 percent of FBS revenue derive from contributions, it is also possible that some of the contributions to the athletics department come at the expense of contributions to the institution's general fund. To the extent that this is so, the institution is absorbing further losses in athletics than those that are reported.

Third, even in those football and men's basketball programs where a true surplus is generated and some of this surplus is meaningfully transferred to support the nonrevenue sports, there is still evidence of substantial siphoning of the surplus. Consider the support given to exorbitant salaries of the head coaches of football and men's basketball teams, their assistant coaches, the athletic directors, and the conference commissioners. While the NCAA and others have attempted to justify these elevated levels of compensation on the basis of market competition, the underlying market forces are artificially created. Hence, there is good reason to believe that these salaries constitute private inurement, which could disqualify athletics departments from 501(c)(3) treatment. This final point is discussed in more detail in the next section.

Private Inurement and the Compensation for Head Coaches and Others

The average salary for FBS head football coaches in 2020–21 was scheduled to be $2.79 million prior to the pandemic. For the sixty-five schools in the Power Five conferences, the head football coach compensation was $4.4 million.[12] The top-thirty head men's basketball coaches received compensation packages between $3 million and $8 million in 2019–20.[13]

These figures exclude bonuses as well as extensive perquisites, including free use of cars, housing subsidies, country-club memberships, private jet service, exceptionally generous severance packages, and more. The coaches also have handsome opportunities to earn outside income via apparel or sneaker endorsements, the lecture circuit, summer camps on campus, and book contracts. For some coaches' contracts, the buyout is the most lucrative element: the former Notre Dame head football coach Charlie Weis is enjoying a nearly $19 million buyout after his release, even though he became the University of Kansas head coach after leaving Notre Dame.[14]

Not surprisingly, assistant coaches have also experienced an explosion in their pay packages in recent years, with many earning over $1 million annually. Athletic directors and conference commissioners are also wealthy beneficiaries of the system. In 2017–18, there were seventeen athletic directors in FBS with compensation over $1 million before bonuses, led by Jack Swarbrick at Notre Dame with a $3.05 million package.[15] There is a clear pattern for schools with higher coach compensation to also have higher athletic director compensation.

Conference commissioners earn even more. Greg Sankey, commissioner of the Southeastern Conference (SEC), made $2.6 million in 2018. John Swafford of the Atlantic Coast Conference (ACC) pulled in $3.8 million. Bob Bowlsby of the Big 12 earned $4.0 million. Larry Scott, the

Pac-12 commissioner, earned $5.4 million, and Jim Delaney, former commissioner of the Big Ten, earned $8.5 million.[16]

This pattern began long ago. Back in 1924, Centenary College in Shreveport, Louisiana, the nation's first liberal-arts college west of the Mississippi, was denied accreditation by the Southern Association of Colleges and Schools because the school placed an "undue emphasis on athletics." The primary evidence of Centenary's misplaced priorities by the Southern Association was that the college paid its football coach more than it paid its college president. The next year the football coach was gone and the college gained accreditation.[17]

The legendary head football coach at the University of Alabama Bear Bryant (1958–82) adhered to a firm policy of always keeping his salary one dollar below that of the school president. Bryant believed that it was symbolically important for the university president to be paid more than the head football coach.[18]

Defenders of the multimillion-dollar head coaches' salaries often argue that coaches' compensation packages are driven by market forces. This may be true, but what drives the market forces? The market for coaches is sustained by several artificial factors: (a) there is no compensation paid to the athletes; (b) intercollegiate sports benefit from substantial tax privileges; (c) there are no shareholders demanding dividend distributions or higher profits to bolster stock prices; (d) athletics departments are nourished by university and state-wide financial support, as well as booster contributions; and (e) coaches' salaries are negotiated by athletic directors whose own worth rises with the salaries of their employees.

In a normal competitive market, college football coaches would not be getting compensated almost at the same level as NFL coaches. During the 2011–12 season, the highest paid NFL coach was Bill Belichick of the Patriots at $7.5 million, and the tenth highest paid coach was Andy Reid of the Eagles at $5.5 million.[19] The top thirty-two college football programs in that year generated revenues in the $40–$90 million range; the average NFL team generated around $270 million. The same logic applies to the

NBA and its coaches. During 2011–12, the top-paid NBA coach was Doc Rivers of the Celtics at $7 million (nearly $3 million below Mike Krzyzewski's compensation at Duke), and the tenth highest paid was Scott Skiles of the Bucks at $4.5 million.[20] The revenue range for the thirty top college basketball teams in that year was $15–$40 million, while the average NBA team generated $130 million.

If there were a rule that college head coaches could be paid no more than three times as much as the average salary of a full professor, it would not affect the quality of coaching or the level of intercollegiate competition. This is because the next best alternative for top college coaches (the reservation wage) is likely to be well below this level—perhaps coaching in Division II or III or in high school and earning between $20,000 and $100,000, without perks. Anything above the reservation wage is what economists call "economic rent." Economic rent does not affect the allocation of resources. Thus, the argument that college coaches' compensation packages appear to constitute private inurement appears to be strong.

2018 Tax Reform

In February 2018, the US Congress passed a reform package that included the elimination of the 80 percent deduction for seat purchases at school games and imposed a 21 percent excise tax on salaries over $1 million to the top-five paid employees. The 80 percent deduction undoubtedly incentivized contributions to athletics departments, which rely heavily on such transfers. Indeed, in 2018–19, FBS athletics departments received 23 percent of their revenue from donations. It remains to be seen what impact the removal of this favorable tax treatment will have on donations. The 21 percent excise tax on salaries over $1 million for the top-five paid employees may also have an effect on compensation policy, but it seems that schools will be able to skirt a significant portion of this tax by arranging for direct compensation from corporate sponsors to coaches and the athletic director.

Conclusion

In this essay, I have presented the nature of the tax privileges enjoyed by college sports and reviewed the basis in the tax laws for this favorable treatment. The foundation for these privileges is the fact that athletics departments are housed within public colleges and universities or within private universities that are considered 501(c)(3) entities. Because it is not clear that the activity of big-time college sports is functionally related to the purpose of the university (education) or to the promotion of amateur sports and because there is a compelling argument that there is private inurement and possibly private benefit in the operation of big-time college sports, there is a case to be made that college sports does not deserve its favorable treatment. The IRS has attempted to capture some tax revenue from parts of the intercollegiate sports business, but it has backed off as a result of either political pressure or new legislation.

We have also seen that some people believe that trying to tax college sports is a paper tiger. That is, even if the IRS or the US Congress decided to tax the net income of college sports, athletics departments would find a way to manipulate their books to show no profit. While efforts at manipulation may occur, accounting rules could limit this ability. Further, if intercollegiate athletics were subjected to UBIT, then activities like corporate sponsorships could be treated as separate entities under the fragmentation principle. The direct costs of obtaining corporate sponsorships are minimal, and it would be difficult to hide the net income generated.

Finally, there is the issue of whether athletics departments should be allowed to use the university's tax-exempt bonding privileges, especially if their activity is judged not to be functionally related to the school's educational mission. It appears that this bonding privilege has only encouraged an arms race to build bigger and better athletics facilities, foisting major funding costs of hundreds of millions of dollars on schools throughout the country.

NOTES

1. There was a third area that was eliminated in the February 2018 tax act and that had allowed purchasers of tickets to school games to deduct 80 percent of the price of those tickets from their taxable income. These transactions were framed as "donations" to the athletics program, but in exchange for the donations, the giver would be entitled to purchase desirable seats at the institution's stadium or arena at a nominal price.

2. John Colombo, "The NCAA, Tax Exemption, and College Athletics," *University of Illinois Law Review*, January 4, 2010, 109.

3. Ibid., 111.

4. Ibid.

5. In the same bill, Congress lifted the previous $150 million limit on tax-exempt bonds for college facility construction.

6. The NCAA estimated that in 2004–5, corporate sponsorship payments to college athletics programs totaled $275 million.

7. Burton Weisbrod, Jeffrey Ballou, and Evelyn Asch, *Mission and Money: Understanding the University* (New York: Cambridge University Press, 2008).

8. "Football Bowl Subdivision," Knight Commission College Athletics Financial Information Database, accessed November 18, 2020, http://cafidatabase.knightcommission.org/fbs#!quicktabs-tab- where_the_money-1.

9. Congressional Budget Office, "Tax Preferences for Collegiate Sports," May 2009.

10. Todd Petr, Director of Research for the NCAA, email to the author, October 29, 2020.

11. Jonathan Orszag and Peter Orszag, "The Empirical Effects of Collegiate Athletics: An Update," National Collegiate Athletic Association, April 2005. Sometimes it is argued that athletics departments support the overall educational mission of the university by generating a surplus that is then transferred to the university's central budget. While it appears to be true that a handful of departments transfer a modest surplus to their university's central fund, in all but a dozen or so of the 351 Division I schools, there is a deficit (when properly accounted) in the athletics department. In 2018–19, the median FBS school athletics department ran an operating deficit of $18.8 million, according to the NCAA's own figures (*Revenues and Expenses Annual Report*, 2020), and this was before the consideration of capital and indirect expenses. Further, sometimes it is claimed that strong athletics programs attract student applications and increase donations to the school. While this is a complicated matter to assess, suffice it to state that the scholarly evidence on each is ambiguous (see chapter 4 in this volume). One reasonable (and complicated) point is that costs can also be overstated when counting the value of athletic scholarships at their sticker price when the average student pays only about 45 percent of the sticker price. After accounting for the fact that many Power Five athletes today receive a cost-of-attendance stipend as well as free room, board, and fees and that athletic scholarships themselves lower the actual pay-to-sticker-price ratio, it is reasonable to maintain that only about 50 percent of the cost attributed to athlete scholarships should be counted. Still, even when this adjustment is made, it has a considerably smaller effect than the cost-increasing adjustments.

12. Steve Berkowitz and Tom Schad, "5 Surprising Findings from College Football Coaches Salaries Report," *USA Today*, October 14, 2020, https://www.usatoday.com/story/sports/ncaaf/2020/10/14/college-football-coaches-salaries-five-surprising-findings-data/5900066002/.

13. "NCAA Salaries," *USA Today*, accessed December 2, 2020, https://sports.usatoday.com/ncaa/salaries/mens-basketball/coach/.

14. Brian Hamilton, "Notre Dame's Weis Buyout May Approach $19 Million," *Chicago Tribune*, May 24, 2013, www.chicagotribune.com.

15. Spencer Fane, "2017–2018 Athletics Directors," accessed September 23, 2020, http://www.sportsinfo.pro/AthleticDirector2018.html.

16. Steve Berkowitz, "Power Five Conferences Had Over $2.9 Billion in Revenue in FY 2019," *USA Today*, July 12, 2020.

17. James Johnson, "The Suicide Season," *Shreveport Times*, September 4, 2008, www.shreveporttimes.com.

18. Allen Barra, *The Last Coach: A Life of Paul "Bear" Bryant* (New York: Norton, 2005).

19. Tom Weir, "Bill Belichick Tops Forbes List of 10 Best-Paid Coaches," *USA Today*, May 16, 2012, www.usatoday.com.

20. Tom Van Riper, "The Highest Paid Coaches in Sports," *Forbes*, May 15, 2012, www.forbes.com.

CHAPTER 2

Reforming College Sports

THE CASE FOR A LIMITED AND CONDITIONAL ANTITRUST EXEMPTION

Jayma Meyer and Andrew Zimbalist

College sports has been undergoing rapid commercialization and reorganization. This transformation has led to sharpening inequality among schools within and between divisions, unstable and unsustainable economics, and burgeoning legal challenges. It is not an exaggeration to state that intercollegiate athletics is at an economic and legal tipping point. This essay first discusses the economic issues confronting college sports. It then turns to consider the plethora of litigation facing the National Collegiate Athletic Association (NCAA) and argues that antitrust and labor laws are inadequate means to respond effectively to the economic and legal challenges surrounding college sports. Finally, the essay makes the case for a limited and conditional antitrust exemption for the NCAA that would promote the primacy of academics and the fair treatment of athletes.

The Economic Environment

Background

To many people, it may seem that big-time college sports is running on a treadmill. Every year more money pours in—whether through new media contracts with national networks, regional sports networks, corporate

---

Antitrust Bulletin, March 2017.

sponsorships, the Football Championship Playoff (FCP), fatter donations, or new ticketing strategies—but the number of the 351 Division I or 130 Football Bowl Subdivision (FBS) programs reporting an operating surplus has stagnated around 25.[1] Moreover, according to the biannual NCAA *Revenues and Expenses Report*, the size of the median program operating deficit in FBS has been steadily growing in recent years, from $5.9 million in 2004 to $9.5 million in 2010, $12.3 million in 2012, $14.7 million in 2014, and $18.8 million in 2019.[2]

It is important to understand what these operating deficits mean. They do not include a substantial share of capital expenses, such as the debt service on stadiums, arenas, training facilities, or tutoring centers that is covered by the institution or the state.[3] Indeed, the 2005 study commissioned by the NCAA estimated that the median capital costs of FBS athletics programs exceeded $20 million annually.

The operating deficits also tend to exclude an array of indirect costs, such as a share of a university president's compensation, office rental and supplies, and staff.[4] Part of the problem is that there are no established counting conventions, so despite instructions from the NCAA, each school uses its own interpretation of the proper accounting methodology. The point is that the reported operating deficits tend to be considerably smaller than actual fully accounted deficits. Some of the financial shortfalls may be offset by increased appropriations from state legislatures, increased student fees, or an uptick in donations to successful programs. This funding, however, is neither robust nor dependable. It applies in a positive way, if at all, to competitively successful programs and applies in a negative way to unsuccessful programs. Moreover, some studies have suggested that donations to athletics can substitute for donations to the general fund, suggesting further financial deficits experienced by the school.

Of course, to be a competitively successful program, schools need to commit to providing abundant resources in the areas of hiring big-name coaches, creating world-class facilities, recruiting aggressively, providing extensive academic tutoring, and so on. That is, with salary payments to athletes prohibited, the most effective way to recruit the best athletes is by providing successful coaches, lavish facilities, and effective support systems. Note that in professional sports in the United States, athlete compensation is controlled by a system of salary caps, debt rules, luxury taxes, and revenue sharing. In college sports, the spending is displaced from athlete compensation to other areas where there are no constraints on spending. This is a system without the necessary restraints for financial success.

Unlike a typical commercial enterprise, college sports programs do not have stockholders who demand a profit at the end of each quarter so that the price of the company's stock will rise or that dividends may be paid out. Rather, college sports programs have stakeholders (e.g., boosters, season-ticket buyers, alumni, administrators, students, and state legislators) who, above all else, want winning teams. The primary pressure placed on athletic directors (ADs) is to find a way to win, not a way to make profits. Moreover, ADs and coaches advance in their careers and are able to command higher and higher compensation packages only if they produce victorious teams. What this means is that when the typical AD at a Power Five–conference school sees additional revenues entering the program, the first and dominant thought is, "How can I put that revenue to use to build a more successful program?" In the hypercompetitive world of big-time college sports and the arms race it engenders, there is always some additional enhancement that an AD is yearning to make.[5]

The result is that the system, even for the 130 richest FBS athletics programs in the country, has growing median operating deficits. In any given year, when properly accounted (e.g., including capital costs), there are probably only half a dozen or so schools that generate a true surplus in their athletics programs.[6]

It bears emphasis that the financial situation of intercollegiate athletics is growing more dire, despite the rapid increase in revenues in recent years. The combination of sharpening inequality across schools and conferences and enormous fees and costs (directly or indirectly) inflicted on athletics programs as a result of various litigations presents an increasingly problematic financial challenge. Changes in telecommunications technology threaten to undermine the long-standing, lucrative model of

TABLE 2.1

REVENUE INEQUALITY AMONG THE APPROXIMATELY TOP 150 ATHLETICS PROGRAMS, 1962–97

Year	*Top school / average school*
1962	1.81
1970	1.92
1980	2.48
1989	3.04
1995	3.29
1997	3.48

expanded basic-cable television and to reduce media revenue streams for college sports in the future. There are too many pressures on the system for it to avoid substantial reform.

Growing Inequality among Athletics Programs

With the NCAA's long-standing national TV policy struck down on antitrust grounds in 1984 by the Supreme Court in *NCAA v. Board of Regents of University of Oklahoma* (*Board of Regents*),[7] schools and conferences were left to fend for themselves. The NCAA television cartel was broken. The leading football colleges and conferences were cut free, and the weaker football colleges lost the protection of the previous NCAA plan.

The data in table 2.1 illustrate the revenue distributional impact of the 1984 *Board of Regents* Supreme Court decision and the conference restructuring of the 1990s.[8] During the eighteen years between 1962 and 1980, there was a steady increase in relative revenue inequality across the top 150 college athletics programs, with the ratio of the top revenue program to the average (mean) revenue program increasing by 0.67 points. During the next seventeen-year period, 1980–97, the ratio increased at a 50 percent faster rate, or by 1.00 point.

It is also noteworthy that the Supreme Court ruling was largely coincident with the explosion in popularity of cable television in the United

States. Whereas in 1980 there were 15.5 million cable-TV homes (or 19.9 percent of TV households), by 1990 there were 52 million cable-TV homes (or 56.4 percent of TV households). As is well known, cable television added a second revenue stream (monthly subscription fees) to the traditional advertising stream, and hence, its expansion helps to explain the rapid growth in television contracts for the elite football conferences in Division I.

Other factors promoting inequality include the Bowl Championship Series (BCS), the Football Championship Playoff (FCP), skewed revenue distributions from the NCAA, the emergence of conference-owned regional sports networks (RSNs), and the explosion of network conference television contracts. Since the inception of the BCS in 1998, and through 2014, it allowed for preferential bowl access and sharply differential revenues to flow to the six original BCS (aka automatic qualifying, or AQ) conferences. The FCP extends the unequal distribution of revenue flows and roughly triples the amount of money distributed.[9]

Although the top/average revenue ratio series ends in 1997, it is possible to extend the trend through 2003 by reference to NCAA data for football and men's basketball programs. Table 2.2 shows that the ratio of the highest revenue program from football and men's basketball to the average revenue program steadily increased from 3.56 in fiscal year 1997 to 3.66 in fiscal year 1999 and to 3.89 in fiscal year 2003.[10]

Since 2003, the NCAA has not reported average (mean) revenues for athletics programs. Instead, it reports only median revenue. With the

TABLE 2.2

FBS FOOTBALL AND MEN'S BASKETBALL REVENUE, 1997–2003

FY	*High*	*Average*	*Ratio (high/average)*
1997	$37,400,000	$10,500,000	3.56
1999	$44,700,000	$12,200,000	3.66
2003	$67,300,000	$17,300,000	3.89

TABLE 2.3

FBS FOOTBALL AND MEN'S BASKETBALL REVENUE, 2004–14 (MILLIONS OF DOLLARS)

FY	*Median generated revenue*	*Top generated revenue*	*Top/median*	*Top–median*
Football				
2004	8.3	46.2	5.6	37.9
2010	16.2	93.9	5.8	77.7
2014	21.7	151	7.0	129.3
Men's basketball				
2004	3.2	16.5	5.2	13.3
2010	4.8	25.9	5.4	21.1
2014	5.8	40.6	7.0	34.8

skewed revenue distribution that prevails in the FBS, the mean is typically considerably above the median, so these two data series are not comparable.

As shown in table 2.3, the ratio of the highest to median revenues in both football and basketball for FBS schools continues its steady ascent between fiscal year 2004 and fiscal year 2014.[11]

This pattern of inequality is underscored by considering the decile breakdown of revenues in football and men's basketball within the 124 FBS schools in fiscal year 2014.[12] In football, 40 percent of the programs had revenues below $7.56 million in fiscal year 2014, while in basketball, 40 percent had revenues below $3.2 million.[13] Meanwhile, the bottom half of FBS schools are trying to remain competitive and are expanding their athletic spending. The average athletic spending per student-athlete in FBS went from $63,000 in 2004 to $85,000 in 2008 to $105,000 in 2012 and to $116,000 in 2014.[14]

As a result of the Football Championship Playoff and mammoth conference television deals (both networks and RSNs), only the schools in the Power Five conferences are generating enough revenues to supply competitive resources to their teams. FBS schools outside the Power Five continue to aspire to the "big time" by building new facilities, hiring high-priced coaches, and attempting to more aggressively recruit, but their prospects for promotion are practically nonexistent. They are wasting resources because, as noted earlier, even among the sixty-five schools in the Power Five, only about twenty are generating an operating surplus, and when capital and other indirect costs are included, the number of programs generating a surplus dwindles to roughly half a dozen.[15]

The inevitable outcome for the overwhelming majority of college athletics programs is that they drain the central educational budget of millions (or tens of millions) of dollars yearly. The drain is only getting larger over time. Universities have attempted to plug the financial leak by raising student fees, increasing tuition, and seeking more taxpayer support from the state legislature. The situation is not financially, politically, or socially sustainable. Nor, as discussed in the following section, is it legally effective.

The Legal Environment

Overview

Litigation tends to trigger NCAA rule changes. Sometimes just the threat of litigation causes reform. Other times, we see new rules after lengthy and expensive litigation that the NCAA has settled or lost. Many times these rules are at the margin (e.g., permitting unlimited snacks for athletes); other times they are more significant (e.g., permitting aid up to the cost of attendance). This is hardly an efficient or effective way to manage college sports, nor is it a satisfactory way to make important public policy decisions regarding higher education.

Litigation involving antitrust laws has been a particular thorn in the NCAA's side. The antitrust laws have been the basis for athletes and others to challenge rules, including payment and benefits to athletes for their play, the length and number of scholarships available to athletes, the length of competitive seasons, the selection of teams to participate in national championships, and the payment of assistant coaches. These litigations have had mixed results. Athletes also have resorted to labor laws to find a friendly basis for pursuing their claims and seeking payment for play and other reforms. Attempts under the Fair Labor Standards Act for college athletes to be declared employees have not yet succeeded at the national level. Attempts by Northwestern University football players to unionize, while finding success at a regional level in Chicago, failed at the national level.

These efforts, described in this section in detail, have helped create a tipping point. Indeed, while the Supreme Court has declined to hear the *O'Bannon* case,[16] lower courts in *Alston*[17] and *Jenkins*,[18] or likely additional new cases,[19] may fundamentally change the landscape of intercollegiate athletics by permitting payment and other benefits beyond the cost of attendance to athletes for their services. Without further Supreme Court guidance, outcomes of these cases are uncertain due to the murkiness in applying current legal frameworks. Moreover, the expense and effort involved in litigating these outcomes are enormous. All of this demonstrates the need for a new approach.

That solution is a limited and conditional antitrust exception. It would permit the NCAA and its member schools to impose certain rules such as prohibiting payment for play (e.g., salaries) to athletes without fear of violating the antitrust laws, while allowing certain types of payments and benefits (e.g., payments for third-party endorsements) to athletes. These exceptions would be provided if cost-spending measures are implemented (e.g., capping coaches' salaries and facilities spending) and player-centric measures are implemented (e.g., protecting the health, safety, and well-being of college athletes and requiring the primacy of academics in intercollegiate athletics).[20] Thus, the proposed limited and conditional exception would promote socially desirable policies that otherwise might not be enacted due to the fear of litigation.

Antitrust Laws and the Judicially Created "Rule of Reason" Framework Are Difficult to Apply to NCAA Rules

The antitrust laws and their judicially created frameworks are not easily applied to intercollegiate sports. The Sherman Act prohibits all contracts, combinations, or conspiracies in restraint of trade that are unreasonable, and it was designed to govern commercial activities. Colleges and universities, most of which are nonprofit organizations, enter into contracts and combinations (i.e., rules) in order jointly to compete in sports.[21] In antitrust cases involving intercollegiate sports, the threshold question is whether the challenged rule is fundamentally commercial in nature. If it is, the overriding question is whether the rule is unreasonable because it causes significant net anticompetitive effects.

Both of these questions require an analysis of factors that are not necessarily comparable and application of a framework originally designed for businesses that does not apply easily to intercollegiate sports. There are no bright-line rules, no clean-cut balancing tests with objective criteria, and few other mechanisms to make these judgments unambiguously. With respect to the threshold question, courts must evaluate rules that have claimed noncommercial purposes (e.g., eligibility rules that preserve amateurism) but that have major commercial effects. While there are no clear definitions of what constitutes a "commercial" restraint, it includes "almost every activity from which [an] actor anticipates economic gain."[22]

Few people would deny that college athletics, especially FBS football and Division I (DI) men's basketball, are commercial enterprises. In fact, despite the economic deficits experienced by many athletics departments, as described earlier, over the past few decades the commerciality of college sports has accelerated.[23] College sports are estimated to be at least a $14 billion industry and growing. Indeed, the NCAA admits that FBS football teams and DI men's basketball teams "command significant commercial interest. That interest exerts pressures that could undermine the distinct and longstanding nature of college athletics, driving them away from being a scholastic endeavor and towards being a professional one."[24] Similarly, the Seventh Circuit Court of Appeals opined in *Agnew v. NCAA*, "No knowledgeable observer could earnestly assert that big-time college football programs . . . do not anticipate economic gain from a successful recruiting program . . . since schools can make millions of dollars as a result of these transactions."[25]

Once a rule is found to be fundamentally commercial, the court must then address the question of whether it is an unreasonable restraint on trade. Here, because the nature of the product—competitive sports—requires joint activity among individual institutions (i.e., a team cannot play by itself), courts apply a "rule of reason" analysis to answer the question.[26] The judicially created rule of reason framework involves three steps. First, the plaintiff has the burden of proving that the restraint creates anticompetitive effects.[27] Second, the burden shifts to the defendant to prove procompetitive benefits flowing from the restraint.[28] Third, if the defendant's justifications are "sufficient,"[29] the burden shifts back to the plaintiff to show that the challenged conduct is not reasonably necessary to achieve the legitimate benefits or that comparable procompetitive benefits could be achieved through a less restrictive alternative (LRA).[30] Courts, at least implicitly, attempt to assess the legitimacy of (or weigh or balance) these pro- and anticompetitive effects and the LRA and therefore determine whether the virtues of the anticompetitive conduct justify the adverse impact.[31] Their judgment turns on whether the dominant or net effect of the restraint, or of the LRA, is to promote competition or hinder it.[32] This informs the ultimate question required by the Sherman Act of whether the challenged behavior is unreasonable.

Although the rule of reason framework—designed to analyze the reasonableness of a restraint—has been embedded in antitrust law for decades, its precise parameters are vague, and its application is inconsistent.[33] As a matter of fact, an operative concept in the Sherman Act—reasonableness—lacks precision. With little guidance on how to quantitatively weigh and balance harms with procompetitive effects and analyze alternatives, many courts purport to apply the framework but, rather subjectively, reach their own conclusions.[34] Indeed, in the second step, with respect to commonly asserted procompetitive justifications in antitrust cases involving intercollegiate sports (such as amateurism, integration of athletics and academics, and competitive balance), lawyers and courts frequently either insufficiently quantify or fail to quantify at all the justifications. Instead, they rely on qualitative assessments of the benefits, making them nearly impossible to weigh against quantitative anticompetitive effects.[35] Accordingly, some courts rather mechanically assume that the procompetitive benefits are sufficient and turn to the third step of analyzing whether less restrictive alternatives exist. This step also suffers from vagueness. Here, too, quantifiable measures are frequently absent, and there is little agreement on how much less restrictive the alternative must be—whether it must be the least anticompetitive restriction, whether it must result in the same procompetitive effects as the challenged restraint, whether it must not impose additional costs, how probable the benefits must be, and so on. As a result, as in earlier steps, frequently courts' rather subjective view of the proposed alternative restriction prevails.[36]

Thus, unquestionably, the fact finder's role in balancing the pro- and anticompetitive effects and alternative restraints is fraught with ambiguity.[37] If fact, despite language to the contrary in many of the cases, and perhaps due to the problems with quantification, true balancing may be rarely, if ever, actually performed: "Rule of reason balancing is perhaps the greatest myth in all of U.S. antitrust law."[38] Some scholars have gone so far as to suggest that balancing should be avoided unless absolutely necessary: "Once we have identified the types and magnitudes of threats to competition, legitimate objectives, and possible alternatives, we have still to reach an 'on balance' judgment about 'reasonableness.' Because both theory and data are usually insufficient and because quantification in terms of a common denominator is usually impossible, balancing will inevitably be crude and should be avoided unless absolutely necessary."[39]

Accordingly, the judicially created analytical framework for the rule of reason, designed to bring clarity to analyzing the reasonableness of restraints under the antitrust laws, is infested with vagueness and subjectivity. Without converting pro- and anticompetitive effects, whether of the original restraint or a less restrictive restraint, into the same measurements, courts weigh incommensurate values[40] or even ignore the process of balancing the effects.

The Supreme Court and Its Progeny Do Not Impart Clarity

The Supreme Court in the seminal case, *NCAA v. Board of Regents*, established that the previously discussed two-step process applies to NCAA rules. First, courts analyzing antitrust challenges to NCAA regulations should distinguish between commercial and noncommercial NCAA regulations.[41] Second, if the rules fall into the commercial bucket, courts should apply the rule of reason to determine if those rules unreasonably restrain competition.[42]

The Supreme Court in *Board of Regents* rather quickly concluded that the challenged contracts that schools jointly negotiated with television networks were commercial rules. However, it made a point to state that not all NCAA rules are commercial: "The specific restraints on football telecasts that are challenged in this case do not, however, fit into the same mold as do rules defining the conditions of the contest, the eligibility of participants, or the manner in which members of a joint enterprise shall share the responsibilities and the benefits of the total venture."[43] This dicta, which was irrelevant to the key issue in the case—legality of the rules regarding TV contracts—opened the door to the NCAA arguing in later cases that its rules, especially "eligibility" rules, are not commercial.

Next, the Court explained that the rule of reason, not the per se illegal rule, should be used because the case "involves an industry in which horizontal restraints on competition are essential if the product is to be available at all."[44] Applying the first step of the rule of reason framework, the Court found that the restraint limited output (reduced the number of games televised) and restricted prices (set a minimum aggregate price)—"paradigmatic examples of restraints of trade that the Sherman Act was intended to prohibit."[45] Shifting to the second step of the rule of reason, the Court stated that the contracts, as "hallmarks of anticompetitive behavior," placed a "heavy burden" on the NCAA to establish an affirmative defense that justifies the deviation from a free market.[46] The Court then upheld the lower court's findings that the procompetitive justifications of protecting a live audience, establishing an efficient marketing strategy, and preserving competitive balance were not supported by the evidence and thus did not "offset" the anticompetitive limitations on price and output. Because step 2 was not satisfied, the Court never reached consideration of a less restrictive alternative, although it stated that it agreed with the lower court's conclusion that if the procompetitive justifications had been supported by the evidence, they could be achieved by a less restrictive alternative.[47] Other than the Supreme Court's admonition that the NCAA carried a "heavy burden" at the second stage, it provided no specific guidance on what weights to assign to or how to balance the pro- and anticompetitive effects. Unlike most litigated cases, here the anticompetitive effects were undeniably strong and the procompetitive effects absent.

While the Court's application of the rule of reason was quite straightforward given the particular facts, its opinion included some discourse that has caused much debate in subsequent cases. Particularly, dicta about payments to athletes, like its dicta noted earlier about eligibility rules, have stirred confusion and unpredictability. Explaining that the distinction between professional sports and college athletics justified the application of the rule of reason,[48] the Court expressed that college athletes "must not be paid, must be required to attend class, and the like."[49] The Court did not analyze whether such rules would be unreasonable under the burden-shifting framework. Rules regarding payments to athletes were irrelevant to the issue at hand—the legality of the rules regarding TV contracts. Yet it is that dicta that the NCAA has regarded as controlling in subsequent cases that explicitly analyze restraints that prohibit payments to athletes.

Accordingly, the Supreme Court's holding has limited precedential value regarding (1) the determination of whether particular rules are commercial (since the restraint there was so obviously commercial) and (2) the precise application of the rule of reason to subsequent cases that have mixed anti- and procompetitive effects (since the effects there were so apparently anticompetitive—restraining prices and output—and the proffered justifications irrelevant to the restraint). While virtually every court that has considered the antitrust legality of NCAA rules since *Board of Regents* has attempted to apply it, without more precise guidance, predictably, there has been insufficient consensus.

Certain courts have given great deference to the dicta in *Board of Regents*. For example, they have found NCAA rules, such as rules prohibiting the use of agents, to be noncommercial and therefore held that the Sherman Act does not apply. They explicitly base their conclusions on the NCAA's argument that the rules are "eligibility" rules that implicate the NCAA's requirement of amateurism (even if they also have a commercial impact).[50]

On the contrary, especially given the pervasiveness of commercialism in FBS football and DI men's basketball, courts more recently have held that a variety of NCAA rules, such as rules limiting the number of athletic scholarships and their time period, are commercial and subject to the Sherman Act despite the NCAA's arguments that the rules are necessary to preserve amateurism and a clear demarcation between college and professional sports. For example, in *Agnew v. NCAA*, a class of football players challenged the NCAA limits on the number of athletic scholarships that schools could award per team and the one-year scholarship rule.[51] The Seventh Circuit rejected the NCAA's argument that the rules were noncommercial and held that the rule of reason applied. Significantly, the court was skeptical about the NCAA's reliance on amateurism to justify the restraint, stating that "whether or not a player receives four years of educational expenses or one year . . . he is still an amateur."[52] The court did not further analyze this issue. Given the procedural posture of the case—a motion to dismiss—the court was required to accept the allegations as true and only to determine the plausibility that the allegations stated a claim.[53]

Not surprisingly, courts find that rules with more direct monetary significance, like setting specific salaries, are easier to analyze and conclude that they are commercial and are unreasonable restraints in violation of the Sherman Act.[54] For example, attempts by the NCAA to set salaries of assistant coaches were analyzed under a quick rule of reason analysis and found to be illegal in *Law v. NCAA*.[55] There, part-time men's basketball coaches challenged an NCAA regulation labeling part-time coaches as "restricted-earnings coaches" and limiting their compensation to $16,000 annually (a reduction of approximately 70 percent for some part-time coaches).[56] The court held that the alleged procompetitive cost-cutting justifications were not sufficient and that the price-fixing restrictions were illegal.[57]

Recent Cases Seek Clarity

The fuzziness in applying the antitrust laws and the judicially created rule of reason framework to NCAA rules, especially those rules that potentially have mixed effects and purposes—for example, socially desirable justifications but clear anticompetitive impact—is starkly illustrated in several recent cases: *O'Bannon*, *Jenkins*, and *Alston*.

O'Bannon. *O'Bannon*'s now tortured history began with a class-action complaint in 2009 filed in the Northern District of California.[58] The complaint challenged the NCAA's rules prohibiting purported classes of FBS football and DI men's basketball players from receiving payments for their names, images, and likenesses (NILs) in video games and live or archived television broadcasts. The NCAA rules prohibiting payments to athletes beyond grant-in-aid (GIA) scholarships did not specifically address, but subsumed, payments for NILs. After an enormous amount of legal maneuvering, and five years after the complaint was filed, the Honorable Judge Claudia Wilken issued a ninety-nine-page opinion in 2014, finding the rules to be commercial and, thus, subject to the Sherman Act and an unreasonable restraint of trade.[59]

The NCAA in *O'Bannon* had attempted to classify its no-payment rules as noncommercial "eligibility" rules that were necessary to protect the amateur product of college athletics. As such, and relying on *Board of Regents* dicta, the NCAA argued the rules were not subject to the Sherman Act and accordingly were legal. Judge Wilken rejected this argument and found that the NCAA was a cartel that engages in commercial restraints.[60]

Judge Wilken then applied the rule of reason to determine whether the alleged prohibitions violated the Sherman Act. She summarized the law by stating that "a restraint violates the rule of reason if the restraint's harm to competition outweighs its procompetitive effects."[61] And she said it was appropriate to rely on a "burden-shifting framework to conduct this balancing."[62]

First, Judge Wilken found that the plaintiffs demonstrated that the prohibitions were a restraint with an anticompetitive effect—a price-fixing agreement. That is, athletes were prohibited from negotiating group licenses for their NILs and received zero compensation for them.[63] Next, under the second step, the burden switched to the NCAA to demonstrate that there were compensating procompetitive justifications for its restrictive rules. The NCAA relied on four justifications; to wit, its rules were necessary to protect

- amateurism;
- integration of athletics with academics and the rest of the student body;
- competitive balance among schools; and
- output or viewership.[64]

Judge Wilken accepted as valid the first two of these justifications, finding that amateurism played a "limited" role in maximizing consumer demand and that integration of athletics and academics was a "narrow" procompetitive goal of increasing the quality of athletes' education.[65] She rejected the last two justifications on the basis that there was an insufficient relation between them and the restraint.[66] Judge Wilken did not reveal an in-depth balancing analysis to support her conclusion that the first two proffered procompetitive effects were "sufficient" and may increase consumer demand for college athletics or quality of educational services, despite her earlier comment that typically courts apply the burden-shifting framework to conduct a balancing of harm and procompetitive effects.[67] Instead, she said that because the defendant established two sufficient procompetitive benefits, it was appropriate to move to the third step required under the rule of reason, which places a burden on the plaintiffs to demonstrate that there are other and better ways through less restrictive means to accomplish the procompetitive justifications.[68] More particularly, she said that the plaintiffs must show that an alternative is substantially less restrictive and as effective without significantly increased costs.[69] While not revealing any explicit balancing here either, her use of "substantially" and "significantly" indicates some type of weighing.[70] Judge Wilken found that two less restrictive means were available to fulfill the NCAA's stated procompetitive justifications of amateurism and integration:

- Payment of scholarships up to cost of attendance (COA) (an increase of between $2,000 and $6,000 per year, depending on the school, over the previous grant-in-aid (GIA) amount)[71]
- Payment of up to $5,000 a year to be held in trust for when the athlete leaves or graduates from college with the requirements that all athletes on a team receive the same amount and that the funds be generated from group licenses[72]

Although celebrated by some people as a big win for the plaintiffs, it was somewhat of a hollow victory because by the time of the decision, the NCAA's rules already had changed to permit scholarships up to the COA. Plus, the trust-fund stipends did not help the athletes while they were in college and had other limitations as described earlier. The true win was to future plaintiffs, in that a court had explicitly held that the NCAA rules prohibiting payments to athletes beyond the direct costs in

GIA, even if called "eligibility rules," are rules with commercial effects and are unreasonable pursuant to a rule of reason antitrust analysis under the Sherman Act.

Both sides then had reason to be dissatisfied and shifted gears to pursue a hotly debated appeal to the Ninth Circuit. The Ninth Circuit, after extensive briefing by the parties, eleven amici curiae briefs,[73] and a lengthy hearing, issued its decision in September 2015.[74] Judges Jay Bybee and Gordon Quist and Chief Judge Sidney Thomas agreed that the restriction of no payments for NILs was a commercial restraint subject to the Sherman Act. This was a loss for the NCAA on a fundamental premise. Further, the Ninth Circuit disagreed with the NCAA's claim that under *Board of Regents*, its "amateurism" rules were valid as a matter of law. Instead, the Ninth Circuit said that *Board of Regents* required such rules to be analyzed under the rule of reason.

In applying the three-step burden-shifting framework, first, the Ninth Circuit agreed with the district court that the restraint had a "significant" anticompetitive effect by eliminating price competition among schools.[75] Moving to the second step in the rule of reason analysis, it accepted that amateurism and integration were procompetitive justifications because they preserve the popularity of intercollegiate sports and broadened choices, respectively. Third, the Ninth Circuit considered the proposed alterative restraints. It upheld Judge Wilken's injunction that the NCAA could restrict the schools' ability to award scholarship amounts above the COA. The Ninth Circuit agreed that this was "substantially" less restrictive than a rule prohibiting payments beyond GIA and would not "significantly" increase costs.[76] The panel's reasoning focused on the necessity of amateurism to college sports: (1) amateurism requires no payment to athletes, so there would be no amateurism if there were payments; and (2) payments up to the COA were "tethered" to academics and therefore preserved the concept of amateurism.[77]

However, the panel split on the issue of trust-fund stipends for NIL rights, with the majority finding that they violated principles of amateurism because they were untethered to academics. Chief Judge Thomas's dissent on this issue challenged the artificiality of the majority's distinction and detailed the evidence that showed that small amounts of cash payments (beyond COA) provided to athletes after they left school would not harm the principle of amateurism. Plus, Chief Judge Thomas pointed out that amateurism, a "nebulous" concept, is relevant as a procompetitive justification in an antitrust analysis only to the extent that it relates to consumer interest (a quantitative effect).[78] He stated that there was no showing that such small, deferred payments would harm consumer interest.

Interestingly, at no point did the Ninth Circuit discuss or engage in any explicit balancing.[79] Indeed, the majority's conclusion stated, "When . . . regulations truly serve procompetitive purposes, courts should not hesitate to uphold them."[80] However, it stressed that a restraint is illegal where it is "patently and inexplicably stricter than is necessary,"[81] implying that some quantification and balancing must be conducted.

Again, both sides had reason to be dissatisfied. Accordingly, after the plaintiffs' request for an en banc rehearing to the full Ninth Circuit Court of Appeals was denied,[82] in a somewhat unusual consensus on the need for review, both the plaintiffs and the NCAA submitted petitions for writ of certiorari to the Supreme Court.[83] On October 3, 2016, the Supreme Court announced that it would not accept certiorari.[84] The Ninth Circuit's decision remains intact, resulting in continued uncertainty generally about the reach of the Court's 1984 holding in *Board of Regents* and the proper application of the rule of reason to NCAA rules, including the extent to which amateurism justifies a restraint on player compensation, the parameters of the less restrictive alternative analysis, and whether, when, and what balancing should take place. More specifically, there continues to be uncertainty, especially outside the Ninth Circuit, about whether schools can agree that college athletes cannot be paid more than cost-of-attendance scholarships and whether the compensation must be tethered to college expenses. As a result, the NCAA is left vulnerable to more challenges.[85]

***Jenkins* and *Alston*.** Among the most recently filed class-action cases to challenge the NCAA's no-pay rules[86] are *Jenkins v. NCAA* [*and the Power Five conferences*][87] and *Alston v. NCAA* [*and the Power Five conferences plus six other conferences*].[88] The cases allege that the NCAA and conferences systematically colluded to set a cap on the amount of compensation a school may provide athletes. The complaints seek to open the compensation issue to the free market. They seek an injunction that strikes down the alleged illegal restraints without specifying what other rules would be lawful.[89] However, the plaintiffs' lawyers, possibly reacting to criticisms of the *O'Bannon* decision that the court had micromanaged the NCAA, have suggested that a possible alternative is that the conferences could unilaterally decide appropriate levels of pay.

While *Jenkins* and *Alston* have been coordinated for pretrial purposes in the Northern District of California before Judge Wilken (the same judge that decided *O'Bannon*), there is a significant difference between the cases. *Jenkins* seeks only injunctive relief.[90] *Alston* seeks not only injunctive relief but also monetary damages for four years (amount of time permitted under the applicable statute of limitations) of the difference between GIA and COA scholarships. The plaintiffs have alleged that this comes to $240 million. Judge Wilken in December 2015 certified three classes of athletes for the injunctive relief claims in *Jenkins* and *Alston*: FBS football players, DI men's basketball players, and DI women's basketball players. Certification of the proper classes for the monetary damage claims in *Alston* continues to be litigated.

There was some initial jockeying once *Jenkins* was coordinated with *Alston*. One result is that the lawyers for the *Jenkins* plaintiffs are now cocounsel with the plaintiffs in *Alston* for the claims seeking injunctive relief. However, it remains unclear how, when, or where the cases will be tried. The injunctive relief sought in *Jenkins* and *Alston* may end up being tried together. Or all the claims may be tried together. And another possibility is that *Jenkins* may go back for trial to the Northern District of New Jersey, where it was originally filed.

Importantly, these cases, if successful, may fundamentally change college sports as we know them. They will be decided by courts that must answer the messy questions: (1) Which rules fundamentally are commercial? (2) If they are commercial, what are the anti- and procompetitive justifications?[91] (3) Are there less restrictive alternatives? and (4) What is the net effect of all this? To the extent the claims remain before Judge Wilken, the Ninth Circuit's decision in *O'Bannon* is binding, including that the NCAA's rules on compensation to intercollegiate athletes are subject to the Sherman Act. On the other hand, among other things, the plaintiffs will be challenged by the Ninth Circuit's holding that payments must be tethered to academics.[92]

Cases Based on Labor Laws Provide No Relief

Athletes, who have found the antitrust laws inhospitable to demands to be paid for their services beyond a COA scholarship, have resorted to the labor laws. For example, in *Berger v. NCAA*, the University of Pennsylvania women's track-and-field athletes alleged that they are "employees" under the Federal Labor Standards Act (FLSA) and therefore entitled to be paid for playing, just like students in work-study programs are paid.[93] The district court in southern Indiana granted the defendants' motions to dismiss on February 16, 2016, and stated that the relationship between athletes and institutions of higher education is fundamentally an "educational experience," more akin to extracurricular student-run programs than to work-study programs. On December 5, 2016, the Seventh Circuit affirmed, agreeing with the district court that intercollegiate sports are extracurricular "play," not "work,"[94] and that their economic reality is based on the revered tradition of amateurism. While the Seventh Circuit agreed that student-athletes are not employees and should not be paid, the concurring opinion muddied the waters by stating that the economic reality and tradition of amateurism in revenue-producing sports like DI men's basketball and FBS football may dictate a different result.[95] Accordingly, we can expect to see more cases brought under the FLSA, especially by revenue-producing athletes.

Efforts to Unionize Fail

Much of the joint activity in the professional sports leagues is exempted from the antitrust laws under a nonstatutory labor exemption. Professional players, through respective unions, negotiate collective bargaining agreements with owners and agree on numerous noncommercial details (e.g., conduct policies) and restrictive commercial rules (e.g., player and team salary caps and reserve clauses) that otherwise would be prohibited under the Sherman Act.

Attempting to gain a similar right to negotiate terms and conditions of play, a group of football players at Northwestern University, under the guidance of the College Athletes Players Association (CAPA), filed a petition in 2013 to gain the right to unionize.

Peter Sung Ohr, regional director in Chicago of the National Labor Relations Board, after extensive briefing and a hearing, held that the Northwestern football players who received scholarships had a right to unionize. He concluded that the athletes were employees under the National Labor Relations Act because, inter alia, they are subject to special rules. For instance, they are required to

- live in on-campus dormitories for freshman and sophomore years;
- obtain permission from the athletics department to obtain outside employment;
- disclose to the department information regarding the vehicle they drive; and
- abide by a social media policy.[96]

Ohr also found that the players are prohibited from engaging in numerous types of activity such as

- swearing in public;
- transferring to another school in order to play football immediately; and
- profiting off their names, images, and likenesses[97]

And he found, among other things, that the players were subject to many other rules, none of which were applicable to the general student body; for example, they must

- wear certain clothes when traveling to away games;
- attend study hall a certain number of hours; and
- stay within a six-hour radius of campus on game days.[98]

Also crucial to Ohr's conclusion that the scholarship football players were employees was the amount of time they devoted to football. Five pages of Ohr's decision detailed those time commitments. He found that the time commitments totaled fifty to sixty hours per week during training camp, forty to fifty hours per week during the season, and twenty-five hours in a number of two-day periods traveling to and from games and competing in the games.[99]

On the basis of these time commitments, the control exercised over the players (through the many rules such as those just listed), and benefits received by the university from the players (e.g., the Northwestern football program generated $30.1 million in operating revenue and $21.7 million in operating expenses in the 2012–13 academic year), Ohr concluded that the scholarship football players were "employees" and entitled to vote on whether to unionize and be represented for collective bargaining purposes by CAPA.[100]

This decision was heralded as a breakthrough for the protection of the rights of college athletes. Such optimism was short-lived, as the NCAA immediately appealed to the full NLRB in Washington, DC. Many observers expected the full board to rather quickly uphold the regional director's conclusions based on his careful and detailed findings.

Instead, the board took seventeen months to "punt." It failed to address the merits of the matter and found that it would not promote labor harmony to accept jurisdiction. In particular, the NLRB made three key observations: (1) intercollegiate athletics was in a transitional phase in 2015; (2) allowing unionization would have engendered systemic instability by permitting only athletes at the 17 private colleges out of 128 FBS schools to unionize; and (3) there was a need to resolve the labor-market issues and academic tensions in the current system.[101] Significantly, the NLRB made a call to the US Congress to clarify the institutional structure of college sports by concluding with a plea that it was addressing the "case in the absence of explicit Congressional direction regarding whether the Board should exercise jurisdiction" and emphasizing that it was leaving open the issue of whether it might find jurisdiction in another case involving scholarship players.[102]

Congressional Intervention Is Necessary

In addition to the inconsistent application of the unsatisfactory analytical rule of reason framework as applied in the sports area (as discussed earlier), other reasons support the need for congressional action in the form of a limited and conditional antitrust exemption.[103] These include that resources are misallocated and spent on litigation instead of academic support or health and safety assistance for athletes' and that courts are ill equipped to make important decisions impacting the future of college sports.

Excessive Time, Money, and Effort Are Spent on Legal Matters

Time, money, and effort by the NCAA, conferences, and schools should be spent on ensuring the integrity of college sports, ensuring the health and safety of college athletes, and maximizing the academic experience of these students. Instead, the NCAA, conferences, and schools are all spending excessive time, money, and effort defending themselves in the many attempts by athletes to be paid (and receive other benefits) for their play, whether via the antitrust or labor laws as detailed earlier.[104] The *O'Bannon* case highlights the misplacement of resources. The complaint was filed in July 2009, and the merits were not resolved until October 2016, when the Supreme Court declined to accept the writs for certiorari. The following list demonstrates the highly litigious—"leave no stone unturned"—approach by both sides in the *O'Bannon* case:[105]

- Trial court
  - 1,161,043 pages of documents were produced by the NCAA.
  - Over seventy-six depositions were conducted.
  - Over ten motions to dismiss were made.
  - Twenty-three live witnesses testified at trial (plaintiffs had nine witnesses, while the NCAA had fifteen witnesses).
  - 287 trial exhibits were admitted.
  - Trial lasted three weeks.
  - Trial transcript was 3,395 pages.
  - At least seventy-six motions were made by the parties.
  - Along the way, there were five Notices of Interlocutory Appeal to the Ninth Circuit (including the appeal of the district court's final decision).
  - Three posttrial briefs were filed.
  - Permanent injunction findings of fact and conclusions of law were ninety-nine pages long.

- Ninth Circuit
  - Both sides appealed the permanent injunction decision to the Ninth Circuit.
  - Eleven amici curiae briefs were submitted in connection with the appeal of permanent injunction.
  - Plaintiffs submitted a motion for an en banc hearing.
  - Both sides hired additional renowned appellate lawyers.

- Supreme Court
  - Both sides submitted petitions for writ of certiorari and briefs in opposition.
  - Four amici curiae briefs were submitted.

Further, the parties have hotly debated the plaintiffs' fees and costs. The plaintiffs made a request for $50.2 million, of which Judge Wilken ordered the NCAA to pay slightly more than $40 million.[106] The NCAA challenged that amount in both the district court and Ninth Circuit.[107] As of November 2016, there was no final decision.

Significantly, the fee request is only for the plaintiffs' attorney fees and costs through the trial. It does not include, inter alia, the plaintiffs' fees and costs posttrial, all the defendants' fees and costs, and the time and expenses of internal NCAA lawyers and witnesses, among others. Since the fee request was made in 2015, both sides have invested substantially more time and expense in this one case, including the appeal to the Ninth Circuit and petitions for writ of certiorari to the Supreme Court.

Further, the fee request does not reflect any of the fees, costs, and settlement amounts paid in related claims. The *O'Bannon* plaintiffs settled with defendants Electronic Arts and the Collegiate Licensing Co. (the NCAA licensing arm) for $40 million. The NCAA settled with the *Keller* plaintiffs (the video-game plaintiffs) for $20 million. The *Keller* claims that had been initially consolidated with the *O'Bannon* claims concerned an alleged violation of publicity rights as a result of the use of NCAA FBS players' and basketball players' names, images, and likenesses in certain NCAA-branded video games by Electronic Arts.[108]

Time, money, and effort, unquestionably, would be much better spent on ensuring the integrity of college athletics and reinforcing the primacy of academics. *O'Bannon* and its extremely lengthy litigation history illustrate a misplacement of resources. There are no indications that *Jenkins* and *Alston* or any of the cases brought under the labor laws will be any less vigorously litigated.

The Judicial System Is Ill Suited to Make Important Decisions Impacting the Future of College Sports

Most courts and applicable judicial processes have limited practical capacity to fully address the desirability and scope of rules protecting college sports.[109] Rules of evidence, constrained testimony, limited briefing, and artfully constructed oral arguments are not conducive to full analyses of all the stakeholders' information, positions, and implications thereof necessary to resolving these important public policy matters.[110] Further, as discussed in detail earlier, courts have latitude in determining whether particular rules are commercial and subject to the Sherman Act. Moreover, the long-standing framework for applying the rule of reason process, particularly analyses and balancing of pro- and anticompetitive effects and less restrictive alternatives, is immensely difficult to apply in any context and much more so in this context.

Scholarly Analyses Demonstrate the Need for Congressional Intervention

Many recent scholarly analyses have focused on the difficulties in applying the antitrust laws to the NCAA's rules on payments to intercollegiate athletes. For example, Scott Hemphill, in his recent article "Less Restrictive Alternatives in Antitrust Law," discusses the "anxiety about balancing" in this context and precisely explained some of the difficulties:

> Although modern antitrust law has economics at its core, applying cost-benefit analysis to real-world conduct is not a straightforward task. Assessing the net effect of mixed conduct is hard. It is challenging to measure the effects of, say, a loss in competition for players arising from limits on compensation. (How much would the players receive? Which ones? What would be the change in output, if any?) Measuring the benefits to competition among sports leagues is also hard. (Would fans otherwise watch less college sports? How much worse is the next-best use of fans' time? What are the effects on advertising markets?) A full analysis requires an assessment of size, probability, and error costs. Such quantification, at least in a rough sense, is necessary in order to compare the two effects.
>
> Implementation is a further, potentially difficult issue. Judges are generalists, see antitrust cases only rarely, are generally unfamiliar with the practice and industry at issue, and are therefore not well equipped

to evaluate these effects. The limited fact-finding capacity of courts is a familiar refrain, as is courts' limited capacity in antitrust cases, particularly if the fact-finding is performed by a jury.[111]

Herbert Hovenkamp, in discussing *O'Bannon* and the "problems at work" in collegiate sports, advocates that antitrust laws are not the solution and says that "any fix that addresses all of [the] problems will probably have to come from Congress."[112] In fact, numerous law professors and economists, in addition to the court of public opinion, have recognized that a new course is necessary to resolve this complex issue in intercollegiate sports.[113]

Judges Recognize the Need for Congressional Intervention

Judges, too, have increasingly recognized the difficulties in applying antitrust laws and legal frameworks to intercollegiate sports and have suggested that Congress may need to intervene.

Judge Wilken, in the District Court for the Northern District of California, after spending five years as the judge in the *O'Bannon* case, expressed her dissatisfaction with the ability of antitrust laws to resolve the NIL pay-for-play issue:

> College sports generate a tremendous amount of interest, as well as revenue and controversy. Interested parties have strong and conflicting opinions about the best policies to apply in regulating these sports. Before the Court in this case is only whether the [NCAA can restrict athletes' payment for NILs to GIA scholarships].
>
> To the extent other criticisms have been leveled against the NCAA and college policies and practices, those are not raised and cannot be remedied based on the antitrust causes of action in this lawsuit. It is likely that the challenged restraints, as well as other perceived inequities in college athletics and higher education generally, could be better addressed as a policy matter by reforms other than those available

> as a remedy for the antitrust violation found here. Such reforms and remedies could be undertaken by the NCAA, its member schools and conferences, or Congress.[114]

Indeed, Judge Wilken, two years after she issued her opinion in *O'Bannon*, said, "Any rule of reason case almost is a tabula rasa, because you're weighing apples against oranges."[115] She further said that because the antitrust analysis has many complications, she did not know how she would have designed jury instructions if the *O'Bannon* case had proceeded to a jury trial.[116]

Similarly, Chief Judge Thomas, of the Ninth Circuit Court of Appeals, in *O'Bannon* pointed out the difficulty in resolving whether athletes should be paid for play: "The national debate about amateurism in college sports is important. But our task as appellate judges is not to resolve it. Nor could we."[117] Also, as noted earlier, the NLRB, in declining to accept jurisdiction over whether the Northwestern University football players could unionize, implied that the issue of whether athletes are employees and therefore should be paid might be most appropriately decided by Congress: "We address this case in the absence of explicit congressional direction regarding whether the Board should exercise jurisdiction."[118]

Quite simply, the adversarial system is not the place to make meaningful and appropriate decisions in the intercollegiate sports arena, where certain cooperation among competitors and jointly enacted rules are necessary to the product and where their elimination would have numerous direct and unintended consequences.

Reform Proposal: A Limited and Conditional Antitrust Exemption

Intercollegiate athletics, as discussed earlier, are increasingly commercial but still a hybrid model, containing elements of both professionalism and amateurism. The tension between these elements has yielded hypocrisy, waste, and exploitation. Effective reform will necessarily move the system toward one end of the spectrum or the other.

Moving toward professionalism and pay for play poses many challenges. First, how would the system be structured? With 17 private schools and 111 public schools in FBS, collective bargaining seems beyond reach. Without collective bargaining, there is no nonstatutory labor exemption, so it is unclear how restraints on a free labor market (such as a salary or team caps) could be imposed lawfully. If restraints were fashioned by a court order (such as in *O'Bannon*), then college labor markets would be determined by judges and lawyers. Absent a rational and democratically determined set of labor-market restraints that takes into account more than just one or several isolated challenged restraints, an open labor market would evolve into a free-for-all. For example, it could accelerate the rapacious recruiting of seventeen-year-old high school athletes. This, in turn, would eventually mean that aggressive player agents would be hanging around high school athletic facilities to sign up fifteen- and sixteen-year-olds. The goal of subordinating athletics to the educational mission of colleges, now hanging on a thin thread, would be obliterated.

Second, there is little question that only the few biggest star athletes on FBS football and male basketball teams are economically exploited. Some of these athletes produce a value of over $1 million per year for their schools.[119] In exchange, they receive a full-ride scholarship that may be worth up to $60,000 or $70,000 per year (assuming optimistically that they actually receive an education). The balance of athletes on these squads are lightly exploited, are not exploited, or, for the majority of the eighty-five football scholarship athletes, receive compensation in the form of scholarship, first-class travel, and perquisites in excess of the value they produce. If there is concern over athlete exploitation, it should be focused on the few top star athletes. But these athletes are professionals in training and will soon be earning multimillion-dollar salaries in the professional leagues. The major issue they confront is the possibility of career-ending injury. This problem can be addressed by offering the star athletes income-replacement insurance for a career-ending disability (such insurance is now permitted by NCAA rules, but the athlete must pay for it)[120] and by permitting regulated third-party payments for NILs to those stars.

Third, introducing pay for play will be expensive. The median operating deficit in FBS was already $14.7 million in fiscal year 2014 and growing. With capital and indirect costs, the median deficit balloons to more than $20 million or $30 million. If athletes become employees, then schools will have to pay salaries as well as make payments for Social Security, workers' compensation, unemployment insurance, and other benefits. Athletes will have to pay income and Social Security taxes on their compensation. Schools may lose some of their favorable Unrelated Business Income Tax (UBIT) treatment by the IRS, along with other tax preferences. In the end, the educational budget and learning process will suffer further damage.[121]

Fourth, there is the question of how pay for play will affect the popularity of college sports as amateur competition. Some people argue that if college athletes are paid, fans will perceive intercollegiate athletics as they perceive minor league sports. Accordingly, attendance and television contracts will fall. Others argue that a similar claim was made when there was discussion of paying Olympic athletes in the 1970s, but the Olympics has only grown in popularity since the 1980s, when Olympic athletes were first allowed to compete as professionals.[122] In truth, while compelling arguments can be made on both sides of the debate, no one knows what the impact on fandom will be from the professionalization of college sports.

Thus, there are many reasons to avoid the further marketization and professionalization of college sports. Fortunately, there is a more attractive reform path: reinforce the educational model.

One logical way to confront the tendency toward the subordination of academics to athletics is to revisit the major source of the post-1984 commercialization juggernaut: the antitrust treatment of college sports.[123] By legislating a partial and conditional antitrust exemption for the governing body of college sports, it would be possible not only to blunt the incentives that are corroding academic integrity but also to arrest the runaway expenses that are burning a deep hole in the pockets of athletics programs and, therefore, also of university budgets.

That is, on the condition that the NCAA enacts certain reforms to promote academic integrity and the fair treatment of athletes, Congress would grant an antitrust exemption in certain commercial areas and elsewhere where commercial and academic concerns overlap. Congressional involvement is necessary because rules such as controlling compensation to athletes, compensation to coaches, the value and number of athletic scholarships, the number of pre- and postseason tournaments, the limit of twenty countable hours of practice and games during the week, and so on are designed to protect the separation between college and professional sports. But, as argued earlier, there are no clear-cut balancing tests or other mechanisms to make policy judgments cleanly about whether they are in fact justified and necessary. The answers end up depending on the judgment of particular courts and not on any clear objective standards.

A limited antitrust exemption would seek to define clearly those NCAA rules that could not be challenged under the Sherman Antitrust Act on the grounds that they are controls necessary to achieve the priority purposes of higher education in the conduct of intercollegiate athletics as an extracurricular activity.

Unquestionably, a fundamental function of the NCAA is to maintain a clear line of demarcation between college sports as an extracurricular activity secondary to the academic responsibilities of students, on the one hand, and professional sports—which require a time and effort priority on athletic excellence and revenue decisions inappropriate for a nonprofit educational institution—on the other hand. Actions that should be considered the legitimate functions of a nonprofit national intercollegiate athletics governance association typically include, among others, those that (1) control the cost of athletics (athletics programs are heavily subsidized by student fees and general funds) so the support of athletics programs does not damage the ability of the institution to support its primary academic programs; (2) prevent the operation of varsity sport programs from conflicting with student academic responsibilities (e.g., controlling sport schedules so they do not conflict with class attendance, restricting athletic participation of students who are not performing academically, limiting the time students spend on sport activities in order to allow sufficient time for attending class and studying); (3) enhance competitive balance among schools and conferences; and (4) protect the health and welfare of college athletes (e.g., providing proper health-insurance coverage and safeguards after injury before returning to play).

Many of these actions also have commercial implications and have been or will be the target of antitrust lawsuits absent a limited antitrust exemption. A limited antitrust exemption that applies only to these legitimate categories of controls will enable institutions of higher education to collectively enact needed reforms without fear of legal liability. Such a limited exemption is both justifiable and necessary. Antitrust lawsuits represent huge costs for legal representation, participation in court cases, and payment of damages.[124] These funds would otherwise be available to advance the NCAA's and its member institutions' nonprofit educational purposes.

Next we elaborate on what areas might be granted an antitrust exemption and on the conditions the NCAA must follow to qualify for the partial exemption.

Potentially Exempt Areas

First, the NCAA would be exempt from imposing limits on the salaries paid to head and assistant football and men's basketball coaches,[125] which often exceed the salaries of the universities' presidents by a factor of five to ten. Over 110 college football and basketball coaches received salaries exceeding $1 million in fiscal year 2014; three dozen exceeded $3 million, and fifteen exceeded $4 million. The highest paid coach was Nick Saban at Alabama, with a salary of $7.2 million plus potential bonuses of $700,000.[126] His contract is guaranteed, with increases through the 2021–22 season. Saban's staff earned an additional $5.2 million in salary in

2014, including a $525,000 salary for the strength and conditioning coach. Thus, total football-coaching compensation at Alabama before handsome benefits and rich perquisites exceeded $13 million. Perquisites generally include free use of cars, housing subsidies, country-club memberships, private jet service, exceptionally generous severance packages, and more.[127] The coaches also have handsome opportunities to earn outside income via apparel or sneaker endorsements, the lecture circuit, summer camps, and book contracts. In forty states, the head football or basketball coach on a college team makes more in guaranteed compensation than the governor does.[128]

Defenders of multimillion-dollar salaries for head coaches argue that coaches' compensation packages are driven by market forces. Perhaps that is true, but the market for coaches is sustained by artificial factors: (1) no compensation is paid to the athletes; (2) intercollegiate sports benefit from substantial tax privileges; (3) no shareholders demand dividend distributions or higher profits to bolster stock prices at the end of every quarter; (4) athletics departments are nourished by university and statewide financial support; and (5) coaches' salaries are frequently negotiated by athletic directors whose own worth rises with the salaries of their employees.

In a normal competitive market, college football and basketball coaches would not be compensated almost at the same level as NFL and NBA coaches. The top thirty-two college football programs generate revenues between $35 million and $150 million; NFL teams generate between $296 million and $620 million.[129] The top thirty college men's basketball teams generate roughly between $10 million and $40 million in revenue, while NBA team revenues are from $110 million up to $293 million. Thus, NFL team revenues are 8.4 times greater than revenues of college football teams at the lower end and 4.1 times at the top end; NBA team revenues are 11.0 times greater than those in college basketball at the lower end and 7.3 times greater at the top end. Yet the compensation packages of college and professional coaches in football and basketball are strikingly similar.

Most FBS college coaches are paid the value created by the players they recruit. Much of the recruiting is done by assistant coaches, and much of the allure of the recruitment effort is a function of the school's history, brand, and facilities. Moreover, the coaches' bloated compensation packages are almost all economic rent. That is, they are paid way beyond what they would have to be paid to induce them to offer their labor in the college coaching market. If the Nick Sabans and John Caliparis of the college coaching world did not coach in an FBS program, their next best alternative employment opportunity probably would be coaching at FCS or Division II or III or even high school.[130] Accordingly, if the NCAA placed, say, a $400,000 limit on coaches' compensation packages,[131] it would not affect the quality of coaching or the level of intercollegiate competition. Stated differently, it would not affect the allocation of coaching resources or diminish the entertainment value of college sports. Further, it would eliminate the sending of twisted signals to undergraduate students about the importance of the college president or the professoriate relative to the head football or basketball coach.

Second, we propose a cap on spending to build new facilities that would be exempt from the antitrust laws.[132] The cap would be geared toward preventing extraordinary expenses on athlete-only facilities, like those built at Clemson that include laser tag, miniature golf, beach volleyball, and other amenities divorced from the playing field and geared toward retaining recruiting advantages.

We propose that a third exempt activity would be rules reducing the size of FBS football teams. NCAA rules currently allow FBS football teams up to 85 scholarships. Capping the number at 60 (or fewer) would not devalue college football.[133] NFL teams have a maximum active roster of 45, plus a maximum inactive roster of 8 additional players.[134] The average FBS team has 35 walk-ons plus 85 scholarship players—120 players in all![135] If football scholarships were cut to 60, the average college would probably save close to $1.5 million annually[136]—easily enough to finance an average FBS soccer team plus an average FBS golf team, or an FBS tennis team plus gymnastics team, and have several hundred thousand dollars left over.[137] Even assuming that the number of walk-ons would not increase with the lower scholarship limit, the average squad size would still be over 90. No rational coach would dare to argue that a football team size of 90-plus players is inadequate.

A fourth exempt policy would be restrictions on the payment of salaries to athletes for the performance in their sport. Athletes could receive full scholarships for participating on their team, including a cost-of-living allowance, third-party payments up to certain limits for NILs, and other elements to be discussed shortly, but they could not be paid directly for what they do on the football field or basketball court. This is basically the concept of amateurism (i.e., no compensation for *playing* a sport) that is applied by the Amateur Athletic Union (AAU) and other amateur sports organizations in the United States.

We further suggest other areas of exemption that lean more toward the academic-integrity end of the spectrum, including restrictions on weeknight football and basketball games, the length of competitive seasons, the number of in-season and out-of-season practice and game hours per week, inter alia.[138]

Conditions for Granting Partial Exemption

One can imagine a variety of conditionality stipulations geared toward ensuring that athletes are treated fairly and that academic fraud is minimized, if not extirpated. For the NCAA to be granted a partial antitrust exemption, it would have to enact and implement certain pro-educational and health, safety, and fairness reforms. Congress would mandate these conditions. A suggested, noninclusive list follows.

Initial eligibility standards need to be strengthened. Since the 2003 sliding scale was introduced, it is possible for athletes to gain full initial eligibility and still receive a zero score on standardized tests by attaining a 3.55 grade point average (GPA).[139] If, however, the high school rigs the athlete's classes and teachers to achieve this GPA, then the initial eligibility standard is a mockery. Similar issues apply to the continuing eligibility standards and to the Academic Progress Rate (APR) metric. New, more meaningful standards need to be set and become conditions for the limited antitrust exemption.

The NCAA would also be required to put in place appropriate due process procedures for all schools, administrators, and athletes who are accused of transgressions. These include notice of allegations, fair hearing processes (including the exchange of evidence and cross-examination rights of both parties), and adequate appeal procedures.

Athletes' rights must be fortified, including the following health, safety, and fairness protections:

- Schools should pay for broad injury insurance coverage.
- Athletes should have the right to work with counsel or an agent prior to deciding on entering a professional draft or participating in a sports league combine.
- All academic-support programs for athletes should be removed from the athletics department and put entirely under academic control.
- Transfer athletes should not lose a year of eligibility.
- Athletes should be guaranteed a four-year scholarship.
- Stricter rules regarding time commitments by athletes should be imposed.
- Whistle-blower protection should be provided to anyone reporting transgressions with retaliation explicitly prohibited.
- Every school should be required to certify Title IX compliance.

Additionally, the NCAA should run the national Championship Football Playoff (CFP) system, inaugurated in 2014–15, just as it runs all other (eighty-nine in total) NCAA championships. The CFP, which is the only national championship not controlled by the NCAA, generates more than $600 million in revenue, over three-fourths of which is distributed to the Power Five conferences. This skewed distribution, at once, enhances the financial incentives toward victory at any cost and, importantly, diminishes funding for Olympic sports and women's sports throughout the NCAA's three divisions. Thus, a condition for receiving a partial antitrust exemption should be to bring the football playoff into the fold.

Finally, NCAA governance should be reformed with more equal balance among the divisions and within Division I. The NCAA's boards, councils, and committees should have more independent yet informed members. We do not recommend a specific structure at this time other than specifying that the entire membership should not be controlled by the Power Five powerhouses. However, we agree with the Dodd-Frank Wall Street Reform and Consumer Protection Act of 2010 (Dodd-Frank),[140] insofar as it requires the boards of directors of for-profit corporations to be composed of a majority of independent directors and requires that compensation and audit committees must be made up entirely of independent directors. Other helpful models include the Amateur Sports Act,[141] which requires that the National Governing Boards for each Olympic sport include individuals who are not affiliated with any amateur sports organizations and who would represent the US public's interests. If the NCAA and its membership are unable to restructure and its board members are unable to exhibit a fiduciary duty to the NCAA as a whole and not just to individual divisions or group of schools, then Congress should consider creating a new federally created nonprofit organization or an independent federal regulatory commission to govern intercollegiate athletics.[142]

Precedent of Antitrust Exemptions

The solution proposed herein is not extraordinary.[143] Congress has enacted limited antitrust exemptions in numerous industries—ranging from the hog industry[144] to railroads[145] to soft drinks[146] to the insurance industry[147] to sports and most significantly to higher education. Certain statutory antitrust exemptions involving the sports industry and higher education are discussed in the following subsections.[148]

Sports Broadcasting Act

The Sports Broadcasting Act of 1961 (SBA) provides limited immunity from antitrust litigation to the four major professional sport leagues for selling horizontally pooled broadcasting rights to over-the-air channels.[149]

The SBA puts restrictions on broadcasting games on Friday nights and Saturday. Its limited immunity is made clear: the SBA "shall [not] be deemed to change, determine, or otherwise affect the applicability or non-applicability of the antitrust laws to any act, contract, agreement, rule, course of conduct, or other activity by, between, or among persons engaging in, conducting, or participating in the organized professional team sports of football, baseball, basketball, or hockey."[150]

NFL-AFL Merger

In 1966, Congress passed a very limited and targeted antitrust exemption to permit the combination of the NFL and AFL.[151]

Ted Stevens Olympic and Amateur Sports Act (ASA)

Particularly to clean up amateur sports, Congress passed the Amateur Sports Act (ASA) in 1978 (subsequently amended in 1998),[152] creating a vertical structure for the management of certain amateur sports in the United States.[153] While Congress did not expressly exempt action taken under the ASA's direction from the federal antitrust laws, nevertheless, courts have found an implicit exemption from antitrust laws where there exists a plain conflict between the antitrust and ASA regulatory provisions.[154]

Curt Flood Act

The Curt Flood Act of 1988 removes Major League Baseball's presumed antitrust exemption (judicially conferred in 1922) in the area of labor relations.[155] There continues to be much litigation regarding this judicial exemption.

Improving America's Schools Act

The Improving America's Schools Act of 1994 exempts from the antitrust laws agreements to admit students on a need-blind basis by institutions of higher education. The act permits, inter alia, schools jointly "to use common principles of analysis for determining the need of such students for financial aid if the agreement to use such principles does not restrict financial aid officers . . . in their exercising independent professional judgment with respect to individual applicants for such financial aid."[156] The act does not permit schools to agree on which particular students are entitled to aid.

Medical Resident Matching Program Exemption

Following an antitrust lawsuit filed by medical students challenging national resident matching programs, Congress in 2004 partially exempted the existing medical resident matching programs from antitrust laws.[157] The law stated that it is not "unlawful under the antitrust laws to sponsor, conduct, or participate in a graduate medical education residency matching program."[158] The amendment also made inadmissible in federal court evidence of exempted conduct to support claims that allege violations of the antitrust laws.[159] The exemption does not permit agreements to fix the amount of the stipend or other benefits received by students participating in such programs.[160]

These acts demonstrate that Congress protects certain activities in sports and higher education from the antitrust laws when it deems fit.[161] It defines antitrust exemptions specifically and narrowly. Here too the exemption should be narrowly defined.

Conclusion

In summary, intercollegiate sports are distinct from other extracurricular activities in higher education and from professional sports. Thorough reform of the existing system is needed. The NCAA has made mostly incremental efforts at reform, while public policy has been inactive regarding intercollegiate athletics. The most substantial challenges for reform have come from piecemeal litigation. It is time for systemic change.

First, we have demonstrated that the economic environment of intercollegiate sports is unstable and unsustainable. Growing deficits in athletics departments are depleting academic resources and undermining the educational process. Indeed, college athletics programs are draining central educational budgets of hundreds of millions of dollars annually. And the drain is only growing.

Second, we have argued that it is unsatisfactory to apply an antitrust framework to college sports with analyses that (1) distinguish between commercial and noncommercial purposes and effects and (2) analyze pro- and anti-competitive effects and less restrictive alternatives. Moreover, court decisions are limited to particular claims. They cannot take into account all the broader social policy implications of their decisions that impact the future of intercollegiate sports with its many dimensions and stakeholders. And tens of millions of dollars—along with the attention of thousands of lawyers, administrators, and others—are being misspent on litigation.

For these reasons, congressional intervention is necessary to address the policy decision of how to preserve the educational pursuit of universities and colleges and their collegeathletes, while saving the aspects of intercollegiate sports that we cherish and that nourish the well-rounded development of college athletes. We believe such intervention should be narrowly tailored and limited to specific concerns facing the NCAA and college athletes today and should be informed by analogous statutory antitrust exemptions and judicial precedents. Accordingly, the exemption should be conditioned on the implementation of (1) cost-saving measures (e.g., capping coaches' salaries and facilities spending) and (2) measures ensuring the health and safety of athletes and the primacy of academics in intercollegiate sports.

NOTES

1. We define "operating surplus" as the NCAA does in its biannual *Revenues and Expenses* report. That is, it refers to generated revenues (including donations) minus operating costs, where operating costs exclude most capital expenses. See NCAA, *Revenues*

and Expenses: 2004–2014 NCAA Division I Intercollegiate Athletics Programs Report 11, 24 (comp. Daniel L. Fulks, 2015), http://www.ncaa.org/sites/default/files/2015%20Division%20I%20RE%20report.pdf (hereinafter NCAA, *Revenues and Expenses* 2015).

2. Note that these figures represent net generated revenue for the FBS athletics programs in each cited fiscal year. *Id.* at 24.

3. There are no set accounting conventions for college athletics departments, and although the NCAA has been encouraging uniformity, there is still substantial variability among departments in their treatment of capital expenses. The most common practice appears to be that when debt service on facility loans are paid directly by the athletics department, they are included in operating costs. In contrast, when the debt service is paid by the university or the state, they tend not to be included.

4. Donations to the athletics program are included on the revenue side. It is also important to point out that the expense side can be overstated when student-athletes on scholarship cannot be replaced by full-paying students. In such a case, the tuition expense is overstated because it does not represent the out-of-pocket cost to the school. Two caveats to this observation are in order. First, while the marginal out-of-pocket cost of adding a football player to a classroom of a few dozen students may be close to zero, it is not close to zero if the alternative is for the school to drop from FBS, the top level of college football, to FCS, in which case there are twenty-two scholarship athletes affected, or if the alternative is to drop to Division III or to drop football altogether, in which cases there are eighty-five scholarship athletes affected. For larger groups of students, extra classrooms, materials, teachers, and tutors are required, presenting substantially augmented costs. Second, if the alternative to enrolling an academically underprepared athlete is to bring in an intellectually gifted minority student from the inner city, then, although there is full scholarship in both cases, there is certainly an indirect cost with regard to the quality of the student body, the eventual productivity of the student when they join the workforce, the intellectual environment in the classroom, and the reputation of the school. Another way to model the actual cost of the athletic scholarships is to observe that colleges on average receive only about 40 percent of the sticker price of tuition, room and board, and fees. Excluding athletic scholarships and adjusting for cost-of-attendance allowance would suggest that around 50 percent of the sticker price, rather than the full sticker price, should be used when calculating the athletic deficit. In any event, even with this reckoning of scholarship cost, the factors suggesting an upward revision in the deficit are stronger than those suggesting a downward revision.

5. Expenditures to increase the quality of intercollegiate teams do not increase output. They merely redistribute talent and generate additional revenue for the successful schools. With athlete pay suppressed, a majority of this revenue flows to coaches. Because of this peculiarity of college sports, putting caps on expenditures would not decrease consumer welfare. This is another reason that supports our call for a conditional and limited antitrust exemption.

6. Note that just over half of FBS football teams (52 percent in 2018–19) and under half of FBS men's basketball teams (44 percent in 2018–19) run an operating surplus, that is, a surplus before capital and certain indirect costs are included. But typical FBS athletics programs support fifteen to thirty sports, virtually all of which run a substantial operating deficit. The result is commonly a deficit for the entire athletics department. Where there is an operating surplus in football and men's basketball, it is used to finance the "nonrevenue" sports. This constitutes a transfer from sports with predominantly students of color to sports with predominantly white students.

7. National Collegiate Athletic Association v. Board of Regents of University of Oklahoma, 468 U.S. 85 (1984).

8. Andrew Zimbalist, *Unpaid Professionals: Commercialism and Conflict in Big-Time College Sports* (1999). See also Mitchell H. Raiborn, NCAA, *Financial Analysis of Intercollegiate Athletics* (1970); Raiborn, NCAA, *Revenues and Expenses of Intercollegiate Athletic Programs, 1970–1977, 1978–1981, 1981–1985, 1985–1989* (1990); Daniel Fulks, NCAA, *Revenues and Expenses of Intercollegiate Athletic Programs, 1993* (1994); Fulks, NCAA, *Revenues and Expenses of Division I and II Intercollegiate Athletic Programs, 1995, 1997* (1998).

9. Revenue distribution data prior to 2000 are scarce, and those that are available are generally tabulated with different metrics than those available since 2000. It is therefore difficult to obtain an accurate picture of how much inequality has increased over the decades. Further, due to inconsistent and incomplete accounting practices within athletics departments and the fact that a good deal of revenue and cost information is treated as proprietary, it is impossible even today to achieve a full and accurate picture of the extent of inequality. Nonetheless, it is possible to compile pieces of information from the periodic NCAA *Revenues and Expenses* reports, the Equity in Athletics Data Act (EADA) reports, and other sources to assemble a broad outline of the trends and the status quo in revenue inequality among FBS programs.

10. Andrew Zimbalist, "Inequality in Intercollegiate Athletics: Origins, Trends and Policies," 6 *Journal of Intercollegiate Sports* 5, 15 (2013).

11. NCAA, *Revenues and Expenses* 2015 *supra* note 1, at 27.

12. By fiscal year 2016, the number of FBS schools had grown to 128.

13. NCAA, *Revenues and Expenses* 2015 *supra* note 1, at 27.

14. *Id.* at 22.

15. To be sure, a prepublication draft of the 2016 NCAA *Revenues and Expenses* report for the academic year 2014–15 indicates that there were twenty-four athletics programs that experienced a net operating surplus in 2014–15, the same number as in 2013–14. The number of FBS athletics programs with a net operating surplus was eighteen in 2003–4 and fourteen in 2008–9.

16. O'Bannon v. National Collegiate Athletic Association, 7 F. Supp 3d 955 (N.D. Cal. 2014), *aff'd in part, vacated in part,* 802 F.3d 1049 (9th Circuit 2015), *cert. denied* (Oct. 3, 2016).

17. Alston v. National Collegiate Athletic Association, Case No. 4:14-md-02541 (N.D. Cal. 2015).

18. Jenkins v. National Collegiate Athletic Association, Case No. 4:14-cv-02758-CW (N.D. Cal. 2014).

19. It is especially likely that new cases will be brought in circuits other than the Ninth Circuit, where *O'Bannon* was decided. *See infra* "Recent Cases Seek Clarity."

20. See Matthew J. Mitten, James L. Musselman & Bruce W. Burton, "Targeted Reform of Commercialized Intercollegiate Athletics," 47 *San Diego Law Review* 779 (2010), for a similar proposal.

21. While nonprofit organizations are not categorically exempt from the Sherman Act, "when they perform acts that are the antithesis of commercial activity, they are immune from antitrust regulations." United States v. Brown University, 5 F.3d 658, 665 (3d Circuit 1993).

22. Phillip E. Areeda & Herbert Hovenkamp, *Antitrust Law* 260b, at 250 (2000).

23. The agreement (May 2016) between UCLA and Under Armour for a fifteen-year, $280 million merchandising/sponsorship agreement is the largest in the history of collegiate sponsorship and highlights the paradox of commercialized college sports. *See* Lucy Schouten, "UCLA Lands NCAA's Biggest Merchandise Contract Ever," *Christian Science Monitor* (May 24, 2016), http://www.csmonitor.com/USA/USA-Update/2016/0524/UCLA-lands-NCAA-s-biggest-merchandise-contract-ever.

24. Brief in Opposition to Petitioner's Petition for Writ of Certiorari at 1, O'Bannon v. National Collegiate Athletic Association, 802 F.3d 1049 (2016) (No. 15-1167).

25. Agnew v. National Collegiate Athletic Association, 683 F.3d 328, 340 (7th Circuit 2012).

26. Traditionally courts have analyzed agreements under either a per se illegality standard or a "rule of reason" analysis (or variation thereof, like a "quick look" rule of reason). Ordinarily, horizontal price fixing and output limitation are automatically per se illegal. However, where horizontal restraints on competition are essential if the product is to exist at all, courts typically apply a rule of reason analysis.

27. Some courts say the plaintiff must prove "significant" anticompetitive effects (*e.g.*, O'Bannon v. National Collegiate Athletic Association, 802 F.3d 1049, 1072 (9th Circuit 2015)) or "substantial" anticompetitive effects (*e.g.*, Law v. National Collegiate Athletic Association, 902 F. Supp. 1394 (D. Kan. 1995), *aff'd* 134 F.3d 1010 (10th Circuit 1998) (emphasis added).

28. Some courts articulate that the challenged restraint be reasonably necessary to achieve a legitimate objective. See, *e.g.*, United States v. Brown University, 5 F.3d 658, 678–79 (3rd Circuit 1993).

29. Some courts state that the procompetitive effects, at this stage, must offset (*e.g.*, California Dental Association v. Federal Trade Commission, 526 U.S. 756, 782 (1999) (Breyer, J., dissenting)); countervail (*e.g.*, Federal Trade Commission v. Indiana Federation of Dentists, 476 U.S. 447, 459 (1986); *Board of Regents*, 468 U.S. 85 (1984)); outweigh (e.g., Eastman Kodak Co. v. Image Technical Services, 504 U.S. 451, 486 (1992); Atlantic Richfield Company v. USA Petroleum Company 495 U.S. 328, 342 (1990); United States v. Microsoft Corp., 253 F.3d 34, 59 (D.C. Circuit 2001); Harriston v. Pacific 10 Conference, 101 F.3d 1315, 1319 (9th Circuit 1996); or justify (e.g., the 10th Circuit's discussion of anticompetitive effects in *Law*, 134 F.3d at 1019–21). The court in *Law* also stated that "justifications . . . may be considered only to the extent that they tend to show that, on balance, 'the challenged restraint enhances competition.'" *Law*, 134 F.3d at 1021 (emphasis added) (citations omitted). On the other hand, some courts make no judgment at this point and move directly to step 3. See C. Scott Hemphill, "Less Restrictive Alternatives in Antitrust Law," 116 *Columbia Law Review* 927, 941–42 (2016).

30. Some courts require the plaintiffs to show a least restrictive alternative. *See, e.g.*, Phillip E. Areeda & Herbert Hovenkamp, *supra* note 22, 1505(b), at 913.

31. Some courts state that the balancing occurs once all the burdens are met. *See, e.g.*, *Law*, 134 F.3d at 1019. Some courts engage in balancing only if no LRA is demonstrated. *See* Hemphill, *supra* note 29, at 941. Indeed, the Model Jury Instructions state that fact-finders must balance benefits and harms if no LRA exists. American Bar Association Section of Antitrust Law, *Model Jury Instructions in Civil Antitrust Cases*, Instruction 3D (2005). And some cases state that no balancing is required once a LRA is proven. *See* Hemphill, *supra* note 29, at 976–77.

32. *California Dental Association*, 526 U.S. at 771; Geneva Pharmaceuticals Technology Corporation v. Barr Laboratories, Inc., 386 F.3d 485, 507 (2d Circuit 2004).

33. This essay does not engage in the scholarly debate about the proper parameters of the rule of reason, including the role and timing of balancing, but instead argues that its uncertain and inconsistent articulation and application support our call for a conditional and limited antitrust exemption.

34. As Phillip Areeda has explained, "Solutions are elusive where allowing the restraint would threaten competition with significant harm of substantial magnitude but where preventing it would apparently deprive society of significant and substantial benefits." Areeda, *The "Rule of Reason" in Antitrust Analysis: General Issues* 3 (Federal Judicial Center 1981) (available at https://www.fjc.gov/sites/default/files/2012/Antitrust

.pdf). And he further stated, "There is no general formula by which one can say what balance of harms and benefits justifies categorical prohibition." *Id.* at 23. *See also* Gary R. Roberts, "The NCAA, Antitrust, and Consumer Welfare," 70 *Tulane Law Review* 2631, 2656 (1966) (discussing the lack of clarity in case law as to how to weigh and balance procompetitive effects and anticompetitive harms and stating: "All a factfinder could do is intuitively sense how 'bad' or 'good' an effect is and then subjectively decide whether his or her sense is that the 'good' effects are greater than the 'bad' based on his or her own life experiences and values.").

35. *See* Rebecca Haw Allensworth, "The Commensurability Myth in Antitrust," 69 *Vanderbilt Law Review* 1 (2016) (discussing the debate surrounding balancing tradeoffs required as part of the rule of reason and stating, "What are offered in antitrust cases as procompetitive and anticompetitive effects are typically qualitatively different, and trading them off is as much an exercise in judgment as mathematics. But despite the inevitability of value judgments in antitrust cases, courts have perpetuated a commensurability myth, claiming to evaluate 'net' competitive effect as if the pros and cons of a restraint of trade are in the same unit of measure. The myth is attractive to courts because it appears to allow the law to avoid the murky, value-laden compromises struck by other areas of regulation.").

36. *See* Herbert Hovenkamp, "Antitrust Balancing," 12 *New York University Journal of Law and Business* 369, 370 (2016) ("Even if the things requiring balancing did come in cardinal units, most times the courts would not have the tools necessary to make and apply the measurements. Instead, balancing approaches are usually binary rather than cardinal. They are more like off and on switches that go in one direction or the other.").

37. Andrew I. Gavil, William E. Kovacic & Jonathan B. Baker, *Antitrust Law in Perspective: Cases, Concepts and Problems in Competition Policy* 207 (2d ed. 2008).

38. Andrew I. Gavil, "Burden of Proof in U.S. Antitrust Law," 1 *Issues in Competition Law and Policy* 125, 147 (ABA Section of Antitrust Law 2008). *See also* Michael A. Carrier, "The Real Rule of Reason: Bridging the Disconnect," 16 *Issues in Competition Law and Policy* 1265, 1267 (1999); Carrier, "The Rule of Reason: An Empirical Update for the 21st Century," 16 *George Mason Law Review* 827, 828 (2009).

39. Phillip E. Areeda & Herbert Hovenkamp, *Fundamentals of Antitrust Law* § 15.04(A) (4th ed.) (2016 Supplement).

40. Justice Scalia described this problem in another context as "judging whether a particular line is longer than a particular rock is heavy." Bendix Autolite Corp. v. Midwesco Enters., Inc., 486 U.S. 888, 897 (1988) (Scalia, J., concurring). *See also* Robert H. Bork, "The Rule of Reason and the Per Se Concept: Price Fixing and Market Division," 74 *Yale Law Journal* 775, 839 (1965).

41. *Board of Regents*, 468 U.S. at 98–99.

42. *Id.* at 103–4.

43. *Id.* at 117.

44. *Id.* at 101.

45. *Id.* at 107–8.

46. *Id.* at 113.

47. *Id.* at 97.

48. The Supreme Court stated, "One clear effect of most, if not all, of these regulations [including those relating to eligibility, recruiting, and scheduling] is to prevent institutions with competitively and economically successful programs from taking advantage of their success by expanding their programs, improving the quality of the product they offer, and increasing their sports revenues. Yet each of these regulations represents a desirable and legitimate attempt 'to keep University athletics from becoming professionalized to the extent that profit making objectives would overshadow

educational objectives.' Significantly, neither the Court of Appeals nor this Court questions the validity of these regulations under the Rule of Reason." *Id.* at 123 (citations omitted).

49. *Id.* at 102.

50. *See, e.g.*, Bassett v. National Collegiate Athletic Association 528 F.3d 426, 433–34 (6th Circuit 2008) (discussing NCAA recruiting regulations); Smith v. National Collegiate Athletic Association, 139 F.3d 180 (3d Circuit 1998) (discussing NCAA graduate transfer rules); Gaines v. National Collegiate Athletic Association, 746 F. Supp. 738 (M.D. Tenn. 1990) (discussing NCAA restrictions on agents). *See also* Areeda & Hovenkamp, *supra* note 22, 262.

51. Agnew v. National Collegiate Athletic Association, 683 F.3d 328 (7th Circuit 2012).

52. *Id.* at 344. *See also* Banks v. National Collegiate Athletic Association, 977 F.2d 1081, 1099 (7th Circuit 1992) (Flaum, J., dissenting) ("The NCAA continues to purvey . . . an outmoded image of intercollegiate sports that no longer jibes with reality. The times have changed. College football . . . is also a vast commercial venture that yields substantial profits for colleges."). Note that NCAA rules now permit multiyear scholarships.

53. Ultimately, the Seventh Circuit upheld the district court's dismissal on the basis that the alleged markets ("bachelor's degrees" and "student athlete labor") were unclear and the complaint did not adequately define the relevant market on which the rules had an anticompetitive effect. *See also* Rock v. National Collegiate Athletic Association, 928 F. Supp. 2d 1010 (S.D. Ind. 2013) (refusing to certify a class of Division I football recruits and holding that rules that limited scholarships to one year at a time and that capped the number of football scholarships are subject to the Sherman Act (same basic allegations as in *Agnew*)).

54. Professional leagues that have collective bargaining agreements that provide salary caps on teams, rookies, etc. are permitted to enter into such price-fixing agreements as a result of the nonstatutory labor exemption from the antitrust laws. But colleges and universities do not have a similar antitrust exception. As discussed later in this chapter, unionization of college athletes and collective bargaining do not appear likely to be an option in college sports.

55. Law v. National Collegiate Athletic Association, 902 F. Supp. 1394 (D. Kan. 1995), *aff'd* 134 F.3d 1010 (10th Circuit 1998).

56. *Law*, F.3d at 1014.

57. *See also* White v. National Collegiate Athletic Association, Case No. CV 06 0999 (C.D. Cal. 2008) (applying the Sherman Act to allegations that the grant-in-aid (GIA) scholarship cap violated antitrust laws. After the NCAA's motion to dismiss was denied and class certification granted, the NCAA settled for $10 million plus requirements that athletes could more easily access a $218 million fund already existing). *Cf.* Banks v. National Collegiate Athletic Association, 977 F.2d 1081, 1089–90 (7th Circuit 1992) (applying the Sherman Act and upholding no-draft and no-agent eligibility rules); McCormack v. National Collegiate Athletic Association, 845 F.2d 1338 (5th Circuit 1988) (applying the Sherman Act and upholding rules restricting compensation because they are a desirable and legitimate attempt to keep athletes from being professionalized).

58. NCAA Player Likeness, 4:09-CV-1967-CW, No. 1158-277 (N.D. Cal. 2015) (which is the consolidation of Keller v. Electronic Arts, 4:09-CV-01967-CW (N.D. Al. 2015) and O'Bannon v. National Collegiate Athletic Association, 4:09-CV-03329-CW (N.D. Cal. 2015).

59. O'Bannon v. National Collegiate Athletic Association, 7 F. Supp. 3d 955 (N.D. Cal. 2014), *aff'd in part, vacated in part*, 802 F.3d 1049 (9th Circuit 2015), *cert. denied* (Oct. 3, 2016).

60. *O'Bannon*, 7 F. Supp. 3d at 988.

61. *Id.* at 985 (quoting Tanaka v. University of Southern California, 252 F.3d 1059, 1066 (9th Circuit 2001)).

62. *Id.*

63. *Id.* at 973.

64. *Id.*

65. *Id.* at 1001, 1003.

66. *Id.* at 1002, 1004.

67. *Id.* at 985.

68. Judge Wilken stated that if the NCAA had failed to meet its burden in step 2, she would not have addressed step 3: the availability of less restrictive alternatives. *Id.* at 1004–5.

69. *Id.* at 1005.

70. Accordingly, the court conducted some type of balancing, at least implicitly, in steps 2 and 3 of the burden-shifting framework.

71. GIA includes room, board, tuition, fees, and required books for courses. COA adds miscellaneous expenses such as travel to and from campus, other books and supplies, laundry expenses, etc. Schools determine their respective COA on the basis of a federally mandated formula. Given the discretion available in applying the formula, some schools are calculating the applicable amount on the high side and allegedly are gaining recruiting advantages. The COA, however, is limited by what is offered to other nonathlete scholarship students. *O'Bannon*, 7 F. Supp. 3d, at 965, 974.

72. Judge Wilken's opinion states that she was enjoining schools from prohibiting payments that are capped at less than $5,000. *Id.* at 1008. While discussion of a cap at less than $5,000 created some confusion, it is clear she meant that the cap could not be more than $5,000; that is, schools must be allowed to pay up to $5,000. *See, e.g.*, the parties' briefs to the Ninth Circuit: Brief for the National Collegiate Athletic Association, O'Bannon v. National Collegiate Athletic Association, 802 F.3d 1049 (2014) (Nos. 14-16601, 14-17068); Plaintiff-Appellees' Opposition Brief in Response to National Collegiate Athletic Association's Opening Appellate Brief, O'Bannon v. National Collegiate Athletic Association, 802 F.3d 1049 (2015) (Nos. 14-16601, 14-17068); Reply Brief for the National Collegiate Athletic Association, 802 F.3d 1049 (2015) (Nos. 14-16601, 14-17068).

73. The amici represented a wide variety of interests, from antitrust and economic scholars to the American Council on Education.

74. O'Bannon v. National Collegiate Athletic Association, 802 F.3d 1049 (9th Circuit 2015).

75. *Id.* at 1070–72.

76. *Id.* at 1074–75.

77. Judge Bybee explained, "The difference between offering student-athletes education-related compensation and offering them cash sums untethered to educational expenses is not minor; it is a quantum leap. Once that line is crossed, we see no basis for returning to a rule of amateurism and no defined stopping point. . . . At that point the NCAA will have surrendered its amateurism principles entirely and transitioned from its 'particular brand of football' to minor league status." *Id.* at 1078–79 (quoting *Board of Regents*, 468 U.S. at 101–2).

78. *Id.* at 1083 (Thomas, J., concurring in part, dissenting in part).

79. While Judge Thomas did not state that he was engaging in any balancing, by noting that the proposed LRA was substantially less restrictive, he, concurring in part and dissenting in part, made a judgment that involved weighing the effects. *Id.* at 1080–82.

80. *Id.* at 1079.

81. *Id.* at 1075.

82. Plaintiff-Appellees' Petition for Rehearing En Banc, National Collegiate Athletic Association v. O'Bannon, 802 F.3d 1049 (9th Circuit 2015), *rehearing denied* (Oct. 14, 2015).

83. The plaintiffs submitted a petition on March 14, 2016: Petition for Writ of Certiorari, O'Bannon v. National Collegiate Athletic Association, 802 F.3d 1049 (Mar. 14, 2016). The NCAA submitted a petition on May 13, 2016: Petition for Writ of Certiorari, National Collegiate Athletic Association v. O'Bannon, 802 F.3d 1049 (May 13, 2016).

84. O'Bannon v. National Collegiate Athletic Association, 802 F.3d 1049 (9th Circuit 2015), *cert. denied* (Oct. 3, 2016).

85. In the NCAA's petition for certiorari, it showed its frustration with the current litigations: "The NCAA should not have to undergo a full trial (and years of litigation) or face treble damages whenever a plaintiff or counsel hits on a supposedly better way to administer college athletics." Petition for Writ of Certiorari, No. 15-1388, at 26–27 (clarifying that the precedent would "preclude[] potentially endless antitrust challenges to NCAA rules").

86. NCAA Bylaw 15.1, as amended in 2015, provides that "a student-athlete shall not be eligible to participate in intercollegiate athletics if he or she receives financial aid that exceeds the value of the cost of attendance." NCAA, *2009–10 NCAA Division Manual* 174 (2009), http://www.ncaapublications.com/productdownloads/D110.pdf.

87. Case No. 4:14-CV-0278-CW (N.D. Cal. 2016). The five power conferences are the Atlantic Coast Conference, Big 12 Conference, Big Ten Conference, Pac-12 Conference, and Southeastern Conference.

88. Case No. 4:14-md-02541-CW (N.D. Cal. 2015). The six other conferences are the American Athletic Conference, Conference USA, Mid-American Conference, Mountain West Conference, Sun Belt Conference, and Western Athletic Conference. The original *Alston* complaint was consolidated with four other complaints, and a consolidated complaint was filed. Steve Berkowitz, "Court Filing: NCAA, Conferences Say Scholarships Could Be Reduced," *USA Today*, Sports (May 1, 2015), http://www.usatoday.com/story/sports/college/2015/05/01/ncaa-suit-shawne-alston-martin-jenkins-kessler-nigel-hayes-claudia-wilken/26685565/.

89. Consolidated Pls.' Memorandum in Opposition to Defendants' Motion for Judgment on the Pleadings, at 2, Jenkins v. National Collegiate Athletic Association, No. 15-80219 (9th Circuit June, 1, 2016) (Doc. 396).

90. The *Jenkins* case is frequently referred to as the *Kessler* case in the popular press. Jeffrey Kessler represents the plaintiffs.

91. The *Jenkins* attorneys have made it clear that they intend to quantify the question of whether amateurism leads to increased output.

92. Although a distinction is that the *O'Bannon* plaintiffs only sought payments for NILs.

93. *Berger v. NCAA*, 2016 U.S. Dist. LEXIS 18194 (S.D. Ind. Feb. 16, 2016) (No. 1:14-cv-1710-WTL-MJD). This case originally was captioned *Sackos/Anderson v. NCAA*. A former soccer player at the University of Houston alleged that the NCAA and Division I universities conspired to violate the Fair Labor Standards Act by failing to at least pay a federal minimum wage of $7.25 per hour. No. 1:14-cv-1710-WTL-MJD (S.D. Ind. filed Oct. 22, 2014). Sackos was replaced by the women track-and-field athletes at Penn as the plaintiffs.

94. Berger v. National Collegiate Athletic Association, 2016 WL 7051905 at *8 (7th Circuit December 5, 2016).

95. *Id.* at *8–9.

96. Northwestern University v. College Athletes Players Association, NLRB No. 13-RC-121359 (Mar. 26, 2014).

97. *Id.* at 5. A similar case, *Dawson v. National Collegiate Athletic Association*, No. 3:16-cv-05487, was brought on September 26, 2016, in the Northern District of California. The plaintiff, a former USC football player, has brought the case on behalf of himself individually and purported classes of college football players, seeking to be defined as employees and to be paid both minimum wages and overtime pay.

98. *Northwestern University*, NLRB No. 13-RC-121359, at 5.

99. *Id.* at 6–7.

100. *Id.* at 13.

101. *Id.* at 4.

102. Subsequently, in August 2016, the NLRB held that graduate and undergraduate teaching and research student assistants were statutory employees pursuant to the National Labor Relations Act. Columbia University and Graduate Workers of Columbia-CWC, UAW, NLRB No. 02-RC-143012 (2016). Significantly, this decision overruled Brown University, 342 NLRB 483 (2004), a case that the NLRB in *Northwestern* said was distinguishable because "scholarship players bear little resemblance to the graduate student assistants." Northwestern had heavily relied on *Brown* in its briefs. *Northwestern University*, NLRB No.13-RC-121359, at 3, 13.

103. *See* Stephen F. Ross & Matt Mitten, "A Regulatory Solution to Better Promote the Educational Values and Economic Sustainability of Intercollegiate Athletics," 92 *Oregon Law Review* 837, 868–69 (2014).

104. In fiscal year 2015, the NCAA's lobbying expenses, while not all devoted to the issues addressed herein, were $580,000—an amount that exceeded the three previous years combined. And, much more significantly, the NCAA's legal expenses totaled $25 million, double from the previous year. Indeed, the NCAA's CFO, Kathleen McNeely, told *USA Today*, "I was naïve in believing that our legal fees would start to come down, I'm willing to admit that. It's a litigious environment." Steve Berkowitz, "NCAA Spends $25 Million on Outside Legal Fees, Double from Previous Year," *USA Today*, Sports (June 11, 2016), http://www.usatoday.com/story/sports/college/2016/06/11/ncaa-legal-fees-obannon/85772006/.

105. Plaintiffs' Motion for Attorneys' Fees, Costs, and Expenses and Memorandum in Support Thereof, O'Bannon v. National Collegiate Athletic Association, 7 F. Supp. 3d 955 (N.D. Cal. 2014) (No. 4:09-cv-03329-CW). *See also* Declaration of Michael D. Hausfeld in Support of Antitrust Plaintiffs' Motion for Attorneys' Fees, Reimbursement of Expenses, and Class Representative Incentive Awards, Nos. 4:09-cv-1967-CW, 4:09-cv-3329-CW (N.D. Cal. 2014).

106. O'Bannon v. National Collegiate Athletic Association, No. C09-3329 CW, 2016 WL 1255454, at 1 (N.D. Cal. Mar. 31, 2016), *appeal docketed*, No. 16-15803 (9th Circuit May 2, 2016).

107. *Id.*

108. In re NCAA Student-Athlete Name & Likeness Licensing Litigation, 724 F.3d 1268 (9th Circuit 2013) (holding that the First Amendment did not prevent a right-of-publicity claim arising from the use of college football players' NILs in video games).

109. Among other issues, Supreme Court judges have waded into economic issues that the justices appear to insufficiently understand. The Court in *Board of Regents* wrote, "The television plan protects ticket sales by limiting output—just as any monopolist increases revenue by reducing output." *Board of Regents*, 468 U.S. at 116–17. The justices misapprehended basic microeconomic theory. Monopolists produce on the elastic portion of the demand curve, meaning that a certain percentage increase in price (from reduced output) yields a larger percentage decrease in quantity demanded. Since revenue equals price times quantity, revenue decreases when a monopolist decreases output. Profits, however, grow because costs decrease by more than revenue decreases.

110. For example, a rule permitting athletes to be paid their fair market value could result in the reduction of overall revenues and, as a consequence, the demise of many women's intercollegiate teams and non-revenue-producing men's teams. Revenues from big-time football and basketball, particularly at DI schools, are currently redistributed to support women's and non-revenue-producing men's teams. Indeed, in *O'Bannon*, the NCAA argued that a procompetitive justification for not paying FBS football players and DI basketball players was the positive revenue sharing on women's sports. The court refused to permit that argument because it did not affect the relevant market at issue. See *O'Bannon*, 802 F.3d at 1070. Order Denying Motion for Leave to File Motion for Reconsideration, In re NCAA Student-Athlete Name & Likeness Licensing Litigation [O'Bannon] (N.D. Cal. 2014) (Docket No. 1033). *See also* Antitrust Plaintiffs' Opposition to Defendant NCAA's Motion to Sever, or Alternatively to Continue Trial, in re NCAA Student-Athlete Name & Likeness Licensing Litigation, 2014 WL 1873825 (N.D. Cal. 2014), No. 4:09-cv-1967-CW; *but see* Order Denying Motion to Sever Trial Issues or Continue Trial Date and Setting Dates, Keller v. National Collegiate Athletic Association, 4:09-cv-01967 (N.D. Cal. 2014) (Docket No. 1029) (consolidated with *O'Bannon*).

111. Hemphill, *supra* note 29, at 947 (citations omitted).

112. Hovenkamp, *supra* note 36, at 379.

113. *See, e.g.*, Brian L. Porto, "Neither Employees nor Indentured Servants: A New Amateurism for a New Millennium in College Sports," 26 *Marquette Sports Law Review* 301 (2016); Nathaniel Grow, "Regulating Professional Sports Leagues," 72 *Washington and Lee Law Review* 573, 574 (2015); Daniel E. Lazaroff, "An Antitrust Exemption for the NCAA: Sound Policy or Letting the Fox Loose in the Henhouse?," 41 *Pepperdine Law Review* 229 (2014); Stephen F. Ross & Matt Mitten, *supra* note 103, at 844; Stephen F. Ross, "Radical Reform of Intercollegiate Athletics: Antitrust and Public Policy Implications," 86 *Tulane Law Review* 933 (2012); Mitten, Musselman & Burton, *supra* note 20, at 779; Roberts, *supra* note 34; Ralph D. Russo, "As NCAA Fends Off Challenges, Antitrust Exemption Debated," *Washington Times* (May 21, 2015), http://www.washingtontimes.com/news/2015/may/21/as-ncaa-fends-off-challenges-antitrust-exemption-d/; Len Elmore, "Exempt the NCAA from Antitrust," *Chronicle of Higher Education* (Dec. 11, 2011), http://www.chronicle.com/article/Exempt-the-NCAA-From-Antitrust/130073/. *See also* Sharon Terlep, "Colleges May Seek Antitrust Exemption for NCAA," *Wall Street Journal* (July 30, 2014), http://www.wsj.com/articles/colleges-may-seek-antitrust-exemption-for-ncaa-1406741252.

114. *O'Bannon*, 7 F. Supp. 3d at 1008–9.

115. Jeff Zalesin, "Antitrust Rule of Reason Cases Tough to Try, Judges Say," *Competition Law* 360 (Apr. 6, 2016), http://www.law360.com/articles/781389/antitrust-rule-of-reason-cases-tough-to-try-judges-say.

116. *Id.*

117. The *O'Bannon* plaintiffs in their petition for certiorari (at 15) compared the NCAA's reliance on amateurism to the defendant's defense in United States v. Trans-Missouri Freight Association, 166 U.S. 290, 340 (1897), wherein the Court said that the antitrust laws do not permit the defendant to establish a legally cognizable interest in the suppression of competition: "These considerations are, however, not for us. If the act ought to read as contended for by the defendants, congress is the body to amend it, and not this court, by a process of judicial legislation wholly unjustifiable." Petition for Writ of Certiorari, *supra* note 83.

118. Northwestern University & College Athletes Players Association, 2015 NLRB LEXIS 613, 204 L.R.R.M. 1001, 2014–15 NLRB Dec. (CCH) P 15,999, 362 NLRB No. 167 (N.L.R.B. Aug. 17, 2015). Additionally, the court in *Berger v. NCAA* cautioned that

whether "college athletes . . . should be compensated in some way" is not properly resolved by a court but instead is a broader "societal debate." Berger v. National Collegiate Athletic Association, 2016 U.S. Dist. LEXIS 18194, at n. 5. *Cf.* PGA Tour, Inc. v. Martin, 532 U.S. 661, n. 51 (2001) ("Petitioner's questioning of the ability of courts to apply the reasonable modification requirement to athletic competition is a complaint more properly directed to Congress.").

119. With NBA and NFL stars earning from $10 million to $20 million annually, and with NBA and NFL teams generating between two and a half and ten times as much revenue as the top-thirty college basketball and football teams, it is apparent that with a normal labor market, the top college hoops and gridiron players would be earning (and, hence, producing a value) well in excess of $1 million.

120. The NCAA provides loans to star athletes who are most likely to be drafted by professional leagues in order to purchase career-ending insurance through its Exceptional Student-Athlete Disability Insurance Program.

121. Eventually, if college athletes were paid, the astronomical compensation now paid to college coaches and athletic administrators would be reduced, alleviating some of the cost pressure. See the discussion in Gerald Gurney, Donna A. Lopiano & Andrew Zimbalist, *Unwinding Madness: What Went Wrong with College Sports and How to Fix It*, chs. 7–8 (2017).

122. In 1984, the International Olympic Committee (IOC) voted to allow the International Federation of each sport to set the eligibility rules for its sport, within some limits. In 1987, the IOC voted to permit professional tennis players to participate in the games, and in 1989, the IOC extended the welcome to all professional athletes. See Andrew Zimbalist, *Circus Maximus: The Economic Gamble behind Hosting the Olympics and the World Cup*, ch. 2 (2015). It should be noted, however, that the compensation of Olympic athletes in the United States is determined by each sport's federation and tends to be nominal. Thus, almost all of the Olympic athletes receive below a livable wage, and while they are "paid," the perception of the public may still be that the athletes are not professionals. Top Olympic athletes from other countries, especially Asian countries, receive more robust compensation, and those who win medals usually receive hundreds of thousands of dollars in reward. In those countries, government funding supports the Olympic program.

123. As noted earlier, a major factor that facilitated and deepened the commercialization of college sports was the 1984 Supreme Court decision in *Board of Regents*, wherein the Supreme Court ruled that the NCAA's existing national television contracts with ABC and CBS were illegal restraints of trade. The ruling set the stage for subsequent conference contracts with the television networks, a mergers-and-acquisitions phase of conference growth that redrew geographical conference lines to maximize the value of media deals and heightened incentives to compromise academic integrity in pursuit of athletic glory.

124. Noteworthy is that antitrust damages are trebled under the Sherman Act. This is an impetus for the parties to reach a settlement. Settlements resolve matters only between the particular parties and do not foreclose future cases brought by a different set of plaintiffs. *See, e.g.*, White v. National Collegiate Athletic Association, Case No. CV-06-0999-RGK (C.D. Cal. 2006) (discussing allegations regarding the GIA cap that settled, allowing for a different set of plaintiffs in *O'Bannon* to bring similar allegations without the existence of contrary precedent).

125. Such limits would be imposed regardless of the source of the funding.

126. For the 2016–17 season, Jim Harbaugh at the University of Michigan was compensated to the tune of $9 million. Mark Snyder & Steve Berkowitz, "Jim Harbaugh, U-M Agreed to $2-Million Additional Compensation in June," *Detroit Free Press* and

USA Today (Aug. 18, 2016), http://www.freep.com/story/sports/college/University-michigan/wolverines/2016/08/17/michigan-jim-harbaugh-contract/88910306/.

127. One eye-popping severance clause appeared in the contract of Mike Sherman, Texas A&M's football coach, who, if terminated, would have been paid $150,000 a month for the remainder of his contract, which would have amounted to a "$7.8 million golden handshake." Andrew Zimbalist, *Circling the Bases: Essays on the Challenges and Prospects of the Sports Industry* 177 (2011).

128. Reuben Fischer-Baum, "Infographic: Is Your State's Highest-Paid Employee a Coach? (Probably)," *Deadspin* (May 9, 2013, 3:23 p.m.), http://deadspin.com/infographic-is-your-states-highest-paid-employee-a-co-489635228. In a 41st state, New Hampshire, the head ice hockey coach earns more than the governor.

129. The revenue estimates for NBA and NFL teams come from the 2015 *Forbes* annual reports. Those for college football and basketball teams come from the 2015 NCAA *Revenues and Expenses* biannual report.

130. Of course, some college coaches would attempt to coach in the NFL or NBA. Both Calipari and Pitino, for instance, have done that and failed. Coaching in college and in the pros require rather different skill sets. In any event, to the extent that some college coaches go to the pros (and Calipari, for one, has continued to receive interest from some NBA owners), the pro coaches they replace would become available to the top college programs. Thus, the talent level of coaching and the quality of the college product would not be materially affected by capping coaches' compensation. Some observers have pointed out that if student-athletes were paid, then the excessive payment of salaries to coaches would self-adjust downward. While this is a likely occurrence, it would take years to fully play out, as existing long-term contracts would have to expire and the culture of the marketplace would have to adjust. The same relationship holds with excessive spending on facilities, but in this case, the adjustment would take decades because the useful life of new stadiums, arenas, and training centers is at least thirty years. During the adjustment periods, larger losses would be sustained by athletics programs.

131. The $400,000 figure is illustrative. The actual cap should approximate the coaches' reservation wage, that is, the compensation they would require in order to induce them to offer their labor. In turn, this level will be approximated by the opportunity cost or the next best compensation package they could receive if they were not coaching at the top college level.

132. This cap may be modified to allow catch-up spending for schools that had not made a certain level of facility investment over the previous period.

133. College coaches have protested that college football teams cannot be properly compared to professional teams. The latter, they say, can always call up reserves when players get injured, but college teams must have players on their rosters to replace the injured. First, NFL teams have only a maximum of 16 players on reserve and practice squads to complement their 45-man active rosters. Second, the NCAA Injury Surveillance System Summary reports that for the 2000–2001 season, the serious-injury rate during games in football was 14.1 per 1,000 exposures, while the rate in football practices was 1.6 per 1,000. If we assume that 60 players enter a game and the team plays thirteen games during the year (that is, including a postseason game), then the average total number of serious injuries (in which a player is out seven or more days) from games is eleven per year. If on average, each such player misses two games, then the average number of game-injured players is 1.69 per game. Performing a similar calculation for practice-injured players' yields 1.48 per game, for a combined average of 3.17 injured players per game. This hardly constitutes a justification for carrying 85 scholarship and 120 total players on an FBS team.

134. NFL teams are also allowed to carry up to eight additional players on their practice squads.

135. NCAA, *2005–06 NCAA Gender Equity Report* 27 (Oct. 2008), http://www.ncaapublications.com/productdownloads/GER06.pdf.

136. This number is based on twenty-five men's scholarships at $40,000 each, plus the possibility of savings on women's scholarships and the probable reduction in athletic support staff and equipment.

137. NCAA, *2004–08 NCAA Revenues and Expenses of Division I Intercollegiate Athletics Programs Report* 37 (October 2009), http://www.ncaapublications.com/productdownloads/RE09.pdf.

138. Many courts might classify these as noncommercial restraints. If so classified, an antitrust exemption would be redundant.

139. This sliding scale eligibility was introduced after a two-decade struggle with the Black Coaches Association that claimed a hard cutoff on standardized tests was arbitrary and discriminatory toward minority athletes. It is interesting to note the growth in the participation of black athletes in college sports actually was more rapid prior to 2003 than it was after 2003.

140. 12 U.S.C. § 5301, et seq. (2010). The Sarbanes-Oxley Act of 2002 first enacted some of these requirements. 15 U.S.C. § 7241 (2002); 18 U.S.C. § 1350 (2002).

141. 36 U.S.C. § 220504(b) (1998).

142. The Drake Group, a national organization committed to academic integrity in collegiate sport, has proposed similar reforms, including the establishment of a Presidential Commission in Intercollegiate Athletics Reform and a bill entitled the College Athletics Act. It further proposes a federally chartered nonprofit organization to replace the NCAA. *See* The Drake Group: Academic Integrity in Collegiate Sport, http://thedrakegroup.org. *See also* Gurney, Lopiano & Zimbalist, *supra* note 121.

143. Arguably, regulating college athletics, including eligibility, scholarships, scheduling, and spending, is not so different from regulating college financial assistance, such as what is covered in the Higher Education Act, which includes rules on loan limits, accreditation, determining who gets money, how much, and when, etc. And regulating gender equality in college sports (e.g., Title IX, 20 U.S.C. § 1681 et seq.) demonstrates that Congress believes it is appropriate to impose legislation in this important area.

144. Anti-Hog-Cholera Serum and Hog-Cholera Virus Act, 7 U.S.C. § 852 (1935).

145. Railroad transportation exemption, 49 U.S.C. § 10706 (1996).

146. Soft Drink Interbrand Competition Act.,15 U.S.C. §§ 3501–3 (1980).

147. McCarran-Ferguson Act, 15 U.S.C. §§ 1011–15 (1945).

148. Various bills have been proposed to provide the NCAA an antitrust exemption that would permit greater benefits to athletes. For example, in 1991, US Representative Tom McMillen (a former professional basketball player) introduced legislation in Congress to grant the NCAA a five-year antitrust exemption in exchange for NCAA reform regarding revenue sharing and due process for those who are accused of violations of NCAA rules. The bill, entitled the Collegiate Athletic Reform Act, would have also authorized the payment of a stipend of $300 per month and five-year athletic scholarships for student-athletes in good academic standing. The proposal failed to become law. Brian L. Porto, *The Supreme Court and the NCAA* (2013) (citing Welch Suggs, "Football, Television, and the Supreme Court," *Chronicle of Higher Education* (July 9, 2004), at A17, A32–A33).

149. Sports Broadcasting Act of 1961, 15 U.S.C. § 1291 (2000) (stating, "The antitrust laws, as defined in section 1 of the [Sherman] Act[,] . . . shall not apply to any joint agreement . . . by which any league of clubs participating in professional football, baseball, basketball, or hockey contests sells or otherwise transfers all or any part of

the rights of such league's member clubs in the sponsored telecasting of the games . . . engaged in or conducted by such clubs").

150. 15 U.S.C. § 1293 (2000).

151. Pub. L. No. 89-800 § 6(b)(1) (codified at 15 U.S.C. § 1291 (1986)).

152. 36 U.S.C. § 220501 et seq. (2006).

153. 36 U.S.C. § 220503 (1998).

154. For example, in *Behagen v. Amateur Basketball Association of the U.S.*, 884 F.2d 524, 529–30 (10th Circuit 1989), the Tenth Circuit held that the degree to which private action was necessary to implement the intent of Congress in passing the ASA meant National Governing Bodies (NGBs) could exercise monolithic control over a particular sport, and NGBs could exercise such control without fear of violating the federal antitrust laws. *See also* Eleven Line v. North Texas State Soccer Association, 213 F.3d 198, 204 (5th Circuit 2000); Gold Metal LLC d/b/a Run Gum v. USA Track & Field, Case No. 6:16-cv-00092-MC (D. Or. 2016) (Doc. 52) (finding an implied antitrust immunity applies to the ASA).

155. Congress ensured the limited scope of its intervention by expressly stating that "the passage of this Act does not change the application of the antitrust laws in any other context or with respect to any other person or entity." 15 U.S.C. § 26b.

156. 20 U.S.C. ch. 70, subch. I § 6301 et seq. (2015).

157. 15 U.S.C. § 37 (1997).

158. 15 U.S.C. § 37b(2) (2004).

159. 15 U.S.C. § 37b(b)(2) (2004).

160. 15 U.S.C. § 37b(b)(3) (2004).

161. There also have been discussions in favor of an antitrust exemption for the NCAA as it relates to Title IX. The Commission on Opportunity in Athletics, empaneled from 2002 to 2003 (and, notably, made up primarily of representatives from Division I-A schools), made a recommendation to the secretary of education that an antitrust exemption be created to reduce spending in intercollegiate athletics. Several years later, the Women's Sports Foundation issued a report in favor of an antitrust exemption that would allow the NCAA to reduce expenditures, including coaches' salaries, due to the negative effects that the arms race can have on student-athletes and the institutions' educational efforts. While these efforts did not gain traction at the time, they too are examples of support for an antitrust exemption, including an exemption for regulations imposing restraints on athletics spending, so long as the cost savings are used in furtherance of education or student-athletes' welfare.

CHAPTER 3

A Win-Win

COLLEGE ATHLETES GET PAID FOR THEIR NAMES, IMAGES, AND LIKENESSES AND COLLEGES MAINTAIN THE PRIMACY OF ACADEMICS

Jayma Meyer and Andrew Zimbalist

California Governor Gavin Newsom signed the Fair Pay to Play Act (SB 206) into law on September 30, 2019. The bill made it illegal for California's universities to prohibit college athletes from receiving compensation for use of their names, images, and likenesses (NILs). Lawmakers soon introduced similar bills in other states[1] and in Congress.[2]

The National Collegiate Athletic Association (NCAA) lobbied vigorously against SB 206 after its introduction in the California state legislature, threatening to prohibit all of the state's fifty-eight member colleges from postseason play if the bill went into effect at the specified date in 2023. The NCAA also threatened to sue to block the law[3] on the basis of the Commerce Clause of the US Constitution,[4] which prohibits states from enacting legislation that unduly impacts commerce beyond its borders.[5]

The Fair Pay to Play Act collides with the NCAA's longtime insistence that college athletes be amateurs and thus not receive pay for playing or their athleticism.[6] Indeed, payments to college athletes for NILs could blow up its amateurism model, which prohibits athletes, unlike other students, from receiving pay for activities including signing endorsements,

Harvard Journal of Sports and Entertainment Law 11, no. 2 (Spring 2020).

permitting video games to use their likeness, sponsoring athletic camps, selling jerseys and other apparel, and monetizing social media.

Confronted with snowballing legislation and lawsuits, along with a growing public consensus that the status quo exploits high-profile college athletes, the NCAA sought to regain control by forming a nineteen-member committee to examine the feasibility of NIL payments to student-athletes (NIL Committee).

After California passed SB 206, the NIL Committee gave the NCAA Board of Governors (Board) an interim report that tentatively greenlit NIL benefits for athletes but also recommended myriad guidelines and restrictions. Specifically, on October 29, 2019, the Board announced that it had voted to allow athletes generally to receive NIL benefits "in a manner consistent with the collegiate model"[7] and requested that each of the NCAA's three divisions[8] draw up plans for implementation by January 2021.

Part of the NCAA's concern with SB 206 and other state initiatives around NIL payments is that it would be unworkable to have a national organization with rules and regulations that differ on a state-by-state basis. Indeed, the bills introduced in the South Carolina and New York state legislatures allow for schools to pay athletes directly,[9] while SB 206 allows schools to make NIL payments to current students (not prospective students) and allows payments from third parties.[10] The New York bill also stipulates that 15 percent of a school's athletics department revenues go to pay for its student athletes.[11] Florida's NIL bill would go into effect on July 1, 2021, much earlier than in other states.[12] Fortunately, the prospect of a patchwork of varying state laws appears unlikely to eventuate because Representative Mark Walker (R-NC) has introduced a NIL bill in the US House of Representatives that would create a uniform federal system.[13] Similarly, Senators Chris Murphy (D-CT), Mitt Romney (R-UT), and Marco Rubio (R-FL) have discussed introducing a NIL bill in the US Senate, and the Senate's Commerce Committee held a hearing on the matter in February 2020.[14]

In this essay, we explain the history and role of amateurism in college athletics; the legal landscape of amateurism and paying college athletes, including NIL payments; the potential scope of NIL payments; and the NCAA NIL Committee's recommendations. We conclude by offering a public policy proposal for implementing circumscribed NIL rights for college athletes.

The History of Amateurism

The Evolution of Amateurism

Whether amateurism rules are necessary for intercollegiate athletics has been the subject of long-standing academic debate and legal challenges.[15] It is instructive to follow the evolution of the NCAA's definition of amateurism from its origins, at which time it prohibited all financial aid based on athletic ability, to its current stance, in which it embraces athletic scholarships and benefits with values generally exceeding those afforded nonathletes.

The NCAA, in its early days, did not enforce many of its policies, rendering definitions and principles of amateurism inconsequential. Article VI of the NCAA's 1906 bylaws burdened each member institution with enforcing violations of its amateurism principles, such as "the offering of inducements to players to enter colleges or universities because of their athletic abilities or maintaining players while students on account of their athletic abilities."[16] Thus, athletic scholarships, as we know them today, violated amateurism rules of the time, while need-based financial aid unrelated to athletics did not.

Not until 1916 did the NCAA define the term "amateurism." Article VI(b) of the bylaws at that time provided that an amateur is "one who participates in competitive physical sports only for the pleasure, and the physical, mental, moral, and social benefits derived therefrom."[17] The NCAA amended this definition in 1922: "An amateur sportsman is one who engages in sport solely for the physical, mental, or social benefits he derives therefrom, and to whom the sport is nothing more than an avocation."[18]

Because the NCAA had no enforcement power during this time, its members ignored and violated these amateurism rules with impunity.

Indeed, a 1929 Carnegie Foundation report on intercollegiate athletics found that three-quarters of the 112 colleges investigated violated the NCAA's amateurism code and principles.[19] After declining during the Depression and much of World War II, college sports' commercialization accelerated as the war ended. At the end of 1946, the sports editor of the *New York Herald Tribune* wrote, "When it comes to chicanery, double-dealing, and undercover work behind the scenes, big-time college football is in a class by itself. . . . Should the Carnegie Foundation launch an investigation of college football right now, the mild breaches of etiquette uncovered [in the 1920s] . . . would assume a remote innocence which would only cause snickers among the post-war pirates of 1946."[20]

The de facto payrolls of several college teams reached $100,000, and the football coach at Oklahoma State estimated that its rival Oklahoma annually spent over $200,000 ($2.86 million in today's dollars) on players.[21]

After the situation had gotten sufficiently out of control, the NCAA finally attempted to both ratify the reality of financial aid to athletes and enforce its code of amateurism.[22] First, in 1948, the NCAA passed its so-called Sanity Code, allowing schools to award athletically related financial aid if the student-athlete qualified for need and the aid was limited to tuition and incidental expenses. Aid exceeding tuition could be granted if it stemmed from superior academic scholarship. In 1950, however, the NCAA effectively abandoned the Sanity Code—which also prohibited schools from withdrawing aid if a student quit participating in athletics—when its membership voted not to expel violating schools.[23]

In 1956, the NCAA finally addressed allowable non-need-based compensation to athletes when it permitted athletic scholarships to cover commonly accepted educational expenses. In 1957, an "Official Interpretation" defined such expenses to include costs for room, board, tuition, books, fees, and $15 a month for "laundry money,"[24] equal to $140 a month, or $1,680 annually, in today's dollars. Few who attended the NCAA's first convention in 1906 could have conceived that, by 1957, NCAA rules would allow a university to use these types of financial inducements to recruit high school athletes.[25]

The 1957 NCAA rules contained provisions specifically meant to counter a possible argument that athletic scholarships constituted "pay for play," which would have exposed its members to workers' compensation claims and Social Security contributions. Financial aid could not be "reduced (gradated) or canceled on the basis of an athlete's contribution to team success, injury, or decision not to participate."[26] Adding form to substance, the NCAA mandated the use of the term "student-athlete."[27]

Then, in 1967, the NCAA drifted further from its original amateurism concept in its response to member-school complaints about athletes who accepted four-year scholarships and then decided against participating. One athletic director opined that this was "morally wrong," adding that "regardless of what anyone says, this is a contract and it is a two-way street."[28] In response, the NCAA passed rules that allowed the immediate cancellation of an athlete's scholarship should he or she voluntarily withdraw from sports or fail to follow a coach's directives.

The NCAA departed still further from its model of amateurism in 1973 by requiring schools to replace athletic scholarships' four-year guarantees with annually renewable terms, effectively empowering coaches to discontinue scholarships for virtually any reason, including injury, performance, fit, or availability of more favorable talent.[29] The contingent contractual nature of this relationship and the control it gave to the coaches over the players' behavior had many trappings of an employment contract.[30]

The Modern Treatment of Amateurism

In response to cries of athlete exploitation and an increasing amount of litigation brought under antitrust and labor laws, the NCAA has sought to tweak its treatment of amateurism in recent years to provide athletes with more protection and expanded benefits. In 2012, for example, the NCAA approved a new rule giving Division I schools the option to award multi-year scholarships.[31] In 2014, the association started allowing expanded food service for athletes, beyond that available to nonathlete students.[32] More significantly, in 2015, for Division I, the NCAA began allowing four-year scholarships and cost-of-attendance (COA) stipends to supplement the traditional grant-in-aid that covered only the cost of tuition, room and board, fees, and required books.[33] The COA stipends aimed to cover items like cost of transportation to and from school, recommended books, and other items that vary from school to school and are set by each school's maximum financial package, but athletes could use the cash payments however they pleased.[34] Depending on the school, the COA stipends, as dictated by the application of federal guidelines, vary, equaling between $2,000 and $6,000.[35] For low-income athletes, these newly allowed COA stipends can supplement Pell Grants,[36] which amounted to $6,195 in 2019–20.[37]

The NCAA has permitted many other modifications to its amateurism rules aimed at particular sports or at individual athletes' situations—particularly successful athletes. For example, it permits athletes who win Olympic medals to receive cash prizes from the United States Olympic and Paralympic Committee under a program called Operation Gold.[38] The amount has increased over the years; today, gold medalists receive $37,500, silver medalists $22,500, and bronze medalists $15,000, while team members split the prize money equally.[39] The NCAA also permits tennis players to receive up to $10,000 annually in prize money before they enter college while retaining amateur status.[40]

Additionally, the NCAA now allows student-athletes to receive gifts for participating in bowl games or championships. For instance, athletic participation awards provide cash and merchandise (such as video games and jewelry, among other prizes) to players in football bowl games and the March Madness basketball tournament. A March 2012 article in the *Sports Business Journal* provided some details: "For example, a senior on a team that runs the table and wins championships for the regular season, postseason conference tournament and NCAA tournament could secure gifts valued at up to $3,780. Last year's comparable total was $3,380. Up to 25 gift packages can be provided to a team by its school and by its conference for participating in this month's conference tournaments, according to NCAA bylaws."[41] The total amount of the awards granted is now estimated at $5,600 yearly per athlete.[42] The NCAA also permits athletes' families to receive payments of up to $4,000 to cover the cost of attending the men's and women's Final Four championship games as well as the College Football Playoffs.[43]

A modification that has particularly large implications for high-profile athletes, especially in basketball and football, is that cash from two funds created by the NCAA—the Student Assistance Fund (SAF)[44] and Academic Enhancement Fund (AEF)[45]—can be given to athletes.[46] Though the NCAA created these resources to help student-athletes cover costs related to personal emergencies (e.g., bereavement-related travel), universities can now allocate these funds discretionarily for their student-athletes' benefit. One highly visible example is schools' provision of funds to athletes to pay premiums on loss-of-value insurance. Indeed, Zion Williamson would have been entitled to collect on an $8 million loss-of-value insurance policy—that Duke University paid $50,000 in premiums for—if he slipped past the number 16 overall pick in the 2019 National Basketball Association (NBA) draft.[47]

The NCAA's Current Bylaws Regarding Amateurism

Today, the NCAA views its amateurism principles as integral to its educationally focused mission. In its bylaws, the NCAA states that it seeks to "provid[e] student-athletes with exemplary educational and intercollegiate-athletics experiences in an environment that recognizes and supports *the primacy of the academic mission* of its member institutions, while enhancing the ability of male and female student-athletes to earn a four-year degree."[48]

The NCAA has several bylaws that address amateurism, including NIL payments.[49] These bylaws restrict athletes in specific ways:

- Financial aid is "not considered to be pay or the promise of pay for athletics skill."[50]
- Payments to athletes for athletic services are prohibited.[51]

- Athletes who accept payments may be subject to revocation of their amateur status and eligibility under severe conditions.[52]
- Athletes are prohibited from receiving money for promoting any "commercial product."[53]
- Athletes who start a business may not use their "name, photograph, appearance or athletics reputation" to promote the business.[54]

Perhaps inconsistent with the NCAA's stated mission (along with modifications to the amateurism policy addressed in the previous sections) are two particular bylaws:

- The NCAA and its member institutions may use athletes to endorse their products and activities in a wide variety of circumstances.[55]
- While athletes may receive certain performance awards for athletics, they generally may not for academic achievement.[56]

The Proper Role of Amateurism

Given the NCAA's history of extensive modifications of what acts do and do not run afoul of being an amateur athlete, it is reasonable to conclude that amateurism in college sports is whatever the NCAA dictates it to be at the time. With regularly shifting goal posts, it seems problematic to argue that this morphing concept of amateurism is necessary for college sports. We believe, however, that amateurism, properly understood, is an important feature of intercollegiate athletics.

The word "amateurism" derives from the Latin word *amator*, which means "lover." In common English, an amateur is someone who engages in activity for pleasure or love rather than for extrinsic reward or money. Ergo, Division I college basketball players remain amateurs as long as they do not receive pay for their participation. So, under this line of reasoning, a Division I college basketball player should be able to receive pay for endorsing a local car dealership because the underlying performance is for executing the endorsement, not for playing basketball. That is, NIL payments do not violate the core meaning of amateurism. Nevertheless, such payments are prohibited under the current NCAA rules.

In our view, as long as playing a college sport remains an extracurricular activity rather than a standalone commercial activity, amateurism should play a role. Many athletes in high-profile college football and basketball programs already are cheated out of a proper learning experience. They may be admitted without adequate academic achievement or ability and hustled into phantom courses and majors. Most are required to spend well in excess of forty hours weekly preparing for and engaging in competition.[57] If their amateur status is lifted and they begin to receive compensation, they will face more pressure to perform for their coaches, who, in turn, will be less restricted by the exigencies of the educational process. This will inevitably create a greater separation between student-athletes and the normal student body. Athletes would also have to pay taxes on their income, introducing a cadre of lawyers, financial advisers, agents, and tax accountants.

For those who believe that athletes must receive pay to avoid exploitation, the only complete solution is the professionalization of major college sports. But this would present problems for both the schools and athletes. Significantly, athletics programs in the NCAA's Division I Football Subdivision (FBS) run a median deficit of $18.8 million,[58] according to the latest NCAA financial report.[59] This deficit, moreover, does not include most capital expenditures and many indirect costs of athletics programs, which would add millions of dollars to the financial drain.[60] If college athletes were to receive a salary, then this deficit, financed out of the school's educational budget, would balloon. Eventually, the extent of the increase in the deficit will diminish as coaches and athletic administrators, who are now paid out of the value of the athletes they recruit, would see their salaries decrease. Further compounding the problematic implications is that as the athletics department deficit grows, there is less funding available for women's sports, which makes Title IX compliance increasingly more difficult.[61]

The argument in favor of paying athletes often references the multimillion-dollar salaries received by coaches and top administrators, as well as current expenditures on ultralavish facilities.[62] Not to pay athletes in the face of these bloated salaries is seen as unjust and unseemly. With this, we agree. Indeed, in 2019, there were 176 college football and men's basketball coaches who received salaries exceeding $1 million, 71 whose salaries exceeded $3 million, and 38 whose salaries exceeded $4 million.[63] The highest paid coach was Dabo Swinney at Clemson University, with a guaranteed salary of $9.3 million plus bonuses of $1.1 million and a potential buyout clause worth $50 million.[64] Swinney's assistant coaches collectively earned $6.8 million, raising the total for all football coaches at Clemson to $17.2 million, not including their handsome perquisites and opportunities for outside income. Perquisites generally include free use of cars, housing subsidies, country-club memberships, private jet services, exceptionally generous severance packages, and more.[65] The coaches also have alluring opportunities to earn outside income via apparel or sneaker endorsements, the lecture circuit, summer camps, and book contracts.[66] In forty states, the head football or basketball coach on a college team within the state makes more in guaranteed compensation than the state's governor.[67]

Defenders of multimillion-dollar coaches' salaries argue that coaches' compensation packages are driven by market forces. While this may be true, the market for coaches is buoyed by artificial factors, including (1) the lack of compensation paid to the athletes; (2) substantial tax privileges given to intercollegiate sports; (3) a lack of shareholder demand for dividend distributions or higher profits to bolster stock prices at the end of every quarter; (4) the university and statewide financial support given to athletics departments; and (5) the incentive of athletic directors who negotiate coaches' salaries and whose own worth rises with the salaries of their employees.

The answer to the bloated spending though, in our view, is not to pay the athletes a salary; it is to cap coaches' and administrators' salaries, to cap the expenditures on lavish facilities used for a single sport, and to reinforce the educational mission of the school.[68] We believe that these restrictions would require an antitrust exemption.[69] Such an exemption should be conditioned on the NCAA ensuring that athletes receive a robust educational and social experience in college, safeguarding athletes' health, and providing health and lost-income-from-injury insurance. Significantly, this plan would permit athletes to receive payments for product endorsements from third parties or other use of athletes' NIL rights with appropriate restrictions. Our proposed plan for NIL payments, along with an antitrust exemption, is explained later in this essay.

Another factor in athlete pay is whether the college-sports brand would suffer if pay-for-play, including the institution paying for athletes' NILs, were introduced.[70] Some people claim that college sports derive much popularity from the presumption that the athletes are students, not "ringers" or professionals who do not attend class. If the athletes are matriculated students who attend and participate in classes alongside non-student-athletes, a link is formed between the athletes and nonathletes. The team is thus perceived to be the school team, which stimulates support from current students, administrators, alumni, and local businesspeople. If the link between athlete and student is disrupted, however, then the special fan attachment to the team could dissipate, and college sports will morph into little more than a minor league professional basketball or football league, with attendant reductions in attendance and television contracts. Proponents of pay-for-play or for NILs retort that this position ignores the experience of the Olympics, where athletes since the 1980s are no longer amateurs, yet the popularity of the Olympic Games has continued to grow in recent decades.[71] Each side of this debate has proffered nondispositive evidence, and it is thus fair to say that this debate has not yet been resolved.[72]

Certain opponents of pay-for-play argue that NIL payments by third parties will diminish the progress that women have made toward gender equality in collegiate sports since Title IX[73] was enacted in 1972.[74] The concern is that high-profile men playing football and basketball will receive the vast majority of NIL payments and that Title IX will not apply to require equity because the discrimination would not be engaged in by the organization receiving federal funds (i.e., educational institutions). Of course, if the institution directly pays athletes for use of their NILs, which is not what this essay proposes, then there is little question that Title IX would apply, mandating equivalent NIL payments to women either as part of its financial-aid or benefits-and-opportunities requirements.[75] Yet it may still be possible that Title IX's requirements would apply if schools do not pay the NIL payments to athletes but are involved in one form or another, directly or indirectly, with respect to the third-party payments—for example, in an administrative or compliance capacity.[76] To the extent that NILs become a recruiting tool, then "there is a question as to whether that school's knowledge creates an obligation [under Title IX] to try to ensure similar opportunities are offered for the other gender."[77] Further, since promotional efforts must be equitable under Title IX for men and women, if schools promote NIL opportunities from third parties for men or men's teams, then they must devote qualitatively similar efforts to women or women's teams.[78]

NIL payments made by third parties, even if generally not as large to female athletes as to males, may meaningfully benefit high-profile female athletes.[79] This is significant given that women today have fewer opportunities to go professional. Just consider how many men play football professionally. Indeed, the sponsor of the California bill, Nancy Skinner, made this point, stating that "women [athletes] really should have a shot at getting something while they're in college" because of the lack of professional opportunities for women after college.[80] As explained by Congresswoman Skinner, any female athletes, whether nationally or locally known, have their moment in the spotlight, with corresponding earning power, when they are in college. For them, the chance to receive NIL payments while in college is a significant benefit. For example, Katelyn Ohashi, a star gymnast at the University of California, Los Angeles, whose perfect (10.0) floor routine in 2019 went viral when posted on YouTube,[81] pointed out that her situation would have been dramatically different if she could have profited from that video.[82] Ohashi said she felt stifled by NCAA regulations as she gained name recognition: "Along with this came a lot of attention and opportunities, but I couldn't capitalize on them. I was handcuffed by the NCAA rules that prevented me from deriving any benefit from my own name and likeness, regardless of the fact that after my final meet, I had no pro league to join."[83]

Finally, some commentators argue that payment for play will reduce the ugly underbelly of surreptitious payments to athletes.[84] Indeed, former US secretary of state Condoleezza Rice, as chairperson for the committee that evaluated the recent basketball scandal,[85] explained that athletes should be entitled to NIL payments for this very reason.[86] She then said that the NCAA's rules relating to NIL payments are "incomprehensible" and noted that, when she sees policies as "confused" as the NCAA's are with respect to NILs, she thinks, "'Why haven't you gone and looked at this before.' It's really time to come to terms with name, image and likeness."[87]

The Legal Landscape of Amateurism and Paying College Athletes, Including for Their NILs, in College Sports

Litigation aimed at providing college athletes with pay or additional benefits and rights has relied on various causes of action pursuant to federal, state, and common laws.[88]

Antitrust laws have been the most widely used to chip away at the NCAA's amateurism rules. In these cases, the NCAA has argued that, even if its rules are anticompetitive, they are necessary to preserve amateurism in order to protect the uniqueness of college sports and thus demand for the brand.[89] Right-of-publicity claims have proved to be more complicated because they turn on state laws and common law, and strong defenses may be available under the First Amendment and copyright laws, depending on the usage (for example, live broadcasts versus video games).

Athletes have also resorted to employment and labor laws in order to find a friendly basis for pursuing their claims to receive payment, including the Fair Labor Standards Act, arguing that they are employees, and the National Labor Relations Act, arguing that they be allowed to unionize. As explained in the following subsections, these employment- and labor-law-based efforts have not been successful to date.[90]

Athletes Have Received Additional Benefits under the Antitrust Lawsuits

Antitrust laws, and their judicially created frameworks, while not easy to apply to intercollegiate sports, have been the most fertile ground for chipping away at the NCAA's amateurism rules.

The Sherman Act,[91] designed to govern commercial activities,[92] prohibits contracts, combinations, or conspiracies that unreasonably restrain trade.[93] Once a court finds a rule fundamentally commercial under the Sherman Act, a court then must address whether the rule unreasonably restrains trade.[94] With respect to the NCAA, because the product—competitive sports—requires joint activity among individual institutions (i.e., a team cannot play against itself), courts apply a rule of reason analysis to determine whether the rule is unreasonably anticompetitive. The judicially created rule of reason framework involves three burden-shifting steps. First, the plaintiff has the burden of proving that the restraint creates anticompetitive effects. If the plaintiff successfully argues this point, the analysis moves to the second step, in which the burden shifts to the defendant to prove procompetitive benefits flowing from the restraint. If the defendant's justifications are "sufficient," the burden shifts back to the plaintiff, in the third step, to show that the challenged conduct is not reasonably necessary to achieve the legitimate benefits or that comparable procompetitive benefits could be achieved through a less restrictive alternative (LRA) that is virtually as effective and as economically efficient. Courts, at least implicitly, try to assess the legitimacy of, or weigh, these pro- and anticompetitive effects and the LRA and therefore determine whether the virtues of the anticompetitive conduct justify the adverse impact. Their judgment turns on whether the dominant or net effect of the restraint, or of the LRA, is to promote competition or hinder it.[95]

The Supreme Court's Decision in *Board of Regents*. The Supreme Court has issued just one antitrust decision relating to college sports: *National Collegiate Athletic Association v. Board of Regents of University of Oklahoma* (*Board of Regents*).[96] It discusses amateurism only in dicta. The case involved the NCAA's control (limitation) of how many games a college could broadcast on national TV and the prices for such broadcasts. The Court quickly concluded that the challenged contracts that schools jointly negotiated with television networks were commercial rules and accordingly that the Sherman Act applied.[97]

Next, the Court applied the rule of reason and its three-step burden-shifting analysis.[98] First, the Court found that the restraint limited output (reduced the number of games televised) and restricted prices (set a minimum aggregate price)—both of which are "paradigmatic examples of restraints of trade that the Sherman Act was intended to prohibit."[99] Shifting to the second step of the rule of reason analysis, the Court stated that the contracts, as "hallmarks of anticompetitive behavior," placed a "heavy burden" on the NCAA to establish an affirmative defense that justifies the deviation from a free market.[100] The Court then upheld the lower court's findings that the procompetitive justifications of protecting a live audience, establishing an efficient marketing strategy, and preserving competitive balance were not supported by the evidence and thus did not "offset" the anticompetitive limitations on price and output.[101]

While the Court's holding was straightforward, its opinion included discourse that the NCAA has since relied on regularly to justify its refusal to pay athletes, including refusal to permit NIL payments to athletes: "One clear effect of most, if not all, of these regulations [including those relating to eligibility] is to prevent institutions with competitively and economically successful programs from taking advantage of their success by expanding their programs, improving the quality of the product they offer, and increasing their sports revenues. Yet each of these regulations represents a desirable and legitimate attempt 'to keep university athletics from becoming professionalized to the extent that profit making objectives would overshadow educational objectives.'"[102]

In further dicta, the Court said that college athletes "*must not be paid*, must be required to attend class, and the like."[103] The Court did not analyze whether pay-for-play rules would be unreasonably anticompetitive and violations under the Sherman Act because payments to athletes were irrelevant to the issue at hand: the legality of the rules on TV contracts.

The Ninth Circuit's Decision in *O'Bannon*. Whether the NCAA rules regarding payments to athletes violated the Sherman Act was at the core of the Ninth Circuit's decision in *O'Bannon v. National Collegiate Athletic Association*.[104] Edward O'Bannon was a basketball player on the University of California, Los Angeles, national championship team in 1995. After discovering that his likeness was used in a commercial video game without his permission and without the promise of any compensation for use of his property rights, he brought an antitrust suit against the NCAA[105] on behalf of purported classes of FBS football and Division I men's basketball players. The case sought to enjoin NCAA rules that prohibited payments to athletes for their NILs in three submarkets: (1) live game telecasts, (2) sports video games, and (3) game rebroadcasts, advertisements, and other archival footage.[106]

The issue in the case, brought under the Sherman Act, was whether the agreement to prevent such payments to athletes for their NILs was an unreasonable restraint of trade.[107] Embedded in the case is whether athletes have rights of publicity for usage in the three submarkets. If they do not, then they would lack standing and suffer no antitrust injury as a result of the agreement.[108] On summary judgment motion, the Northern District of California court found that the athletes had standing and satisfied the antitrust injury without specifying in which submarket the harm occurred.[109]

After much legal maneuvering,[110] the parties proceeded to a bench trial on the merits of the antitrust claim. Judge Claudia Wilken issued a ninety-nine-page opinion in 2014, finding the NCAA rules to be commercial and then applying the three-part rule of reason analysis to determine whether the alleged prohibitions violated the Sherman Act. First, she found that the prohibitions constituted an anticompetitive restraint—a price-fixing agreement. The schools had agreed to rules prohibiting NIL payments to athletes for group licenses.[111] Next, under the second step,[112] Judge Wilken accepted as valid two of the NCAA's justifications, finding that amateurism played a "limited" role in maximizing consumer demand[113] and that integrating athletics and academics was a "narrow" procompetitive goal of increasing the quality of athletes' education.[114]

Moving to the third step under the rule of reason analysis, Judge Wilken found that two less restrictive alternatives were available to fulfill the NCAA's stated procompetitive justifications of amateurism and integration:

- Payment of scholarships up to cost of attendance (COA) (an increase of between $2,000 and $6,000 per year, depending on the school, over the previous grant-in-aid (GIA) amount)[115]
- Payment of up to $5,000 a year to be held in trust for when the athlete leaves or graduates from college, with the requirements that all athletes on a team receive the same amount and that the funds be generated from group licenses

Both sides then had reason to be dissatisfied and appealed to the Ninth Circuit. On appeal, the Ninth Circuit agreed that the restriction of no payments for group licensing of NILs was a commercial restraint subject to the Sherman Act.

In applying the three-step burden-shifting framework, first, the Ninth Circuit said that the restraint had a "significant" anticompetitive effect by eliminating price competition among schools.[116] Moving to the second step in the rule of reason analysis, it accepted that amateurism and integration were procompetitive justifications because they preserve the popularity of intercollegiate sports and broadened choices, respectively. Third, the Ninth Circuit considered the proposed LRAs. Ultimately, the court upheld Judge Wilken's holding that the NCAA could restrict the schools' ability to award scholarship amounts above the COA, agreeing that this was "substantially" less restrictive than a rule prohibiting payments beyond GIA and would not "significantly" increase costs.[117] The panel's reasoning focused on the need for amateurism in college sports: (1) amateurism requires no payment to athletes, so there would be no amateurism if there were payments; and (2) payments up to the COA were "tethered" to academics and therefore preserved the concept of amateurism. Writing for the panel, Judge Jay Bybee explained, "The difference between offering student-athletes education-related compensation and offering them cash sums untethered to educational expenses is not minor; it is a quantum leap. Once that line is crossed, we see no basis for returning to a rule of amateurism and no defined stopping point. . . . At that point the NCAA will have surrendered its amateurism principles and transitioned from its 'particular brand of football' to minor league status."[118]

That said, the panel split on trust-fund stipends for NIL rights, with the majority finding that they violated principles of amateurism because they were untethered to academics. Chief Judge Sidney Thomas's dissent on this issue challenged the artificiality of the majority's distinction and detailed the evidence that showed that small amounts of cash payments (beyond COA) provided to athletes after they left school would not harm the principle of amateurism. Plus, Chief Judge Thomas pointed out, amateurism, a "nebulous" concept, is relevant as a procompetitive justification in an antitrust analysis only to the extent that it relates to consumer interest, which is a quantitative effect.[119] He stated that there was no showing that such small, deferred payments would harm consumer interest. Finally, Chief Judge Thomas stressed the difficulty in resolving whether athletes should be paid for play: "The national debate about amateurism in college sports is important. But our task as appellate judges is not to resolve it. Nor could we."[120]

Again, both sides had reason to be dissatisfied. Accordingly, after the plaintiffs' request for an en banc rehearing to the full Ninth Circuit Court of Appeals was denied,[121] in a somewhat unusual consensus on the need for review, both the plaintiffs and the NCAA submitted petitions for a writ of certiorari to the Supreme Court.[122] But both petitions were ultimately denied.[123] As a result, the NCAA's regulations were left vulnerable to more challenges.[124]

***Jenkins* and *Alston*: NCAA "grant-in-aid" litigation.** Two recent antitrust class-action cases have further challenged the NCAA's amateurism rules, *Jenkins v. National Collegiate Athletic Association* and *Alston v. National Collegiate Athletic Association*.[125] They were coordinated before Judge Wilken in the Northern District of California (*NCAA Grant-in-Aid*).[126] The plaintiffs alleged that the NCAA and eleven athletic conferences systematically colluded to cap the compensation that a school may provide athletes and sought to open compensation to the free market.[127] These cases, accordingly, were broader than *O'Bannon*, as they were not limited to NIL payments. Judge Wilken certified three classes: FBS football players, Division I men's basketball players, and Division I women's basketball players.

On March 8, 2019, after a bench trial, Judge Wilken held that the NCAA's rules capping the amount of compensation that student-athletes can receive in exchange for their athletic services violated the Sherman Act. As she did in *O'Bannon*,[128] she found that the NCAA rules were commercial, had anticompetitive effects, and were subject to the rule of reason analysis. Judge Wilken devoted most of her analysis to the asserted procompetitive justifications. This time, the defendants relied only on the two justifications that the Ninth Circuit in *O'Bannon* had upheld: the compensation rules promote (1) amateurism because it is a key part of demand for college sports and (2) integration of student-athletes with their academic communities because it improves the college education that student-athletes receive.[129]

In analyzing the defendants' first purported procompetitive effect, Judge Wilken expressed great frustration. She noted that the defendants failed to offer "an affirmative definition of amateurism" and that "no link appears" between the "Principle of Amateurism" described in the NCAA's Division I Constitution and the challenged compensation limits: "the principle does not mention or address compensation; nor does it prohibit or even discourage compensation."[130] Judge Wilken expressed her concern that the defendants defined amateurism based on what it is not: the "only thing that can be inferred is that compensation constitutes 'pay for play' or 'pay' if the NCAA has decided to forbid it, and compensation is not 'pay for play' or 'pay' if the NCAA has decided to permit it."[131]

Judge Wilken then analyzed whether the amateurism rules affected consumer demand and agreed with the plaintiffs that consumer demand, despite modifications in the rules permitting more benefits since *O'Bannon*, had not decreased.[132] But she concluded, based mostly on anecdotal evidence, that "when compared with having no limits on compensation, *some* of the challenged compensation rules may have *some* effect on preserving consumer demand for college sports as distinct from professional sports to the extent that they prevent unlimited cash payments unrelated to education such as those seen in professional sports leagues."[133]

As for the defendants' second procompetitive justification, integration of athletes and other students, Judge Wilken dismissively rejected it, stating that considerable economic disparities already existed on college campuses due to students' socioeconomic backgrounds and other sources of wealth.[134]

Judge Wilken then turned to the third step of the rule of reason analysis: the plaintiffs' proposed less restrictive alternatives. She rejected the plaintiffs' "alternative that would prohibit the NCAA from placing any limits on compensation or benefits, whether or not related to education, given in exchange for athletic services,"[135] noting (consistent with the Ninth Circuit's decision in *O'Bannon*) that *unlimited* cash payments unrelated to education would harm the demarcation between college and professional sports.[136]

Judge Wilken issued a rather complicated injunction. Basically, she permitted virtually every conceivable type of noncash benefit as long as it was in some form or manner incidental or related to education,[137] but she capped cash benefits for achievement in academics up to the value of those currently provided for team-based performance (commonly viewed to be up to $5,600 over COA).[138] Judge Wilken left in place the NCAA's rules that prohibit non-education-related cash compensation for individual athletic achievement. The injunction also allowed any NCAA member conference to impose stricter limits.[139]

Both sides appealed to the Ninth Circuit, and the oral argument was held on March 9, 2020. The panel was composed of Judges Milan Smith and Roland Gould and the same Chief Judge Sidney Thomas who wrote the partially dissenting opinion in *O'Bannon* and would have permitted the proposed $5,000 payments for group NILs as long as they were held in trust for athletes until they leave school or graduate. Judge Smith was the only active questioner, including questions about the impact of California's SB 206 on the case. Seth Waxman, attorney for the NCAA and conferences, stated that SB 206 is "flatly inconsistent" with the NCAA's principles of amateurism. Amateurism, as defined by the NCAA, continues to be raison d'etre of its argument. In contrast, Jeffrey Kessler, one of the plaintiffs' attorneys, argued that the court should enjoin all NCAA restraints on compensation (which would allow the NIL compensation in SB 206). He stressed that the NCAA already, especially since *O'Bannon* was decided, permits benefits not related to education and that consumer demand has only increased. He conceded that it would be appropriate to let the conferences respectively decide on appropriate limits. Based on the oral argument, it is unclear how the panel will rule; what is clear is that it is reasonable to expect at least one of the parties will petition for certiorari to the Supreme Court once the Ninth Circuit issues its decision.

In sum, these antitrust cases show the instability of the scope of amateurism and its relationship to consumer demand. Intercollegiate athletics, as discussed earlier, are increasingly commercial but still a hybrid model, containing elements of both professionalism and amateurism. There is much tension between these elements. Effective reform, including the payment for NILs, will move the system along the spectrum toward professionalism. But, as explained later in this essay, we propose that the more defensible concern should focus on the difference between professionalism and the primacy of education in college sports.

Claims to Rights of Publicity Are Inconclusive

College athletes also have attempted to use rights-of-publicity claims to obtain compensation for their NILs. Athletes have asserted their rights of publicity within antitrust lawsuits, as argued in *O'Bannon*, by alleging that the NCAA has agreed or conspired to refuse to pay for rights of publicity, under the Sherman Act. Significantly, the Sherman Act permits treble damages and attorney's fees.[140] Other times, athletes assert their rights of publicity claims directly under particular state laws.

Publicity rights, under common law or state statutory laws, protect a person's ability to control the use of their NIL for commercial gain. Thus, a right-of-publicity claim is an allegation of unauthorized misappropriation of the commercial value of a person's identity.[141] This right is generally recognized as not extending to use in newsworthy activities like news reporting or commentary or in entertainment, creative works, or other transformative uses, where the First Amendment is a defense to a right of publicity.[142] Thus, athletes' rights to their own publicity vary depending on the respective state law, on how the athletes' NIL is employed, and how much the athletes' likeness or character has been transformed.[143]

These issues were addressed by the Ninth Circuit in *Keller v. Electronic Arts*[144] and by the Third Circuit in *Hart v. Electronic Arts*.[145] Both courts held on motions that former college athletes had a right-of-publicity claim against Electronic Arts (EA) based on the creation of avatars for the video game *NCAA Football* that looked like particular players, played like those players, and played in college stadiums that looked like the ones those players played in.[146] The defendants had not obtained permission from the players to use their images or likenesses but argued that video games, like movies and books, are expressive works fully protected by the

First Amendment.[147] Both the *Keller* court and the *Hart* court rejected EA's defense that it had sufficiently transformed the avatars to have a First Amendment right to publish the video games without the players' permission and without compensating them.[148] The courts noted that the avatars in the video games were not sufficiently transformed; they were too accurate and faithful to reality.[149]

Chief Judge Thomas of the Ninth Circuit, as in *O'Bannon*, issued a dissenting opinion in *Keller*. He would have permitted EA's defense based on the First Amendment and would not have found that the athletes were entitled to publicity rights in the particular EA football video games.[150] He said that the players were unidentified and anonymous (despite the availability of third-party software that allowed gamers to determine the identity of the player) and stated that the game as a whole was sufficiently transformative.[151]

Significantly, in *Keller*, EA and the Collegiate Licensing Co., the NCAA's licensing arm, settled before trial for $40 million,[152] and the NCAA settled for $20 million.[153] As a result of the litigation, EA also agreed to stop producing its video games with avatars similar to former college athletes. Subsequently, the NCAA agreed to discontinue selling jerseys on its website with numbers of star athletes that matched the numbers used in games and school designations.[154] Further, the NCAA said that it would allow a blanket eligibility waiver for any currently enrolled student-athletes who receive funds connected with the settlement, adding, "In no event do we consider this settlement pay of athletics performance."[155] *Hart* was wrapped into the settlement as well.

A broader discussion of whether college athletes have a right of publicity can be found in *O'Bannon*. The Ninth Circuit said that athletes have a right of publicity in the EA-produced NCAA football and basketball video games and, based on the realistic nature of the players, rejected the NCAA's argument that the First Amendment would preclude any publicity right for video games. Because it found that the athletes had standing and had suffered injury under the antitrust laws as a result of not being paid for their NILs in the video games, the Ninth Circuit declined to reach "the thornier questions of whether participants in live TV broadcasts . . . have enforceable rights of publicity or whether the plaintiffs are injured by the NCAA's current licensing arrangement for archival footage."[156] Notably, the district court in *O'Bannon*[157] stated that athletes would have a right to create and sell group licenses for the use of their NILs in live game broadcasts absent NCAA rules prohibiting such.[158] District Judge Wilken specifically rejected the NCAA's defense that the First Amendment barred plaintiffs' claims.

A few years later, in *Marshall v. ESPN*,[159] the Sixth Circuit held differently. In *Marshall*, a group of Division I football and basketball players alleged that an agreement to force athletes to sign waivers of their otherwise existing right to compensation for their publicity rights for in-game broadcasts violated the Sherman Act. The Sixth Circuit held that the athletes did not have a cognizable right of publicity in the broadcast use of their likenesses. Significantly, Tennessee's right-of-publicity law had a carve-out that stated, "it is deemed a fair use and no violation of an individual's rights shall be found . . . if the use of a name, photograph or license is in connection with a . . . sports broadcast or account."[160] Thus, the decision is limited due to the specific state law, although many states have similar laws.[161]

The NCAA's guidelines on NILs, as recently proposed and discussed later in this essay, directly caution that the new rules must account for athletes' rights of publicity and any defense of the First Amendment. As explained earlier, the applicability of these legal theories depends on the state in which the event occurs, the type of use (e.g., matters of public interest, like in-game live broadcast, versus commercial activities, like video games with players altered as avatars) and the extent of transformation of the images.[162]

Employment Law Claims Have Failed to Yield Pay for College Athletes

With athletes finding federal antitrust laws and rights of publicity insufficiently hospitable to their demands to be paid for their services, they have also resorted to employment law, seeking to categorize athletes as employees. Their efforts have thus far failed. For example, in *Berger v. National Collegiate Athletic Association*,[163] the University of Pennsylvania women's track-and-field athletes alleged that they were "employees" under the Federal Labor Standards Act (FLSA) and were thus entitled to compensation for playing, similar to students who are compensated in work-study programs. In December 2016, the Seventh Circuit rejected this claim and held that, based on the revered tradition of amateurism, the athletes were not employees, emphasizing that intercollegiate sports are extracurricular "play," not "work."[164] The concurring opinion, however, muddied the waters by stating that the economic reality and tradition of amateurism in revenue-producing sports like Division I men's basketball and FBS football may dictate a different result.[165]

In *Dawson v. NCAA*,[166] the Ninth Circuit addressed the situation raised by the concurring opinion in *Berger*. The Ninth Circuit panel that included Chief Judge Thomas (who would have permitted both the $5,000 stipend in *O'Bannon* and the First Amendment defense in *Keller* and who is now on the panel in *NCAA Grant-in-Aid*) held that FBS football players were not employees and therefore not owed a minimum wage or overtime pay. The court explained that the FLSA requires an analysis of the economic realities of the situation to discern the true nature of the parties' relationship. The court focused heavily on the fact that neither of the two defendants (the NCAA and the Pac-12 Conference) had the power to hire or fire Dawson and then explicitly left open the possibility for similar claims to succeed against schools.[167] Presumably, athletes would have to show that they do not already, through GIA and other benefits, receive the equivalent of the minimum wage.

Efforts to Unionize Fail: Northwestern Football Players

Yet another way in which college athletes have sought to obtain increased benefits, including pay, is through unionization. Specifically, a group of football players at Northwestern University,[168] under the guidance of the

College Athletes Players Association (CAPA), petitioned in 2013 to gain the right to unionize pursuant to the National Labor Relations Act (NLRA), seeking to gain similar rights to those held by professional athletes.[169]

The Regional Office in Chicago of the National Labor Relations Board (NLRB), after extensive briefing and a hearing, found that Northwestern (1) exerted great control over the athletes on issues including what they wore, where they traveled, when and how much they practiced, and (2) received great benefits from the players (e.g., the Northwestern football program generated $30.1 million in operating revenue during the 2012–13 season alone).[170] The regional director concluded that the scholarship football players were "employees" and entitled to vote on whether to unionize and be represented for collective bargaining purposes by CAPA.[171]

This decision was heralded as a breakthrough for college athletes' rights, but this optimism was short-lived. The full NLRB overruled the regional director[172] in an opinion that most observers view as a "punt." The NLRB chose not to address the merits of the matter, instead finding that unionization would not promote labor harmony. The NLRB made three key observations: (1) intercollegiate athletics was in a transitional phase in 2015; (2) allowing unionization would have engendered systemic instability by only permitting unionization at the 17 private colleges among 128 FBS schools; and (3) there was a need to resolve the labor-market issues and academic tensions in the current system.[173] Significantly, the NLRB called on the US Congress to clarify the institutional structure of college sports with a plea that it was addressing the "case in the absence of explicit Congressional direction regarding whether the Board should exercise jurisdiction," emphasizing that it was leaving open the issue of whether it might find jurisdiction in another case involving scholarship players.[174]

Notably, if athletes become "employees" under any of the preceding scenarios, schools will have to make payments for Social Security, workers' compensation, Medicare, unemployment insurance, and other benefits, along with pay; athletes will have to pay income and Social Security taxes on their compensation; and schools may lose some of their favorable

Unrelated Business Income Tax (UBIT) treatment by the IRS, along with other tax preferences.[175] In the end, we believe that the educational budget and learning process will suffer from such a result.[176]

The Potential Scope of NILs

Athletes seek to sell their NILs to entities for a host of activities other than in-game broadcasts, including endorsements, advertisements, items of clothing with their names on them, appearing at clinics, appearing in video games, or commercializing an athlete's social media site. There is a lot yet to be determined regarding the application of NIL rights to these types of activities before college athletes are compensated. Consider the following:

- How will the eventual NCAA rulings or guidelines restrict athletes from receiving pay in exchange for their NIL rights? In a October 29, 2019, statement, the NCAA Board of Governors simply said that the three divisions[177] should develop rules that would permit NIL "benefits" for athletes, without further elaboration of the term "benefits."[178] The district court in *NCAA Grant-in-Aid*, while not directly addressing NILs, permitted unlimited benefits like laptops, smart phones, unlimited numbers of scholarships to graduate school, payment for semesters to study abroad, and so on, as long as they are related to education, on top of (1) cash benefits up to $5,600 that do not have to be related to education as long as they are team-based performance awards and (2) cash benefits up to $5,600 stemming from academic achievement awards.[179] How this translates to NIL payments presents a host of complications. Such noncash benefits are all potentially valuable, but, of course, they would be more valuable to some students than to others.
- Will Division I seek to permit at least some cash payments as "benefits"? If so, will it require these payments be tethered to education, allowed while the student is still enrolled, or will the money

accumulate in a trust fund, not available until after the athlete leaves school or graduates? Chief Judge Thomas in his dissent in *O'Bannon* would have required payments for group licenses to be held in trust and provided to the athlete once they leave school or graduate.[180]

- If the new regime for NIL payments emanates from national legislation, in addition to the foregoing questions, will payments for NILs be restricted to nongame use of names, images, and likenesses? If so, what will be the scope of the restriction? Would commercials for in-game broadcasts and the like be allowed? In *O'Bannon*, the district court said that athletes have NIL rights for in-game broadcasts, while the Ninth Circuit specifically refused to address this issue—calling it a "thornier" question.[181] Many states, like Tennessee in *Marshall*, as discussed earlier, have laws that explicitly exclude rights of publicity in live broadcasts.[182] Plus, First Amendment rights, copyright laws, and fair use standards may come into play to prohibit payments for in-game NILs. By contrast, NIL payments for names and rights of publicity on jerseys, likenesses in video games, endorsements on billboards, and advertisements on social media, among others, are much more established. They are not live action. In most likelihood, any practical definition of NIL rights will be limited to nongame NIL rights.
- Will NIL rights be restricted to contracting with third parties, such that schools cannot contract with athletes either directly or as an intermediary? The potential implications here are twofold. First, if schools are involved in the contracting, then the school seemingly becomes similar to an athlete's employer.[183] Second, if schools pay athletes directly for NILs, then Title IX would require parallel payments for women athletes.
- Even if third parties make the payments, would Title IX apply? If schools are involved—for example, administer, enforce, or promote the NIL contracts—or the payments are disguised as indirect recruiting efforts by schools, or if additional promotion efforts are provided to men and men's teams regarding the availability of NIL payments,

then would Title IX apply as it does with fundraising efforts by third parties?

- If the schools pay out NIL money, how do they protect against growing financial deficits? Of course, the athletics department may lose some revenue in any case, to the extent that companies substitute athletes for whole programs as the vehicle to promote their products.[184]
- Will athletes be restricted as to when they can contract or activate their NIL rights? Will they have to do so only after the competitive playing season is over or only when classes are out of session? Can they do so as high school students?
- Will athletes be able to use university names, marks, and brands while exploiting NIL rights with outside companies?
- Will athletes on their social media that is being monetized be permitted to state that they play a certain sport at their respective schools?
- Will athletes be able to sign up with companies in competition with companies that are already in sponsorship deals with the school? What role will the compliance staff in athletics departments play in such evaluation?
- Should athletes be allowed to contract their individual NIL rights as well as join with other athletes to contract group NIL rights? The latter would apply, for example, to multiple athletes appearing in one advertisement, in one video game, or in a set of playing cards.
- Will the price that is paid to athletes for their NILs be regulated, or will the total NIL income earned per year be bounded?[185] Absent any restraints, it is easy to imagine an all-out competition of manipulated contracts among athletics department recruiters for star high school athletes. Consider this hypothetical: Big Ten schools from medium-sized Midwest cities contact various local businesses and arrange for these businesses to offer NIL contracts to prospects. The schools make a deal with these businesses, such as cheaper advertising space at the stadium or free luxury-suite passes, if the businesses offer the school's top prospect $10,000 for a public appearance to sign autographs that

would normally fetch only $500 in a competitive market. This type of behavior could quickly transform itself into a surrogate pay-for-play market. Some schools, particularly those in larger markets or a more lucrative conference, would gain another competitive advantage. Schools might find their sponsorship and luxury-suite revenue from companies sacrificed at the altar of this new, circuitous system of athlete compensation. To be sure, even if there is no such underhanded manipulation of market prices in the market for NILs, some schools in larger markets, such as the University of Southern California or the University of California, Los Angeles, will benefit over other schools in smaller markets, such as Oregon State University or Washington State University.

- Will the law permit athletes to unionize to help them identify opportunities and negotiate group NIL payments? Will athletes have a right to form trade associations to do the same?
- Will athletes have a right to hire agents to help them identify and negotiate NIL contracts? The NCAA's strict rules prohibiting agents, except in very narrow circumstances, could be an obstacle to athletes receiving expert advice. If agents are permitted, how would they be prevented from exploiting teenagers who are unsophisticated and inexperienced in business? If permitted, will athletes be allowed to contract with agents prior to their matriculation in college? If they are, then the agents could become surrogates for the university during recruitment and trigger open market competition.

The list of possible machinations and infelicitous outcomes is virtually endless. Clearly, there is a strong argument for imposing certain constraints on a newly emerged NIL marketplace. We suggest solutions to many of these concerns later in this essay.

The NCAA's Recommendation for Implementation of NIL Payments

In response to the many pressures on the NCAA, including lawsuits, legislation, and the court of public opinion, the NCAA formed a committee (NIL Committee), headed by Big East Commissioner Val Ackerman and Ohio State Athletic Director Gene Smith, to examine the feasibility of NIL payments to NCAA student-athletes.[186] This committee, on October 29, 2019, presented an interim report to the NCAA Board of Governors that was unanimously adopted.[187] The interim report from the NIL Committee and the Board's affirmative vote on the report potentially represent a turning point in the NCAA's definition of and insistence on amateurism. Still, there remains great uncertainty around the report's details, which will be further detailed in the next year.

The momentous report stated, "It is the policy of the Association that NCAA member schools may permit students participating in athletics the opportunity to benefit from the use of their name, image and/or likeness in a manner consistent with the values and beliefs of intercollegiate athletics."[188] The Board voted that each of the three divisions should modify and modernize the relevant NCAA bylaws and rules and do the following:

- Ensure student-athletes are treated similarly to nonathlete students unless a compelling reason exists to differentiate
- Maintain the priorities of education and the collegiate experience to provide opportunities for student-athlete success
- Ensure rules are transparent, focused, and enforceable and facilitate fair and balanced competition
- Make clear the distinction between collegiate and professional opportunities
- Make clear that compensation for athletics performance or participation is impermissible

- Reaffirm that student-athletes are students first and not employees of the university
- Enhance principles of diversity, inclusion, and gender equity
- Protect the recruiting environment and prohibit inducements to select, remain at, or transfer to a specific institution[189]

Attempting to control the future modifications, the NIL Committee provided more "guidance" in its report to the Board.[190] The guidance appears to stem from the cases discussed earlier, including that payments be tethered to education (as in *O'Bannon* and *NCAA Grant-in-Aid*), that athletes not be employees and not be compensated for their athletic performances (as in the FLSA and NLRA cases), and that First Amendment rights of third parties be considered (as in *Keller*, *Hart*, and *Marshall*).

The NIL Committee made a point of noting that the NCAA's current bylaws permit athletes to engage in outside employment and business activity.[191] The NIL Committee then provided examples of situations in which NIL payments might fit under the current bylaws but could also conceivably be used unfairly to compensate an athlete directly or indirectly for participation in athletics or involve inappropriate payments by boosters and therefore should be prohibited. The examples of possible acceptable use include athletes using their NILs in connection with writing and publishing a book or charging a fee for a lesson that is unrelated to sports; creating a social media channel to serve as the platform for their own business; promoting their own nonprofit organization; and creating and producing a video series containing nutritional tips for athletes and distributing the content via social media.[192]

The NIL Committee also said that each of the NCAA's three divisions should develop its own rules and consider, inter alia, whether the rules require that athletes must receive prior approval from the athletic director, faculty athletics representative, or their designee for NIL payments and whether there must be no involvement of schools, employees, or boosters in the development or promotion of NIL opportunities.[193]

While commentators and member institutions are generally optimistic about these potentially important changes, many are quick to note that the "devil is in the details."[194] The final proposals will need to be very specific, especially to avoid unintended consequences. We believe that the NIL Committee has taken a useful step forward in suggesting guidelines.[195] Our biggest concerns are with the following suggestions:

- Athletics department approval must be required.
- All deals must not relate to athletics and must be tethered to education.
- Schools can make NIL payments to athletes.
- All compensation for athletic performance or participation, even outside the school arena, is impermissible.

The availability of cash payments for NIL use may be prohibited, as the report refers only to "benefits" that can be received.

Directly addressing these concerns, we believe the following:

- Athletics departments should not play a role in approving NIL payments but instead should receive copies of proposed NIL deals only to determine whether they conflict with the school's current contracts. Congress should appoint an independent commission to set appropriate restrictions; analyze the impact, including unintended consequences, of the new rules; and act as a clearinghouse.
- Athletes should have complete control to receive payments for their own NILs, including use of or reference to their athletic abilities (e.g., basketball players can autograph a picture of themselves dribbling a basketball). One exception is that, as explained in the following section, there should be reasonable restrictions set by the independent commission to ensure that the payments are at fair market value and not disguised recruiting bonuses or other improper payments.[196]
- Schools should not engage in paying athletes directly or indirectly for their NILs. Such behavior would bring the relationship between the school and athletes closer to an employer/employee relationship,

with all the attendant consequences. Also, it would raise questions regarding schools' UBIT responsibilities and other tax issues. College athletes should not be permitted to be professional athletes, employed by professional leagues, while eligible for college sports but otherwise should not be restricted from receiving payment at the going rate for participation in athletics outside of school.
- Athletes should be permitted to receive cash as one form of benefit. They already receive cash, through COA stipends, of which use is not regulated.[197]

A Proposal for Federal Implementation of NIL Rights

In this section, we propose a detailed framework[198] for the payment to college athletes for their NILs.[199] The framework includes principles and conditions for both institutions and athletes and a proposal for an independent commission that would set specific standards and adjudicate compliance with those standards.

Guiding Principles

We propose that intercollegiate athletics operate according to the following basic principles and rules:

- College athletes should be treated like other students as much as possible with regard to their independent efforts to engage in nonschool efforts to receive payments for their NILs.
- Extracurricular activities generally, and intercollegiate athletics programs particularly, are important contributors to student development.[200]
- Higher-education institutions should have the right to own and commercially exploit performance events involving students participating in the institution's curricular and extracurricular activities through the sale of tickets, parking, game or event programs, posting on the

school's social media accounts, advertising, and sponsorship rights, and rights to live and delayed electronic telecasts. The revenues from such activities should be used to defray the costs of the extracurricular activity or otherwise advance the mission of the nonprofit higher-education institution, including caring for the health and welfare of participants.
- College athletes should not be permitted to use the logos, brands, or marks of their institution for private gain. But, under fair use, they should be able to include the fact that they are athletes at their respective school. College athletes should otherwise have the right to use their NILs for private gain, conditioned on the athlete obtaining such opportunity without assistance from the institution (i.e., such activities are not arranged by employees or others engaged by the athlete's institution for that purpose) and other conditions that protect the primacy of education.

Specific Proposal

1. Higher-Education Institution Use of Athlete NILs

Higher-education institutions should be permitted to condition participation in their athletics programs on athletes providing the limited use of their NILs related to such participation. Such limited use shall include the following:

- Audio or videocast or otherwise recorded for live or delayed electronic distribution or photographed for print or digital publication of the regular-season (including postseason) athletic events in which the athlete is participating during that season.
- Advertising or promotion of the regular-season and postseason athletic events in which the athlete is participating during that season.
- Publication and sale of event programs sold with or during the regular season and postseason at athletic events in which the athlete is participating during that season.

- Perpetual print and electronic publication rights for the athlete's historical performance and participation statistics and photographs of prior champions or championship teams, which may not be commercially exploited in any way other than athletic event programs. Such historical license should not extend to commercial documentary products that exist separate from the current athletic event. The inclusion of historical data on the institution's official athletics internet site, which may be supported by sponsorship revenues, shall not be considered prohibited commercial exploitation.
- Official team apparel or equipment to teams or to be the exclusive seller of such products at official athletic events and activities in which the athlete is participating.[201] Athletes' obligations to wear official team apparel shall extend throughout the academic year for official team practices, exhibition or nontraditional season contests, and appearances at official university events in which this apparel must be worn by all attending players.

Other conditions on institutions that we propose are the following:

- Higher-education institutions should be prohibited from otherwise exploiting current students' NILs (other than as detailed in the preceding list for official team events and activities) such as entering into licensing agreements using student NILs for video games, licensed apparel, licensed products, and more.
- The NCAA, athletic conferences, and member schools can jointly license their regular-season and postseason collective intellectual property (NCAA, school, and conference names, marks, logos, and more) to third parties, conditioned on such agreements not including royalty or other payments to athletes.
- Any rules that schools or conferences employ regarding restrictions on social media usage during athletic contests, travel, or any other official team events will continue to apply.[202]

2. College Athlete Independent Use of Own NIL

College athletes should be permitted to obtain employment and accept pay for the commercial use of their NIL in advertisements, appearances, or speaking engagements and for endorsement of commercial products ("commercial arrangements") with certain conditions:

- College athletes (or their agents) must independently obtain such arrangements (such arrangements cannot be arranged, directly or indirectly, by the institution's employees, donors, athletics program sponsors, or advertisers or other representatives of its athletics interests).[203]
- College athletes' commercial arrangements must not conflict with the institution's rights as specified in proposal 1 for official team events or activities. This shall not preclude a college athlete's agent or the athletes themselves from independently soliciting work from any company that also supports the institution.
- College athletes may earn pay for work from third parties, including for work related to the athlete's skill and notoriety and NIL agreements related to endorsements, product licensing, personal appearances, books, movies, television or radio shows, providing autographs, endorsing commercial products, or being the owner or partner of a sports business, among others.
- College athletes may not enter into NIL arrangements with third parties that are inappropriate as determined by the Commission with respect to the character and integrity of the third party and the type of the activity.
- College athletes must report, in writing, their NIL arrangements above a de minimis amount set by the Commission and submit such arrangements to both the school and the Commission or entity such as an Eligibility Center.[204]
- College athletes must be in good academic standing, meeting all rules

related to athletics eligibility, including normal progress and full-time enrollment provisions.
- College athletes may enter into group licensing agreements with other athletes. Such group agreements shall also conform to the policies herein.[205]
- College athletes may hire agents and lawyers without impacting their eligibility.

3. An Independent Commission Should Set Appropriate Standards for NIL Payments to Athletes

Congress should establish an independent NIL Commission to set standards for the payment of college athletes' NILs.[206] Higher education has an important obligation to promulgate rules that place a student's academic success above the athletic success of the institution's sports teams. The proper limitations that permit students to engage fully in athletics and to complete academic requirements for a degree, while also using their NILs for payment, can best be developed and enforced by an independent commission that does not also have the competing objective of creating winning athletic teams.

a. Standards

We suggest that the independent NIL Commission be charged with the following:

- Set the maximum income that can be paid to athletes for use of their NILs on an annual, local basis.[207] Absent such control, the NIL market runs the risk of devolving into a surrogate labor market in which colleges will approach high school recruits with financial packages based on promised NIL contracts.[208]
- Set standards related to the appropriateness of college athletes' required activities, including a requirement that no classes, exams, or participation in other required academic activity be missed to perform agreement-related activities.[209]

- Set standards for the character and integrity of any third party; the standards shall not be more onerous than the NCAA's advertising and promotional standards.
- Set standards for the registration and recognition of college athletes' approved sports agents.
- Set standards for agent and attorney agreements that specify recommended ranges for hourly rates or percentage commissions.
- Set a value (e.g., $1,000) that is considered de minimis for reporting purposes.
- Collect all non–de minimis NIL arrangements and make them publicly available.
- Receive and monitor complaints concerning agents, attorneys, and other third parties related to compliance with the standards set by the Commission.
- Adjudicate generally compliance with its standards.[210]

b. Composition of the NIL Commission

The NIL Commission shall consist of a majority of independent experts. At least one independent member shall be appointed by each of the Faculty Athletic Representatives Association, the National Association for Athletics Compliance, the National Association of Collegiate Directors of Athletics, the Sports Lawyers Association, CAPA, and Women Leaders in College Sports. The term "independent" shall mean at least two years removed from employment by the NCAA, a NCAA member athletic conference, or a member institution's athletics department. The member must also agree not to return to this employment within two years of leaving the NIL Commission.

c. A Necessary Antitrust Exemption

The NIL Commission could effectively operate only if Congress (and the NCAA to the extent that its rules require athletes to abide by the NIL Commission's requirements) grants it a limited and conditional antitrust exemption.[211] A limited antitrust exemption would specifically permit implementing the preceding standards.[212] Further, the exemption would eliminate any restrictions and ambiguity resulting from the current cases, including those from *O'Bannon* and *NCAA Grant-in-Aid*.

If an antitrust exemption is granted that allows the setting of market restraints, such as caps on local NIL income, then we believe the exemption should also apply to setting caps on coaches' and administrators' income. As discussed earlier, the extraordinary income paid to Division I football and basketball coaches results largely from the suppression of pay to athletes. It would be unconscionable to pass an exemption permitting the capping of local athlete NIL income while not permitting the capping of coach and administrator income.

The exemption would also allow for the establishment of uniformity of rules regarding agreements on NIL rights for live in-game broadcasts that are now dependent on underlying common law and statutory law.[213]

A limited and conditional antitrust exemption that applies to the legitimate categories of controls discussed in this proposal will enable the NIL Commission and the NCAA collectively to enact needed reforms without fear of future legal liability. Such an exemption is both justifiable and necessary. Antitrust lawsuits represent huge costs for legal representation, participation in court cases, and payment of damages.[214] These funds would otherwise be available to advance the NCAA's and its member institutions' nonprofit educational purposes.

A solution that includes an antitrust exemption would not be extraordinary.[215] Congress has enacted limited antitrust exemptions in many industries—ranging from the hog industry[216] to railroads[217] to soft drinks[218] to the insurance industry[219] to professional sports[220] and, most significantly, to higher education.[221] Statutory antitrust exemptions involving the sports industry or higher education include (a) the Sports Broadcasting Act of 1961 (SBA), which provides limited immunity from antitrust litigation to the four major professional sport leagues for selling horizontally pooled broadcasting rights to over-the-air channels;[222] (b) a narrow and targeted antitrust exemption in 1966 that permitted the combination of the National Football League and American Football League;[223] (c) the Ted Stevens Olympic and Amateur Sports Act in 1978 (subsequently amended in 1998), which created a vertical structure for the management of certain amateur sports in the United States;[224] (d) the Curt Flood Act of 1998, which removes Major League Baseball's presumed antitrust exemption (judicially conferred in 1922) in the area of labor relations;[225] (e) the Improving America's Schools Act of 1994, which exempts from antitrust laws agreements to admit students on a need-blind basis by institutions of higher education;[226] and (f) the Medical Resident Matching Program Exemption in 2004.[227]

These acts demonstrate that Congress protects certain activities in sports and higher education from the antitrust laws when it deems fit. It defines antitrust exemptions specifically and narrowly. Here, too, the exemption should be narrowly defined.

Conclusion

In this essay, we have reviewed the legal history of amateurism in collegiate sports and its relationship to NILs. The *Keller* and *O'Bannon* cases brought the NIL issue to the fore, and the September 30, 2019, signing of the California Fair Pay to Play Act by Governor Newsom broke the long-standing legislative inertia surrounding NCAA amateurism. Threatened with losing control over NIL and broader compensation issues, on October 29, 2019, the NCAA Board of Governors relented and suggested, at least nominally, that the NCAA's enduring prohibition on athlete compensation from NILs be changed.

While the Board did not announce specific measures to implement NIL rights for athletes, it did charge each of the NCAA's three divisions with proposing guidelines for implementation by January 2021. These guidelines are to be consistent with the NCAA's conception of amateurism and only allow "benefits" that are tethered to education. At its annual meeting in January 2021, the NCAA decided to table the recommended changes to

NIL policy until after the Supreme Court decision in *Alston* and any action by the US Congress.

We critique this approach as far too narrow and failing to grant college athletes the same NIL rights as granted to other students (with a few exceptions). The NCAA has applied a constantly morphing definition of amateurism over the years. The only sensible definition of amateurism for a college athlete would require that athletes not be paid by member institutions a cash income for playing their sport.

Accordingly, we propose a NIL policy that affords many more opportunities for college athletes. Athletes should have the same right to be paid by third parties as other students are, save for a few narrow exceptions. Importantly, NIL income contracted with third parties should not conflict with students' pursuits of a college education.[228] Any difference that persists between students who are not athletes, on the one hand, and students who are athletes, on the other hand, is necessary due to the extraordinary time demands placed on athletes.[229] To ensure both that our more open system does not ignore athletes' abilities to attend and study for their classes and that a surrogate, indirect pay-for-play system does not evolve, it is necessary to impose a regulatory structure. Such a structure would be most effective if it were mandated by Congress and were independent. Unfortunately, the oversight structure means a modicum of bureaucracy.[230] While it would be desirable to have a world where no regulatory controls were necessary, we do not live in such a world, and the challenge then becomes not to abolish regulation but to make it function effectively.

NOTES

1. Through November 2020, thirty-eight states have introduced similar bills to the one passed in California. *See* Matt Norlander, "Fair Pay to Play Act: States Bucking NCAA to Let Athletes Be Paid For Name, Image, Likeness," CBS Sports (October 3, 2019), https://www.cbssports.com/college-football/news/fair-pay-to-play-act-states-bucking-ncaa-to-let-athletes-be-paid-for-name-image-likeness/ [https://perma.cc/66SE-6G68].

2. Student-Athlete Equity Act, H.R. 1804, 116th Cong. (2019); Aspen Institute, "Future of College Sports: Government's Role in Athletic Pay" (Dec. 17, 2019), https://www.aspeninstitute.org/events/future-of-college-sports-governments-role-in-athlete-pay/ [https://perma.cc/8Y3F-ZX2J].

3. Jon Brodkin, "NCAA Fights California over New Law That Helps Athletes Get Paid," *Ars Technica* (Sept. 30, 2019), https://arstechnica.com/tech-policy/2019/09/ncaa-athletes-could-be-paid-for-being-in-video-games-under-new-calif-law/ [https://perma.cc/3UWP-28CF].

4. U.S. Const. art. I, § 8, cl. 3.

5. In *National Collegiate Athletic Association v. Miller*, 795 F. Supp. 1476 (D. Nev. 1992), Nevada enacted a statute that would have "impose[d] certain minimum 'due process' procedural standards on the NCAA when the NCAA is investigating a Nevada NCAA member institution." *Id.* at 1483. Although the court found that the statute did "not facially or directly discriminate against interstate commerce," it held that the statute was unconstitutional under the Commerce Clause because it impaired the contractual relationship between the NCAA and its Nevada member institutions. *Id.*

6. A fundamental tenet of the NCAA is the "principle of amateurism," which, under the NCAA's bylaws, is the theory that "student-athletes shall be amateurs in an intercollegiate sport, and their participation should be motivated primarily by education and by the physical, mental and social benefits to be derived. Student participation in intercollegiate athletics is an avocation, and student-athletes should be protected from exploitation by professional and commercial enterprises." National Collegiate Athletic Association Academic and Membership Affairs Staff, 2019–2020 NCAA Division I Manual 2.9 (2019) (hereinafter Division I Manual).

7. *See* NCAA, Report of the NCAA Board of Governors October 29, 2019 Meeting 4 (2019) [hereinafter NCAA NIL Report], https://ncaaorg.s3.amazonaws.com/committees/ncaa/exec_boardgov/Oct2019BOG_Report.pdf [https://perma.cc/R3CF-J8UQ].

8. The NCAA's three divisions are Division I, Division II, and Division III. NCAA, "Our Three Divisions," https://www.ncaa.org/sites/default/files/18-00037%20NCAA%20101%20-%20Our%20Three%20Divisions%20Updates%20_WEB.pdf [https://perma.cc/3CYW-SGR3]; *see* National Collegiate Athletic Association, "Divisional Differences and the History of Multidivision Classification," http://www.ncaa.org/about/who-we-are/membership/divisional-differences-and-history-multidivision-classification [https://perma.cc/78FM-E7J2] (explaining the differences between the NCAA's three divisions).

9. *See* Jenna West, "South Carolina Lawmakers to File Proposal Similar to California's Fair Pay to Play Act," *Sports Illustrated* (Sept. 13, 2019), https://www.si.com/college/2019/09/13/south-carolina-proposal-pay-college-athletes-fair-pay-play-act [https://perma.cc/652W-XUSC]; Joseph Nardone, "New York Senator Proposes Bill to Have College Athletes Paid Directly by Schools," *Forbes* (Sept. 18, 2019), https://www.forbes.com/sites/josephnardone/2019/09/18/new-york-senator-proposes-bill-to-have-college-athletes-paid-directly-by-schools/#415a854a4d17 [https://perma.cc/XHT9-ZBX6].

10. J. Brady McCollough, "News Analysis: What's Next for NCAA and College Athletics Now That SB 206 Is Law?," *L.A. Times* (Sept. 30, 2019, 5:40 PM), https://www.latimes.com/sports/story/2019-09-30/what-next-for-ncaa-college-athletics-now-that-sb-206-is-law [https://perma.cc/EXC8-VH6J].

11. Nardone, *supra* note 9.

12. *See, e.g.*, "Florida Gov. Endorses Proposed NIL Bill That Would Take Effect in '20," *Sports Business Journal* (Oct. 24, 2019), https://www.sportsbusinessdaily.com/Daily/Issues/2019/10/24/Colleges/Florida-NIL.aspx [https://perma.cc/6JLX-FXWY].

13. Student-Athlete Equity Act, H.R. 1804, 116th Cong. (2019).

14. Alex Daugherty & Brian Murphy, "Marco Rubio Leads Senate Effort to Compensate College Athletes," *Tampa Bay Times* (Nov. 8, 2019), https://www.tampabay.com/

florida-politics/buzz/2019/11/09/marco-rubio-leads-charge-to-compensate-college-athletes/ [https://perma.cc/FN2S-76AT]. Also, the US representative and former Ohio State football player Anthony Gonzalez announced a plan to propose a federal law to allow college athletes the opportunity to earn a profit from endorsements. Dan Murphy, "Congressman to Propose Federal Legislation for Paying College Athletes," ESPN (Oct. 2, 2019), https://www.espn.com/college-sports/story/_/id/27751454/congressman-propose-federal-legislation-paying-college-athletes [https://perma.cc/8Y9G-PGES].

15. Portions of the "History of Amateurism" section are based on one of the author's previous work. *See* Gerald Gurney, Donna A. Lopiano & Andrew Zimbalist, *Unwinding Madness: What Went Wrong with College Sports and How to Fix It*, 13–15 (2017).

16. Proceedings of the First Annual Convention of the National Collegiate Athletic Association 22 (Dec. 29, 1906).

17. Proceedings of the Eleventh Annual Convention of the National Collegiate Athletic Association 118 (Dec. 28, 1916).

18. Proceedings of the Seventeenth Annual Convention of the National Collegiate Athletic Association 118 (Dec. 29, 1922).

19. Gurney, Lopiano & Zimbalist, *supra* note 15, at 12.

20. Murray Sperber, *Onward to Victory: The Creation of Modern College Sports* 168 (1998).

21. Andrew Zimbalist, *Unpaid Professionals: Commercialism and Conflict in Big-Time College Sports* 9 (1999).

22. Arguably, this effort began at the 1939 NCAA Convention when the association passed a rule enabling athletes to receive financial aid based on need, but the aid could not be conditioned on athletic participation. Hence, in principle, it was not a form of athletic aid; rather, it was need-based aid that could be allocated to all students, including athletes.

23. NCAA, 1947–48 Yearbook 212–13.

24. NCAA, 1956–57 Yearbook 4–5. It is notable that in the NCAA's 1957 rules it did not prohibit payment to athletes for appearances and endorsements. This prohibition did not come until 1964. Of course, the amount of money available for athlete NILs at the time was diminutive. *See* Roger Noll, "Collusion in College Sports: Edward O'Bannon, et al. v. NCAA, et al.," in *The Antitrust Revolution: Economics, Competition, and Policy* (John Kwoka & Lawrence White eds., 7th ed. 2018); Corrected Direct and Rebuttal Testimony of Dr. Roger G. Noll to Reflect Final Trial Exhibit Numbers, *In re* NCAA Athletic Grant-in-Aid Cap Antitrust Litigation, 311 F.R.D. 532 (N.D. Cal. 2015) (No. 4:14-md-02541).

25. Walter Byers, the executive director of the NCAA from 1951 to 1987, has characterized the awarding of athletic scholarships as the beginning of a nationwide money-laundering scheme whereby boosters who formerly gave money directly to athletes could now funnel it to athletes through legitimate university channels. *See* Walter Byers, *Unsportsmanlike Conduct: Exploiting College Athletes* 73 (1995). Significantly, the schools in the Ivy League do not permit scholarships for athletic participation. Ivy League, "Prospective Athlete Information," https://ivyleague.com/sports/2017/7/28/information-psa-index.aspx [https://perma.cc/8X3H-DWLH].

26. Byers, *supra* note 25, at 69.

27. *Id.* at 75.

28. Letter from Clyde Smith to Walter Byers (July 6, 1964), *in* Walter Byers Papers, Long Range Planning Folder, NCAA Headquarter, Overland Park, KS, 163–64.

29. *Id.* at 164.

30. Robert A. McCormick & Amy Christian McCormack, "The Myth of the Student Athlete: The College Athlete as Employee," *Washington Law Review* 71 (2006).

Further control was afforded by the long-standing rule that required any athlete changing schools to sit out a year of competition once enrolling at the new school. This rule, dating back to the NCAA's original constitution in 1906, was intended to deter the use of tramp athletes, i.e., athletes who were not matriculated students and were paid under the table to play for school teams. The rule is still in place in 2019 and enforces an asymmetry wherein coaches can jump from school to school without a year of ineligibility but athletes cannot. For transfer terms, see NCAA, "Transfer Terms," http://www.ncaa.org/student-athletes/current/transfer-terms [https://perma.cc/2EGN-TQAF]. Athletes who do not like playing for a coach or who are not playing as regularly as they would like face the penalty of a year's ineligibility if they choose to transfer to a new school. Of course, on some occasions, the athlete may want to transfer due to an issue with the academic program and would face a similar disincentive.

31. *See* Michelle Brutlag Hosick, "Multiyear Scholarship Rule Narrowly Upheld," NCAA (Feb. 17, 2012), http://www.ncaa.org/about/resources/media-center/news/multiyear-scholarship-rule-narrowly-upheld [https://perma.cc/83R8-EPF5].

32. This tweak was widely seen to gain public support when a star University of Connecticut basketball player very publicly asserted that he went to bed hungry every night. Rodger Sherman, "Shabazz Napier: 'There's Hungry Nights Where I'm Not Able to Eat,'" *SB Nation* (Apr. 7, 2014), https://www.sbnation.com/college-basketball/2014/4/7/5591774/shabazz-napier-uconn-basketball-hungry-nights [https://perma.cc/CYV7-T3CS]; *see* Zach Schonbrun, "N.C.A.A Ensures Athletes Will Get All They Can Eat," *N.Y. Times* (Apr. 24, 2014), https://www.nytimes.com/2014/04/25/sports/ncaa-ensures-athletes-will-get-all-they-can-eat.html [https://perma.cc/3AZT-6662].

33. These COA stipends are basically a reincarnation of the so-called laundry money, which was ended in 1973.

34. Given that there are no controls on how the money is spent or even that it be related to education, there are reports that athletes use the COA money to buy things like video games and hoverboards. *See* Nina Mandell, "Jokes about NCAA Athletes Buying Hoverboards Show That College Sports Still Have a Big Problem," *For the Win, USA Today* (Dec. 10, 2015), https://ftw.usatoday.com/2015/12/jokes-about-ncaa-athletes-buying-hoverboards-show-that-college-sports-still-have-a-big-problem [https://perma.cc/R9E6-3BND].

35. 20 U.S.C. § 1087-1 (2018).

36. Federal Pell Grants are awarded to low-income undergraduate students with exceptional financial need. Unlike a loan, federal Pell Grants do not have to be repaid. The maximum grant awarded for the 2019–20 academic year is $6,195, and the amount recipients are awarded varies depending on their contribution, attendance costs, whether they are full- or part-time students, and whether they plan to be enrolled in school for the full academic year. *See* Federal Student Aid, US Department of Education, "Federal Pell Grants," https://studentaid.ed.gov/sa/types/grants-scholarships/pell [https://perma.cc/5TRH-ATB5].

37. Kevin Allen, "Here Are Some Benefits NCAA Athletes Already Are Eligible for That You Might Not Know About," *USA Today* (Oct. 1, 2019), https://www.usatoday.com/story/sports/college/2019/10/01/ncaa-football-basketball-benefits-college-athletes-now-can-receive/2439120001/ [https://perma.cc/S8UU-5VGV]; *see* O'Bannon v. National Collegiate Athletic Association, 7 F. Supp. 3d. 955, 974 (N.D. Cal. 2014).

38. *See* Steve Berkowitz, "Olympic Swimmer Joseph Schooling Scores Big in Butterfly with $740,000 in Win over Phelps," *USA Today* (Aug. 13, 2016), https://www.usatoday.com/story/sports/olympics/rio-2016/2016/08/12/singapore-olympic-swimming-texas-ncaa-cash-bonuses-butterfly/88647594/ [https://perma.cc/Q3HV-T77B].

39. The NCAA also permits college athletes to receive awards for medaling in world

championships and foreign swimmers to receive what their respective countries award them. For example, the NCAA permitted a swimmer at the University of Texas to accept $740,000 from Singapore, the country for which he competed at the Rio 2016 Olympic Games. *See* Berkowitz, *supra* note 38. Given this essay's focus on athlete publicity rights, it is noteworthy that in October 2019, the United States Olympic and Paralympic Committee (USOPC) announced that it would interpret the International Olympic Committee's (IOC's) Rule 40 (which does not allow athletes to publicize any endorsement agreements with companies they may have during the Olympic Games) to allow athletes to publicize their corporate ties in most circumstances as long as the company in question first registered with the USOPC. The traditional IOC concern with such situations (often referred to as "ambush marketing") was that the exercise of athlete publicity rights would diminish the value of exclusive IOC sponsorship arrangements.

40. Division I Manual, *supra* note 6, ¶ 12.1.2.4.2 ("In tennis, prior to full-time collegiate enrollment, an individual may accept up to $10,000 per calendar year in prize money based on his or her place finish or performance in athletics events.").

41. David Broughton, "Higher Limits Bring Gift Package Upgrades," *Sports Business Journal* (Mar. 5, 2012), https://www.sportsbusinessdaily.com/Journal/Issues/2012/03/05/Colleges/College-gifts.aspx [https://perma.cc/SZ6F-ZJ86]. In 2012, the NCAA allowed each bowl to award up to $550 worth of gifts to 125 participants per school. In addition, participants were allowed to receive awards worth up to $400 from the school and up to $400 from the conference for postseason play, covering both conference title games and any bowl game. *See* David Broughton, "Players Share the Wealth with Bowl Gifts," *Sports Business Journal* (Dec. 3, 2012), https://www.sportsbusinessdaily.com/Journal/Issues/2012/12/03/In-Depth/Bowl-gifts.aspx [https://perma.cc/QU5K-5QXZ].

42. *See* Redacted Plaintiffs' Response Brief and Opening Brief on Cross-Appeal at 15, 17–18, *In re* NCAA Athletic Grant-in-Aid Cap Antitrust Litigation, 2019 WL 5598019 (9th Circuit Oct. 23, 2019) (Nos. 19-15566, 19-15662) (Jenkins' Appeal Brief).

43. Michelle Brutlag Hosick, "Council Adopts Final Four Family Travel Proposal," NCAA (Jan. 23, 2019), http://www.ncaa.org/about/resources/media-center/news/council-adopts-final-four-family-travel-proposal [https://perma.cc/D2SH-GK4N].

44. *See generally* David McCoy, "NCAA's Little-Known Student Assistance Fund," CBS Minnesota (Jan. 12, 2014), https://minnesota.cbslocal.com/2014/01/12/ncaas-little-known-student-assistance-fund/ [https://perma.cc/Z22T-XTUY].

45. *See* Michelle Brutlag Hosick, "DI to Distribute Revenue Based on Academics," NCAA (Oct. 27, 2016), http://www.ncaa.org/about/resources/media-center/news/di-distribute-revenue-based-academics [https://perma.cc/NMJ8-3DV5].

46. *See* NCAA, *2019 Division I Revenue Distribution Plan* (2019), https://ncaaorg.s3.amazonaws.com/ncaa/finance/d1/2019D1Fin_RevenueDistributionPlan.pdf [https://perma.cc/5GPY-L7UL].

47. Mike Chiari, "Report: Zion Williamson's $8M Insurance Policy Revealed after Injury vs. UNC," *Bleacher Report* (Feb. 21, 2019), https://bleacherreport.com/articles/2821748-report-zion-williamsons-8m-insurance-policy-revealed-after-injury-vs-unc [https://perma.cc/CDU4-SYV2]; *see also* Jenkins' Appeal Brief, *supra* note 42, at 15.

48. Division I Manual, *supra* note 6, 14.01.4 (emphasis added).

49. Prior to 2015–16, the NCAA required athletes to explicitly release claims for the NILs to their schools, conferences, and the NCAA for live-in-game broadcasts. *See* Greg Lush, "Reclaiming Student Athletes' Rights to Their Names, Images and Likenesses, Post O'Bannon v. NCAA: Analyzing NCAA Forms for Unconscionability," 24 *Southern California Interdisciplinary Law Journal* 767, 767–69 (2015).

50. Division I Manual, *SUPRA* note 6, 12.01.4.

51. *Id.* 12.1.2.

52. *Id.* 12.1.2. This bylaw revokes amateur status and NCAA eligibility when a student-athlete: (1) "uses his or her athletic skill (directly or indirectly) for pay in any form in that sport"; (2) "accepts a promise of pay even if such pay is to be received following completion of intercollegiate athletics participation"; (3) "signs a contract or commitment of any kind to play professional athletics, regardless of its legal enforceability or any consideration received, except as permitted in Division I Manual § 12.2.5.1"; (4) "receives directly or indirectly, a salary, reimbursement of expenses, or any other form of financial assistance from a professional sports organization based on athletics skill or participation, except as permitted by NCAA rules and regulations"; (5) "competes on any professional athletics team per Bylaw 12.02.11, even if no pay or remuneration for expenses was received, except as permitted in Division I Manual § 12.2.3.2.1"; (6) "after initial full-time collegiate enrollment, enters into a professional draft (*see* Division I Manual § 12.2.4)"; or (7) "enters into an agreement with an agent." *Id.*

53. *Id.* 12.5.2.1.

54. *Id.* 12.4.4.

55. *Id.* 12.5.1.1; *see also* Mike McIntire, "The College Sports Tax Dodge," *N.Y. Times* (Dec. 28, 2017), https://www.nytimes.com/2017/12/28/sunday-review/college-sports-tax-dodge.html [https://perma.cc/F49X-RAXB]. Nonprofit educational institutions have a special tax status such that athletics department revenues from commercial activities like sale of tickets and apparel are not subject to the Unrelated Business Income Tax (UBIT) because college athletics are an integral part of the education program of educational institutions (i.e., such revenues are substantially related to the educational program). *See infra* note 198 and accompanying text. If an educational institution pays athletes with its revenues instead of using them for educational purposes, it could lose its special tax status. In fact, in 2018, Congress tightened tax-exempt status for college athletics by imposing an excise tax on salaries above $1 million and eliminating a partial deduction for booster donations tied to the sale of game tickets. *See* Associated Press, "College Coaches' Salaries Increase Despite Threat of New Tax," *USA Today* (Dec. 13, 2017), https://www.usatoday.com/story/sports/ncaaf/2017/12/13/college-coaches-salaries-increase-despite-threat-of-new-tax/108562894/ [https://perma.cc/W5RH-ZYKP].

56. *See* Brief of Amici Curiae, *In re* NCAA Athletic Grant-in-Aid Cap Antitrust Litigation, 375 F. Supp. 3d 1058 (N.D. Cal. 2019) (No. 4:14-md-02541). *But see* NCAA Bylaw § 15.02.5.4, which lists "honorary award for outstanding academic achievement" as one exempted institutional financial aid.

57. Penn Schoen Berland, "Student-Athlete Time Demands," Pac-12 Conference (Apr. 2015), https://sports.cbsimg.net/images/Pac-12-Student-Athlete-Time-Demands-Obtained-by-CBS-Sports.pdf [https://perma.cc/NSG3-GWKA].

58. Andrew Zimbalist, "The NCAA Sports Model Is Broken, and It's Time for Congress to Step In," *Forbes* (Dec. 20, 2019), https://www.forbes.com/sites/andrewzimbalist/2019/12/20/the-ncaa-sports-model-is-broken-and-its-time-for-congress-to-step-in/#4118eea23d09 [https://perma.cc/YQ76-2H4M]. *But see* Andy Schwarz, "The NCAA Isn't Going Broke, No Matter How Much You Hear It," *FiveThirtyEight* (Apr. 20, 2016), https://fivethirtyeight.com/features/the-ncaa-isnt-going-broke-no-matter-how-much-you-hear-it/ [https://perma.cc/K3LL-6L9J].

59. NCAA Research, *14-Year Trends in Division I Athletics Finances* 9 (2019).

60. Note that the athletics department financial books count athletic scholarships at their quoted rate based on tuition, room and board, fees, and required books rather than their actual expense to the school, based on marginal costs. In this sense, actual athletic costs are overstated. But the understatement from incomplete accounting of capital costs (facility construction and maintenance) and indirect costs (charging

a share of the college administration's salaries, offices, travel, etc.) far outweighs any undercounting. Also note that the NCAA reporting system includes donations to athletics as revenue generated, but some of the athletic donations may displace donations to a school's general fund. While it is true that big-time college athletics revenues have been growing rapidly in recent decades, expenses have grown more rapidly. The basic problem is that college athletics departments do not have stockholders who seek reports of quarterly profits to bolster stock prices and dividends; instead, they have stakeholders who seek victories. Athletic directors respond accordingly, resulting in little cost discipline.

61. 20 U.S.C. §§ 1681–88 (2018). In *O'Bannon v. National Collegiate Athletic Association*, 7 F. Supp. 3d 955 (N.D. Cal. 2014), *affirmed in part, vacated in part*, 802 F.3d 1049 (9th Circuit 2015), Judge Claudia Wilken rejected the NCAA's procompetitive justification that its amateurism limits enable increased support for women's sports, stating that the NCAA could mandate that schools direct a greater portion of their licensing revenue generated by football and basketball to the other sports. *Id.* at 1000–1001.

62. For example, in 2017, Clemson University opened its ultraextravagant $55 million, 142,000-square-foot Reeves Football Complex, which includes a miniature golf course, bowling lanes, a barber shop, a nap room, and Wiffle ball court. Following Clemson's lead, the University of South Carolina's new $50 million football operations center opened in January 2019, equipped with a recording studio and barber shop. Manie Robinson, "Staying Power: Clemson Football Has Changed the Game in Facilities," *Greenville News* (July 30, 2019), https://www.greenvilleonline.com/story/sports/college/clemson/2019/07/30/staying-power-clemson-football-facility-college-athletics-facilities/1839960001/ [https://perma.cc/AM6E-Z6UY].

63. "NCAAF Coaches' Salaries," *USA Today*, https://sports.usatoday.com/ncaa/salaries/ [https://perma.cc/MG9M-4EEC].

64. *Id.*

65. One eye-popping severance clause appeared in the contract of Mike Sherman, Texas A&M's football coach, who, if terminated, would have been paid $150,000 a month for the remainder of his contract that would have amounted to a "$7.8 million golden handshake." Andrew Zimbalist, *Circling the Bases: Essays on the Challenges and Prospects of the Sports Industry* 177 (2011).

66. To be clear, outside of basketball and football, coaches do not receive such lavish remuneration. In Divisions II and III, no coaches benefit from this largesse.

67. Reuben Fischer-Baum, "Infographic: Is Your State's Highest-Paid Employee a Coach? (Probably)," *Deadspin* (May 9, 2013), http://deadspin.com/infographic-is-your-states-highest-paid-employee-a-co-489635228 [https://perma.cc/4Z3N-PL9R].

68. *See* Jayma Meyer & Andrew Zimbalist, "Reforming College Sports: The Case for a Limited and Conditional Antitrust Exemption," 62 *Antitrust Bulletin* (2017). Also, note that such a cap on coaches' salaries would have no discernible impact on the quality of college coaches. The best alternative employment for these coaches would be coaching at lower levels at much-lower salaries. If a few went to the professional leagues, the existing professional coaches would become available to coach at the college level.

69. The NCAA has already lost an antitrust case when it tried to impose compensation limits on assistant basketball coaches in the 1990s. *See* Law v. National Collegiate Athletic Association, 134 F.3d 1010 (10th Circuit 1998). Price fixing is a restraint of trade and generally seen as a per se violation of antitrust laws. *See* discussion *infra* later.

70. This issue is further discussed from a legal standpoint *supra*.

71. In 1984, the IOC voted to allow the International Federation of each sport to set the eligibility rules for its sport, within some limits. In 1987, the IOC voted to permit professional tennis players to participate in the games, and in 1989, the IOC extended

the welcome to all professional athletes. *See* Andrew Zimbalist, *Circus Maximus: The Economic Gamble Behind Hosting the Olympics and the World Cup* ch. 2 (2015). It should be noted, however, that the compensation of Olympic athletes in the United States is determined by each sport's federation and tends to be nominal. Thus, almost all of the Olympic athletes receive below a livable wage, and while they are "paid," the perception of the public may still be that the athletes are not professionals. Top Olympic athletes from other countries, especially Asian countries, receive more robust compensation, and those who win medals usually receive hundreds of thousands of dollars in rewards. In those countries, government funding supports the Olympic program.

72. Experts, equipped with survey evidence, in the antitrust cases present much conflicting evidence on this hypothetical question. *See* Cody J. McDavis, "Paying Students to Play Would Ruin College Sports," *N.Y. Times* (Feb. 25, 2019), https://www.nytimes.com/2019/02/25/opinion/pay-college-athletes.html [https://perma.cc/PLQ3-Z9ZT].

73. Title IX requires that women and men be provided equitable opportunities to participate in sport, to receive financial aid proportional to their participation numbers and equivalent treatment with respect to overall benefits. Equivalent benefits and treatment that must be provided specifically include publicity and promotions, support services, and recruitment of athletes. For a fuller explanation, see generally Women's Sports Foundation, https://www.womenssportsfoundation.org/ [https://perma.cc/L3ZZ-SCN2].

74. This is in addition to the arguments made earlier regarding the possibility that group licenses paid by educational institutions to athletes, especially in football and basketball, or third-party payments now made to individuals will diminish athletics department revenues and therefore harm women's sports. *See supra*.

75. The schools then might need to either match the amount paid by third parties to men or require that the respective third party equally make payments for women athletes or teams. This would not be dissimilar to Title IX's requirements regarding fundraising. *See* Donna Lopiano, Gerald Gurney, Fritz Polite, David B. Ridpath, Allen Sack, Sandy Thatcher & Andrew Zimbalist, "A Critical Analysis of Proposed Models of College Athlete Compensation," Drake Group (Mar. 2, 2019), https://www.thedrakegroup.org/wp-content/uploads/2019/10/COMPENSATION-POSITION-PAPER-March-2.pdf [https://perma.cc/K52T-NGJF].

76. In a situation involving very different facts, the Office of Civil Rights in 2017 pointed out that if a member institution assists an outside organization in making employment available to any of its students, it must make certain that the employment is available without discrimination on the basis of sex. *Id.*; *see also* Michael McCann, "Key Questions, Takeaways from the NCAA's NIL Announcement," *Sports Illustrated* (Oct. 29, 2019), https://www.si.com/college/2019/10/30/ncaa-name-image-likeness-announcement-takeaways-questions [https://perma.cc/9FDH-YF3W]; Mark Emmert, "If College Athletes Could Profit Off Their Marketability, How Much Would They Be Worth? In Some Cases, Millions," *USA Today* (Oct. 9, 2019), https://www.usatoday.com/story/sports/college/2019/10/09/college-athletes-with-name-image-likeness-control-could-make-millions/3909807002/ [https://perma.cc/D9ME-MVBL]; Jenny Dial Creech, "More Progress Must Be Made to Secure Equal Pay for Women's Sports," *Houston Chronicle* (June 10, 2018), https://www.houstonchronicle.com/sports/columnists/dialcreech/article/More-progress-must-be-made-to-secure-equal-pay-12982980.php [https://perma.cc/BU5Z-N9EE].

77. Paul Steinbach, "What Title IX Fallout Might NIL Legislation Pose?," *Athletic Business* (Jan. 2020), https://www.athleticbusiness.com/college/how-might-nil-legislation-be-impacted-by-title-ix.html [https://perma.cc/AW5X-SF9L].

78. *Id.*

79. *See supra* note 73; *see also* Dan Murphy, "What California Bill Means for NCAA Image and Likeness Debate," ESPN (Oct. 1, 2019), https://www.espn.com/college-football/story/_/id/27585301/what-california-bill-means-ncaa-image-likeness-debate [https://perma.cc/4VZY-XQ9X] ("Senator Skinner, co-author Senator Steven Bradford, and Governor Newsom all said they felt the *law actually opens more doors for female athletes* who can now promote themselves rather than relying on the schools, which typically spend most of their marketing budget on revenue sports like football and men's basketball."); Cecelia Townes, "Why California's Fair Pay to Play Act Could Be a Financial Win for Female Athletes," *Forbes* (Sept. 16, 2019) https://www.forbes.com/sites/ceceliatownes/2019/09/16/why-the-california-fair-pay-to-play-act-could-be-a-financial-win-for-female-athletes/#388a592d4c72 [https://perma.cc/6PHN-YCUV] ("Endorsements (and other opportunities to earn income from one's NIL) may be the only opportunity that a talented female athlete has to be compensated for her skills.")

80. See Emmert, *supra* note 76; Elliot Almond, "What Does the NCAA Board's Vote on Paying Athletes Actually Mean?," *Mercury News* (Oct. 29, 2019), https://www.mercurynews.com/2019/10/29/what-does-the-ncaa-boards-vote-on-paying-athletes-actually-mean/ [https://perma.cc/P7L2-TFPX].

81. UCLA Athletics, "Katelyn Ohashi—10.0 Floor," YouTube (Jan. 12, 2019), https://www.youtube.com/watch?v=4ic7RNS4Dfo [https://perma.cc/M5QX-Z6XC].

82. Michelle R. Martinelli, "Viral Former UCLA Gymnast Katelyn Ohashi Slams NCAA, Felt 'Handcuffed' by Profit Rules," *USA Today* (Oct. 9, 2019) https://ftw.usatoday.com/2019/10/katelyn-ohashi-ucla-viral-gymnast-slams-ncaa-fair-pay-to-play [https://perma.cc/7PY4-NC3C].

83. *Id.* One cannot help but ask whether it would have been different for Olympic swimmer Missy Franklin if she had not faced the choice of making money from her NIL only by dropping out of University of California, Berkeley. She dropped out after two years in order to sign with an agent and pursue attractive endorsement deals in 2015. She never regained the same level of swimming success. Or would it have been different for Katie Ledecky, another Olympic swimmer, who in 2018 stopped competing for Stanford, where she earned numerous NCAA titles and records, in order to accept professional endorsements and sponsorship opportunities? *See* Dial Creech, *supra* note 76.

84. *See generally* Ryan Swanson, "Want to Clean Up College Athletics? Pay the Players," *Washington Post* (Oct. 2, 2017), https://www.washingtonpost.com/news/made-by-history/wp/2017/10/02/want-to-clean-up-college-athletics-pay-the-players/ [https://perma.cc/P3UL-BKVQ].

85. On September 26, 2017, the Federal Bureau of Investigation announced ten arrests involving various big-name Division I basketball programs and Adidas executives on various corruption and fraud charges including bribery, money laundering, and wire fraud. *See* Lauren Thomas, "FBI Arrests NCAA Basketball Coaches and Adidas Rep in Bribery Probe Involving Recruitment," CNBC (Sept. 26, 2017), https://www.cnbc.com/2017/09/26/ncaa-basketball-officials-arrested-on-fraud-and-corruption-charges.html [https://perma.cc/7VUV-TLBR]. The core allegations were that student-athletes were being paid to attend certain schools and participate in their basketball programs. *See id.*

86. Christine Brennan, "NCAA Rules Are 'Incomprehensible,' Says Condoleezza Rice," *USA Today* (May 9, 2018), https://www.usatoday.com/story/sports/ncaab/2018/05/09/ncaa-mens-basketball-rules-incomprehensible-condoleezza-rice/596549002/ [https://perma.cc/7B5E-CGNT]. The NCAA granted a waiver to Notre Dame basketball star Arike Ogunbowale to earn money from *Dancing with the Stars* soon after Notre Dame won the Final Four tournament, during which Ogunbowale hit a winning three-point

shot that went viral. The NCAA reasoned that the show was unrelated to her basketball abilities. Rice used this as an example of the incomprehensibleness of the rules. *See id.*

87. *Id.*

88. *See* Meyer & Zimbalist, *supra* note 68 (including certain of the same analysis as in this section but with more detail).

89. The rules that have been challenged under the antitrust laws include not only payment and benefits to athletes for their play but also the length and number of scholarships available to athletes, the length of competitive seasons, the selection of teams to participate in national championships, the transfer of athletes between schools, and the payment of assistant coaches. *Id.*, at n.51–54.

90. *See, e.g.*, Ben Strauss, "N.L.R.B. Rejects Northwestern Football Players' Union Bid," *N.Y. Times* (Aug. 17, 2005), https://www.nytimes.com/2015/08/18/sports/ncaafootball/nlrb-says-northwestern-football-players-cannot-unionize.html [https://perma.cc/5UDB-GBZV].

91. Codified in 15 U.S.C. §§ 1–38 (2018), the Sherman Antitrust Act is a federal antitrust statute that prohibits acts that restrict interstate commerce and competition. Section 1 of the act states, "Every contract, combination in the form of trust or otherwise, or conspiracy, in restraint of trade or commerce among the several States, or with foreign nations, is declared to be illegal." *Id.*

92. While nonprofit organizations, like many universities and colleges, are not categorically exempt from the Sherman Act, "when they perform acts that are the antithesis of commercial activity, they are immune from antitrust regulations." United States v. Brown University in Providence in State of R.I., 5 F.3d 658, 665 (3d Circuit 1993).

93. *See generally* Meyer & Zimbalist, *supra* note 68, at 41. Also, see Agnew v. National Collegiate Athletic Association, 683 F.3d 328, 340 (7th Circuit 2012) (opining that "no knowledgeable observer could earnestly assert that big-time college football programs . . . do not anticipate economic gain from a successful recruiting program. Despite the nonprofit status of NCAA member schools, the transactions those schools make with premier athletes—full scholarships in exchange for athletic services—are not noncommercial, since schools can make millions of dollars as a result of these transactions").

94. *See generally* O'Bannon v. National Collegiate Athletic Association, 802 F.3d 1049 (9th Circuit 2015).

95. *See* Meyer & Zimbalist *supra* note 68, at 36–39.

96. National Collegiate Athletic Association v. Board of Regents of University of Oklahoma, 468 U.S. 85 (1984).

97. "The specific restraints on football telecasts that are challenged in this case do not, however, fit into the same mold as do rules defining the conditions of the contest, *the eligibility of participants*, or the manner in which members of a joint enterprise shall share the responsibilities and the benefits of the total venture." *Id.* at 117 (emphasis added); *see infra* notes 104–25 and accompanying text.

98. *See Board of Regents*, 468 U.S. at 101.

99. *Id.* at 107–8.

100. *Id.* at 113.

101. Because step 2 was not satisfied, the Court never reached consideration of a less restrictive alternative, although it stated that it agreed with the lower court's conclusion that if the procompetitive justifications had been supported by the evidence, they could be achieved by a less restrictive alternative. *Id.* at 102.

102. *Id.* at 123.

103. *Id.* (emphasis added).

104. *See* O'Bannon v. National Collegiate Athletic Association, 7 F. Supp. 3d 955 (N.D. Cal. 2014), *affirmed in part, vacated in part*, 802 F.3d 1049 (9th Circuit 2015), *cert.*

denied, 137 S. Ct. 277 (2016); *In re* NCAA Student-Athlete Name & Likeness Litigation, 4:09-CV-1967 CW, 4:09-cv-3329 CW, 2015 WL 5005901 (N.D. Cal. Aug. 19, 2015) (which is the consolidation with Keller v. Electronic Arts, Inc., 4:09-cv-1967-CW, 2015 WL 5005057 (N.D. Cal. Aug. 18, 2015)).

105. At the same time, Michael Keller, Ed O'Bannon, and others brought a separate lawsuit against Electronic Arts (EA) alleging an infringement of their rights of publicity in EA-produced video games under California's anti-SLAPP law. Keller v. Electronic Arts, Inc., 724 F.3d 1268, 1276 (9th Circuit 2013).

106. *O'Bannon*, 7 F. Supp. 3d. at 963.

107. *Id.*

108. Also, the court analyzed the three proposed submarkets to determine if there was injury to competition since groups of athletes would not compete with each other to sell their rights. The court concluded that groups of athletes would have an incentive to cooperate to sell packages of rights to the buyers. *Id.* at 994.

109. *In re* NCAA Student-Athlete Name & Likeness Licensing Litigation, 37 F. Supp. 3d 1126, 1155 (N.D. Cal. 2014). The NCAA unsuccessfully sought an interlocutory appeal on this matter. *In re* NCAA Student-Athlete Name & Likeness Licensing Litigation, No. C 09-1967 CW, 2014 WL 1949804 (N.D. Cal. May 23, 2014) (leave to file for reconsideration denied); *In re* NCAA Student-Athlete Name & Likeness Licensing Litigation, No. C 09-1967 CW, 2014 WL 12642228 (N.D. Cal. May 23, 2014) (motion to certify appeal denied). It argued that neither the Supreme Court nor any circuit court had squarely addressed whether athletes have a right of publicity for the use of the NILs in sports broadcasts. Defendant NCAA's Notice of Motion and Motion to Certify Pursuant to 28 U.S.C. § 1292(b) Court's Order Resolving Cross Motions for Summary Judgment at 4, *In re* NCAA Student-Athlete Name & Likeness Licensing Litigation, 37 F. Supp. 3d 1126 (N.D. Cal. 2014) (No. 1032).

110. The procedural posture of this case is long and complicated, including motions to dismiss and for summary judgment and interlocutory appeals.

111. *O'Bannon*, 7 F. Supp. 3d. at 973. *But see* Keller v. Electronic Arts, Inc., 724 F.3d 1268, 1284 (9th Circuit 2013) (focusing only on the video-game market).

112. *O'Bannon*, 7 F. Supp. 3d. at 973.

113. *Id.* at 1001.

114. *Id.* at 1003.

115. GIA includes room, board, tuition, fees, and required books for courses. COA adds miscellaneous expenses such as travel to and from campus, other books and supplies, laundry expenses, etc. Schools determine their respective COA on the basis of a federally mandated formula. Given the discretion available in applying the formula, some schools are calculating the applicable amount on the high side and allegedly are gaining recruiting advantages. The COA, however, is limited by what is offered to other nonathlete scholarship students. *Id.* at 965, 974.

116. O'Bannon v. National Collegiate Athletic Association, 802 F.3d 1049, 1070–72 (9th Circuit 2015).

117. *Id.* at 1074–75.

118. *Id.* at 1078–79 (quoting *Board of Regents*, 468 U.S. at 101–2).

119. *Id.* at 1083 (Thomas, J., concurring in part and dissenting in part).

120. *Id.* The *O'Bannon* plaintiffs compared the NCAA's reliance on amateurism to the defendant's defense in *United States v. Trans-Missouri Freight Association*, 166 U.S. 290 (1897), wherein the Court said that the antitrust laws do not permit the defendant to establish a legally cognizable interest in the suppression of competition. "These considerations are, however, not for us. If the act ought to read as contended for by the defendants, Congress is the body to amend it, and not this court, by a process

of judicial legislation wholly unjustifiable." 166 U.S. at 340. *See* Petition for Certiorari at 15, O'Bannon v. National Collegiate Athletic Association, 137 S. Ct. 277 (2016) (No. 15-1167).

121. Plaintiff-Appellees' Petition for Rehearing En Banc, NCAA v. O'Bannon, 802 F.3d 1049 (9th Circuit 2015), *rehearing denied*, No. 4:09-cv-03329-CW (9th Circuit Dec. 16, 2015) (Nos. 14-16601, 14-17068).

122. The plaintiffs submitted a petition on March 14, 2016: Petition for Writ of Certiorari, National Collegiate Athletic Association v. O'Bannon,137 S. Ct. 277 (2016) (No. 15-1167). The NCAA submitted a petition on May 13, 2016: Petition for Writ of Certiorari, National Collegiate Athletic Association v. O'Bannon, 137 S. Ct. 277 (2016) (No. 15-1388).

123. O'Bannon v. National Collegiate Athletic Association, 137 S. Ct. 277 (2016).

124. In the NCAA's petition for certiorari, it showed its frustration with the current litigations: "The NCAA should not have to undergo a full trial (and years of litigation) or face treble damages whenever a plaintiff or counsel hits on a supposedly better way to administer college athletics." Petition for Writ of Certiorari at 26–27, *O'Bannon*, 137 S. Ct. 277 (No. 15-1388) (clarifying that the precedent would "preclude[] potentially endless antitrust challenges to NCAA rules").

125. *In re* NCAA Athletic Grant-in-Aid Cap Antitrust Litigation, 375 F. Supp. 3d 1058 (N.D. Cal. 2019); *In re* NCAA Athletic Grant-in-Aid Cap Antitrust Litigation, 311 F.R.D. 532 (N.D. Cal. 2015). The five power conferences are the Atlantic Coast Conference, Big 12 Conference, Big Ten Conference, Pac-12 Conference, and Southeastern Conference. The six other conferences are the American Athletic Conference, Conference USA, Mid-American Conference, Mountain West Conference, Sun Belt Conference, and Western Athletic Conference. The original *Alston* complaint was consolidated with four other complaints, and a consolidated complaint was filed. Steve Berkowitz, "Court Filing: NCAA, Conferences Say Scholarships Could Be Reduced," *USA Today* (May 1, 2015), http://www.usatoday.com/story/sports/college/2015/05/01/ncaa-suit-shawne-alston-martin-jenkins-kessler-nigel-hayes-claudia-wilken/26685565/ [https://perma.cc/695Z-833L]. While *Jenkins* and *Alston* were coordinated for pretrial purposes in the Northern District of California before Judge Wilken (the same judge that decided *O'Bannon*), there is a significant difference between the cases. *Jenkins* sought only injunctive relief. *Alston* sought injunctive relief and monetary damages for four years (the amount of time permitted under the applicable statute of limitations) of the difference between GIA and COA scholarships. Prior to trial, the damages portion of *Alston* was settled for approximately $208 million. Conceivably, the *Jenkins* case could still be remanded to New Jersey for trial.

126. *In re NCAA Athletic Grant-in-Aid Cap Antitrust Litigation*, 375 F. Supp. 3d 1058.

127. NCAA Bylaw 15.1, as amended in 2015, provides, "A student-athlete shall not be eligible to participate in intercollegiate athletics if he or she receives financial aid that exceeds the value of the cost of attendance." NCAA, 2009–10 NCAA Division Manual 174 (2009).

128. For a fuller discussion of Judge Wilken's decision, see Harrison (Buzz) Frahn, Michael R. Morey, Loren Shokes & Omar Kanjwal, "The Northern District of California Enjoins the NCAA from Capping the Amount of Education-Related Compensation that Student-Athletes Can Receive," California Law Association (June 25, 2019), https://calawyers.org/antitrust-ucl-and-privacy/the-northern-district-of-california-enjoins-the-ncaa-from-capping-the-amount-of-education-related-compensation-that-student-athletes-can-receive/ [https://perma.cc/MGE4-XUE8].

129. *In re NCAA Athletic Grant-in-Aid Cap Antitrust Litigation*, 375 F. Supp. 3d at 1098–1103.

130. *Id.* at 1098–99.

131. Judge Wilken noted that the NCAA, in fact, permits "cash or cash-equivalent compensation that exceeds the cost of attendance by thousands of dollars," some of which are "directly correlated with athletic performance," something the bylaws would protect and, on their face, "pay for play." *Id.* at 1099.

132. *Id.* at 1100.

133. *Id.* at 1101 (emphasis added). Also, she found that "limits or prohibitions on most other benefits related to education that can be provided on top of a grant-in-aid, such as those on tutoring, graduate school tuition, and paid internships, have not been shown to have an effect on enhancing consumer demand for college sports as a distinct product." *Id.* at 1102.

134. Indeed, Judge Wilken next explained that, if anything, the record supported that the challenged compensation limitations increased separation among students because they allowed schools to spend significant resources on opulent, athletes-only facilities. *Id.* at 1102–3.

135. *Id.* at 1086.

136. *Id.*

137. This included "computers, science equipment, musical instruments and other tangible items not included in the cost of attendance calculation but nonetheless related to the pursuit of academic studies; post-eligibility scholarships to complete undergraduate or graduate degrees at any school; scholarships to attend vocational school; tutoring; expenses related to studying abroad that are not included in the cost of attendance calculation; and paid post-eligibility internships." Michael McCann, "Why the NCAA Lost Its Latest Landmark Case in the Battle over What Schools Can Offer Students," *Sports Illustrated* (Mar. 8, 2019), https://www.si.com/college/2019/03/09/ncaa-antitrust-lawsuit-claudia-wilken-alston-jenkins.

138. *In re* NCAA Athletic Grant-in-Aid Cap Antitrust Litigation, No. 14-md-02541 CW, 2019 WL 1593939, at *1 (N.D. Cal. Mar. 8, 2019); *see also* Jenkins' Appeal Brief, *supra* note 42 at 11.

139. More specifically, the injunction stated that the NCAA member conferences may "fix or limit academic or graduation awards or incentives that may be made available from that conference or its member schools to Division I women's and men's basketball and FBS football student-athletes on top of a grant-in-aid." *In re NCAA Athletic Grant-in-Aid Cap Antitrust Litigation*, 2019 WL 1593939, at *1; *see also* Jenkins' Appeal Brief, *supra* note 42.

140. 15 U.S.C. § 15(a) (2018).

141. *See* Restatement (Third) of Unfair Competition § 46 (American Law Institute 1995).

142. *Id.* § 46 cmt. C; *see generally* Marc Edelman, "Closing the 'Free Speech' Loophole: The Case for Protecting College Athletes Publicity Rights in Commercial Video Games," 65 *Florida Law Review* 554 (2013); Eugene Volokh, "The First Amendment, the Right of Publicity, Video Games and the Supreme Court," *Washington Post* (Jan. 4, 2016), https://www.washingtonpost.com/news/volokh-conspiracy/wp/2016/01/04/the-first-amendment-the-right-of-publicity-video-games-and-the-supreme-court/ [https://perma.cc/ST5Y-DUNU]; Michael Marrero, "A Primer on NCAA Athletes' Right of Publicity," *Law360* (July 16, 2013), https://www.law360.com/articles/456776/a-primer-on-ncaa-athlete's-right-of-publicity [https://perma.cc/7K59-DYZS].

143. Specific analysis of rights of publicity, the First Amendment, federal and state consumer protection laws, copyright and trademark laws, fair use doctrines, and federal and state tax laws as applied to institutions, athletes, and donors is beyond the scope of this article.

144. Keller v. Electronic Arts, Inc., 724 F.3d 1268, 1276 (9th Circuit 2013). As noted, *Keller* was consolidated with *O'Bannon*. *See supra* note 104.

145. Hart v. Electronic Arts, Inc., 717 F.3d 141 (3d Circuit 2013); *see also* Daniels v. Fanduel, Inc., 909 F.3d 876 (7th Circuit 2018).

146. *Hart*, 717 F.3d at 151; *Keller*, 724 F.3d at 1284.

147. *Hart*, 717 F.3d at 145; *Keller*, 724 F.3d at 1271.

148. *Keller*, 724 F.3d at 1271.

149. *Hart*, 717 F.3d at 170; *Keller*, 724 F.3d at 1284.

150. *Keller*, 724 F.3d at 1284 (Thomas, J., dissenting). In *O'Bannon*, Chief Judge Thomas would have provided additional rights to athletes (up to $5,000 held in trust) without specifying the particular submarket in which the revenues would be earned. O'Bannon v. National Collegiate Athletic Association, 802 F.3d 1049, 1079 (9th Circuit 2015) (Thomas, J., concurring in part and dissenting in part).

151. *Keller*, 724 F.3d at 1288–90 (Thomas, J., dissenting).

152. Tom Farrey, "Players, Game Makers Settle for $40M," ESPN (May 30, 2014), https://www.espn.com/espn/otl/story/_/id/11010455/college-athletes-reach-40-million-settlement-ea-sports-ncaa-licensing-arm [https://perma.cc/GS6C-Y7T6].

153. Jon Solomon, "NCAA Reaches $20 Million Settlement with Players in Video Game Suit," CBS Sports (June 9, 2014), https://www.cbssports.com/college-football/news/ncaa-reaches-20-million-settlement-with-players-in-video-game-suit/ [https://perma.cc/YE8V-LEDZ].

154. Significantly, the dissent in *Keller* noted the inequity in a system wherein colleges, universities, coaches, television networks, and others all make money from the talent and hard work of athletes, many of whom come from inner-city neighborhoods and rural towns, while the athletes are precluded from sharing in the revenues. *Keller*, 724 F.3d at 1289, n.5 (Thomas, J., dissenting).

155. Jon Solomon, "NCAA Reaches Settlement in Electronic Arts Video Game Lawsuit," NCAA (June 9, 2014), http://www.ncaa.org/about/resources/media-center/press-releases/ncaa-reaches-settlement-ea-video-game-lawsuit [https://perma.cc/GMT7-HYV4]. It is easy to agree that the pay was not for performance on the field, but arguably it was pay for use of the athletes' NILs.

156. The court declined to consider NCAA's other argument that the Copyright Act preempts right-of-publicity claims. The court said this was irrelevant to the standing argument and other main issues of the case and is convoluted and complex. It did note that Electronic Arts pays professional players in the National Football League (NFL) and NBA for the right to use their NILs in its video games, indicating that the Copyright Act may not preempt such claims. *O'Bannon*, 802 F.3d at 1067.

157. Two points to emphasize from *O'Bannon* that are relevant to this essay's proposal of NIL payments are that the allegations in the case involved payments from the NCAA or member institutions (not third parties) and only group licenses between the NCAA or member schools and the athletes (not third-party payments to individual athletes).

158. A case filed in 2017 by the former football great Chris Spielman against Ohio State would have elucidated many of the issues left open in *O'Bannon*, but the case settled. Jennifer Smola, "Spielman and Ohio State Reach $140k Settlement in Lawsuit over Athletes' Images," *Columbus Dispatch* (Nov. 30, 2018), https://www.dispatch.com/news/20181130/spielman-and-ohio-state-reach-140k-settlement-in-lawsuit-over-athletes-images [https://perma.cc/YUN8-492L]. There, Spielman, on behalf of a class of current and former Ohio State football players in federal court in Ohio (which is in the Sixth Circuit and not bound by the Ninth Circuit's opinion in *O'Bannon*), sued Ohio State; IMG, Ohio State's sports marketing agency; Nike, with which Ohio State had a licensed apparel contract that included the sale of jerseys with former players

depicted; and Honda, which sponsored banners at Ohio State with former players' names and photos. Spielman alleged that Ohio State unfairly profited from the use of the former players' NILs used on banners hanging at the school, sales of DVDs that showed replays of games, and the sale of photos and jerseys. A year later and before much motion practice or discovery, the parties settled. Spielman donated his settlement award of $140,000 to charity. Speculation was that numerous similar lawsuits would be filed at other schools, but perhaps due to the huge cost of litigation and loyalty by most athletes to their schools, we have seen no such explosion.

159. Marshall v. ESPN, 668 Federal Appendix 155 (6th Circuit 2016) (brought against two-dozen entities including conferences, networks, and licensing agencies; the NCAA was not sued).

160. Tennessee Code Annotated § 47-25-1107 (2019).

161. *See supra* notes 9–14. Also to note is that the NCAA argued that California, in fact, has a state law that is similar to Tennessee law and protects live broadcasts as fair use; however, Minnesota where two of the plaintiffs lived, did not have a similar law.

162. Providing historical facts through game programs and video clips may command a substantial public interest and be a form of expression with First Amendment protection. Also, as noted earlier, copyright law recognizes that broadcast rights are held by the copyright owner. 17 U.S.C. § 106 (2018).

163. Berger v. National Collegiate Athletic Association,162 F. Supp. 3d 845 (S.D. Ind. 2016).

164. This case originally was captioned *Sackos/Anderson v. NCAA*. A former soccer player at the University of Houston alleged that the NCAA and Division I universities conspired to violate the Fair Labor Standards Act by failing to at least pay a federal minimum wage of $7.25 per hour. No. 1:14-cv-1710-WTL-MJD (S.D. Ind., Oct. 22, 2014). Sackos was replaced by the women track-and-field athletes at the University of Pennsylvania as the plaintiffs. Berger v. National Collegiate Athletic Association, 843 F.3d 285 (7th Circuit 2016). The district court granted the defendants' motions to dismiss on February 16, 2016, and stated that the relationship between athletes and institutions of higher education is fundamentally an "educational experience," more akin to extracurricular student-run programs than to work-study programs. *Berger*, 162 F. Supp. 3d at 856.

165. *Berger*, 843 F.3d at 294.

166. Dawson v. National Collegiate Athletic Association, 932 F.3d 905 (9th Circuit 2019).

167. *Id.* Failing in the Ninth Circuit, two months later, certain FBS football players brought a similar lawsuit in the Third Circuit. In November 2019, a former Villanova football player, Trey Johnson, filed a 116-page complaint in the Eastern District of Pennsylvania on behalf of a purported class of football players from twenty-two Division I schools (all located in the Third Circuit) against the NCAA. *See* Complaint, Johnson v. National Collegiate Athletic Association, No. 2:19-cv-05230 (E.D. Pa. Nov. 6, 2019). In great detail, the complaint alleges that the NCAA failed to pay the minimum wage to the athletes as required by the Pennsylvania Minimum Wage Act and the FLSA. The plaintiffs assert that they are employees the same as, if not more so than, students in work-study programs. The complaint alleges, "Notably, student ticket takers, seating attendants and food concession workers at NCAA contest are paid a minimum wage . . . under Work Study. At the same time, the Student Athlete, whose athletic work creates those Work Study jobs at the ticket gate, in the seats and at concession stands, are paid *nothing*." Ryan Boysen, "NCAA Must Pay Minimum Wage, Ex-Villanova Player Says," *Law360* (Nov. 7, 2019), https://www.law360.com/articles/1217930/ncaa-must-pay-minimum-wage-ex-villanova-player-says [https://perma.cc/5GKE-92FE]. While this

complaint does not address NIL payments, clearly any reasoning that compares non-student pay to athlete pay is relevant.

168. *See* Roberto L. Corrada, "The Northwestern University Football Case: A Dissent," 11 *Harvard Journal of Sports and Entertainment Law* 15 (2020) (describing Northwestern University students' unionization efforts).

169. Professional players, through respective unions, negotiate collective bargaining agreements with owners and agree on restrictive commercial rules (e.g., player and team salary caps and reserve clauses) that otherwise would be prohibited under the Sherman Act.

170. *Northwestern University & College Athletes Players Association (CAPA)*, 13-RC-121359, 2014–15 NLRB Dec. P 15781, 2014 WL 1246914, at *13 (Mar. 26, 2014).

171. *Id.*

172. *Northwestern University & College Athletes Players Association (CAPA)*, 362 N.L.R.B. 1350, 1368 (2015).

173. *Id.* at 1355.

174. Subsequently, in August 2016, the NLRB held that graduate and undergraduate teaching and research student assistants were statutory employees pursuant to the NLRA. *Trustees of Columbia University in the City of New York and Graduate Workers of Columbia GWC, UAW*, 364 N.L.R.B. 90 (2016). Significantly, this decision overruled *Brown University and International Union, United Auto., Aerospace and Agriculture Implement Workers of America, UAW AFL-CIO, Petitioner*, 342 N.L.R.B. 483 (2004), a case that the NLRB in *Northwestern* said was distinguishable because "scholarship players bear little resemblance to the graduate student assistants." Northwestern had heavily relied on *Brown* in its briefs. *Northwestern University*, 362 N.L.R.B. at 1365.

175. *See generally* John D. Colombo, "The NCAA, Tax Exemption, and College Athletics," *University of Illinois Law Review* 109 (2010).

176. Eventually, if college athletes were paid, the astronomical compensation now paid to college coaches and athletic administrators probably would be reduced, alleviating some of the cost pressure. See the discussion in Gurney, Lopiano & Zimbalist, SUPRA note 15, at chs. 7–8.

177. *See* NCAA NIL Report, *supra* note 7, at 3.

178. *See id.* at 4.

179. *In re* NCAA Athletic Grant-in-Aid Cap Antitrust Litigation, 375 F. Supp. 3d 1058, 1099 (N.D. Cal. 2019).

180. O'Bannon v. National Collegiate Athletic Association, 802 F.3d 1049, 1080 (9th Circuit 2015).

181. *Id.*

182. *See, e.g.*, Tennessee Code Annotated § 47-25-1107(a) (2019) ("It is deemed a fair use and no violation of an individual's rights shall be found, for purposes of this part, if the use of a name, photograph, or likeness is in connection with any news, public affairs, or sports broadcast or account.").

183. See *supra* note 175 and accompanying text for tax implications to the employer (schools) and employees (athletes).

184. This substitution effect may be mollified if the popularity of college sports grows as a result of more fan interface with the athletes.

185. If they are so regulated, without an antitrust exemption, we are likely to see a continuation of lawsuits brought on antitrust grounds. Then the NCAA, no doubt, would argue that amateurism is a procompetitive justification for the restrictions. Even if the NCAA were successful (which given the trend of the cases may not be likely), much time and money would be spent on the case(s).

186. There is additional pressure to pay athletes for their NILs due to the limited

options that high school students have to play professional sports upon graduation. Indeed, both high school and college athletes with dreams of going professional are subject to entry rules created by the different professional leagues, e.g., the NBA's "one-and-done" rule or the NFL's requirement that athletes be out of high school for three years or the MLB rule, which allows athletes after high school, but once they are enrolled in college, they must remain until they complete their junior year or reach twenty-one years of age, unless they attend junior college, in which case they can enter the draft after two years. Kelly Hines, "Going Pro: Which Sport Gets Draft Rules Right?," *Tulsa World* (Apr. 20, 2013), https://www.tulsaworld.com/sportsextra/collegebasketball/going-pro-which-sport-gets-draft-rules-right/article_ea5642ca-4a94-5084-bd1f-f3f3213cbec3.html [https://perma.cc/96P7-QWAL]. The NBA rule, in particular, requiring just one year after high school before receiving eligibility, has received a lot of negative attention because, for the elite players that would otherwise go straight into the NBA, they are forced to either play in the NCAA, patronizing the notion of primacy of education, or play with professional teams located overseas. The NFL does not have a significant international market, so athletes out of high school have few choices but to enter college, risking serious injury, if they wish to one day turn professional. The NCAA, in response to these criticisms, has encouraged schools to seek out additional "opportunities to allow prospective and current student-athletes to go directly into professional leagues." *See* NCAA, *Federal and State Legislative Working Group Report to the NCAA Board of Governors* 2 (2019) [hereinafter NCAA NIL Working Group Report], https://ncaaorg.s3.amazonaws.com/committees/ncaa/exec_boardgov/Oct2019BOG_Report.pdf [https://perma.cc/R3CF-J8UQ].

187. *See* NCAA NIL Report, *supra* note 7, at 3.

188. *Id.*

189. *Id.* at 3–4.

190. NCAA NIL Working Group Report at 3.

191. *Id.* at 5.

192. *Id.*

193. *Id.*

194. *See, e.g.*, Greg Hunter, "Lyons Addresses Ever-Changing Landscape of College Athletics," *Morgantown News* (Nov. 30, 2019), https://www.wvnews.com/morgantownnews/sports/lyons-addresses-ever-changing-landscape-of-college-athletics/article_db3bdc30-efa1-53e7-ac46-a54dd5f9c046.html [https://perma.cc/J4BV-W5L4] (interview with Shane Lyons, chairman of the NCAA Division I Football Oversight Committee and West Virginia University director of athletics).

195. In November 2019, the NCAA released a timeline for schools and divisions to provide feedback and prepare for the future rules. Key dates are September 2020, deadline for Divisions II and III presidents to sponsor legislation; November 2020, deadline for Division I to submit proposals; January 2021, discussion at the NCAA Convention of the proposals. Notably there is no deadline for Division I to sponsor legislation, although the NCAA notes that the Division I legislative process allows the Division I Board of Directors discretion to adopt legislation at any time. In fact, there is no deadline for voting on the proposals. *See* NCAA NIL Report, *supra* note 7, at 4.

196. This would help better resolve situations like that of University of Central Florida backup kicker Donald De La Haye, who lost his eligibility after refusing to stop monetizing his YouTube channel. *See* Dan Gartland, "UCF Kicker Ruled Ineligible after YouTube Channel Gets Him in Trouble with NCAA," *Sports Illustrated* (July 31, 2017), https://www.si.com/college/2017/07/31/ucf-kicker-donald-de-la-haye-ineligible-ncaa-youtube-videos [https://perma.cc/NB7D-F8WF]. The NCAA based its decision on the fact that there were football-related videos on the channel. *See id.* Even US Senator

Marco Rubio tweeted, "The @NCAA is out of control," in response to this decision. Marco Rubio (@marcorubio), Twitter (Aug. 1, 2017, 7:58 AM), https://twitter.com/marcorubio/status/892353886589116417 [https://perma.cc/MG5M-VMMQ]

197. *See* Mandell, *supra* note 34.

198. This proposal is similar to the Drake Group position paper "Compensation of College Athletes Including Revenues Earned from Commercial Use of Their Names, Image and Likenesses and Outside Employment," (Nov. 4, 2019), https://www.thedrakegroup.org/2019/10/14/compensation-of-college-athletes-including-revenues-earned-from-commercial-use-of-their-names-images-and-likenesses-and-outside-employment/ [https://perma.cc/8BU2-8NBU]. The position paper provides considerably more detail for a proposed solution.

199. This framework is most applicable for Division I athletes and can be easily modified for Divisions II and III, if necessary. Given that our proposal does not require institutions to pay athletes, no modification may be necessary.

200. *See* "College Extracurricular Activities—Impact on Students, Types of Extracurricular Activities," StateUniversity.com, http://education.stateuniversity.com/pages/1855/College-Extracurricular-Activities.html#ixzz3RYLjNs8c [https://perma.cc/VSE9-V7D8].

201. Athletes shall retain the right to use their own sports equipment. Shoes are subject to a medical exception, in which case athletes shall be required to cover the brand of the conflicting sponsor during participation if during such regular-season (including postseason) athletic events.

202. *See, e.g.*, Marc Stein, "NBA Social Media Guidelines Out," ESPN (Sept. 30, 2009), https://www.espn.com/nba/news/story?id=4520907 [https://perma.cc/WY8P-S3SL] (explaining that the NBA introduced a policy prohibiting players, coaches, and team personnel from using electronic communication devices and accessing social media beginning forty-five minutes before the start of a game and only concluding after players and coaches have completed their postgame media obligations).

203. Marketing companies are jumping at the opportunity to assist college athletes to monetize their NIL rights either individually or as a group. *See* Michael Smith & Liz Mullen, "College Sports: Sharper Resolution," *Sports Business Journal* (Dec. 2, 2019), https://www.sportsbusinessdaily.com/Journal/Issues/2019/12/02/In-Depth/NIL.aspx [https://perma.cc/D7N9-C3J8].

204. *See generally* Gabe Feldman, "The NCAA and 'Non-Game Related' Student Athlete Name, Image and Likeness Restrictions," Knight Commission on Intercollegiate Athletics (May 2016), https://www.knightcommission.org/wp-content/uploads/2008/10/feldman_nil_white_paper_may_2016.pdf [https://perma.cc/23RX-UTZH] (proposing numerous restrictions, many of which are similar to those suggested here but also proposing group licensing arrangements between schools and athletes in addition to individual agreements between athletes and third parties).

205. *Id.*

206. The NIL Commission should consider establishing a clearinghouse for NILs that could be similar to the NCAA's current Eligibility Center or the Drug Free Sport International. All athletes could be required to submit their NIL agreements to the clearinghouse for review. Also, the agreements would be posted on a website that is searchable. This transparency hopefully will help reveal potential abuses. The Commission could set appropriate standards for the redaction of competitively sensitive information as long as such redaction does not interfere with the purpose in making the contracts publicly available. This transparency hopefully will help reveal potential abuses.

207. It is important to control local, as opposed to national, income because it is local income that enters into consideration during athlete recruitment. Local would be

delineated by a mile radius around the university, with an exception for social media income, which, while generated locally, can engage national sources of revenue. We believe that those athletes with a national reputation should be able to fully exploit their notoriety nationally without limitation.

208. Also, setting a cap on the amount that athletes can earn from local sources may minimize the concern that donations made directly to schools will be reduced, which in turn could particularly impact nonrevenue sports.

209. The authors have considered other restrictions, including limitations on the amount of time that athletes may devote to NIL-profiting activities and the number of these activities. While it may be something that the Commission in the future finds desirable, we do not suggest such regulations at this time.

210. These activities could be delegated to the clearinghouse discussed earlier. *See supra* note 206. We do not envision the Commission initiating such adjudication, as the burden would be too great. Rather, we suggest that certain designated third parties could bring appeals that would be adjudicated by the Commission.

211. Ideally, Congress would consider a limited Commission and conditional antitrust exemption that would be much broader and address holistically all the key reforms needed in college sports. *See generally* Meyer & Zimbalist, *supra* note 68.

212. An act of Congress that creates a national NIL Commission and grants a federal antitrust exemption would preempt state laws that attempt to regulate NILs.

213. Interestingly, the NCAA no longer requires athletes to sign Form 15-3(a), in which athletes agreed to give up any NIL rights they might have regarding broadcasts and promotions thereof. This is consistent with the argument made by the NCAA at the oral argument on behalf of the summary judgment motion in *Keller*, at which the NCAA's attorney stated, "The student athletes don't have any NIL rights in the live broadcasts of the games." He explained that live broadcasts are noncommercial events, noncommercial speech that involves a matter of public interest. Reporter's Transcript of Proceedings at 31, Keller v. Electronic Arts, Inc., 4:09-cv-01967 CW (N.D. Cal. Aug. 18, 2015).

214. Noteworthy is that antitrust damages are trebled under the Sherman Act. *See* 15 U.S.C. § 15 (2018). This is an impetus for the parties to reach a settlement. Settlements resolve matters only between the particular parties and do not foreclose future cases brought by a different set of plaintiffs. *See, e.g.*, White v. National Collegiate Athletic Association, No. CV 06-0999-RGK, 2006 WL 8066803 (C.D. Cal. Oct. 19, 2006) (discussing allegations regarding the GIA cap that settled, allowing for a different set of plaintiffs in *O'Bannon* to bring similar allegations without the existence of contrary precedent).

215. Arguably, regulating college athletics, including eligibility, scholarships, scheduling, and spending, is not so different from regulating college financial assistance, such as is covered in the Higher Education Act, which includes rules on loan limits, accreditation, determining who gets money, how much, and when, etc. And regulating gender equality in college sports (e.g., Title IX, 20 U.S.C. § 1681 et seq.) demonstrates that Congress believes it is appropriate to impose legislation in this important area.

216. Anti-Hog-Cholera Serum and Hog-Cholera Virus Act, 49 Stat. 781 (1935) (codified at 7 U.S.C. § 852 (2018)).

217. ICC Termination Act of 1995, Public Law No. 104-88, 109 Stat. 812 (codified at 49 U.S.C. § 10706 (2018)).

218. Soft Drink Interbrand Competition Act, Public Law No. 96-308, 94 Stat. 939 (1980) (codified at 15 U.S.C. §§ 3501–3 (2018)).

219. McCarran-Ferguson Act, 59 Stat. 33 (1945) (codified at 15 U.S.C. §§ 1011–15 (2018)).

220. *See infra* notes 222–25.
221. *See infra* notes 226–27.
222. Sports Broadcasting Act of 1961, Public Law No. 87-331, 75 Stat. 732 (codified as amended at 15 U.S.C. § 1291) (stating, "The antitrust laws, as defined in section 1 of the [Sherman] Act[,] . . . shall not apply to any joint agreement . . . by which any league of clubs participating in professional football, baseball, basketball, or hockey contests sells or otherwise transfers all or any part of the rights of such league's member clubs in the sponsored telecasting of the games . . . engaged in or conducted by such clubs").
223. Public Law No. 89-800 § 6(b)(1), 80 Stat. 1515 (1966) (codified as amended at 15 U.S.C. § 1291 (2018)).
224. Ted Stevens Olympic and Amateur Sports Act, Public Law No. 105-225, 112 Stat. 1466 (1998) (codified as amended at 36 U.S.C. §§ 220501–12 (2018)).
225. 15 U.S.C. § 26b (2018). Congress ensured the limited scope of its intervention by expressly stating, "The passage of this Act does not change the application of the antitrust laws in any other context or with respect to any other person or entity." Curt Flood Act, Public Law No. 105-297, § 2, 112 Stat. 2824 (1998). The Supreme Court had previously presumed that Major League Baseball was exempt from the antitrust laws. *See* Fed. Baseball Club v. Nat'l League, 259 U.S. 200 (1922).
226. Improving America's Schools Act of 1994, Public Law No. 103-382, tit. V, § 568(a), 108 Stat. 4060) (codified at 15 U.S.C. § 1 (2018) (note)). The act permits, inter alia, schools jointly "to use common principles of analysis for determining the need of such students for financial aid if the agreement to use such principles does not restrict financial aid officers . . . in their exercising independent professional judgment with respect to individual applicants for such financial aid." The act does not permit schools to agree on which particular students are entitled to aid.
227. 15 U.S.C. § 37 (2018).
228. See earlier discussion for a few other narrowly drawn circumstances in which third-party NIL income may be restricted to ensure no conflicts with the school's intellectual property.
229. It is recognized that athletics departments that earn revenues from broadcasts and apparel deals have legitimate concerns in protecting those.
230. As noted earlier, the Commission would be charged with analyzing the impact of the regulations and the need for any additional requirements.

CHAPTER 4

The Impact of College Athletic Success on Donations and Applicant Quality

Benjamin Baumer and Andrew Zimbalist

Intercollegiate athletics is in a turbulent period. Recruiting and academic scandals along with antitrust litigations are erupting with unprecedented frequency. The Rice Commission on reforming college basketball called for a panoply of structural reforms.

Meanwhile, the financial outcomes of college athletics departments remain bleak for the vast majority of institutions. NCAA reports consistently show that in recent years only about 20 out of roughly 130 athletics departments in FBS (the Football Bowl Subdivision of Division I, the most commercial subdivision in the NCAA) run an operating surplus. FBS itself is subdivided into the Power Five or Autonomous Conferences (Pac-12, Big Ten, SEC, ACC, and Big 12) with sixty-five schools and the five Non-Autonomous Conferences with sixty-four schools. The Power Five command the large television contracts, control the football championship playoff, and enjoy much-larger attendance at their games.

During the 2015–16 school year, the median reported operating deficit at all FBS athletics programs was $14.4 million. At the Power Five schools, the median reported operating deficit was $3.6 million. There were twenty-four Power Five schools during 2015–16 that experienced an operating surplus—the median surplus for these schools was $10 million.[1]

International Journal of Financial Studies 7, no. 1 (2019).

Because of accounting irregularities, however, it appears that most FBS athletics departments do not include significant shares of their capital costs in their reports to the NCAA. According to one NCAA study, capital costs, properly reckoned, exceed $20 million annually at the average FBS school.[2] If these and other indirect costs were included, most estimates suggest that no more than half a dozen programs would have a true surplus.

To be sure, there is an active debate about the underlying economic reality of intercollegiate athletics programs. For instance, many economists assert that it is improper to include the cost of athletic scholarships in the financial reports because they do not represent the actual marginal costs to the school. That is, even though the school may charge $50,000 tuition, the incremental cost of educating an additional student is close to zero. Put differently, an economics professor will get paid, say, $150,000, whether she has 120 or 121 students in her introductory macroeconomics class, and there are no additional facility costs incurred by the extra student.

While this is a fair point, it is also reasonable to note that fielding an FBS football team requires eighty-five scholarships. If the relevant alternative is having no football team, then it is no longer true that the incremental cost of educating eighty-five students is zero. Indeed, it is misleading to think that the marginal cost of educating a single football player is zero. The school expends considerable resources on tutoring centers and academic support to keep players eligible.

It might also be relevant to consider the opportunity cost of a football scholarship. If low-income and highly qualified students do not get scholarships, and thus do not attend the school, then the school may suffer from lower graduation rates, fewer serious students in the classroom, and a lower profile for its student body in terms of standardized test scores and school rank.

Further, even if all athletic aid were eliminated from the financials, it would only amount to a median savings of $4.6 million—well below the median operating deficit of $14.4 million in FBS. Moreover, standard athletic accounting does not include a host of indirect expenses, such as a share of the school president's time, travel, office, and administrative assistants' salaries.

The reality is that intercollegiate athletics departments are not profit maximizers. They do not have shareholders who demand quarterly profits to boost stock prices or corporate dividends. Instead, they have stakeholders who want victories. Subject to some constraints, athletic directors are win maximizers. The conventional method for maximizing wins is to hire well-known coaches at multimillion-dollar salaries, invest lavishly in athletic and tutoring facilities, and spend freely on recruitment. Thus, when revenues rise, the athletic director finds more than enough ways to spend the bounty. And even if the football or men's basketball team yields a surplus, much of it is drained by the deficits experienced by the fifteen or more "nonrevenue" men's and women's sports. The consequence is that the vast majority of programs run in deficit.

How, then, can these hypercommercialized, massive athletics programs be justified? One line of defense holds that while the programs might run financial deficits, they provide invaluable exposure and advertising for the university. This branding value, in turn, produces an increase in applications. These applications fill empty beds in the dormitories and enable the college to be more selective in its admissions policies, yielding an improvement in the quality of the student body (usually measured in standardized test scores). Additionally, alumni and athletic boosters become excited by team success or media prominence and open up their wallets, leading to increased donations and endowment growth. And, in some cases, this line of reasoning goes, state legislators also become enthused and allocate more budgetary assistance to the university.

Of course, even if it could be verified that athletic success leads to these salutary outcomes, it would not justify the tens of millions of dollars of investment that most FBS universities make annually. This is because only roughly half of all teams have a winning record and only a handful of teams achieve top ranking. If regression analysis shows that winning is positively correlated with applications, this implies both that applications tend to go up when wins increase and that applications tend to go down when wins decrease. Further, many, if not most, FBS universities bend the rules or cheat in order to promote athletic success. Some of these schools get caught, and scandals ensue. The resulting ignominy may have negative enduring effects on applications, donations, and legislative appropriations. The lowering of admissions standards for athletes and the creation of sham courses also serve to dilute the educational experience and intellectual spirit on the campus.

In this essay, we endeavor to expand on, clarify, and update the existing scholarly literature on whether athletic success in football and men's basketball leads to increased applications, enhanced quality of the student body, more donations, and greater state support. This updating is important because the organization and rules affecting college sports have been in flux in the twenty-first century. We consider evidence from 2005–6 through 2015–16 for the sixty-five Power Five schools in the FBS. These schools are athletically the most successful and best known by a considerable margin and, therefore, the most likely to garner the positive publicity effects from athletic success.

In what follows, we review the existing scholarship, describe our data sources and our data profile, discuss our models and results, and draw conclusions. The evolution of the literature is not linear, and the current state of knowledge remains ambiguous.

Review of the Literature

Athletic Success and the Quantity and Quality of Applications

One of the first and most frequently cited studies on the impact of athletic success on admissions is one by McCormick and Tinsley.[3] They gather data on 150 schools for 1971. On the basis of a multiple regression test with several control variables, they estimate that a school with a "big-time" athletics program had 3 percent higher SAT scores than schools without such a program. They identified sixty-three of the schools in their sample to have a big-time program. A difficulty with this cross-sectional analysis is that characteristics not identified by the control variables of a school lead to an incomplete model specification. In an attempt to rectify this deficiency, McCormick and Tinsley test a second model with data from 1981 to 1984, focusing exclusively on schools with big-time programs. They explore the link between changes in SAT scores and changes in athletic performance over this period. None of the estimated coefficients are statistically different from zero at standard confidence levels.

Bremmer and Kesselring essayed a retest of the McCormick and Tinsley hypotheses, using data from 1989 for 132 schools and from 1981–89 for 53 schools.[4] They find no evidence that basketball or football success led to increased SAT scores of matriculated students.

Tucker and Amato adapt the McCormick and Tinsley model by using a new metric of athletic success—whether the school was in the Associated Press top-twenty ranking in football or basketball.[5] They find no relationship between basketball success and SAT scores but find that a football program ranked in the top twenty for ten consecutive years (1980–89) would attract a freshman class with 3 percent higher average SAT scores than a program that never ranked in the top twenty.

Murphy and Trandel construct a ten-year panel, 1978–87, and use team win percentage as the measure of athletic success.[6] They use school fixed effects and, thereby, control more effectively for unobserved differences among institutions. Murphy and Trandel find that a 50 percent increase in a team's win percentage results in a rather small increase of only 1.3 percent in the number of its applicants.

Mixon employs a different measure of basketball success—the number of rounds through which the school's team advanced in March Madness in the spring before the applications were filed the next fall.[7] Mixon's estimate was positive and statistically significant, suggesting that the average SAT score in the entering class increased by 1.7 points for each additional round the school's team was in the tournament.

Toma and Cross examine the records for the thirteen different universities that won the FBS football championship between 1979 and 1992 and the eleven different universities that won the NCAA men's basketball tournament over the same period.[8] They track the quantity and quality of undergraduate applications for five years preceding and succeeding the championship for each of these schools. They find a clear correlation between winning a championship and the number of applicants but are unable to identify any measurable impact of a championship on the quality of admitted or entering students.

Zimbalist uses data from eighty-six FBS colleges from 1980 through 1995 and performs a variety of fixed-effect multiple regressions, using different measures of athletic success.[9] The tests reveal that, while there is some tendency for athletic success to increase applications, there is no significant relationship between athletic success and average SAT scores.

In a study under commission from the NCAA, Litan, Orszag, and Orszag use a fixed-effects model for 1993–2001 and are unable to find a statistically significant relationship between football winning percentage and SAT scores of the incoming class.[10]

Tucker considers evidence from 1990, 1996, 2000, 2001, and 2002 from seventy-eight Division I schools.[11] He finds that after 1996, football success has a positive impact on the average SAT scores of the incoming class. He argues that the perfection of the Bowl Championship Series played a central role in bringing increased attention and, hence, advertising exposure to the top football programs.

Smith, in contrast, considers data from Division I schools during 1994–2005 and finds little evidence to support a link between different measures of men's basketball success and four measurements of student quality.[12] The one exception was that schools that had a "breakout" year (lagged two years) experienced an 8.86 point average increase in the SAT scores of the seventy-fifth percentile of the entering class. "Breakout" was defined in various ways but basically denoted that a school went from a perennial losing record to a strong winning record.

Pope and Pope, using a data set from 330 Division I schools during 1983–2002, find that certain types of athletic success appear to increase interest in a school from applicants with high, medium, and low SAT scores but that the increase in enrollments from the students with SAT scores above 600 in English and in math is weaker and less reliable.[13] Indeed, for some of the athletic-performance variables, the relationship between athletic success and the log of enrollment is significantly negative. Further, any impact tends to be in the next year, with no significant effect after two or three years. In the end, Pope and Pope conclude that "the summary data . . . would suggest that athletically successful schools actually saw slightly lower long-run growth in applications and enrollments."[14] One important caveat in interpreting these results is that Pope and Pope test fixed-effect multiple regressions with control variables and thirty-two athletic-performance variables. At a .10 level of significance, one would anticipate that 3.2 variables would achieve statistical significance randomly. The authors should have, but did not, control for the multiplicity problem.[15] Multicollinearity among the performance variables presents another challenge in interpreting the coefficients.[16]

Pope and Pope use a Division I data set of 332 schools during 1994–2001 to test the impact of men's basketball and football on the propensity of high school applicants to send their SAT scores to a school.[17] They find that a school with stellar results in either sport receives on average up to 10 percent higher SAT scores. They also find that the relationship is stronger for some demographic subgroups, such as males, people of color, out-of-state students, and high school athletes. They do not test for actual applications to the school or for eventual enrollments. Pope and Pope model one- to three-year lags and find that the statistical significance of sports success "decays very quickly across time."[18]

In sum, the various studies lend some support to the notion that robust athletic success can lead to an increase in applications to a school. The correlate of this proposition is that poor athletic performance can lead to falling applications. There is only weak support, if any, for the claim that sport success leads to an increase in the quality of students. The increase in applications in some cases, however, may assist a school in filling empty beds in its dormitories. These conclusions are supported anecdotally by a self study done at the University of Massachusetts following its ascent to basketball fame in the mid-1990s under John Calipari.

> The period from fall 1988 to fall 1990 did not include outstanding basketball years. In 1991, UMass was a semi-finalist in the NIT and in the four years since has been featured consistently on national television, has been ranked consistently in the top twenty and has gone to the NCAA tournament. . . . It is clear that after double digit declines in out-of-state applications from fall 1988 to fall 1991, we experienced two years of double digit increases in fall 1993 and 1994. It has been suggested that this bump in applications might be related to, among other things, the greater awareness of the university beyond Massachusetts, at least partially as a result of the success in basketball.
>
> It has been reported that the University of Connecticut experienced a similar application increase after their very successful Elite Eight season in 1991, with a 26 percent increase in out-of-state and 6 percent increase of in-state applications. Despite the growth of applications correlated with UConn basketball success, the conclusion was that there was no impact on yield (enrollment divided by admittances). With the numbers of applications up, it would also be expected that the quality of students enrolled might increase because of a larger pool on which to draw. The Connecticut experience indicates no changes in the quality of students. In the UMass figures there was a decrease in the SAT scores of applicants and enrolled students for both in- and out-of-state students. In fact, this [1995–96] was the first year that the SAT scores of out-of-state students fell below in-state. None of this suggests that team success carries beyond the application stage. In fact, in the year following the "Dream Season," UConn applications dropped back to earlier numbers. Their conclusion was that there was no lasting impact on the admission numbers.[19]

Athletic Success and Alumni Giving

Studies on alumni or other giving are less numerous and less complete. The primary reason for this is that the availability of data on alumni giving is spotty. Sigelman and Carter assemble data from the Council for Financial Aid to Education (CFAE) from 1966–67 to 1975–76 and test the relationship between the yearly change in total giving to the annual fund and athletic success, measured by win percentages in football and men's basketball and a dummy variable indicating whether the team participated in the postseason.[20] Sigelman and Carter do not find any statistically significant relationships between giving and athletic success and even note that some of the coefficients were negative.

Brooker and Klastorin critique the Sigelman and Carter study on the grounds that it does not control for institutional heterogeneity.[21] They adjust for this by using institutional fixed effects and find some positive and some negative relationships between athletic success and giving. Together, they run tests on 1,740 coefficients and find only 1.7 percent of them to be significant at the .10 level, which is fewer than the number that would be expected by chance. The authors do not report the magnitude of the effects.

Sigelman and Bookheimer introduce a fixed-effects model and break down alumni contributions into two components, restricted gifts to the athletics department and unrestricted gifts to the annual fund.[22] They find that the two types of giving are uncorrelated with each other and that only gifts to the athletics department are correlated with sport success (football, not basketball). More precisely, they estimate that a 10 percent increase in football win percentage over the previous four years leads to a $125,000 increase in donations to the athletics department (measured in 1983 dollars).

Grimes and Chressanthis focus on one school, Mississippi State, over a thirty-year period between 1962 and 1991.[23] They consider success of the football, basketball, and baseball teams. Winning success in football had a negative coefficient that was not statistically significant. Basketball's coefficient was significant at the .05 level and positive but extremely small.

Baade and Sundberg construct a data set from Division I schools during 1973–79.[24] They employ both winning percentage and bowl or March Madness appearances as measures of sport success. They find no impact on giving from increased winning percentages but a modest effect for postseason appearances. They do not distinguish between athletic and academic giving.

Rhoads and Gerking follow the modeling of Baade and Sundberg with data for 1986–87 to 1995–96.[25] They run their tests first without institutional fixed effects and find impacts very similar to those of Baade and Sundberg. They run the tests again with fixed effects, and none of the athletic success variables are statistically significant predictors of giving. Rhoads and Gerking also estimate that being placed on NCAA probation for a basketball violation reduces total giving by $1.6 million (measured in 1987 dollars).

Turner, Meserve, and Bowen consider a data set of fifteen private schools during 1988–89 to 1997–98.[26] Using a fixed-effects model, they find that football win percentage has no significant effect on the *rate* of giving among alumni in FBS programs but that it has a highly significant (at .01) and negative effect on the giving *amount* among alumni. Specifically, an increase of twelve wins is associated with a *decrease* in giving by $270 for an average person.

Humphreys and Mondello, based on 320 Division I schools from 1976 to 1996, find that postseason play was positively correlated with giving to athletics but not to giving to academics.[27] Stinson and Howard investigate 208 institutions from Divisions I-AA and I-AAA and find no correlation between giving to athletics and giving to academics.[28]

Athletic Success and State Budgetary Support

Three scholarly articles have explored the impact of university athletic success on legislative appropriations. Humphreys estimates a reduced form model with data from 1975 to 1996 that controls for state and institution specific characteristics.[29] He finds that state appropriations are 8 percent higher for institutions in FBS (formerly Division IA), other things equal. The presence of an increase in state support for having an FBS football team of $2.6 million on average (in 1982 dollars) may do little more than offset the additional net costs of fielding the team. Humphreys, however, does not find that either appearance in a bowl game or achieving a national ranking in the top twenty-five has a statistically significant impact on state appropriations.

Alexander and Kern consider 117 schools from FBS, FCS, and Division II for the period 1983–84 to 2006–7.[30] They do not explain why their sample is more heavily weighted to FBS or why certain schools were omitted. They find that increases in basketball and football win percentage for schools in FBS do produce a statistically significant increase in state appropriations, but appearances in major bowl games or in the NCAA Final Four do not. The three models that they test yield R-squares of .05, .05 and .08, suggesting that they are underspecified and calling into question the reliability of their coefficient estimates.

Jones uses a difference-in-difference model that focuses on six universities that transitioned from FCS to FBS between 2000 and 2010.[31] Jones finds that when the six schools are compared to all other FCS schools, there is no significant correlation between FBS affiliation and state appropriations. When the six schools are compared only to other FCS schools in the same region, there is still no significant correlation. Only when the comparison is made between FCS schools in the same region and within the same propensity score range does the move to FBS yield a significant relationship with state appropriations.[32] Jones concludes that this result provides some support for the hypothesis of a positive effect between NCAA subdivision and state support.

Anderson on Athletic Benefits

Anderson deploys the most sophisticated econometric treatment of the relationships between athletic success and various school outcome variables in the extant literature, uses the most recent data, and has been cited numerous times as representing the state of current knowledge on these matters.[33] Hence, his paper warrants a separate and more detailed discussion. He considers a data set for FBS schools from 1986 to 2009 and employs a propensity-score model to estimate these relationships. Anderson's motivation for adopting this framework is the difficulty of unraveling causality from observational data, especially given that selection bias (e.g., recruiting skill of coaches and administrators), reverse causality (e.g., athletic success begets donations, which are in turn spent to achieve greater athletic success), and confounding variables are probably present.[34]

Anderson's basic approach is to use bookmaker spreads for individual football games to establish (via a fifth-order polynomial logistic model) a probability of winning (the propensity score). Actual wins are then conditioned on the propensity score and used as the independent variable (or treatment). This method depends on the assumption that gambling is efficient (the bookmaker spread represents full and rationally processed information to determine the likelihood of contest outcome; put differently, all the relevant variables that impact a game's result are subsumed into the point spread).[35] Anderson then essentially runs school applications, SAT scores, and donations on the difference between the actual and the expected wins during a season. Thus, Anderson is estimating the effect of unexpected wins (losses) on his school outcome variables.

While it is interesting to know what the effect of unexpected wins is, it is probably a different effect than wins or general athletic success. Few people would question, for instance, that a football or men's basketball team that rises from sport oblivion to prominence in one year will experience an uptick in applications, donations, or state appropriations (see previous discussion of UMass/UConn.)[36] This is a different matter than a team perennially appearing in March's Elite Eight or Final Four or in the Football Championship Playoff.

Anderson does indeed find that unexpected wins are associated with increased applications, higher SAT scores, and increased donations to the athletics department (but not to the general fund). Notably, Anderson's strongest result is for donations to the athletics department, but this finding relies on a very incomplete data set on donations (495 observations for BCS[37] athletic donations versus 1,560 observations possible for sixty-five schools over twenty-four years). He also runs tests separately for the Power Five conferences within FBS and for the remaining FBS (or "Group of Five") conferences and finds that his relationships only hold for the Power Five schools.

Three other points from Anderson are worth noting. First, he finds little evidence that the positive effect of unexpected wins lasts more than one year. Second, his positive results appear to be considerably weaker than he claims. Thus, after correcting for multiple testing, none of his treatment variables are significant at the .05 level. His Alumni Athletic Operating Donations variable comes closest, with significance at the .053 level, but this variable is missing more than two-thirds of its possible observations, creating a possible selection bias.[38] Third, in his conclusion, Anderson misrepresents his own results when he states, "Consider a school that improves its season wins by three games. . . . This school may expect alumni athletic donations to increase by $409,000 (17%), applications to increase by 406 (3%)."[39] But Anderson is not looking at the net benefit of three wins; he is looking the net benefit of three wins over expectation. That is, if a team wins three more games but the betting markets expected that the team would win three more games, there would be no net benefit.

Summary of the Existing Literature

Overall, the literature on the impact of college sport success on the quantity and quality of applications and enrollments, donations to the athletics department and general fund, and state appropriations is mixed and somewhat inconclusive. When significant results have been found, they have tended to be small in practical magnitude. Much of the existing scholarship is limited by methodological issues and data availability, and most studies have not considered evidence from the 2000s. Each new study appears to use a new set of schools, conferences, or divisions; a different set of athletic success variables; distinct issues with missing data; and different modeling of the relationship between the treatment and outcome variable. Given the restructuring of the NCAA subdivisions and conferences, the emergence of conference-owned regional sports networks (RSNs) and attendant spurt in television revenues, the increased autonomy of the Power Five conferences, and the enhanced role of athletics in university finances and governance since 2000, it makes sense to examine the stability of the relationships between success in sports and possible indirect benefits for the school with more recent data. In what follows, we attempt to overcome some of the methodological issues of previous work and to construct a more up-to-date data set.

Our Data

Anderson found that for 1986–2009, the Power Five conferences are the most athletically prominent and the most likely to experience benefits from athletic success.[40] As an update, our data cover the eleven academic years from 2005–6 through 2015–16 (plus the three preceding years for lagged variables) for the sixty-five schools that were members of Power Five conferences in 2015–16.[41] Our data sources are the Council for Advancement and Support of Education annual Voluntary Support of Education (VSE) surveys, Integrated Postsecondary Education Data System (IPEDS) surveys, the National Center for Education Statistics for high school graduates, the US Census Bureau for demographic information, and Sports-Reference.com. The data are available through the colleges package for R, available on GitHub.[42]

Our school benefit response variables—summarized in table 4.1—include the number of applications (Applied, measured in thousands),

TABLE 4.1

DATA PROFILE, RESPONSE VARIABLES

Statistic	*N*	*Mean*	*St. dev.*	*Percentile (25)*	*Percentile (75)*
Applied	711	21.786	11.470	13.058	28.030
SAT75p	675	661.211	50.828	630.000	696.667
Donations	605	178.522	152.569	85.672	230.596
Athletics	356	20.128	14.453	11.939	26.523
NonAthletics	356	154.485	159.349	66.488	197.043
State	558	279.541	137.115	174.574	371.532
StatePC	557	58.073	26.899	39.911	71.806
Yield	711	0.408	0.111	0.338	0.459
Admit	711	0.591	0.214	0.453	0.762

the average seventy-fifth percentile SAT score across three portions of the exam (SAT75p), the admissions rate (Admit) and yield (Yield), donations to athletics by alumni (Athletics, in millions of dollars), total donations by alumni (Alumni, in millions of dollars), total nonathletic donations by alumni (NonAthletics) and total state appropriations to the school (State, in millions of dollars), also computed per student (StatePC, in thousands).

We note that for variables derived from IPEDS (acceptance rate, number of applicants, yield, and seventy-fifth percentile SAT score), we have nearly complete coverage, with only one school (Maryland) failing to report in multiple years. Notably, as is the case with Anderson's data set, the extent of the missing data for donations is much larger. We have athletic donations data for only 356 school years and total donations data for 605 school years out of a total possible 715 observations. The pattern of missing data in donations suggests a possible bias, as certain schools (mostly private, notably Notre Dame, Boston College, Miami [FL], Syracuse, Wake Forest) simply did not report donation data (the data are certainly not missing at random). Hence, our findings for the athletic donations response variable should be interpreted with caution. Of course, private schools do not receive state funding, but this does not fully account for the missing data for that variable—state-related schools like Penn State and Pittsburgh also did not report state funding. Many of these variables are strongly right-skewed, and in these cases, we have fit the model to their logarithm.

Our athletic success treatment variables—summarized in table 4.1—include measures of being good, great, and the best at both basketball and football. Specifically, for both sports, we record the cumulative winning percentage over the previous three seasons (BBWpct, FBWpct), as well as any Final Four appearances and national championships in any of the three preceding seasons.[43] Thus, we consider one-, two-, and three-year lags on the Final Four (BBFF1, BBFF2, BBFF3, and FBFF1, FBFF2, FBFF3 respectively) and championship variables (BBChamps1, BBChamps2, BBChamps3, and FBChamps1, FBChamps2, FBChamps3, respectively). The choice to include cumulative winning percentage over three years—as opposed to, say, winning percentage in each of the previous three years—was designed to smooth out year-to-year noise in winning percentage, while still reflecting relevant recent history.

Our control variables include median income per capita in the state (Income, in thousands of dollars), number of high school diplomas issued in the state in the previous year (HSDiplomas, in thousands), and state funding, both overall and per student (State and StatePC, respectively). These variables help account for variation in the income and population of each state, in addition to the support from state government (only relevant for public schools). While it may be the case that state household income is less relevant for private schools, such schools often draw regional interest and represent only about one-fifth of the schools considered. Further, to control for the unobserved heterogeneity of the sixty-five institutions, we tested both school (School) and year (Year) fixed effects, with both variables treated as categorical.[44] The fixed effect for School should capture the effect of the long-term branding value of the school's athletics program (i.e., Duke basketball), as well as many other attributes. The fixed effect for Year should capture changes due to inflation and other economic conditions.

TABLE 4.2

DATA PROFILE, EXPLANATORY VARIABLES

Statistic	*N*	*Mean*	*St. Dev.*	*Percentile (25)*	*Percentile (75)*
HSDiplomas	715	106.500	100.914	39.227	127.515
Income	715	26.349	3.709	23.797	28.351
BBFF1	715	0.046	0.210	0	0
BBFF2	715	0.045	0.207	0	0
BBFF3	715	0.045	0.207	0	0
BBWpct	715	0.599	0.124	0.514	0.694
BBChamps1	715	0.013	0.112	0	0
BBChamps2	715	0.011	0.105	0	0
BBChamps3	715	0.013	0.112	0	0
FBFF1	715	0.060	0.238	0	0
FBFF2	715	0.060	0.238	0	0
FBFF3	715	0.060	0.238	0	0
FBWpct	715	0.570	0.175	0.444	0.700
FBChamps1	715	0.015	0.123	0	0
FBChamps2	715	0.015	0.123	0	0
FBChamps3	715	0.015	0.123	0	0

The data in table 4.2 come exclusively from Sports-Reference and the US Census Bureau, and there are no missing data. As the number of high school diplomas awarded is right-skewed, we use the logarithm of this variable in our models.

Our Models

We tested a wide variety of models, including semi-logs, different lag patterns, and interactive effects, and focus here on the most important results (please see our data appendix for additional information).[45] Unless otherwise indicated, our standard errors are robust (using the HC1 sandwich variance-covariance matrix),[46] and our p-values are corrected for multiplicity via the Benjamini-Hochberg method, which controls the false discovery rate.[47] All computations were performed in R version 3.4.

See the following equation for our general regression model, where α is a vector of length 10 containing the fixed effects associated with each academic year (relative to 2005–6), γ is a vector of length 64 containing the fixed effects associated with each school (relative to the University of Alabama, which comes first alphabetically),[48] β_1 and β_2 are control variables associated with the number of high school diplomas granted in the previous year and the per capita income in the corresponding state, the θs are associated with the school's recent success in basketball, the λs are associated with the school's recent success in football, and the error term $\varepsilon \sim N(0, \sigma_\varepsilon)$, for some fixed value of σ_ε.[49]

$$y = \beta \cdot X + \varepsilon$$
$$y = \beta_0 + \alpha \cdot Year + \gamma \cdot School + \beta_1 \cdot \log(HSDiplomas) + \beta_2 \cdot Income$$
$$y + \theta_1 \cdot BBWpct + \theta_2 \cdot BBChamps1 + \theta_3 \cdot BBChamps2 + \theta_4 \cdot BBChamps3$$
$$y + \theta_5 \cdot BBFF1 + \theta_6 \cdot BBFF2 + \theta_7 \cdot BBFF3$$
$$y + \lambda_1 \cdot FBWpct + \lambda_2 \cdot FBChamps1 + \lambda_3 \cdot FBChamps2 + \lambda_4 \cdot FBChamps3$$
$$y + \lambda_5 \cdot FBFF1 + \lambda_6 \cdot FBFF2 + \lambda_7 \cdot FBFF3$$
$$y + \varepsilon,$$

Our Results

In each of the models we fit, School and Year (which is treated as a categorical variable) were statistically significant. For clarity of presentation, we relegate these results to our data appendix, but these effects capture much of the variability in the data. There are obvious broad trends, such as a general increase in the number of applications over time, and obvious school-specific effects for which these variables control. Multicollinearity among the explanatory variables of interest—as measured by generalized variance inflation factors[50]—does not appear to be problematic in these models.[51]

Athletic Success and the Quantity and Quality of Applications

Our first model, shown in the following equation, tests the effect of athletic success on school applications, and the results from this model are shown in table 4.3.

$$y_1 = log(Applied) = \beta_1 \cdot X + \varepsilon_1.$$

Out of the fourteen athletic-performance variables, only two are statistically significant at the .10 level: BBChamps2 and FBWpct. BBChamps2 is significant at the .05 level, and its coefficient (θ_3) indicates a national championship two years earlier is associated with a 10 percent increase in applications.[52] FBWpct is significant at the .001 level, and its coefficient (λ_1) indicates an additional win per year on average over the previous three seasons is associated with a 1.1 percent increase in applications.[53]

These results are consistent with the bulk of previous literature that big-time football and men's basketball success does provide an advertising (and/or anticipated quality-of-life) effect that boosts applications to a university. Two additional observations are in order. First, the effect for increasing win percentage in the regular season does not apply to basketball (after controlling for football), and for football, the magnitude of the effect is rather modest. Thus, direct advertising of a school's academic programs and campus life might be more effective in generating applications than investing in its basketball or football success is. Second, the other observed impact occurs only for the rarest of accomplishments (one out of sixty-five in each year): a national championship. Investing in creating a national championship basketball or football team entails very high risk for rather ordinary returns. Further, the returns in the form of increased applications appear to delay for one year and then dissipate by year three.

Table 4.3 also shows the results for a model for the rate of admissions. These results are highly consistent with the previous ones, due to the obvious functional dependence between the rate of admission and the number

TABLE 4.3

MODELS FOR APPLICANTS

	Dependent variable	
	LOG(APPLIED)	ADMIT
	(1)	(2)
log(HSDiplomas)	0.127 (0.124) p = 0.440	−0.086 (0.075) p = 0.399
Income	0.012 (0.011) p = 0.424	0.003 (0.006) p = 0.763
BBFF1	−0.014 (0.022) p = 0.676	−0.002 (0.013) p = 0.954
BBFF2	−0.030 (0.019) p = 0.209	−0.001 (0.020) p = 0.990
BBFF3	0.018 (0.024) p = 0.593	−0.008 (0.017) p = 0.826
BBWpct	0.067 (0.059) p = 0.412	−0.009 (0.036) p = 0.919
BBChamps1	0.059 (0.033) p = 0.145	−0.008 (0.020) p = 0.857
BBChamps2	0.095 (0.035) p = 0.016**	−0.003 (0.023) p = 0.094
BBChamps3	−0.010 (0.046) p = 0.855	0.018 (0.022) p = 0.605
FBFF1	0.031 (0.022) p = 0.270	−0.008 (0.009) p = 0.596
FBFF2	0.010 (0.021) p = 0.778	0.004 (0.008) p = 0.810
FBFF3	0.023 (0.020) p = 0.412	−0.005 (0.008) p = 0.713
FBWpct	0.144 (0.044) p = 0.004***	−0.053 (0.024) p = 0.077*
FBChamps1	0.013 (0.042) p = 0.832	−0.021 (0.015) p = 0.322
FBChamps2	0.045 (0.042) p = 0.424	−0.009 (0.017) p = 0.763
FBChamps3	0.042 (0.043) p = 0.459	0.004 (0.018) p = 0.919
Constant	1.810 (0.571) p = 0.005***	0.930 (0.336) p = 0.020**
Observations	711	711
R^2	0.955	0.920
Adjusted R^2	0.949	0.909
Residual Std. Error (df = 620)	0.115	0.065
F Statistic (df = 90; 620)	147.817***	79.434***

* $p < 0.1$; ** $p < 0.05$; *** $p < 0.01$

of applicants (the number of students is largely fixed at most schools). The negative coefficient for football winning percentage—the only variable to achieve statistical significance at the .10 level—implies that greater success in football is associated with higher selectivity.

Albeit tenuous, the existence of a statistically significant link between athletic success and applications leads to the next question: whether athletic success improves a school's admission yield (the percentage of admitted students who enroll). We ran the following equation to test this relationship.

$$y_3 = Yield = \beta_3 \cdot X + \varepsilon_3$$

Results for this model as shown in table 4.4. Of the fourteen athletic-performance variables, only one is statistically significant at the .10 level. FBWpct is significant at the .05 level with an association between an extra regular-season win on average over the previous three years and an increased yield of 0.476 percentage points; that is, a yield of 30 percent would increase to 30.476 percent. While football's impact appears to be statistically significant but small, performance of the men's basketball team does not have a statistically significant impact on yield.

If athletic success may lead to an uptick in applications, even with a steady yield, the school may become more selective. Greater selectivity, in turn, may lead to an improvement in the quality of the student body, often represented by a school's SAT scores.

In the following equation, we test what impact athletic success has on the seventy-fifth percentile of SAT scores across the three sections of the exam (math, English, writing) for the sixty-five Power Five schools in our sample.

$$y_4 = SAT75p = \beta_4 \cdot X + \varepsilon_4$$

The results from this model are also shown in table 4.4. Only one of the fourteen athletic-performance variables achieve statistical significance at the .10 level: BBWpct. The coefficient of BBWpct (θ_1) implies that every

TABLE 4.4

MODELS FOR ADMISSIONS

	Dependent variable	
	SAT75P	YIELD
	(1)	(2)
log(HSDiplomas)	17.070 (14.516)	0.082 (0.059)
	p = 0.397	p = 0.255
Income	−1.457 (1.033)	0.001 (0.005)
	p = 0.286	p = 0.880
BBFF1	0.108 (3.459)	0.003 (0.012)
	p = 0.980	p = 0.902
BBFF2	−0.100 (3.914)	0.015 (0.022)
	p = 0.980	p = 0.627
BBFF3	1.963 (3.631)	0.0002 (0.013)
	p = 0.741	p = 0.887
BBWpct	17.937 (7.451)	−0.002 (0.013)
	p = 0.041**	p = 0.987
BBChamps1	−7.067 (6.423)	0.0003 (0.017)
	p = 0.418	p = 0.987
BBChamps2	−0.140 (5.528)	−0.019 (0.022)
	p = 0.980	p = 0.512
BBChamps3	−2.869 (6.094)	−0.001 (0.015)
	p = 0.787	p = 0.980
FBFF1	−9.598 (7.237)	−0.001 (0.009)
	p = 0.327	p = 0.944
FBFF2	1.231 (3.781)	−0.005 (0.007)
	p = 0.874	p = 0.573
FBFF3	−7.317 (6.818)	−0.011 (0.008)
	p = 0.426	p = 0.241
FBWpct	−4.963 (6.418)	0.062 (0.023)
	p = 0.600	p = 0.019**
FBChamps1	7.934 (9.794)	−0.002 (0.014)
	p = 0.589	p = 0.944
FBChamps2	−1.843 (4.135)	−0.012 (0.016)
	p = 0.798	p = 0.586
FBChamps3	−0.445 (9.155)	−0.020 (0.011)
	p = 0.980	p = 0.139
Constant	580.580 (55.642)	0.152 (0.265)
	p = 0.000***	p = 0.698
Observations	675	711
R^2	0.925	0.803
Adjusted R^2	0.914	0.775
Residual Std. Error (df = 620)	14.941 (df = 585)	0.053 (df = 620)
F Statistic (df = 90; 620)	81.070*** (df = 89; 585)	28.153*** (df = 90; 620)

* p < 0.1; ** p < 0.05; *** p < 0.01

regular-season win on average over three years is associated with a 0.6 point increase in the average across the English, writing, and math portions of the SAT for the seventy-fifth percentile of the school's student body—a statistically significant effect with no practical impact.

Athletic Success and Alumni Giving

Our next test explores the relationship between alumni donations and athletic success. As was the case with Anderson,[54] who also relied on data from the annual survey of the Council for Aid to Education, there is a substantial problem with missing data. Many of the respondent schools simply do not answer the survey questions on alumni donations or do not do so completely or on a regular annual basis. In Anderson's data set, approximately two-thirds of donation data are missing; in ours, approximately 15 percent of overall donations and about half of athletics donations are missing (359 out of 715). Accordingly, although there is no obvious pattern to which schools did not report, our results must be interpreted with caution. The following equation examines the relationship between alumni donations to athletics and athletic performance, with the standard control variables. Its results are shown in table 4.5.

$$y_5 = log(Athletics) = \beta_5 \cdot X + \varepsilon_5$$

None of the fourteen athletic-performance variables is statistically significant at the .10 level.[55]

The following equation examines the relationship between donations to the school's general fund minus athletic donations (Non-Athletic Donations) and athletic performance.

$$y_6 = log(NonAthletics) = \beta_6 \cdot X + \varepsilon_6$$

Only one of the fourteen athletic-performance variables is statistically significant at the .10 level: FBWpct. However, the effect size—an expected increase of 1.94 percent for each additional victory per year—is small. Nine of the fourteen coefficients had negative signs.

TABLE 4.5

MODELS FOR DONATIONS

	Dependent variable	
	LOG(ATHLETICS) (1)	LOG(NONATHLETICS) (2)
log(HSDiplomas)	−0.453 (1.144) p = 0.932	0.508 (0.331) p = 0.269
Income	0.040 (0.090) p = 0.919	0.068 (0.029) p = 0.058*
BBFF1	−0.118 (0.307) p = 0.932	0.123 (0.085) p = 0.292
BBFF2	0.014 (0.151) p = 0.978	−0.027 (0.068) p = 0.887
BBFF3	0.113 (0.137) p = 0.919	0.010 (0.058) p = 0.929
BBWpct	0.331 (0.510) p = 0.919	−0.020 (0.183) p = 0.952
BBChamps1	−0.092 (0.290) p = 0.932	−0.052 (0.171) p = 0.893
BBChamps2	−0.153 (0.254) p = 0.919	0.036 (0.080) p = 0.876
BBChamps3	−0.349 (0.194) p = 0.629	0.020 (0.075) p = 0.893
FBFF1	0.027 (0.328) p = 0.978	−0.087 (0.086) p = 0.584
FBFF2	0.349 (0.333) p = 0.919	−0.046 (0.067) p = 0.759
FBFF3	0.203 (0.269) p = 0.919	−0.120 (0.071) p = 0.201
FBWpct	0.321 (0.273) p = 0.919	0.250 (0.111) p = 0.071*
FBChamps1	−0.310 (0.589) p = 0.919	−0.053 (0.103) p = 0.838
FBChamps2	0.045 (0.408) p = 0.978	−0.141 (0.094) p = 0.274
FBChamps3	0.365 (0.382) p = 0.919	−0.027 (0.123) p = 0.917
Constant	3.079 (5.783) p = 0.919	1.039 (1.559) p = 0.759
Observations	356	356
R^2	0.709	0.939
Adjusted R^2	0.636	0.924
Residual Std. Error (df = 284)	0.589	0.213
F Statistic (df = 71; 284)	9.725***	61.789***

* p < 0.1; ** p < 0.05; *** p < 0.01

Athletic Success and State Budgetary Support

Our final model in the following equation was on the relationship between academic performance and state funding for public universities. The results are shown in table 4.6.

$$y_7 = State = \beta_7 \cdot X + \varepsilon_7$$

Three of the fourteen athletic-performance variables were significant at the .10 level: BBFF1, FBFF1, and FBFF2.

The nominal interpretation of the first coefficient (θ_5) is that a Final Four appearance in the previous basketball season is associated with a 5.3 percent increase in state funding. However, this is nearly offset by a −3.9 decrease associated with actually winning the championship, although this effect is not statistically significant. It is hard to square the idea that teams that reach the Final Four tend to receive greater increases in state funding than teams that win the championship do.

Further muddying the waters is the fact that the effects on the football side show the same offsetting pattern but in the opposite direction (negative for reaching the Final Four, positive for winning the championship).

When we consider the state funding per capita (as in table 4.6), the statistical significance of all variables save for FBFF1 disappears, and the direction of the effect remains negative.

Conclusion

Previous literature on the effect of athletic success on applications, quality of the student body, donations, and state funding has been inconclusive. Researchers have employed different methodologies and models, and most have been limited by incomplete data. We develop a recent data set for the Power Five conferences during the eleven years from 2006 through 2016 and use fixed-effects linear regression models to retest these relationships. We report robust standard errors and control for multiple testing.

TABLE 4.6

MODELS FOR FUNDING

	Dependent variable	
	LOG(STATE)	LOG(STATEPC)
	(1)	(2)
log(HSDiplomas)	−0.103 (0.198) p = 0.705	−0.024 (0.177) p = 0.905
Income	−0.028 (0.031) p = 0.471	−0.032 (0.023) p = 0.214
BBFF1	0.052 (0.023) p = 0.044**	0.049 (0.030) p = 0.154
BBFF2	0.032 (0.029) p = 0.377	0.037 (0.034) p = 0.338
BBFF3	−0.005 (0.041) p = 0.937	−0.011 (0.050) p = 0.870
BBWpct	0.042 (0.117) p = 0.800	0.059 (0.095) p = 0.623
BBChamps1	−0.040 (0.043) p = 0.471	−0.071 (0.058) p = 0.296
BBChamps2	−2.869 (6.094) p = 0.787	−0.058 (0.052) p = 0.334
BBChamps3	−0.016 (0.052) p = 0.823	−0.017 (0.069) p = 0.867
FBFF1	−0.064 (0.031) p = 0.073*	−0.079 (0.031) p = 0.019**
FBFF2	−0.059 (0.029) p = 0.079*	−0.039 (0.031) p = 0.276
FBFF3	−0.035 (0.027) p = 0.286	−0.028 (0.025) p = 0.338
FBWpct	−0.159 (0.155) p = 0.411	−0.023 (0.109) p = 0.870
FBChamps1	0.073 (0.041) p = 0.129	0.094 (0.056) p = 0.151
FBChamps2	0.057 (0.052) p = 0.387	0.041 (0.067) p = 0.623
FBChamps3	0.011 (0.034) p = 0.823	0.006 (0.045) p = 0.905
Constant	5.863 (1.225) p = 0.00001***	4.190 (0.966) p = 0.00005***
Observations	558	557
R^2	0.949	0.942
Adjusted R^2	0.941	0.933
Residual Std. Error (df = 481)	0.216	0.177
F Statistic (df = = 76; 481)	117.728***	103.449***

* $p < 0.1$; ** $p < 0.05$; *** $p < 0.01$

We find that certain measures of football success have a modest positive and short-lived impact on student applications but no clear impact on admission yield or on the quality of the student body. Although hampered by incomplete data, we also find that athletic success does not have a statistically significant effect on donations. Final Four appearances in both basketball and football show some statistical significance associated with state funding, but the direction and robustness of these findings is unclear.

Please see the ANOVA tables in appendix A for all models discussed in this chapter. Note the persistent statistical significance of the Year and School terms.

Appendix A: ANOVA Tables

TABLE 4.A.1

ANOVA TABLE FOR LOG (APPLIED)

	Df	*Sum Sq*	*Mean Sq*	*F Value*	*Pr(>F)*
Year	10	26.197	2.620	198.729	0.000
school_name	64	148.990	2.328	176.601	0.000
log(hs_diplomas_lag1)	1	0.008	0.008	0.578	0.447
per_capita_income	1	0.008	0.008	0.602	0.438
bball_avg_wpct_lag3	1	0.020	0.020	1.5474	0.214
bb_champs_lag1	1	0.011	0.011	0.867	0.352
bb_champs_lag2	1	0.056	0.056	4.278	0.039
bb_champs_lag3	1	0.008	0.008	0.613	0.434
fball_avg_wpct_lag3	1	0.288	0.288	21.859	0.000
fb_champs_lag1	1	0.016	0.016	1.241	0.266
fb_champs_lag2	1	0.023	0.023	1.777	0.183
fb_champs_lag3	1	0.036	0.036	2.749	0.098
Residuals	626	8.252	0.013		

TABLE 4.A.2

ANOVA TABLE FOR SAT75P

	Df	*Sum Sq*	*Mean Sq*	*F Value*	*Pr(>F)*
Year	10	12,802.322	12,802.322	5.654	0.000
school_name	63	1,591,052.696	25,254.805	111.543	0.000
log(hs_diplomas_lag1)	1	417.541	417.541	1.844	0.175
per_capita_income	1	400.511	400.511	1.769	0.184
bball_avg_wpct_lag3	1	1199.903	1199.903	5.300	0.022
bb_champs_lag1	1	278.781	278.781	1.231	0.268
bb_champs_lag2	1	8.558	8.558	0.038	0.846
bb_champs_lag3	1	20.627	20.627	0.091	0.763
fball_avg_wpct_lag3	1	865.252	865.252	3.822	0.051
fb_champs_lag1	1	0.010	0.010	0.000	0.995
fb_champs_lag2	1	7.444	7.444	0.033	0.856
fb_champs_lag3	1	394.777	394.777	1.744	0.187
Residuals	591	133,810.192	226.413		

TABLE 4.A.3

ANOVA TABLE FOR LOG (DONATIONS)

	Df	*Sum Sq*	*Mean Sq*	*F Value*	*Pr(>F)*
Year	10	9.510	9.510	33.107	0.000
school_name	59	241.490	4.093	142.499	0.000
log(hs_diplomas_lag1)	1	0.176	0.176	6.141	0.014
per_capita_income	1	0.302	0.302	10.500	0.001
bball_avg_wpct_lag3	1	0.000	0.000	0.011	0.918
bb_champs_lag1	1	0.005	0.005	0.180	0.671
bb_champs_lag2	1	0.015	0.015	0.510	0.476
bb_champs_lag3	1	0.028	0.028	0.988	0.321
fball_avg_wpct_lag3	1	0.204	0.204	7.100	0.008
fb_champs_lag1	1	0.016	0.016	0.573	0.450
fb_champs_lag2	1	0.001	0.001	0.027	0.870
fb_champs_lag3	1	0.030	0.030	1.033	0.310
Residuals	525	15.080	0.029		

TABLE 4.A.4

ANOVA TABLE FOR LOG (ATHLETICS)

	Df	*Sum Sq*	*Mean Sq*	*F Value*	*Pr(>F)*
Year	10	10.467	1.047	3.028	0.001
school_name	45	225.721	5.016	14.513	0.000
log(hs_diplomas_lag1)	1	0.051	0.051	0.147	0.702
per_capita_income	1	0.071	0.071	0.204	0.652
bball_avg_wpct_lag3	1	0.125	0.125	0.362	0.548
bb_champs_lag1	1	0.045	0.045	0.129	0.720
bb_champs_lag2	1	0.002	0.002	0.005	0.941
bb_champs_lag3	1	0.078	0.078	0.226	0.635
fball_avg_wpct_lag3	1	0.647	0.647	1.8722	0.172
fb_champs_lag1	1	0.446	0.446	1.289	0.257
fb_champs_lag2	1	0.150	0.150	0.433	0.511
fb_champs_lag3	1	0.4360	0.436	1.263	0.262
Residuals	290	100.232	0.346		

TABLE 4.A.5

ANOVA TABLE FOR LOG (NONATHLETICS)

	Df	*Sum Sq*	*Mean Sq*	*F Value*	*Pr(>F)*
Year	10	8.851	0.885	19.548	0.000
school_name	45	188.907	4.198	92.717	0.000
log(hs_diplomas_lag1)	1	0.066	0.066	1.457	0.228
per_capita_income	1	0.316	0.316	6.979	0.009
bball_avg_wpct_lag3	1	0.000	0.000	0.001	0.977
bb_champs_lag1	1	0.006	0.006	0.140	0.708
bb_champs_lag2	1	0.001	0.001	0.016	0.898
bb_champs_lag3	1	0.010	0.010	0.226	0.635
fball_avg_wpct_lag3	1	0.157	0.157	3.462	0.064
fb_champs_lag1	1	0.024	0.024	0.523	0.470
fb_champs_lag2	1	0.066	0.066	1.459	0.228
fb_champs_lag3	1	0.023	0.023	0.517	0.473
Residuals	290	13.130	0.045		

TABLE 4.A.6

ANOVA TABLE FOR LOG (STATE)

	Df	*Sum Sq*	*Mean Sq*	*F Value*	*Pr(>F)*
Year	10	1.997	0.200	4.294	0.000
school_name	50	414.854	8.297	178.446	0.000
log(hs_diplomas_lag1)	1	0.003	0.003	0.066	0.798
per_capita_income	1	0.094	0.094	2.013	0.157
bball_avg_wpct_lag3	1	0.006	0.006	0.125	0.724
bb_champs_lag1	1	0.004	0.004	0.096	0.756
bb_champs_lag2	1	0.003	0.003	0.067	0.796
bb_champs_lag3	1	0.000	0.000	0.004	0.950
fball_avg_wpct_lag3	1	0.075	0.075	1.607	0.205
fb_champs_lag1	1	0.003	0.003	0.063	0.801
fb_champs_lag2	1	0.001	0.001	0.019	0.891
fb_champs_lag3	1	0.004	0.004	0.086	0.770
Residuals	487	22.644	0.046		

TABLE 4.A.7

ANOVA TABLE FOR LOG (STATEPC)

	Df	*Sum Sq*	*Mean Sq*	*F Value*	*Pr(>F)*
Year	10	5.056	5.056	16.124	0.000
school_name	50	240.754	4.815	153.543	0.000
log(hs_diplomas_lag1)	1	0.002	0.002	0.061	0.804
per_capita_income	1	0.106	0.106	3.387	0.066
bball_avg_wpct_lag3	1	0.022	0.022	0.690	0.407
bb_champs_lag1	1	0.000	0.000	0.004	0.953
bb_champs_lag2	1	0.006	0.006	0.202	0.653
bb_champs_lag3	1	0.004	0.004	0.139	0.710
fball_avg_wpct_lag3	1	0.027	0.027	0.861	0.354
fb_champs_lag1	1	0.005	0.005	0.167	0.683
fb_champs_lag2	1	0.001	0.001	0.042	0.838
fb_champs_lag3	1	0.003	0.003	0.083	0.774
Residuals	486	15.241	0.031		

TABLE 4.A.8

ANOVA TABLE FOR YIELD

	Df	*Sum Sq*	*Mean Sq*	*F Value*	*Pr(>F)*
Year	10	0.823	0.082	29.646	0.000
school_name	64	6.200	6.200	34.880	0.000
log(hs_diplomas_lag1)	1	0.007	0.007	2.608	0.107
per_capita_income	1	0.000	0.000	0.151	0.698
bball_avg_wpct_lag3	1	0.000	0.000	0.117	0.732
bb_champs_lag1	1	0.001	0.001	0.395	0.530
bb_champs_lag2	1	0.000	0.000	0.021	0.884
bb_champs_lag3	1	0.000	0.000	0.001	0.976
fball_avg_wpct_lag3	1	0.022	0.022	7.883	0.005
fb_champs_lag1	1	0.000	0.000	0.057	0.812
fb_champs_lag2	1	0.002	0.002	0.825	0.364
fb_champs_lag3	1	0.008	0.008	2.791	0.095
Residuals	626	1.739	0.003		

TABLE 4.A.9

ANOVA TABLE FOR ADMIT

	Df	*Sum Sq*	*Mean Sq*	*F Value*	*Pr(>F)*
Year	10	0.364	0.036	8.796	0.000
school_name	64	29.422	0.460	111.044	0.000
log(hs_diplomas_lag1)	1	0.009	0.009	2.088	0.149
per_capita_income	1	0.002	0.002	0.494	0.482
bball_avg_wpct_lag3	1	0.001	0.001	0.257	0.612
bb_champs_lag1	1	0.002	0.002	0.367	0.545
bb_champs_lag2	1	0.001	0.001	0.256	0.613
bb_champs_lag3	1	0.000	0.000	0.017	0.896
fball_avg_wpct_lag3	1	0.034	0.034	8.164	0.004
fb_champs_lag1	1	0.007	0.007	1.604	0.206
fb_champs_lag2	1	0.001	0.001	0.321	0.571
fb_champs_lag3	1	0.000	0.000	0.000	0.990
Residuals	626	2.592	0.004		

NOTES

1. NCAA, *Revenues and Expenses of Division I Intercollegiate Athletics Program, 2004–2016* (Indianapolis: NCAA, 2017).

2. Jonathan M. Orszag and Peter R. Orszag, *The Physical Capital Stock Used in Collegiate Athletics* (Indianapolis: NCAA, 2005).
3. Robert E. McCormick and Maurice Tinsley, "Athletics Versus Academics? Evidence from SAT Scores," *Journal of Political Economy* 95:1103–16, 1987.
4. Dale S. Bremmer and Randall G. Kesselring, "The Advertising Effect of University Athletic Success: A Reappraisal of the Evidence," *Quarterly Review of Economics and Finance* 33:409–21, 1993.
5. Irvin B. Tucker and Louis Amato, "Does Big-Time Success in Football or Basketball Affect SAT Scores?," *Economics of Education Review* 12:177–81, 1993.
6. Robert G. Murphy and Gregory A. Trandel, "The Relation between a University's Football Record and the Size of Its Applicant Pool," *Economics of Education Review* 13:265–70, 1994.
7. Franklin G. Mixon Jr., "Athletics versus Academics? Rejoining the Evidence from SAT Scores," *Education Economics* 3:277–83, 1995. Mixon also coauthored two cross-sectional studies based on data from 1990 and 1993 that found a relationship between athletic success or prominence and the attraction of a school to out-of-state residents. Franklin Mixon and Yu Hsing, "The Determinants of Out-of-State Enrollments in Higher Education: A Tobit Analysis," *Economics of Education Review* 13:329–35, 1994; Franklin Mixon and Rand Ressler, "An Empirical Note on the Impact of College Athletics on Tuition Revenues," *Applied Economics Letters* 2:383–87, 1995.
8. J. Douglas Toma and Michael E. Cross, "Intercollegiate Athletics and Student College Choice: Exploring the Impact of Championship Seasons on Undergraduate Applications," *Research in Higher Education* 39:633–61, 1998.
9. Andrew Zimbalist, *Unpaid Professionals: Commercialism and Conflict in Big-Time College Sports* (Princeton, NJ: Princeton University Press, 2001).
10. Robert E. Litan, Jonathan M. Orszag, and Peter R. Orszag, *The Empirical Effects of Collegiate Athletics: An Interim Report* (Washington, DC: Sebago Associates, 2003). For a summary of the literature through 2004, see Robert Frank, *Challenging the Myth: A Review of the Links among College Athletic Success, Student Quality, and Donations* (Miami: Knight Foundation Commission on Intercollegiate Athletics, 2004).
11. Irvin B. Tucker, "Big-Time Pigskin Success: Is There an Advertising Effect?," *Journal of Sports Economics* 6:222–29, 2005.
12. D. Randall Smith, "Big-Time College Basketball and the Advertising Effect: Does Success Really Matter?," *Journal of Sports Economics* 9:387–406, 2008.
13. Devin G. Pope and Jaren C. Pope, "Understanding College Application Decisions: Why College Sports Success Matters," *Journal of Sports Economics* 15:107–31, 2014.
14. Devin G. Pope and Jaren C. Pope, "The Impact of College Sports Success on the Quantity and Quality of Student Applications," *Southern Economic Journal* 75:773, 2009.
15. See, for instance, Yoav Benjamini and Yosef Hochberg, "Controlling the False Discovery Rate: A Practical and Powerful Approach to Multiple Testing," *Journal of the Royal Statistical Society. Series B (Methodological)* 57:289–300, 1995.
16. Castle and Kostelnik examine fourteen Division II schools in Pennsylvania during 1995–2004 and find weak evidence that some measures of athletic success were correlated with an increase in applications and the SAT scores of the entering class. Joshua Castle and Robert Kostelnik, "The Effects of an Institution's Athletic Success on the Future Freshmen Application Pool at NCAA Division II Universities," *Journal of Issues in Intercollegiate Athletics* 4:411–27, 2011. Three studies found that football success was associated with lower student grades; see Charles Clotfelter, *Big-Time College Sports in American Universities* (New York: Cambridge University Press, 2011); Jason M. Lindo, Isaac D. Swensen, and Glen R. Waddell, "Are Big-Time Sports a Threat to

Student Achievement?," *American Economic Journal: Applied Economics* 4:254–74, 2012; and Rey Hernández-Julián and Kurt W. Rotthoff, "The Impact of College Football on Academic Achievement," *Economics of Education Review* 43:141–47, 2014.

17. Pope and Pope, "Understanding College Application Decisions."

18. Ibid., 128.

19. Massachusetts Football Task Force, *Final Report of the I-A Football Task Force* (Boston: University of Massachusetts, 1996).

20. Lee Sigelman and Robert Carter, "Win One for the Giver? Alumni Giving and Big-Time College Sports," *Social Science Quarterly* 60:284–94, 1979.

21. George W. Brooker and Theodore D. Klastorin, "To the Victors Belong the Spoils? College Athletics and Alumni Giving," *Social Science Quarterly* 62:744–50, 1981.

22. Sigelman and Carter, "Win One for the Giver?"

23. Paul W. Grimes and George A. Chressanthis, "Alumni Contributions to Academics: The Role of Intercollegiate Sports and NCAA Sanctions," *American Journal of Economics and Sociology* 53:27–40, 1994.

24. Robert A. Baade and Jeffrey O. Sundberg, "What Determines Alumni Generosity?," *Economics of Education Review* 15:75–82, 1996.

25. Thomas A. Rhoads and Shelby Gerking, "Educational Contributions, Academic Quality, and Athletic Success," *Contemporary Economic Policy* 18:248–58, 2000. Goff also considers the impact of sport success on the endowment. Goff, however, looks at endowment data only for two schools, Georgia Tech and Northwestern. While he finds no statistically significant relationship between sport success and donations at Georgia Tech, Goff does find one at Northwestern. However, Goff notes that the finding for Northwestern may have been affected by an accounting change at the school (moving a substantial amount of cash into long-term equity during the period studied). In any event, the data base is much too thin to assign much importance to these results. Brian Goff, "Effects of University Athletics on the University: A Review and Extension of Empirical Assessment," *Journal of Sport Management* 14:85–104, 2000.

26. Sarah E. Turner, Lauren A. Meserve, and William G. Bowen, "Winning and Giving a Study of the Responsiveness of Giving to Performance on the Field," *Social Science Quarterly* 82:812–26, 2001.

27. Brad R. Humphreys and Michael Mondello, "Intercollegiate Athletic Success and Donations at NCAA Division I Institutions," *Journal of Sport Management* 21:265–80, 2007.

28. Jeffrey L. Stinson and Dennis R. Howard, "Winning Does Matter: Patterns in Private Giving to Athletic and Academic Programs at NCAA Division I-AA and I-AAA Institutions," *Sport Management Review* 11:1–20, 2008. Koo and Dittmore, based on an unexplained sample of 155 schools from Divisions I, II, and III during 2002–3 to 2011–12, purport to find a positive correlation between athletic giving lagged one year and current academic giving. They conclude that athletic giving does not crowd out academic giving. They do not offer an explanation of why they lag athletic giving; any crowding out would presumably happen in the same year. It is also not clear what their full model is and whether, for instance, they detrended their data or used time-fixed effects. Gi-Yong Koo and Stephen W. Dittmore, "Effects of Intercollegiate Athletics on Private Giving in Higher Education," *Journal of Issues in Intercollegiate Athletics* 7:1–16, 2014. Walker uses a sample of between 954 and 1,052 schools during 2002–11 and finds that appearances in the Final Four are significantly associated with increases in private donations, but, again, he does not break out athletic and academic donations and does not provide a full description of his model. Adam G. Walker, "Division I Intercollegiate Athletics Success and the Financial Impact on Universities," *SAGE Open* 5:1–13, 2015.

29. Brad R. Humphreys, "The Relationship between Big-Time College Football and State Appropriations for Higher Education," *International Journal of Sport Finance* 1:119–28, 2006. There was a prior study to Humphreys's, but it was based on only one year (1980–81) and fifty-two Division IA schools. Cletus C. Coughlin and O. Homer Erekson, "Determinants of State Aid and Voluntary Support of Higher Education," *Economics of Education Review* 5:179–90, 1986.

30. Donald L. Alexander and William Kern, "Does Athletic Success Generate Legislative Largess from Sports-Crazed Representatives? The Impact of Athletic Success on State Appropriations to Colleges and Universities," *International Journal of Sport Finance* 5:253–67, 2010.

31. Willis A. Jones, "High-Level Football and Appropriations to Universities: Are Sports-Crazed Representatives Responsive to NCAA Divisional Affiliation?," *Journal of Education Finance* 40:438–55, 2015.

32. Jones's propensity score includes a number of school characteristics, including size, percentage of full-time students, percentage of graduate students, degree of institutional urbanization, freshmen retention rate, and total education expenditures.

33. Michael L. Anderson, "The Benefits of College Athletic Success: An Application of the Propensity Score Design," *Review of Economics and Statistics* 99:119–34, 2017.

34. Reverse causality would not appear to be a significant issue when considering applications or SAT scores and athletic success. That is, while it may be logical to expect athletic success to increase applications or SAT scores, it does not seem plausible that more applications or higher SAT scores would engender greater athletic success. Top football and basketball players in FBS are recruited and, by all accounts, base their decisions on factors related to the athletics program. The effects of confounding variables, such as the managerial talent of a school president or provost, along with other unquantifiable attributes, could be accounted for by team fixed effects. Reverse causality may be an issue with athletic success and donations. In such a case, however, one would expect that the presence of reverse causality would strengthen the estimated correlation between the variables. Since Anderson's use of a propensity score is intended to mitigate the impact of reverse causality, other things equal, one would expect his model to imply a weaker correlation between athletic success and donations, contrary to his findings.

35. For this crucial assumption to be statistically valid, the R^2 from this equation must be very high, approaching 1. Anderson, however, does not mention what the R^2 is in this test. It is nonetheless true that the literature on sports betting markets indicates that they operate efficiently. See, for example, the discussion in Michael Lopez, Gregory J. Matthews, and Benjamin S. Baumer, "How Often Does the Best Team Win? A Unified Approach to Understanding Randomness in North American Sport," *Annals of Applied Statistics*, arXiv:1701.05976, 2018.

36. Such a finding would be consistent with the empirical work of Smith ("Big-Time College Basketball and the Advertising Effect") and his "breakout" variable.

37. BCS stands for "Bowl Championship Series" and refers to universities prior to 2014 in today's Power Five conferences plus the former Big East conference. The BCS conferences were sometimes referred to as the "AQ" or "automatic qualifying" conferences.

38. Anderson, "Benefits of College Athletic Success," Table 3, 127. In his conclusion (132), Anderson suggests that school investments in athletics may have net revenue payoffs, but to conclude this, he misleads because the NCAA definition of revenue includes athletic donations and, indeed, is a major share of athletics department revenues for FBS schools.

39. Ibid., 130.

40. Ibid.

41. Conference alignment was retroactively fixed to the 2015–16 alignment. A school like the University of Utah, which moved from the Mountain West Conference to the Pac-12 in 2012, is considered to have always belonged to the Pac-12 for the purposes of this study.

42. Benjamin Baumer, "Colleges: Data about College Enrollments, Donations, and Athletics," GitHub, 2018, http://github.com/beanumber/colleges.

43. Final Four appearances in basketball are measured by performance in the NCAA Tournament. Final Four appearances in football are measured by end-of-season national ranking by the Associated Press.

44. We also collected many variables that were not included in our regression models, for example, cost of attendance and state population. These variables are included in the colleges package (Baumer, "Colleges") but are often incomplete and/or strongly correlated with our other explanatory variables.

45. None of the models we explored but are not reporting offered substantially different or contradictory results to the ones offered here.

46. Achim Zeileis and Torsten Hothorn, "Diagnostic Checking in Regression Relationships," *R News* 2:7–10, 2002.

47. Yoav Benjamini and Yosef Hochberg, "Controlling the False Discovery Rate: A Practical and Powerful Approach to Multiple Testing," *Journal of the Royal Statistical Society. Series B (Methodological)* 57:289–300, 1995. All reported p-values were adjusted using the p.adjust() function in the stats package.

48. The success of the University of Alabama's football team impacts our interpretation of the football-related variables. However, using Alabama as the reference group has no impact on any term's statistically significance, since we consider only the significance of the School variable as a whole.

49. Note that our models do not directly account for the possibility that a school is not simultaneously investing in competitive athletics and other areas of school achievement or marketing. That is, if a school hired a new football coach for $10 million, leading to an appearance in the national football playoffs, at the same time that it hired two Nobel Prize–winning professors and began a multimillion-dollar marketing campaign, then attributing an increase in applications, in entering students' SAT scores, or in alumni donations to football success would be spurious. There are two caveats to such an endogeneity concern. First, we do employ institutional fixed effects that may attenuate or eliminate such a problem. Second, we do not know of any evidence that such behavior occurred. In any event, we are not attributing causality to the treatment variables in our models; rather, we are noting the presence or absence of statistically significant relationships and the magnitude of such relationships.

50. John Fox and Georges Monette, "Generalized Collineratiry Diagnostics," *Journal of the American Statistical Association*, March 1992.

51. We computed generalized variance inflation factors raised to the $1/(2 \cdot \text{df})$ power, as recommend by Fox and Monette ("Generalized Collineratiry Diagnostics") for all explanatory variables in all models. Those factors were only above 2 for the control variables number of high school diplomas (ranging from 20.8 to 23.9) and per capita income (8.9 to 10.0).

52. The coefficient was 0.095 and $\exp(0.095) = 1.1$.

53. The coefficient was 0.144 and $\exp(0.144 / 13) = 1.011$ (divided by an average of thirteen regular season games).

54. Anderson, "Benefits of College Athletic Success," 133.

55. The high adjusted p-values for the coefficients in the Athletics regression are a result of the unadjusted p-values being relatively uniformly distributed with a large mean (0.48).

PART II

Position Papers by The Drake Group

CHAPTER 5

The "Big Five" Power Grab

THE REAL THREAT TO COLLEGE SPORTS

Brian Porto, Gerald Gurney, Donna Lopiano, David Ridpath, Allen Sack, Mary Willingham, and Andrew Zimbalist

It is hard to see the forest for the trees in college sports these days. The *O'Bannon v. NCAA* lawsuit, concerning college players' ownership of their images, and the unionization drive by football players at Northwestern University have obscured a more important issue. That is the effort by the "Big Five" conferences (Atlantic Coast Conference, Big Ten, Big 12, Pac-12, and Southeastern Conference) to secure legislative autonomy, perhaps even a new Division IV, within the National Collegiate Athletic Association. They threaten that, if rebuffed, they will leave the NCAA and form their own organization. This power grab is a greater threat to the future of college sports than any court decision or unionization campaign is.

The threat exists because the Big Five have foolishly put the financial interests of their football and basketball programs ahead of the well-being of college athletes. Members of these conferences wield great power in NCAA councils and on their own campuses, as evinced by the more than $1.5 billion in media revenue they shared in 2012–13. One result of that financial clout is their veiled warning to the NCAA's other one-thousand-plus members: "Give us autonomy or you will lose your primary funding source."

Instead of giving in to the Big Five, the NCAA should clip their wings by denying the group autonomy. Otherwise, the primacy of commerce over

---

Chronicle of Higher Education, June 19, 2014.

education will accelerate, and athletics programs will become even more divorced from the educational aims of colleges and universities. Moreover, the considerable wealth gap that already exists between the Big Five and the rest of NCAA Division I would widen as the former reap most of the profits from the new College Football Playoff.

The veiled threat by the Big Five to leave the NCAA if denied autonomy is nothing new. In 1997, the Football Bowl Subdivision of Division I, which includes the Big Five, persuaded most NCAA members to replace the traditional one-member-one-vote rule with an FBS-dominated executive committee and a promise that Divisions II and III (68 percent of 1,076 NCAA active members) would receive at least 7.5 percent of NCAA revenue distributions. In 2012–13, members of Division I (32 percent of NCAA active members) received 69 percent of NCAA revenues, and members of the Big Five conferences (6 percent of NCAA active members) received 31 percent of the Division I distributions.

The Big Five quest for autonomy is actually a grab for more power and an even larger portion of the revenue pie than the five conferences enjoy now. The Big Five dominate the FBS, which owns the current four-team College Football Playoff. The sixty-five Big Five institutions receive 75 percent of the $470 million that the playoff earns in annual revenue, while the other sixty FBS institutions share the remaining 25 percent. The Big Five also receive most of the revenues from the NCAA Men's Basketball Tournament, regular-season football and basketball games, and football bowl games. And the conferences will soon get richer, at least in football, as most experts predict that the playoff will eventually expand to eight teams or more, creating an annual payday in the range of $1 billion. Thus, the Big Five conferences view autonomy as a means to control the anticipated pot of gold at the end of the playoff rainbow.

Naturally, they will not acknowledge that publicly. Instead, they claim that if permitted autonomy, they would use revenues from the football playoff to enhance athletes' welfare by providing athletic scholarships covering the full cost of college attendance and lifelong scholarship support for former athletes wishing to complete undergraduate degrees.

That claim is disingenuous. The overriding goal of the Big Five is to win football and basketball games, and the conferences will spend as much as they earn to achieve that. Otherwise, they would have proposed, as we have, that the NCAA own the College Football Playoff and use the proceeds to provide expanded scholarship support to all Division I athletes. Instead, the Big Five seek to enhance their existing advantage by providing their athletes with benefits that members of other conferences in Division I cannot match.

Still, since the Big Five usually earn the most revenue, many people argue that they should reap the bulk of the profits. But that reasoning presupposes a purely commercial model of college sports. If the games are to remain faithful to the educational setting in which they were born, all members of Division I should share in the bounty from the football playoff so as to increase scholarship support and medical benefits to all athletes. Such improvements would assist more athletes than a victory for the plaintiffs in the *O'Bannon* case.

The most likely beneficiaries of a plaintiffs victory in *O'Bannon* are athletes from the Big Five conferences. Their teams play on television frequently; hence, they would be best able to profit from the commercial use of their names, images, and likenesses. In contrast, expanded scholarship and medical benefits would assist every athlete in Division I. And the availability of these benefits might well make athlete unionization a moot point.

To improve college-athlete welfare, we propose that Congress tie NCAA adoption of the following reforms to continued institutional eligibility for federal financial assistance and tax preferences under the Higher Education Act of 1965. The NCAA would own the College Football Playoff and would be required to use playoff revenues to meet the following critical needs:

- *Athlete injury insurance.* The NCAA would provide primary coverage for all 450,000 NCAA student-athletes and could specify that member institutions defray uncovered expenses without causing them to incur any additional costs.

- *Cost of attendance.* All 346 Division I institutions would receive a cost-of-attendance subsidy enabling them to raise the value of full athletics scholarships to federally defined cost-of-education limits.
- *Academic trust fund.* The NCAA would establish an academic trust fund for all Division I athletes to allow a return to college to complete undergraduate degrees.
- *Right to arbitration.* The NCAA would guarantee athletes the right to binding arbitration by mediators approved by the American Arbitration Association to determine whether institutional decisions regarding athletic ineligibility (for nonacademic violations only) or termination of financial aid were made properly.

Football Bowl Subdivision institutions would still receive the $470 million in national-championship revenue distributed by the NCAA but would have to use it to benefit athletes directly, not to increase coaches' salaries or build new athletics facilities. They would retain more than $1 billion in annual conference and institutional regular-season and bowl media revenues.

Notwithstanding the *O'Bannon* litigation and the possibility of athlete unionization, the most pressing needs in college sports today are to ensure academic integrity in big-time sports and to enhance athletes' welfare. Only the US Congress can achieve these goals by conditioning institutions' continued eligibility for federal financial assistance on their adoption of the aforementioned reforms. If the Big Five conferences object, they can leave the NCAA and face the loss of federal funding generally and federal tax preferences for their athletics programs. Perhaps then they will see the forest, too, through the trees.

CHAPTER 6

Why the NCAA Academic Progress Rate (APR) and the Graduation Success Rate (GSR) Should Be Abandoned and Replaced with More Effective Academic Metrics

Gerald Gurney, Donna Lopiano, Mary Willingham, Jayma Meyer, Brian Porto, David Ridpath, Allen Sack, and Andrew Zimbalist

One of the NCAA's stated basic principles for the conduct of intercollegiate athletics is,

> 2.5 The Principle of Sound Academic Standards.
>
> Intercollegiate athletics programs shall be maintained as a vital component of the educational program, and student-athletes shall be an integral part of the student body. The admission, academic standing and academic progress of student-athletes shall be consistent with the policies and standards adopted by the institution for the student body in general.[1]

For more than fifty years, the NCAA has wrestled with the issue of minimum academic eligibility requirements for intercollegiate athletic participation. The association has created and modified standards for initial

The Drake Group (2015; revised 2017, 2019).

eligibility at member institutions for athletes entering from high school or junior college or transferring from four-year institutions. It has also created and modified standards for continuing eligibility once the athlete is enrolled at an institution. Over time, these standards and their chosen metrics have ceased to compare athletes to their nonathlete peers. The standards have also failed to consider institutional characteristics that may affect an athlete's ability to succeed academically. The departure of NCAA academic metrics from sound academic standards has created a negative correlation: as athlete exploitation increases, the academic integrity of the member institution decreases, subjugating the institution to media and public scrutiny.

The NCAA created the Graduation Success Rate (GSR) and the Academic Progress Rate (APR) to minimize the potential negative headlines resulting from reporting lower graduation rates for athletes compared to nonathletes. The APR aims to be a real-time predictor of GSR; it is supposed to allow the institution to track the athlete's progress toward graduation. These independent metrics allowed the NCAA to avoid raising significant academic standards required to participate in athletics. They also allowed the NCAA to publish misleading information regarding the academic success of athletes compared to nonathletes. Contrary to the NCAA's suggestion, the measures used to compare athletes and nonathletes are not equivalent because they account for differing variables in their calculations.

In 2010, the NCAA developed and implemented an additional reform measure, the Coaches' APR. This measure was intended to hold coaches accountable for the academic performance of their athletes. It sought to provide a public-exposure incentive for coaches to recruit and retain academically qualified athletes. Unfortunately, using this measure has not resulted in improved graduation rates. Instead, it has provided student-athletes and athletics staff the impetus to perpetrate academic fraud, sacrificing institutional integrity in a classic example of an unintended consequence of a policy decision.

Throughout the history of collegiate athletics, the NCAA has used flawed metrics to measure the academic success of college athletes. It has skewed the numbers to overstate performance. It then touts its academic reforms, even though the evidence suggests otherwise. For instance, national trends exist toward rising graduation rates for college students, grade inflation, and the creation of less rigorous majors. Perhaps more alarming is the NCAA's failure to mention that graduation rates and academic-performance measures for Division I football and men's basketball are significantly below those of the general student body and other nonrevenue college athletes.

Not all of the NCAA's academic standards apply to all NCAA membership divisions (Division I, II, and III). For purposes of this analysis, we examined only Division I standards and results, recognizing that revenue growth and perceived publicity benefits enjoyed by successful athletics programs in this division have created huge pressures to keep athletes eligible, often resulting in abuses to "beat" the academic metric.

This report aims to (a) enhance the reader's understanding of college athlete eligibility and success standards, (b) identify the strengths and weaknesses of these standards, and (c) recommend how the NCAA should measure academic success. Further, the Drake Group will examine whether the NCAA and institutions are using academic progress measures as public relations smokescreens, hiding underachievement, exploitation, and academic fraud by institutions focused on the financial success of Division I athletics programs, their coaches, and administrators.

NCAA Academic Measures: Definitions, History, Effectiveness, Alternatives

Initial Eligibility Standards: High School Students

In 2003, the NCAA enacted the most recent set of initial eligibility reforms for high school students entering its member institutions, which actually lowered academic standards. A high school student was required to have completed sixteen core courses with a minimum GPA of 2.0, to have earned a corresponding minimum standardized test score on a sliding scale, and to have graduated from high school. Theoretically, a student could fail every question on a standardized test and still qualify. Previously, a minimum composite score of 17 on the ACT or 820 on the SAT was required. The sliding scale was a response to the criticism that standardized-exam requirements disproportionately disqualify minority athletes from eligibility.[2] The stated purpose of the 2003 initial eligibility changes was to increase the number of minority athletes who graduate from college. The actual results have been the following:

- Lower test-score standards, coupled with high school grade inflation, resulting in more athletes who meet NCAA eligibility standards with very low test scores. These students possess inadequate skills to manage college academics, increasing the need for academic-support services at institutions that are already struggling with tight budgets.[3]
- Negligible gains in minority access to higher education through big-time college sports. The NCAA's "Student-Athlete Ethnicity Report" included as variables the participation rates of self-reported ethnicity classifications, by team, each year from 1999 to 2009. It revealed that the adoption of less rigorous eligibility standards had minimal impact (positive) on African American access to participation in football and basketball. Rarely mentioned is that for four years leading up the 2003 reforms, the number of minority participants who met the higher minimum test score standard had increased steadily. Between 1999 and 2002, the African American participation rate in Division I men's basketball increased 2.9 percentage points, from 55.0 to 57.9 percent.[4] But between 2003 and 2009, after the reforms, it rose only three points, to 60.9 percent. The same growth trend was evident in football: between 1999 and 2002, African American participation increased from 39.5 percent to 43.8 percent, but between 2003 and 2009, it increased only two points, to 45.8 percent. According to the NCAA's

reports on federal graduation rates of African American student-athletes in Division I, the most recent data for men's basketball revealed a one-point decline in the 2003 cohort, to 43 percent, and for football a one-point increase, to 48 percent, over the previous year.[5]

- Removing the minimum standardized test requirement has challenged the academic integrity of higher education by widening the gap between the average academic profiles of athletes and nonathletes. The result is a depreciation of a "degree's worth," coupled with an invitation to institutions to maintain an athlete's eligibility by committing academic fraud. This academic fraud includes counseling underprepared athletes to (1) enroll in less demanding academic majors, (2) select the least demanding courses available regardless if they are needed to earn a degree, (3) enroll in courses with faculty who are "easy" graders or who require little to no work to complete course requirements and select increased online and independent study courses to free more time devoted to athletic activities, and (4) participate in acts of academic dishonesty in conjunction with academic tutors, coaches, and staff members hired by the athletics department. As a result, member institutions often fail to provide their athletes with a meaningful education. The richest athletics programs have developed multimillion-dollar academic-support programs, hiring academic-support professionals and counselors who focus on keeping athletes eligible.
- At the high school level, preparatory schools now offer higher GPAs at a price. The result is massive grade inflation, as individuals have learned the system and recognize that an artificially high GPA can negate a poor performance on a standardized test.
- As of August 2016, the NCAA will raise to 2.3 the minimum grade point average for eligibility to practice, compete, and receive financial aid and will require the completion of ten core units prior to the start of the college athlete's senior year.
- The NCAA also created an academic redshirt year from competition for college athletes who would otherwise qualify under the former

GPA/test-score sliding scale. The athlete who fails to meet minimum 2.3 GPA is eligible for financial aid, has no restrictions on practice time, and is not required to seek remediation or academic support.[6]

The NCAA membership should reinstate the minimum standardized-test scores of 17 composite on the ACT and 820 combined verbal and math on the SAT for freshman athletics eligibility. This requirement is necessary to establish minimum reading and mathematics capabilities for incoming students. It would ensure that college athletes have at least rudimentary academic skills or, at a minimum, would require institutions to apply their own entrance requirements equally to both athletes and nonathletes. Absent minimum scores on standardized tests, institutions must address the admission of underprepared athletes in some other rational way. Otherwise, they will continue to exploit predominantly minority football and men's basketball players, and academic fraud designed to keep athletes eligible to play will persist.

Recommendation 1: Require Institutional Match for Initial Eligibility of High School Students

Any student whose academic profile (high school grade point average and standardized-test score) is more than one standard deviation below the mean academic profile (based on high school grade point averages and standardized-test scores) of the previous year's incoming class at the recruiting institution should be ineligible for athletic participation during the freshman year. The institution that admits the athlete must provide (1) athletic scholarship assistance during the year of transition; (2) academic skills and learning disability testing; (3) if necessary, a remediation program supervised by academic authorities; (4) a reduced for-credit course load to accommodate the time required for remediation; (5) a ten-hour-per-week participation restriction applicable to athletics-related activities (practice, meetings, etc.); and (6) tenured faculty oversight of the student's academic progress throughout their enrollment at the institution.[7]

Initial Eligibility Standards: Junior College Transfers

The most recent reforms became effective in August 2012. To be immediately eligible to participate upon transfer to an NCAA member institution, a student must have attended a two-year college full-time for at least one semester or quarter. The student must also have earned an average of at least twelve semester or quarter credit hours for each full-time term at the two-year college and at least a 2.5 GPA in all transferable hours, including no more than two physical-education activity credit hours from the two-year college, to meet the requirements for immediate eligibility.

The NCAA summarized key research findings regarding two-year college transfers to NCAA member institutions as follows:

- Two-four transfer students enter NCAA Division I schools with lower high school grades and test scores than other groups of students.
- Two-four transfers leave college ineligible at higher rates than any other group of student-athletes.
- Two-four transfer graduation rates lag behind those of student-athletes who enter a Division I school from high school.
- The grade-point average at the two-year institution is the best predictor of all first-year outcomes examined.
- Ineligibility rates decrease significantly as grade-point averages earned at two-year institutions increase.
- Student-athletes with more core academic credits[8] perform better at four-year institutions. Science is a strong predictor.
- Students with a high number of physical education activity credits tend to have less academic success at the four-year institution than their two-year institution grade-point average would predict.
- Generally, data pertaining to high school academic performance do not add appreciably to the prediction equation once academic behavior at the two-year institution is known.[9]

Recommendation 2: Carefully Monitor the New Higher Standards Governing Initial Eligibility of Two-Year College Transfers

In consideration of the preceding information, athletics administrators and the NCAA should pay particular attention to the new rule requiring a 2.5 cumulative GPA to transfer from a two-year institution to a four-year institution. They should monitor this rule to ensure it fosters success at four-year colleges. Those who have a vested interest in academic integrity should consider requiring the student to graduate from junior college or meet the normal transfer admission standards of the four-year institution. The following academic profile rule should be implemented:

> Any student whose academic profile (high school grade point average and standardized test score) is more than one standard deviation below the academic profile of the four-year institution's entering class of the previous year should be ineligible for athletic participation *if* that result stands when compared to the academic profile of the incoming transfer class. Under these circumstances, the institution should provide (1) athletic scholarship assistance to support the athlete during the transition; (2) academic skills and learning disability testing; (3) if necessary, a remediation program supervised by academic authorities; (4) if necessary, a reduced for-credit course load to accommodate the time required for remediation; (5) a ten-hours-per-week participation restriction applicable to athletics (practice, meetings, etc.); and (6) oversight by tenured faculty of the student's academic progress while enrolled at the institution.

Initial Eligibility Standards: Four-Year College Transfers

Currently, the NCAA specifies that if the transfer student in sports other than baseball, basketball, FBS football, or men's ice hockey, who attended the previous four-year institution for at least one year, met progress-toward-degree requirements at the previous four-year institution at the time of transfer, and was academically eligible to return to the previous institution and participate in athletics, that student is immediately eligible to participate. The Drake Group does not recommend a change in this provision.

Recommendation 3: Close the Four-Year to Four-Year Transfer Loophole

If the transfer student attended the previous four-year institution for less than one academic year and did not previously graduate from junior college and the student's academic profile (high school grade point average and standardized-test score) is more than one standard deviation below the academic profile of the four-year institution's class that corresponds with the transfer student's class, the student is ineligible for athletic participation during the first year at the four-year institution. The institution that admits the athlete must provide (1) athletic scholarship assistance during the year of transition and remedial learning if necessary; (2) academic skills and learning disability testing; (3) if necessary, a remediation program supervised by academic authorities; (4) if necessary, a reduced for-credit course load to allow time for remediation; (5) a ten-hours-per-week participation restriction applicable to athletics (practice, meetings, etc.); and (6) oversight by tenured faculty of the student's academic progress while enrolled at the institution.[10]

Continuing Eligibility Standards: GPA and Satisfactory Progress

The NCAA currently requires continuing academic eligibility standards. These standards disregard the current high school standard required for initial eligibility: a cumulative GPA of 2.0. When universities require students to remain in "good academic standing," they often use as a floor the minimum acceptable GPA required for graduation within a particular major. At the sophomore level, many institutions allow athletes to participate with a 1.8 cumulative GPA. Considering the time and energy constraints associated with playing a sport in college, to permit the adoption of a lower standard during college than is required for initial eligibility is ludicrous. It validates prioritizing athletics over academics.

Recommendation 4: Adopt the Commonly Accepted Measure of Good Academic Standing

To be eligible for athletics, a student should be required to attain a minimum cumulative GPA of 2.0 during all semesters in which the student attends the institution. Any athlete not meeting the 2.0 standard can participate in practice no more than ten hours per week, may be prohibited from traveling with the team or engaging in other team activities, and may be required to participate in an academic-support program.

Graduation Rate Measures

An important difference distinguishes the Federal Graduation Rate (FGR), which is part of the Higher Education Act (HEA) of 1972, from the Graduation Success Rate (GSR), which the NCAA developed. The FGR applies to all students, whereas the GSR applies only to athletes, allowing no comparison to nonathlete peers. An institution's FGR is tabulated as the number of fall-semester, full-time freshmen students in an entering cohort who eventually graduate from their original institutions within six years, divided by the number of students in the original entering cohort. The HEA requires all institutions that participate in federal student-aid programs to use the FGR to disclose graduation rates for the student body and to disaggregate the data by gender, race, and ethnicity.[11]

The HEA disclosure requirements also apply to schools that offer athletically related student aid in any form. Thus, the FGR for athletes, whether used to examine the FGR for an entire athletics program or for a particular team, includes only athletes who receive athletically related aid. All students in the athlete FGR cohorts must be first-time, full-time freshmen entering in a given fall term while receiving athletically related financial aid.[12] College athletes who do not receive such aid at entry or who transfer into the institution are excluded from the cohort. Whether for athletes or nonathletes, the retention of all students who were admitted and who persisted to graduation is the most important measure of institutional success.

Admittedly, the FGR is limited because it includes only students who enter college in the fall as first-time, full-time undergraduates. Still, it is the only current nationally available graduation measure that permits a comparison between the academic success of recruited athletes who receive athletic financial aid and that of their nonathlete counterparts. The NCAA does not use this measure, though. Instead, it developed and uses the Graduation Success Rate (GSR), which it insists measures academic success more effectively.

The GSR includes only those athletes who receive athletic financial aid or recruited athletes from Division I institutions that do not offer athletic-related aid. It removes from the calculation for an institution any athlete who dropped out of the institution academically eligible to continue athletics participation at the original institution if the athlete had remained there (termed "left eligible"). It includes in the calculation for an institution any athlete who transferred to that institution and received athletics-related aid. As a result, nearly 40 percent more students figure into the GSR than are part of the federal calculation, and the GSR is roughly twenty percentage points higher at most institutions than the FGR is. However, the GSR lacks a comparison measure for the nonathlete portion of the student body. Further, the GSR is even more flawed than the FGR. The GSR adjusts institutional rates for "Transfers Out" even though institutions have no means of verifying that athletes who leave the institution actually graduate.

The GSR calculation inflates graduation rates by removing from a school's cohort all athletes who leave while academically eligible for sports participation. It also adds to the cohort athletes who transfer in from other schools. The NCAA contends that "student-athletes who depart a school while in good academic standing, Left Eligibles (LEs), . . . are essentially passed from that school's cohort to another school's cohort."[13] This implies that almost all LEs will become "Transfers-In." But this is not the case. What the NCAA does not acknowledge is the fact that the number of Transfers-In is significantly smaller than the number of LEs. Most Left Eligibles are not passed to another school's cohort but rather remain unaccounted-for college dropouts. This is not a small number and causes the GSR rates to be significantly inflated.

Tellingly, the NCAA does not make public GSR data or calculations for FBS football and men's basketball, sports in which public concern about athlete exploitation is the greatest. It only provides aggregated data for *all* Division I sports, male and female.[14] For example, in the cohort comprising the 2006–9 entering classes (the latest available GSR calculation), the total number of athletes is 95,782 and the GSR is 84 percent. What the NCAA conveniently ignores is that its data set includes 23,112 LEs but only 8,165 Transfers-In. In other words, there are 14,947 more LEs than Transfers-In. Astoundingly, about 65 percent of all LEs are unaccounted for in the NCAA's graduation "success" data.[15] The NCAA metric is inaccurately reporting the academic success of athletes who leave by absolving the original schools of responsibility for failing to retain them. Because the GSR adjusts for transfers out, it also encourages institutions to push out athletes who might not graduate or who are easily replaced.

To make matters worse, the GSR is inflated compared to the FGR because athletes are required to be full-time students progressing toward a degree, making them more likely than nonathletes to graduate in six years. The FGR, on the other hand, has a lower rate because it includes many entering full-time students who must work and who often drop down to part-time status and take longer to graduate. The GSR also includes eleven thousand Ivy League and Military Academy students who (1) do not receive athletic-related aid, (2) are not admitted as athletes, and (3) are considered properly as regular students in the FGR. Finally, use of the GSR to represent athletes' graduation success overall is misleading because female athletes graduate at significantly higher rates than male athletes do. The GSR masks the significant academic underperformance of male athletes.

Thus, the NCAA has created a graduation measure that misleads the public into thinking that athletes graduate at higher rates than the general student body does. See table 6.1, which compares FGR and GSR data using 2015 NCAA Division I Final Four Basketball Championship as an example.[16]

TABLE 6.1

FEDERAL GRADUATION RATES COMPARED TO NCAA GRADUATION SUCCESS RATES: 2015 NCAA FINAL FOUR FIELD

	2015 NCAA FINAL FOUR—FIELD OF 64				
	Federal Graduation Rates (FGR)			*NCAA graduation success*	
School	4-YR. STUDENT BODY	4-YR. MEN'S BASKETBALL	DIFFERENCE FROM STUDENT BODY	GSR	DIFFERENCE FROM M-88 FGR
Xavier	78%	67%	-11%	89%	22%
Wyoming	54%	25%	-29%	64%	39%
Wofford	82%	62%	-20%	91%	29%
Wisconsin	83%	33%	-50%	40%	7%
Wichita St.	43%	25%	-18%	64%	39%
West VA	57 %	62%	5%	89%	27%
Virginia	93%	64%	-29%	82%	18%
Villanova	90%	69%	-21%	100%	31%
VCU	54%	62%	8%	87%	25%
Valparaiso	71%	67%	-4%	90%	23%
Utah	58%	42%	-16%	88%	46%
Univ. Cinti	60%	8%	-52%	43%	35%
UNI	67%	42%	-25%	60%	18%
UNC	89%	54%	-35%	88%	34%
UCLA	90%	43%	-47%	60%	17%
UC Irvine	85%	30%	-55%	82%	52%
UAB	47%	50%	3%	53%	3%
TX Southern	12%	50%	38%	52%	2%
Texas	80%	41%	-39%	100%	59%
St. John's	57%	60%	3%	83%	23%
St. F. Austin	44%	56%	12%	53%	-3%
SMU	77 %	69%	-8%	75%	6%
SD St.	66%	55%	-11%	63%	8%
Robt. Morris	58%	33%	-25%	54%	21%
Purdue	70%	46%	-24%	73%	27%
Providence	86%	47%	-39%	67%	20%
OU	66%	60%	6%	77%	17%
Oregon	67%	56%	-11%	73%	17%
Oklahoma St	69%	9%	-60%	30%	21%
Ohio St.	81%	36%	-45%	53%	17%
Northwestern	94%	75%	-19%	82%	7%
Notre Dame	95%	85%	-10%	100%	15%

(continued)

TABLE 6.1 (CONTINUED)

School	*Federal Graduation Rates (FGR)*			*NCAA graduation success*	
	4-YR. STUDENT BODY	4-YR. MEN'S BASKETBALL	DIFFERENCE FROM STUDENT BODY	GSR	DIFFERENCE FROM M-88 FGR
New Mexico	46%	46%	0%	64%	18%
NC St.	73%	54%	−19%	80%	26%
N. Dakota St.	53%	92%	39%	85%	−7%
Miss.	58%	36%	−22%	75%	39%
Mich. St.	78%	62%	−16%	73%	11%
Maryland	82%	82%	0%	100%	18%
LSU	67%	36%	−31%	50%	14%
Louisville	51%	38%	−13%	58%	20%
Lafayette	89%	64%	−25%	90%	26%
Kentucky	59 %	40%	−19 %	89%	49%
Kansas	62%	43%	−19%	100%	57%
Iowa	70%	64%	−6%	100%	36%
Indiana	74%	8%	−66%	42%	34%
IA St.	69%	13%	−56%	64%	51%
Hampton	58%	54%	4%	67%	13%
Gonzaga	82%	73%	−9%	91%	18%
Georgia St.	50%	70%	20%	77%	7%
Georgia	83%	33%	−50%	71%	38%
Georgetown	93%	38%	−55%	70%	32%
E. Wash.	46%	13 %	−33%	72%	59 %
Duke	94%	67%	−27%	100%	33%
Dayton	76 %	62 %	−14 %	100 %	38%
Davidson	92%	85%	−7%	100%	15%
Coastal Car	46%	50%	4%	80%	30%
Butler	74%	75%	1%	100 %	25%
Buffalo	69%	64%	−5%	64%	0%
Belmont	68%	100%	32%	100%	0%
Baylor	73 %	73%	0%	92%	19%
Arkansas	59%	25%	−34%	55%	30%
Arizona	61%	50%	−11%	82%	32%
Albany	65%	54%	−11%	80%	26%
				Avg. difference	24%
Harvard	97%	* does not award athletically related financial aid			

Despite this masking of low graduation rates at individual institutions, the NCAA regularly trumpets the results of aggregated GSR data to argue that overall, college athletes perform better than nonathletes in the classroom. For the most recently available six-year cohort (2007), the NCAA reports a 66 percent FGR for athletes nationwide, compared to a 65 percent FGR for all students and an 82 percent NCAA GSR.[17] By not reporting the progression of all athletes who leave the institution and by allowing numerous other adjustments to mitigate low graduation rates (such as not counting against an institution's total an undergraduate who leaves to join a professional team), the GSR fails to measure graduation rates accurately.

Beyond overstating college athletes' graduation rates, the GSR blinds the higher-education community to critical issues. For instance, Bimper notes that of the seventy colleges and universities that competed in football bowl games after the 2012 season, more than half had a twenty-percentage-point gap between the graduation rates of Black and white athletes, respectively. One quarter of all teams had a thirty-percentage-point gap.[18] In another example of the critical value of being able to compare the academic performance of athletes to that of the general student body, Harper, Williams, and Blackman found the following:

- Between 2007 and 2010, Black men were 2.8 percent of full-time, degree-seeking undergraduate students but 57.1 percent of football teams and 64.3 percent of basketball teams.
- Across four cohorts, 50.2 percent of Black male student-athletes graduated within six years, compared to 66.9 percent of student-athletes overall, 72.8 percent of undergraduate students overall, and 55.5 percent of Black undergraduate men overall.
- Among NCAA Division I colleges and universities, 96.1 percent graduated Black male student-athletes at rates lower than student-athletes overall.
- 97.4 percent of all FBS institutions graduated Black male student-athletes at rates lower than undergraduate students overall. On no

campus were rates exactly comparable for these two comparison groups.

- At one university, Black male student-athletes graduated at a rate comparable to that of Black undergraduate men overall. On 72.4 percent of the other campuses, graduation rates for Black male student-athletes were lower than rates for Black undergraduate men overall.[19]

Equally distressing is that athletics programs with the most financial resources can manipulate the GSR to their advantage. For instance, an institution can push out an unwanted (from a talent perspective) and academically weak basketball or football athlete by combining a threat with an incentive. The institution informs the player that it will not renew his or her financial aid unless the athlete attends summer school and raises a deficient GPA enough that the current institution will not suffer a GSR (or APR) loss. This ploy is most prevalent in football and men's basketball, sports in which recruiting underprepared athletes is common due to the financial payoff from winning. Even without such summer-school and transfer shenanigans, richer athletics programs can afford a cadre of academic-support staff devoted to keeping athletes eligible to play.

Worse yet, the mechanisms used to ensure that underprepared athletes remain eligible frequently involve academic fraud and misconduct such as (1) counseling athletes to select the least demanding academic majors, (2) counseling athletes to register for the least demanding academic courses or courses conducted by professors with lax grading reputations, (3) creating intensive tutoring programs that raise questions whether the work produced is the athlete's or the tutor's, (4) using athletics department funds to support academic departments that enroll many athletes in their courses,[20] and (5) counseling athletes to register for independent study courses with professors who require a minimal work product. Athletics departments, not campus academic units, often operate these \$1–\$2 million-per-year academic support programs, which lack management or oversight by tenured faculty. One need only examine the FGR and GSR rates of historically Black colleges and universities (HBCUs) to recognize the impact of financial resources on athlete graduation rates and on continued eligibility prior to transfer (see table 6.2).

TABLE 6.2

FEDERAL GRADUATION RATES COMPARED TO NCAA GRADUATION SUCCESS RATES AT HISTORICALLY BLACK COLLEGES AND UNIVERSITIES (HBCUS): 2013–14 DATA

	Federal Graduation Rates (FGR)			*NCAA Graduation Success Rate (GSR)*	
School	4-YR. STUDENT BODY	4-YR. MEN'S BASKET-BALL	DIFFERENCE	GSR	DIFFERENCE FROM MEN'S BB FGR
University of New Orleans	28%	13%	1 5%	33%	20%
U of Maryland Eastern Shore	33%	14%	19%	100%	86%
U of Arkansas at Pine Bluff	25%	55%	−30%	50%	−5%
Texas Southern U	12%	50%	−38%	52%	2%
Tennessee State University	32%	25%	7%	50%	25%
Southern U at Baton Rouge	28%	29%	−1%	45%	16%
South Carolina State	36%	33%	3%	92%	59%
Savannah State University	31%	50%	−19%	69 %	19%
Prairie View A&M	35%	29%	6%	50%	21%
North Carolina Central	41%	38%	3%	53%	15%
North Carolina A&T	41%	33%	8%	38%	5%
Norfolk State University	36%	33%	3%	55%	22%
Morgan State	31%	18%	13%	31%	13%
Mississippi Valley State U	25%	60%	−35%	48%	−12%
Jackson State	43%	46%	−3%	54%	8%
Howard University	64%	50%	14%	50%	0%
Hampton University	58%	54%	4%	67%	13%
Grambling State U	29%	8%	21%	9%	1%
Florida A&M	34%	40%	−6%	36%	−4%
Delaware State	36%	33%	3%	50%	17%
Coppin State	15%	31%	−16%	67%	36%
Bethune-Cookman	42%	43%	−1%	67%	24%
Alcorn State	35%	60%	−25%	50%	−10%
Alabama State U	22%	22%	0%	45%	23%
Alabama A&M	41%	31%	10%	33%	2%
				Avg. difference	−16%

Recommendation 5: Abandon the GSR

The NCAA should discard the GSR as a metric because of its deceptive statistical reliability and validity. But the NCAA should not invent its own academic metric designed to portray the academic performance of athletes in a better light than the data support. The NCAA must follow its own statement of sound academic principles by using "consistent standards adopted by the institution" for the student body in general. Higher education should commit to measuring the academic success of athletes and nonathletes by means of the same instrument. The GSR has no comparable measure for nonathletes; therefore, it prohibits a comparison to their college athlete peers.

Academic Progress Rate (APR)

Established in 2003 and enforced beginning in 2005, the APR is a direct measure of retention and an indirect measure of scholarship athletes' academic eligibility, including both minimum grade point average and satisfactory progress toward a degree. It is also a real-time predictor of GSR, the NCAA's inflated graduation metric. "Each student-athlete receiving athletically related financial aid earns one retention point for staying in school and one eligibility point for being academically eligible. A team's total points are divided by points possible and then multiplied by one thousand to equal the team's Academic Progress Rate score."[21] Teams failing to achieve the minimum APR requirement, which has been increased from an initial standard of 900 to 930 in 2014–15, are declared ineligible for postseason championship play,[22] and a three-level penalty system corresponding to each consecutive year in which the benchmark is unmet is imposed:

Level One: Team is limited to sixteen hours of practice a week over five days, with the lost four hours to be replaced by academic activities, representing a reduction of four hours and one day per week of practice time.

Level Two: Competition reductions, either in the traditional or nontraditional season, added to the first-level penalties.

Level Three: Penalty options as determined by the NCAA Committee on Academics. Options include coaching suspensions, financial aid reductions, and restricted NCAA membership.

Thus, like the GSR, the APR is flawed in that athletics programs with significant financial resources are better able than less affluent institutions to keep athletes eligible through manipulation of the existing rules. Larger, wealthier institutions also provide additional course offerings, which may allow for an easier pathway to a degree at such institutions. For large-roster teams like football, affluent institutions can increase their APR scores by recruiting some academically gifted players to compensate for those who are not. The NCAA has received heavy criticism about the lack of affluent, high-profile Football Bowl Subdivision teams among those penalized for failing to meet the APR benchmark. Besides directing athletes to easy courses and majors and providing excessive tutoring help, these institutions manipulate the APR by the following means:

- *Extensive use of summer-school financial aid.* Liberal use of summer-school financial aid to boost athlete GPAs and ensure that transfers leave with GPAs that do not cause APR point losses is commonplace among the highly resourced FBS institutions but is less of an option for the HBCUs and smaller Football Championship Subdivision and Division I nonfootball institutions.
- *Learning disability and other waivers.* Athletes who fail to meet initial eligibility standards and can demonstrate a learning disability will often be exempt from meeting standard initial eligibility requirements through an initial eligibility waiver. The NCAA may also waive the requirement to maintain a full-time academic load of twelve credit hours. A successfully written progress-toward-degree waiver can often allow athletes with certified learning disabilities who fail to meet NCAA standards to be granted continuing eligibility by passing enough degree-applicable credit hours. It takes highly

skilled staff to maximize these opportunities. As Gurney and Southall revealed,

> Navigating this educational landscape is a bureaucratic challenge for many NCAA institutions. However, the disparity between compliance staffing at FBS schools and "limited-resource" HBCU institutions is enormous. For example, the University of Oklahoma compliance staff consists of 11 professionals, including several lawyers. The University of Southern California is similarly staffed with 11 compliance officers. The University of Alabama maintains a staff of eight. The University of Texas' Risk Management and Compliance Services staff has seven full-time professionals. Conversely, limited-resource universities must make due with almost nonexistent staffs. For example: Arkansas–Pine Bluff has a total of two compliance staff, Hampton University has a single compliance staff "coordinator" and a total of three full-time academic support staff and Mississippi Valley State University has only one compliance officer.
>
> As a result of their personnel largess, "un-limited-resource" institutions have staff whose primary duties involve writing admissions waivers and exceptions, as well as monitoring athletes' satisfactory progress toward degree. At one Big 12 institution, a typical year's waiver writing assignments for a compliance attorney included one initial eligibility waiver and up to seven reduced-hour or other progress-toward-degree waivers and exceptions. Having someone specifically assigned to these tasks is necessary in order to make certain the institution does not suffer embarrassing penalties or fail to compete in postseason competition. Overworked and understaffed, HBCU athletics departments simply lack the human resources to address these issues. Being overwhelmed by the minutia of NCAA eligibility paperwork, they find it impossible to even address waivers.[23]

- *Medical and missed term exceptions.* Two common exceptions for satisfactory progress primarily used to manipulate APR scores are the medical exception and the missed term exception. "Athletes or members of their families who become ill with incapacitating injuries or illnesses may also escape APR eligibility penalties through being granted an exception. Athletes who experience depression or suffer other mental illness may avoid progress-toward-degree consequences by withdrawing from classes or dropping down to a part-time academic load. Alcoholism, depression or substance abuse, for example, may be considered an incapacitating illness. The missed term exception permits an athlete to miss one or more semesters one time during their career if they leave eligible. The missed term exception may be used even if the athlete's absence is due to a suspension for academic dishonesty if they were eligible prior to the absence."[24] Again, processing such appeals takes considerable staff time.

- *Supporting nongraduates' return to school.* Affluent schools also manipulate APR scores by providing financial aid to nongraduates who have exhausted their athletics eligibility so they can return to the institution and earn their degrees. Such degree-completion programs may not be feasible for underfunded athletics programs. An example of the benefits of institutional affluence is the University of California at Berkeley, which recently implemented a Degree Completion Program (DCP) for athletes who had exhausted their eligibility without obtaining a degree.[25] For many institutions, degree-completion programs are not economically feasible because of the escalating costs associated with running athletics departments.

However, the most serious flaw of the APR is that it is not the metric it purports to be. The 900 APR was supposed to correspond to a FGR of 50 percent. Even the recently elevated 930 APR is nowhere near reflecting a FGR of 50 percent. When the NCAA realized that the 900 APR standard was nowhere near the goal metric, instead of adjusting the APR to correspond to a 50 percent FGR, it pegged the APR to a 50 percent *GSR* that only approximates a 40 percent FGR. This is a "bait and switch" of the worst kind. Arguments that the GSR takes into consideration athletes leaving in good academic standing and athletes who transfer into an institution and that it encompasses a larger percentage of athletes cannot and should not hold any weight if comparisons to the general student body are impossible.

As a result, since the introduction of the GSR, NCAA athletes' reported graduation success has dramatically increased. What has been lost amid the NCAA's public relations campaign is the continued existence of large (30–40 percent) negative graduation gaps between NCAA Division I football and men's basketball players and the general student population. In some cases, teams report graduation rates of zero. Simply put, the athletes on whose skill the entire commercial enterprise depends, college football and men's basketball players, are dramatically less likely than other students to obtain a degree. This is to say nothing about the quality of the education to which they have access.

By consistently simply asserting that the GSR "more accurately assesses the academic success" of college athletes and steadfastly referring to GSR rates, NCAA members have convinced the media to almost exclusively use the new, more favorable metric. Intentionally or not, the NCAA's APR and GSR metrics confuse the media, fans, and the general public. Using the GSR and APR to tout graduation success and increased academic standards is undoubtedly savvy marketing and public relations, but these metrics are fundamentally nothing more than measures of how successful athletics departments are at keeping athletes eligible and have increasingly fostered acts of academic dishonesty and devalued higher education in a frantic search for eligibility and retention points.[26]

If the FGR is used instead of the GSR, exceptions should not be allowed for several reasons:

1. No FGR exclusions are permitted for members of the general student body who experience family issues, medical issues, and learning disabilities.

2. Athletes have a huge retention advantage compared to the general student body in that they are required to be full-time students and they receive financial aid, so they do not have to work. Furthermore, athletes benefit from sophisticated academic-support programs. The FGR does not reflect such general student advantages; indeed, it is artificially low as a comparable standard because many initially full-time students drop down to part-time and are unable to graduate in six years but must still be counted.
3. Some commentators argue that the FGR should be adjusted if the athlete returns to school after six years and graduates. But many nonathlete students do the same, yet the FGR is not adjusted. The FGR is useful because institutions cannot easily tamper with it; that is precisely why the NCAA should adopt it. It will thwart athletics department gamesmanship.

Thus, to further advantage athletes with exclusions or exceptions to the FGR is unjustified.

Lastly, because the APR is pegged to retention and current eligibility to compete, any penalty imposed on a current team (i.e., banning the team from postseason play) for failures of previous members of the team penalizes students who are not responsible for the benchmark failure. The institution, not the athletes, should suffer the penalty.

Recommendation 6: Discard the APR as an Academic Metric, Establish the FGR as the Proper Metric to Impose Coach and Institutional Penalties, and Require Mandatory Five-Year Scholarships

The APR should be discarded because its original purpose was to be a real-time predictor of GSR, which is a flawed metric for the reasons discussed earlier, most notably that it does not compare the academic performances of athletes and nonathletes. Besides being easily manipulated by affluent institutions, the APR, in eliminating teams from postseason play, unfairly penalizes less affluent institutions and current athletes who are not responsible for their institutions' failure to recruit academically prepared athletes. Enforcement of the higher 2.0 cumulative GPA standard for athletic eligibility (see recommendation 4) is sufficient to maintain the integrity of regular-season and postseason championship eligibility. The 2.0 cumulative GPA properly holds the athlete accountable for his or her academic responsibilities, with loss of individual eligibility for competition as the proper penalty. The FGR can hold institutions and coaches accountable for fulfilling the promise of an education to the athletes they recruit.

Thus, the NCAA should establish a rule that requires each sport program of a member institution to compute and maintain an FGR, without any exceptions for athletes, that equals or exceeds the national average FGR or the institution's own FGR, whichever is lower. Failure to achieve this benchmark should *not* be used to declare a team ineligible for postseason play. Rather, institutions should absorb the penalties for such failure, which penalties should increase if benchmark failure continues for consecutive years:

First year: The institution is prohibited from receiving 25 percent of (a) any national championship, bowl, or other post- or preseason NCAA sponsored or sanctioned event media rights fees, sponsorships, advertising, licensing, or gate-receipt revenue distributions in that sport, (b) any conference regular-season or championship media rights fees, sponsorships, advertising, licensing, or gate-receipt revenue distributions in that sport and (c) any non-sports-specific NCAA revenue distributions. The institution may not decrease academic-support program expenditures.

Second consecutive year: The institution is prohibited from receiving 50 percent of (a) any national championship, bowl, or other post- or preseason NCAA sponsored or sanctioned event media rights fees, sponsorships, advertising, licensing or gate receipt revenue distributions in that sport, (b) any conference regular-season or championship media rights fees, sponsorships, advertising, licensing, or gate-receipt revenue distributions in that sport, and (c) any non-sports-specific NCAA revenue distributions. The institution may not decrease academic support program expenditures.

Third consecutive year: The institution is prohibited from receiving 100 percent of (a) any national championship, bowl, or other post- or preseason NCAA sponsored or sanctioned event media rights fees, sponsorships, advertising, licensing, or gate-receipt revenue distributions in that sport, (b) any conference regular-season or championship media rights fees, sponsorships, advertising, licensing, or gate-receipt revenue distributions in that sport, and (c) any non-sports-specific NCAA revenue distributions. Additional penalties, as determined by the NCAA Committee on Academics, may be levied, including coaching suspensions, financial aid reductions, recruiting limitations, and restricted NCAA membership.

Because more than eleven hundred institutions offer academic programs of varying academic rigor, the institutional comparator FGR is of critical import. The optional use of the national average FGR in lieu of the institutional FGR gives reasonable leeway to highly selective institutions. Use of the FGR, which emphasizes athlete retention and graduation from one's original institution, will reduce the current practice of discarding athletes for whom an institution finds more talented replacements. Most importantly, it will require institutions to recruit student-athletes capable of competing academically with other students attending and graduating from that institution. This standard will create academic expectations of athletes that are equal to those the institution has for the rest of the student body.

Key to the desired effect on graduation is to replace the current option of guaranteeing athletic scholarships for five years with a requirement that athletic scholarships be guaranteed for five years. Institutions must be encouraged to recruit athletes who are capable of graduating and to invest in athletes' academic success for the duration of their college careers.

The Coaches' Academic Progress Rate

In 2010 the NCAA established the Coaches' Academic Progress Rate. Established by the Committee on Academic Performance at the request of the Division I Board of Directors, the database aims "to create more transparency in the Academic Performance Program and strengthen the accountability of coaches for the academic performance of their student-athletes."[27] The Head Coach APR Portfolio includes the single-year team APR for a head coach at each institution where he or she has held that post, along with the average single-year APR in the coach's specific sport for comparison purposes. Interim head coaches are not included in the database.

The current NCAA coaches' metric is fundamentally flawed for the following reasons:

- The coach is evaluated based on the academic progress of athletes recruited by others as well as the academic progress of athletes the coach recruited himself or herself.
- The APR metric is pegged to the NCAA Graduation Success Rate, itself a flawed metric for reasons already stated.

Recommendation 7: Adopt the Proper Coach Metric

The NCAA should abandon the Coaches' Academic Progress Rate as currently constructed and should replace it with a Coaches' Graduation Rate. A coach should be held responsible for the academic success and graduation of every athlete that coach recruits, earning a 1.0 for every recruit who graduates within six years of initial enrollment from the institution to which the coach recruited him or her. That number would be divided by the total number of athletes recruited. The institution should be required to publish the Coaches' Graduation Rate for each head coach or former head coach (i.e., one who has been fired or has moved to another institution) in its program.

Transparency of Academic Metrics

Academic integrity in intercollegiate athletics requires a system of checks and balances and transparent academic metrics. These safeguards will ensure that learning occurs, not just that athletic eligibility is maintained.

Institutions often use the Federal Education Rights Protection Act (FERPA) to hide evidence of academic corruption and exploitation of football and men's basketball athletes from public scrutiny, while releasing only good news. They will release information about the A student but will not discuss the number of athletes clustered in an eligibility-friendly major. FERPA has also enabled institutions to deny knowledge of academic misconduct committed by athletics department staff, coaches, and even faculty members. The public cannot evaluate claims of academic improvement without knowing the classes that players take, the names of instructors, and overall course and team GPAs. Thus, true academic reform cannot occur without public accountability.

A careful reading of FERPA shows that only identifiable educational information is prohibited from being disclosed. Jon Ericson, former provost at Drake University, and the attorney Matthew Salzwedel have presented a plan for academic disclosure that would comply with FERPA. In their article entitled "Cleaning Up Buckley: How the Family Educational Rights and Privacy Act Shields Academic Corruption in College Athletics," they argue that the Buckley Amendment allows an appropriate level of academic disclosure regarding college sports, which disclosure will shame institutions into changing their behavior.[28]

A sound academic disclosure plan should not disclose individual athletes' academic information. Academic disclosure is *about institutional behavior*, namely, the complicity of administrators and faculty in academic corruption and the resulting denial to many college athletes of a meaningful college education. Institutional resistance to full disclosure has occurred in past academic scandals, most notably at Auburn University and the University of North Carolina. Both universities were embarrassed, and both made positive changes once their "eligibility manipulation" became public, albeit after some kicking and screaming. Faculty and others who desire to provide bona fide educational opportunities for college athletes need an effective tool for achieving that end. History shows that public humiliation prompts universities to operate with integrity.[29]

The NCAA currently requires athletes to consent to share their academic information with institutional employees who are responsible for determining eligibility. That same requirement should apply to the disclosure of that information, as long as such disclosure does not reveal the identity of the athlete. Because disclosure would not reveal athletes' names, no harm would occur to any individual student, nor would anyone's privacy be invaded. Such use would be in keeping with the letter and spirit of FERPA. Yet the aggregated use of individual data would expose institutional misbehavior by identifying athletes' course selections, their choices of professors and academic majors, their advisers, and team GPAs. Without identifying any student by name, this information would expose academic clustering, suspect courses, and issues like those that occurred at Auburn and the University of North Carolina.

Recommendation 8: Academic Disclosure

The NCAA should require every member institution to establish an academic check-and-balance system consisting of an Academic Oversight Committee composed of tenured faculty, a peer-review certification program, and regularly issued public reports. At each institution, members of the faculty senate or the highest faculty governance authority would elect the Academic Oversight Committee. This committee would meet annually with the head coach of each team to review the academic progress of all athletes on that team. The committee would be required to report to the faculty senate (or other highest faculty authority) annually on the academic progress and admission qualifications of college athletes and, when possible, to compare athletes to nonathletes. The methods of comparison would include average SAT and ACT scores by sport, Federal Graduation Rates by sport, independent studies and/or online courses taken by sport, the professors offering the independent studies and their average grade assigned, admissions profiles, athletes' progress toward a degree, trends in selected majors by sport, average grade distributions of faculty by major, incomplete grades by sport, grade changes by professors, and the name of each athlete's faculty adviser.

The NCAA certification program, which included a more comprehensive examination of athletics programs' academic elements than that conducted by the regional accreditation agencies, was discarded in 2010, but the association should reinstitute it. This program would require each Division I institution to undergo an athletics certification process at least once every ten years. That process should include peer review, by an external body funded by the NCAA, of a campus-wide self-evaluation conducted by various institutional committees assembled for that purpose. A majority of the members of these campus committees should be tenured faculty members.

Each NCAA member institution should also make public an annual report, to include the following data:

1. Certification status of each member institution
2. Federal Graduation Rate for all students, all athletes, athletes by sport, and all athletes admitted with a waiver of admissions standards
3. Number of recruited athletes required to complete one year in residency prior to initial eligibility
4. Number of recruited athletes admitted to the institution with a waiver of published admissions standards compared to the number of students overall receiving such admissions
5. Coaches' Graduation Rates of all head coaches employed by the institution.

What Changes May Result from the Adoption of These Recommended Academic Metrics and Recommendations?

Assuming that the eight recommendations are adopted in their entirety, the following outcomes are anticipated:

1. Coaches will be more likely to recruit academically qualified athletes who will be eligible in their first year of college.
2. Coaches will be less likely to pressure marginal athletes to transfer because of the negative impact of that practice on the Coaches' Graduation Rate.
3. Athletes eligible as freshmen will possess adequate reading, writing, and math skills and will be more likely to compete with their nonathlete peers in the classroom.
4. Athletes who are not eligible as freshman will receive the remedial education necessary to remedy their academic deficiencies, the promise of financial aid, and continuing academic support throughout their five-year tenure at the institution. Therefore, they will be more likely to graduate from the institution that recruited them.
5. Athletes who are not eligible as freshmen will not be required to enroll in a full-time program of college coursework that counts toward a degree or to earn a minimum GPA. Yet they will be able to receive a remedial education, diminishing the institutional temptation to commit academic fraud in order to meet athletic-eligibility and satisfactory-progress requirements.
6. The graduation rates of athletes who are currently underperforming in more selective institutions of higher education will improve.
7. Highly selective institutions will be less likely to exploit underprepared football and basketball players even when they waive normal admissions standards to recruit those players.
8. Academic data on the academic progress of college athletes will be more transparent, facilitating evaluation by faculty, administrators, and the public.

Conclusion

The NCAA's GSR and APR, or any metric that assumes that college athletes are unique and should be treated as academically distinct from the rest of the student body, invites the exploitation of athletes and violations of academic integrity. When no comparator metric to the nonathlete student body exists, no "speed limit" is available to keep athletics programs honest. Unless academic standards for athletes are anchored to institutional academic standards and expectations for all students, athlete academic standards will float with the tide of institutional greed. The standard for athletes will become the one that will allow coaches and institutions to attract the most talented athletes so they can win and prosper. On the contrary, higher education's promise to any student, athlete or nonathlete, must be a meaningful education that satisfies legitimate standards set by the faculty and leads to good academic standing and graduation.

Furthermore, institutions must acknowledge the importance of matching the academic abilities of their athletes to the academic profile of the larger student body for "a good fit." If institutions continue to waive admission requirements for athletes or recruit athletes whose academic profiles do not match those of their nonathlete classmates, then institutions must remediate the academic skills of these athletes before allowing them to compete. Otherwise, athletes will suffer exploitation, as institutions trade in the promise of a meaningful education for the easiest majors and courses, resulting in continued athletics eligibility but little or no preparation for life after the cheering stops.

NOTES

1. NCAA, *2014–15 NCAA Division I Manual* (Indianapolis: NCAA, 2014).
2. Gerald S. Gurney, "Stop Lowering the Bar for College Athletes," *Chronicle of Higher Education* (April 10, 2011), http://chronicle.com/article/Stop-Lowering-the-Bar-for/127058/.
3. Ibid.
4. The first year for which the NCAA provides data is 1999.
5. Gurney, "Stop Lowering the Bar for College Athletes." Of course, another factor possibly affecting these numbers is that the percentage-point increase may occur more readily when the starting level is lower.

6. NCAA, *2015–16 NCAA Division 1 Manual* (Indianapolis: NCAA, 2015), 155–61.

7. For a more complete discussion of freshman eligibility issues, see Gerald Gurney, Mary Willingham, Donna Lopiano, Brian Porto, B. David Ridpath, Allen Sack, and Andrew Zimbalist, "Freshmen Ineligibility in Intercollegiate Athletics," Drake Group (April 20, 2015), http://thedrakegroup.org.

8. New NCAA academic standards were implemented on August 1, 2016. These standards require the completion of ten core courses before the beginning of the senior year.

9. Jennifer Strawley and Diane Dickman, "Two-Year Transfer Summit" (PowerPoint presentation), NCAA, 2012 (2012 Mesa College Two-Year Transfer Summit).

10. Ibid.

11. 20 U.S.C. § 1092; 34 C.F.R. §§ 668.41; 668.45.

12. 20 U.S.C. § 1092 (e) and 34 § CFR 668.48.

13. NCAA, "How Are NCAA Graduation Rates Calculated?" (November 2015), 6, http://www.ncaa.org/sites/default/files/How%20is%20grad%20rate%20calculated_nov_2015.pdf.

14. NCAA Research, "Trends in Graduation Success Rates and Federal Graduation Rates at NCAA Division I Institutions" (November 2016), 5, http://www.ncaa.org/sites/default/files/2016RES_GSRandFedTrends-Final_sc_20161114.pdf.

15. Authors' calculations based on data from NCAA GSR table.

16. Note that these data are based on the most recent six-year 2007 cohort and that the four-year student body and men's basketball percentages represent an average of the last four years.

17. NCAA, "Division: Overall Division I Graduation Rates," 2014.

18. Albert Bimper Jr., "Kansas State Scholar Examines the Classroom Experiences of Black Student Athletes," *Research & Studies* (May 2, 2013), http://www.jbhe.com/2013/05/kansas-state-scholar-examines-the-classroom-experiences-of-black-student-athletes/.

19. Shaun R. Harper, Collin D. Williams Jr., and Horatio W. Blackman, *Black Male Student-Athletes and Racial Inequities in NCAA Division I College Sports* (Philadelphia: University of Pennsylvania, Center for the Study of Race and Equity in Education).

20. Ben Cohen, "At Auburn, Athletics and Academics Collide," *Wall Street Journal* (August 28, 2015), http://www.wsj.com/articles/at-auburn-athletics-and-academics-collide-1440635278.

21. NCAA, "Frequently Asked Questions about Academic Progress Rate," 2015, http://www.ncaa.org/about/resources/research/frequently-asked-questions-about-academic-progress-rate-apr.

22. It should be noted that an institution can appeal this penalty due to unusual circumstances.

23. Gerald S. Gurney and Richard M. Southall, "College Sports' Bait and Switch," *ESPN.com* (August 9, 2012), http://espn.go.com/college-sports/story/_/id/8248046/college-sports-programs-find-multitude-ways-game-ncaa-apr.

24. Ibid.

25. Coby McDonald, "Back in the Game: Cal Program Helps Former Student-Athletes Graduate," *California Magazine* (Cal, Alumni Association, UC Berkeley), 2015, http://alumni.berkeley.edu/california-magazine/spring-2015-dropouts-and-drop-ins/back-game-cal-program-helps-former-student.

26. Ibid.

27. Michelle Brutlag Hosick, "NCAA Releases Academic Progress Rates for Coaches," NCAA (December 15, 2010), http://www.ncaa.com/news/basketball-women/article/2010-08-05/ncaa-releases-academic-progress-rates-coaches.

28. Matthew Salzwedel and Jon Ericson, "Cleaning Up Buckley: How the Family Educational Rights and Privacy Act Shields Academic Corruption in College Athletics," *Wisconsin Law Review* 2003, no. 6 (2003): 1054–13.
29. Ibid.

CHAPTER 7

Fixing the Dysfunctional NCAA Enforcement System

Brian Porto, Gerald Gurney, Donna Lopiano, David Ridpath, Allen Sack, Mary Willingham, and Andrew Zimbalist

The NCAA is the largest and best known of four independent organizations that regulate intercollegiate athletics. Part of its self-governance structure is its membership-approved enforcement process, which assesses penalties for violations of the association's bylaws. This process has been much maligned since the 1970s by journalists, state and federal courts, academic commentators, and NCAA member institutions themselves.

A primary criticism of the NCAA enforcement process has been that it is arbitrary and capricious. That is, it is inconsistent and fails to provide due process for individuals and institutions accused of NCAA rules violations.

To be sure, enforcement is a challenging task for the NCAA. The temptation to violate NCAA rules so as to gain a competitive advantage is ever present and has grown exponentially along with the financial rewards associated with success in big-time college sports. As a result, recruiting scandals, academic fraud, and impermissible eligibility certifications have occurred more frequently in recent decades. Before the television era, NCAA member institutions and affiliated athletic conferences enjoyed considerable autonomy when enforcing NCAA rules and regulations. In a sense, NCAA policy mirrored the legislative policy toward local government commonly known as "home rule."

The Drake Group (April 7, 2015).

The United States Supreme Court's decision in *Tarkanian v. NCAA* in 1984 established the NCAA as a private entity authorized to conduct investigations without providing due process. Nevertheless, the NCAA examined its internal enforcement practices soon after the Court's decision. Former solicitor general Rex Lee chaired the Special Committee to Review the NCAA Enforcement and Infractions Process. The Lee Committee recommended improving the process by providing greater protections for involved institutions and individuals. The Lee Committee advised the NCAA to do the following:

1. Provide initial notice of allegations. The NCAA membership agreed to enhance its notice of inquiry process to ensure all parties are notified prior to an investigation.
2. Establish a summary disposition process. This was suggested as a method for accelerating the infractions process by adjudicating major violations at a reasonably early stage in the investigation.
3. Allow audio recordings and shared documentation of interviews.
4. Use former judges or other eminent legal authorities as hearing officers in cases involving major violations that are not resolved at the summary disposition process. Although the NCAA adopted the hearing-officer recommendation, the hearing-officer positions no longer exist. More importantly, the NCAA never adopted the recommendation of a truly independent trier of fact.
5. Create an appellate process. An NCAA Infractions Appeals Committee was developed in 1993.

Even though the NCAA agreed to allow audio recording of interviews and to add outside individuals to the Committee on Infractions and the Infractions Appeals Committee, it rejected both an independent trier of fact and open hearings. The NCAA believed that open hearings would inhibit investigations and dissuade people with allegations and knowledge of misconduct from cooperating. The NCAA also worried that an independent trier of fact would be expensive and that the persons performing that function would not understand the complexities of college sports. However, the existing system is flawed because members of the Committee on Infractions and the Infractions Appeals Committee are employees of peer member institutions that have an inherent conflict of interest in adjudicating infractions cases. Their judgment can bar a competitor institution from competition, revenue sharing, and recruiting or reduce its scholarships, rendering its teams less competitive over the long term.

Although the Lee Committee's recommendations have arguably made the NCAA enforcement process fairer during the past two decades, numerous flaws continue to plague NCAA jurisprudence. Besides the glaring omissions of an independent trier of fact and open hearings, respectively, the rights of confrontation and cross-examination are notably absent from this quasi-judicial process. The NCAA's current "cooperative principle" requires member institutions to self-report violations of association rules, investigate themselves, and assist the NCAA in such investigations or face enhanced penalties for not cooperating or for failing to correct faulty procedures. Still, institutions cannot force external third parties to cooperate with or supply information to NCAA investigations.

NCAA penalties can have numerous consequences. They can damage the reputations of institutions of higher education and cause coaches and athletic administrators to lose their jobs. They can also cause college athletes to lose participation and scholarship benefits. Accordingly, the Drake Group believes the NCAA must put in place strong processes designed to protect the rights of individuals and institutions. To restore public confidence in the governance of college sport, these processes should include discovery and enhanced procedural protections for individuals and institutions, to be overseen by former judges hired by the NCAA as independent contractors. Congress should mandate these enforcement-system reforms by tying them to eligibility for Higher Education Act funding. Both discovery and the use of experienced judges would ensure due process for all and consistency of punishment.

Proposed New Due Process Rules and Procedures

Institutional protections. The following new due process rules and procedures should be in place before the NCAA (a) issues a "show cause" order; (b) suspends a coach, athlete, or other athletics personnel from representing a member institution in athletics events; (c) suspends the telecommunications privileges of a member institution pertaining to athletic events; (d) levies a substantial financial penalty, or (e) suspends a member institution from participating in a collegiate athletic event.

1. Experienced third-party investigators should conduct investigations, and individuals with experience as trial or appellate judges or administrative law judges should conduct infractions hearings and appeal hearings. The NCAA should hire both the investigators and the judges as independent contractors to remove the appearance or actuality of conflict of interest by NCAA staff or committees. These judges and investigators would participate in enforcement cases involving severe and significant breaches of conduct enforcement cases (i.e., Level I and Level II cases) but would be excluded from participating in breaches of conduct and incidental issues for which penalties are not onerous (Level III and Level IV cases). They would preside at hearings and appeals, issue subpoenas when necessary (such authority should be requested from Congress), and possess exclusive authority to adjudicate, resolve, and issue final judgments, including penalties in enforcement cases under their jurisdiction. Subpoena power is an important part of these proposed guidelines. It would enable the NCAA to compel witnesses to appear at hearings and testify, thereby ensuring the production of a complete and accurate record of events.
2. In cases of severe or significant breaches of conduct (Level I and Level II cases), a prehearing "discovery" process (authority should be requested from Congress) should occur. It would include depositions

and document production and the gathering and exchange of pertinent information by NCAA staff and counsel for accused parties.

3. In cases of severe or significant breaches of conduct (Level I and Level II cases), accused parties, including coaches, athletes, institutional employees, and institutions themselves, should be permitted to confront and cross-examine opposing witnesses at hearings.
4. At the discretion of the hearing judge, a nonparty whom the NCAA or the accused institution has identified as having engaged in wrongdoing or as having enabled wrongdoing to occur may be permitted to present an oral or written statement at the hearing, subject to rebuttal by the institution. At any party's request, the judge shall require the statements to be given under oath or affirmation (authority should be requested of Congress).
5. Member institutions should be prohibited from firing or permanently reassigning employees or disassociating themselves from representatives of the institutions' athletic interests whom the NCAA or the accused institution has identified as having engaged in or enabled wrongdoing until after the case has been resolved and the nonparty's role in it has been determined.
6. All hearings and appellate proceedings should be open to the public, except when an accused party objects. This rule should not apply to the posthearing deliberations of the appellate panels, which would be closed to the public in accordance with the established procedures of appellate tribunals regarding postargument deliberations.
7. The NCAA should be prohibited from using its executive authority to sanction a member institution (such as occurred in the Penn State / Sandusky case) unless it has followed its established enforcement procedure.

Individual college athlete protections. The due process provisions just outlined would not be required in the cases of reductions to an athlete's financial aid dollar amount or award period or claims for reinstatement of athletic eligibility, which claims should be the exclusive responsibility of arbitration panels. These eligibility and financial aid decisions require timely action because the loss of eligibility or of financial support for one's education could be immediate. Therefore, the following due process provisions should be adopted to protect the rights of individual college athletes:

1. The NCAA should be required to hire and to provide salary, benefits, and administrative expenses for, and NCAA member institutions should be required to provide all athletes with contact information for, one or more Athlete Welfare Advocates, who shall provide independent legal advice to college athletes at no cost to the athlete regarding the application of NCAA rules and the athletes' due process rights.
2. Athletes declared ineligible for competition by their respective educational institutions or a national athletic association for reasons other than an insufficient grade point average, failure to make satisfactory progress toward a degree, or similar academic failure should have the right to appeal the eligibility determination and seek reinstatement by means of binding arbitration only.
3. A panel of arbitrators certified by the American Arbitration Association (AAA) and approved by the athlete and the athletic association would conduct the arbitration process in accordance with the AAA Commercial Arbitration Rules and Mediation Procedures. Binding arbitration would replace an appeal to any NCAA committee that reviews an institution's requests for the reinstatement of athletic eligibility in accordance with NCAA rules.
4. The arbitration panel's decision should be final and would bind the athlete involved, the athlete's educational institution, and any national athletic association of which the institution is a member.

Whistle-blower protection. Another important provision that should be required of any national governance organization and its member institutions is *whistle-blower protection*. College athletes, faculty, and other employees of NCAA member institutions who disclose unethical behavior or violations of NCAA or institutional rules related to the conduct of athletics programs should be protected from retaliation by their member institutions or institutional employees.

New Enforcement System Provisions Well Within the Financial Capacity of the NCAA

The estimated $9.1 million cost of such an enforcement system is well within the capacity of a national organization that is generating close to $1 billion annually and returning 90 percent to its Division I members.[1]

Calculation of Approximate Cost of Changes in NCAA Enforcement Process

Trying to determine the likely costs of implementing the due process changes called for by the preceding detailed reform provisions is difficult because it is hard to know with certainty how many judges will be needed and how many days they will work. Similarly, we do not know the number of binding arbitrations that might be required. Nonetheless, the following "ballpark figures" represent an educated guess, at the high end, of what such an enforcement system might cost in addition to current NCAA staff and operating expenses for these functions.

Summary of Estimated Costs

The total cost is estimated to be $9,160,900, and the summary of costs is outlined in table 7.1.

Detailed Explanation of Estimates

First, consider retired judges.

- The current NCAA Infractions Committee provides for up to twenty-four members, or eight panels of three members each. In contrast, retired judges under the new due process legislation will be highly

TABLE 7.1

SUMMARY OF ESTIMATED COSTS

30 hearings per year	
Hearing judges: 6, with each judge hearing 5 cases per year @ 7 days per case @ $2,000 per day ($70,000 per judge)	$420,000
Hearing judges' expenses: meals and incidentals @ $152 per day × 210 days	$31,920
20 appeals per year	
Appeals judges: 6, with each judge working 10 appeals at 4 days per appeal @ $2,500 per day ($100,000 per judge)	$600,000
Appeals judges' expenses: meals and incidentals @ $152 per day × 240 days	$36,480
Judge transportation expenses: 30 hearing judge trips and 60 appeals judge trips (3 judges per panel × 20 cases) @ $250 per trip	$22,500
Investigators: 30 cases per year at 250 hours per case @ $500 per hour	$3,750,000
Investigator travel and per diem costs: 30 cases × $15,000 per case	$450,000
Security guards and costs for hearings open to the public	
Athlete advocate expenses: see below, but the intent is to have a pool of names that work pro bono or at a low cost for an hourly or predetermined amount; incidental and travel expenses apply	$3,000,000
Binding arbitration for eligibility issues/reinstatement: @ $2,000 per day per case; total is estimated as a total pool amount	$250,000
Total	$9,160,900

experienced at considering disputes; therefore, only one hearing judge per case is proposed, just as in a civil or criminal court. The number of teams under NCAA penalty in recent years has been twenty to twenty-five. Overestimating case load, six hearing judges could consider thirty cases per year, although provision could be made for up to eight if necessary.

- The current Infractions Appeals Committee has five members, all of whom hear all appeals. Having six appeals judges would ensure that the same three-person panel would not sit on every case, thereby reducing the likelihood that one or two highly influential members would affect the outcome of every appeal. The United States Courts of Appeals use this system of rotating three-member panels.

- Assume six hearing judges, with each one hearing five cases per year, each of which would involve seven days of work (including prehearing discovery). Further assume that the hearing judges are paid at the high end of what arbitrators earn in labor-management disputes involving the NFL, NHL, or MLB, which would be $2,000 a day. They would be paid a per diem because they would be independent contractors.
- On the basis of these assumptions, each hearing judge would hear five cases per year, working seven days per case, or thirty-five days at $2,000 per day, for an annual total of $70,000. Adding to that the $152 Indianapolis per diem for meals and incidentals under Indiana law boosts the total by $5,320 ($152 × 35). Thus, the annual total for each hearing judge would be $75,320. Multiplied by six, the annual total for the hearing judges is $451,920.
- Regarding the appeals judges, note that not every case is appealed. Thus, assume twenty appeals per year, with each judge participating in half of them. Assuming four days of work per case at $2,500 per day (appellate judges earn more than trial judges), each judge would earn $10,000 per appeal for ten appeals, or $100,000 per year. Adding the $152 per diem for meals and incidentals times 240 days of work (twenty appeals times four days per appeal times three judges per appeal) results in $36,480 in per diem costs. Multiplying by six judges yields a total for the appeals judges of $640,800 per year.
- As to transportation costs, the NCAA would presumably be able to find enough retired judges in Indiana and the neighboring states to handle these matters. Thus, a transportation budget of $250 per judge per case (thirty hearings requiring thirty judges and twenty appeals requiring sixty judges), or $22,500, would cover these estimated costs.
- Finally, adding the costs for both sets of judges produces a total annual judicial cost of $1,110,900.

Next, consider binding arbitration.

- This cost is based on a rate of $2,000 per day per professional arbitrator, which is a high-end estimate. Most eligibility appeals can be heard in one day, although additional time will be required for the three-member panel to deliberate, reach a decision, and issue that decision in writing.

Then, examine third-party investigators.

- The investigators are likely to be lawyers. Presumably, the NCAA could hire retired lawyers as independent contractors to do this work. It probably would not make sense to hire someone who already has a busy law practice. Nor should the NCAA hire law professors from NCAA member institutions. One model would be to hire, say, six retired lawyers, with each one working alone, supported by the NCAA's clerical staff, as needed. Another model would be to have two-person investigative teams consisting of a retired lawyer and a retired law enforcement officer, perhaps, to assist.
- Assuming the model adopted is a lawyer working alone and assuming thirty cases per year, each investigating lawyer would handle five cases. Five cases, at 250 hours per case, and $500 per hour (a middle-range rate in employment arbitration cases, which seem like a reasonable analog) gets us to $125,000 per case for the investigator. Multiplying that by five cases equals $625,000 per investigator per year. Then multiplying $625,000 per investigator per year by six investigators gets us to $3,750,000 per year in investigative costs.
- Adding $15,000 per case in travel expenses, multiplied by thirty cases, we get $450,000 in travel expenses. Finally, adding $450,000 to $3,750,000 gets us to $4,200,000 in annual investigative costs.
- This estimate is probably a bit high, but it is in the ballpark. Two-person investigative teams would make it higher, although the retired law enforcement officers would not command the same hourly rate

that the retired lawyers would (probably half or less), so the cost per investigation would not double.

And then, there are athlete advocates.

- This is a critical aspect of due process so that involved athletes who do not have access to appropriate and knowledgeable counsel can be represented effectively. NCAA rules are nebulous on who can pay for and provide counsel for athletes involved in NCAA investigations. The intent would be to develop a potential pool of athlete advocates who are willing to work pro bono or with a preestablished contingency fee to control costs. There will be substantial incidental and transportation costs, so again this is just an estimate.
- Potential athlete advocates include attorneys, professors, and administrators of the College Athletes Players Association, the Drake Group, and various sports law practices. There will probably be no shortage of available, interested, and qualified people for this important task.

And there are other costs.

- Two other costs could also arise. To open enforcement hearings to the public, the NCAA may have to hire additional security guards. Assuming salaries and benefits totaling $100,000 per person and the hiring of six guards, these costs could be as high as $600,000.

NOTES

1. See NCAA, "Finances," accessed January 3, 2015, http://www.ncaa.org/about/resources/finances.

CHAPTER 8

College Athlete Health and Protection from Physical and Psychological Harm

Donna Lopiano, Janet Blade, Gerald Gurney, Sheila Hudson, Brian Porto, Allen Sack, David Ridpath, and Andrew Zimbalist

Reports of failures by college coaches and other athletics personnel, institutional administrative and oversight mechanisms, and national collegiate athletics governance policies to protect the health and well-being of college athletes have reached epidemic proportions. These reports note traumatic and nontraumatic deaths,[1] athletes requiring hospitalization for rhabdomyolysis (an avoidable condition that results from overexertion and can cause kidney damage or death), cardiac arrest, failures to treat heat-related illness, inadequate efforts to address repetitive head contact and concussion in numerous sports, inadequate sickle-cell-trait protocols, coach abuse, humiliation, and other professional misconduct. The reports have also noted sexual harassment and assault, inadequate athletic-injury insurance, and the mental and physical health costs of excessive athletics department demands on the time of college athletes.

Periodically, the national media and the public are transfixed by a single occurrence, such as the tragic avoidable death in 2018 from heatstroke of the University of Maryland football player Jordan McNair. A local investigative reporter's 2019 multiple-episode coverage of a punishment workout and subsequent hospitalization for exertional rhabdomyolysis of

---

The Drake Group (October 1, 2019).

twelve female University of Houston soccer players also garnered much attention.

A typical scenario unfolds. The public and the higher-education community are momentarily shocked, and the offending institution promises a full, unbiased investigation and a change of policy. The coach might be fired, or, if a popular, winning coach is involved, a lower-level employee might be sacrificed.

Either way, the NCAA typically takes no responsibility, turning its head the other way and claiming that only the institution is responsible for protecting athletes. If the NCAA is sued in its capacity as a governance organization, it might settle out of court while acknowledging no fault, thereby avoiding an embarrassing display of evidence at trial or an adverse judgment. If media coverage includes calls for NCAA rules that put athlete-protective policies in place for member institutions, the NCAA might appoint a study committee or blue-ribbon commission and wait until the media storm blows over before issuing a report that results in minimal change, if any. Even though the NCAA was founded in 1906 because the president of the United States threatened to ban colleges from playing football if the deaths of athletes were not addressed, it has not taken responsibility for protecting the health and wellness of college athletes.

The Drake Group confronts these issues on the basis of its belief that educators, educational institutions, and education-related governance organizations should have as their highest priority protection of the health and well-being of students. Intercollegiate athletics programs should neither ignore nor increase the health risks of college athletes.

We would be remiss not to acknowledge that many well-trained and conscientious coaches and sports-management professionals at the institutional level run a "tight ship" regarding these health-protection obligations. Similarly, individuals within conference and national governance organizations are ringing warning bells regarding the absence of rules and regulations necessary to mandate members' adoption of best practices in sports medicine. The focus of this essay, however, is on continued failures by the intercollegiate athletics system to protect the health and well-being of college athletes.

Finally, although we do not make a legal argument for or against NCAA responsibility for athlete health and wellness, we consistently refer to a "duty of care." This term reflects our view that individuals, higher-education institutions, and intercollegiate athletics governance associations have an ethical responsibility to protect the physical and educational well-being of college athletes.

Duty of Care

Besides protecting the educational well-bring of college athletes as students, the coaches and other professionals who work in college athletics programs have a responsibility to protect students on their teams from foreseeable injuries or other harm. Higher-education institutions and athletics governance organizations have that same duty of care. Educational institutions address these risks by establishing policies and procedures that define appropriate coaching conduct and employee responsibilities, specify credentials and background checks required for employment of athletics personnel, and require employee education. Other policies and procedures assign personnel responsible for inspecting facilities, establish expectations for the safe operation of all programs, monitor coach pedagogy, and administer employee discipline in the case of improper conduct. National governance organizations and conferences use their rule-making and enforcement authorities to require all members to respond to recognized causes of harm in specific ways. These organizations also collect, aggregate, and monitor research about and incidents of athletics injury and similar harms to improve policy, educate members, ensure the development of safe rules of play, and guarantee competent officiating. This essay addresses issues of potential harm to college athletes of which athletics professionals and governance entities are fully aware and examines whether those individuals and entities are meeting their responsibilities to prevent such harm.

Athletics Culture and Moral Injury

When coaches and other athletics program personnel use the power of their positions either to directly harm athletes, knowing they will not be held accountable, or to ignore or hide athlete mistreatment, they inflict moral injury as well as physical or psychological harm. Such moral injury is a betrayal of trust in leaders whom college athletes expect to be guided by a higher-order duty to prevent harm and comply with rules.[2] When coaches or other administrators place their own self-interest or an interest in protecting the brand of the athletics program, institution, or governance organization above their duty to protect college athletes, the resulting failure has a core value impact that is more damaging than even traditional mental (depression, anxiety, etc.) or physical harm. An extreme example is the failure of Michigan State University to protect more than four hundred gymnasts from the team physician Larry Nassar's sexual abuse. How did that failure affect the athletes' trust in the educational institution they attended when they realized that at the highest levels of the institution, leaders knew, refused to act, and were complicit in a cover-up? How do the silence, denial, and inaction compound the psychological impact of the harm itself?

Equally distressing is the reasonable assumption that the majority of Division I college athletes are fully aware of the highly commercialized and exploitative college sport system and do not expect fair treatment from powerful coaches and administrators. Perhaps the value of a scholarship, a small chance of entering the professional ranks, momentary fame, and privileged status among one's classmates are the quid pro quo for acceptance of moral injury. Is there any choice but complicity for the predominantly minority Division I football and basketball players who know they do not meet regular academic admission standards, are specially admitted through academic waivers, and then accede to the institution's system of academic fraud dedicated to maintaining their eligibility to play? This acceptance of moral injury means that the current intercollegiate athletics system must change fundamentally. Just expecting the institutions to improve their management of the system's negative moral, physical, and mental health consequences is unrealistic.

The Absence of Standards for the Certification of Athletic Coaches or Mechanisms to Address Professional Misconduct

Lack of Accredited Certification

One of the significant failures of the US education system has been to embed athletics in our educational institutions without applying any substantive professional preparation or licensure standards to coaches. We require classroom teachers to demonstrate sufficient levels of education, credentials appropriate to the grade levels in which they teach, and the completion of continuing education requirements. Educational institutions accredited to perform this preparation function train teachers, who must then apply for licensure or certification from the state in which they wish to teach. Coaches have no similar requirements, although they operate in a much higher risk environment than classroom teachers do. Coaches are not required to be teachers or physical educators. Some states merely require that coaches in K–12 settings be school-district employees who pass criminal background checks and have completed first aid, CPR, or other emergency or concussion/heat-related-illness response training programs and maybe an online course in coaching fundamentals. The online course may or may not be offered by an accredited institution of higher education.[3] College coaches have similar minimal requirements, but instead of the online coaching-fundamentals course, an undergraduate degree is usually required. The undergraduate degree, though, does not have to be in a field related to athletics, as coaching experience is often an acceptable substitute. Coaches learn the Xs and Os when they attend conventions and workshops or seek coaching credentials from open amateur sport national governing bodies, but they are not required to have training in protecting athletes from physical and psychological harm. They coach as they have been coached or try to emulate the coaches they admire. Increasingly, college coaches come from youth-travel-team programs that embrace a "more is better" philosophy and a year-round commitment to one sport in pursuit of a college athletic scholarship. The predictable results are "burnout" and chronic overuse injuries at an early age. Athletics directors and other administrators are well aware of the challenges posed by unprepared coaches using questionable pedagogy.

Lack of Standards for Professional Conduct

Athletics managers are also aware of common instances of coaching malpractice, such as verbal abuse and the use of conditioning activities as punishment for perceived lack of effort or performance errors. The absence of coaching preparation standards, however, does not fully explain such malpractice. Coaches who win are often allowed to continue questionable practices and are protected by their institutions when such practices are revealed via student complaints or media coverage. Worse yet, too many winning coaches are allowed to intimidate and overrule athletic trainers and other support staff who are hired to serve athletes. Lavish financial and reputational investments in Division I basketball and football programs also corrupt athlete-protection efforts related to coach pedagogy. The label "winning at all costs" is the commonly used descriptor; it is an invitation to the abuse of athletes.

Professional Misconduct

The exercise of a coach's or staff member's power over the college athlete often crosses the line into professional misconduct. The US Center for Safe Sport's "SafeSport Code" applies to open amateur and Olympic/Paralympic sport programs operated by entities outside the US education system.[4] Unfortunately, the NCAA has not promulgated an analogous document that specifically defines professional misconduct by college coaches. The "SafeSport Code" defines and prohibits sexual or gender-related harassment, nonconsensual sexual contact or intercourse, sexual exploitation, bullying, hazing, and emotional and physical abuse and provides the mechanisms for college athletes to confidentially report such abuse. It also identifies the responsibility of all adults associated with the sport program to be mandatory reporters and specifies an adjudication process that could result in permanently banning the offending coach from employment in any covered sport programs. Absent national governance association rules, college coaches are left to the jurisdiction of their employer institutions, which may or may not have policies dealing with abusive behaviors. Institutional employee policies are often deficient in that they do not identify behaviors specific to athletic environments, such as the use of physical exercise for punishment or the types of verbal and emotional abuse commonly practiced by coaches. Athletics department policy manuals may or may not exist and may or may not include a code of professional conduct. If a coach's employment is terminated for such misconduct, no system prevents the coach from moving to another institution and continuing such behaviors. No NCAA system exists for processing college athlete complaints about such treatment. Some institutions lack such complaint processes for athletes.

Institutions Often Enable Coach Misconduct

Ignorance of the information required to competently coach elite athletes does not absolve the coach from a duty of care. The athletics manager is fully aware of the lack of credentials, so the onus is clearly on the higher-education institution to address such deficiencies or be held liable for coach negligence. The answer is not a simple matter of institutions stiffening educational requirements on coach position descriptions used in the hiring process. Institutions often fail to enforce educational competency requirements if winning coaches lack them. They simply accept proven team success in lieu of peer-reviewed accredited credentialing.

A similar practice of looking the other way may prevail even if the institution has a complaint-reporting system for athletes. Administrators may pressure athletes to withdraw complaints with a promise that the administration will address verbal, physical, or emotional abuse and that it will not continue. Athletics managers recognize that the coach's power can be so significant that few athletes have the courage to report mistreatment for fear they might lose their athletic scholarships, a starting role on the team, or a coach committed to their training and success. Even if the complaint advances to an investigation conducted outside the athletics department or by a so-called external independent agency (often an institution-friendly law firm), institutions seldom find fault with themselves. Instead, they protect the institutional brand from bad press or litigation by failing to find any wrongdoing despite reports of coach/employee misconduct (sexual or otherwise) toward athletes.

Absence of Skilled Oversight and an Athletics Program Culture That Inhibits the Reporting of Misconduct

Responsibility for oversight of coach pedagogy at the institutional level most often lies with an assistant athletic director who is charged with supervising multiple sport programs. This administrator seldom attends team practices and almost never attends separate strength and conditioning practices. Even if the administrator does attend such training sessions, the administrator is highly unlikely to have the training to recognize dangerous sport-specific or strength and conditioning practices. Few institutions can provide a certified athletic trainer for every practice and competition and all strength and conditioning sessions. Although a certified athletic trainer has the training to police the pedagogy of coaches and strength and conditioning specialists, this individual is subject to the same power imbalance as the college athlete. Trainers who observe misconduct may fear losing their jobs or a prestigious assignment to the team of a winning coach if they report the coach for dangerous workouts. Such institution-level realities cannot be overcome unless the national governance association installs mechanisms similar to the SafeSport program.

Strength and Conditioning Coaches: Enforcers or Performance Specialists?

Multiple concerns surround the position of athletics program strength and conditioning coaches: (1) lack of accredited certification, (2) use as enforcers of physical penalties on athletes, (3) hiring and supervision by head coaches instead of the medical team, (4) heightened concern about rhabdomyolysis, which results from unrealistic physical demands and a failure to acclimate before strenuous exercise, and (5) the use of strength and conditioning programs as a means of evading hour limits on athletics-related activities.

Lack of Accredited Certification

Not until 2014 did the NCAA require that strength and conditioning coaches "be certified and maintain current certification through a nationally accredited strength and conditioning certification program."[5] The NCAA acknowledges the ineffectiveness of the rule in its recently released *Interassociation Recommendations: Preventing Catastrophic Injury and Death in Collegiate Athletes*:

> The current state of credentialing across the strength and conditioning profession makes it difficult to ensure that all strength and conditioning professionals have the requisite competency to safely and effectively conduct conditioning sessions. Many organizations currently offer "strength and conditioning" credentials, though there is significant variability in both the content represented by these credentials and the rigor required to attain them. The complete absence of state regulation further complicates this landscape because there is no clearly established strength and conditioning scope of practice, and therefore, there is no authoritative accounting of the knowledge and skill domains required for the safe and effective practice of a strength and conditioning professional.[6]

Further, the policy suggests that closing the credentials loophole would require an NCAA rule to specify certification through a program accredited by the National Commission for Certifying Agencies.[7] No such NCAA rule currently exists.

Role of "Enforcer"

In the case of football and basketball especially, the head coach need not participate in the physical abuse of athletes. Assistant coaches and strength and conditioning coaches (the latter not counted against limits on the number of coaches) can "do the dirty work." Unfortunately, athletes and coaches have bought into the false narrative that physical punishment is acceptable and that extra conditioning workloads will only help. Even the NCAA knows this is not true. Adopted by the NCAA, the *Interassociation Recommendations* state that "physical activity never should be used for punitive purposes. Exercise as punishment invariably abandons sound physiologic principles and elevates risk above any reasonable performance reward."[8] The NCAA FAQ document accompanying the recommendations provides more details about why exercise should not be punitive:

> The recommendations note that punishment workouts are based on intent and unsound physiological principles. However, beyond that, no formal definition is provided. Punishment workouts are more than just "extra exercise." In general terms, punitive workouts are motivated by anger or frustration and may include a volume and intensity of exercise corresponding to that anger and frustration. Such volume and intensity is not part of a planned workout and is not based on sound principles of exercise science and physiology, but rather is used to make athletes "tougher" or to create a team culture of "accountability." Punitive exercises are unplanned, spontaneous, are inconsistent with the conditioning level of the athlete or team, are not logically progressive in intensity, and are not sport-specific in their nature. Common sense should prevail.[9]

Hiring and Supervision by Head Coaches

The *Interassociation Recommendations* policy clearly states the problem with coaches hiring or supervising strength and conditioning staff members:

> An additional problem arises through the increasingly close alignment between sport coaches and strength and conditioning professionals, especially in the sport of football. Strength and conditioning professionals frequently are hired by the head football coach, and/or subject to their administrative oversight. This alignment is problematic because it contributes to the perception that strength and conditioning professionals are members of the coaching staff rather than independently credentialed strength and conditioning professionals. Such singular alignment and reporting are not consistent with this document. All strength and conditioning professionals should have a reporting line into the sports medicine or sport performance lines of the institution. This includes sport coaches who have responsibility for providing strength and conditioning services across all sport teams.[10]

Rhabdomyolysis and Acclimatization Concerns

The increased emphasis on strength and conditioning via the hiring of specialized personnel and an expectation that athletes will engage in year-round workouts reflect coaches' efforts to achieve a winning edge. Presumably, adding strength and conditioning specialists to an athletics staff provides expertise that will keep athletes safe. Not so. Preventable nontraumatic deaths, occurring primarily during out-of-season or preseason workouts, remain a major concern. Rhabdomyolysis (overexertion syndrome that damages or destroys muscle fibers, releasing proteins into the bloodstream that can result in kidney failure) is life-threatening and totally preventable. Heat-related illnesses, such as heat stroke and heat exhaustion, dangerously elevate the body's core temperature and are similarly life-threatening but preventable. Yet we continue to see these occurrences in college athletics programs, and they are not being successfully addressed:

- Between 2001 and 2017, the ratio of nontraumatic to traumatic deaths in collegiate football was 5:1—thirty-five nontraumatic deaths compared with seven traumatic fatalities.[11]
- Following a January 2017 workout, which included over an hour of continuous push-ups and up-downs, three University of Oregon football players were hospitalized with rhabdomyolysis. A strength training coach whose only credential was a twenty-one-hour strength training course was in charge of the session. He was suspended for one month following the incident and is now the head strength and conditioning coach at Florida State University.[12]
- On August 1, 2019, a Garden City Community College football player died of exertional heat stroke following a conditioning session in which players were asked to run thirty-five fifty-yard sprints with little rest, on a hot, muggy night.[13]
- In February 2019, twelve University of Houston women's soccer players were hospitalized with rhabdomyolysis after everyone on the team was forced to perform one hundred "up-downs" (similar to burpees) as a penalty for two players taking food designated for the football team.[14]
- On May 29, 2018, the University of Maryland football player Jordan McNair died of heatstroke during a football workout supervised by strength and conditioning staff members. After warm-up, players were told to run ten 110-yard sprints.[15]

Evasion of Practice Limitations

Division I football and basketball programs now operate year-round, contrary to NCAA season limits and rules that exclude out-of-season team practices, evading the spirit, if not the letter, of the rules. For the proffered reason of athlete safety, strength and conditioning coaches are permitted to be present at so-called voluntary athlete workouts during the summer and during the regular academic year when team practices are prohibited. The message is clear to athletes that participation in these strength and conditioning workouts is anything but voluntary. Often, financial support for athletes' summer-school attendance cements the expectation.

Coaches and athletic administrators defend year-round training, maintaining that going "academic light" during the semester when the sport is in season prevents sport from negatively affecting studies (fewer classes missed, athletes can take more difficult classes in the summer or during noncompetition / less competition semester, etc.) by spacing out courses over twelve months. The justification would make sense if athletics departments were not openly engaged in academic fraud. Standard operating practice for high-priority-for-success sports programs is to waive academic admissions standards for talented athletes, the majority of whom are minority football and basketball players, which, in turn, begins a pattern of exploitation about which the institution is well aware. Athletics departments (rather than academic departments) conduct their own tutoring and advising programs—a direct conflict of interest. Athletes are encouraged or required to enroll in less demanding majors and courses and take courses with friendly professors or take online courses or "independent studies," which do not demand classroom attendance. Athletes take the minimum required number of courses to fulfill the "full-time student" status required for athletics eligibility during the regular academic year. Then they receive scholarships to attend summer classes to ensure they meet the requirements to show "normal progress" toward a degree. This academic system is artfully branded as an athlete "benefit" to hide its true purposes—enabling coaches to facilitate year-round conditioning expectations and non-coach-directed sport practices, thereby disguising the academic exploitation of academically underprepared athletes and allowing coaches to better control the athletes' lives. The more rigorous the academic program and the more selective the institution, the greater is the insult to this group, whose members are ill prepared to compete in the classroom with their nonathlete peers. These athletes are also isolated from the college educational experience within athletes-only computer centers and study halls and athletic facilities, so isolated that student-athlete life now effectively continues throughout the summer as well as during the regular academic year.

Athlete Mental Health

Athlete mental health concerns deserve discussion from three perspectives: prevention, awareness of mental health services, and treatment.

Prevention

The most recent research literature[16] related to the mental health of elite athletes supports the identification of the following controllable sport-specific factors that pose high risks to athlete mental health: (a) the stigma associated with seeking counseling, (b) lack of access to mental health services, (c) lack of early identification and referral of athletes with mental health symptoms, (d) insufficient sleep, (e) injury and the associated relationship of injury with premature return and overuse, (f) competitive failure, (g) pain, (h) concussion, (i) retirement, (j) overtraining, (k) body-shaming pressure from coaches and team weigh-ins, and the three most common forms of nonaccidental violence perpetuated by adults (usually coaches) with power over athletes: (l) psychological abuse, (m) physical abuse, and (n) sexual abuse.

The literature also teaches that the culture of sports can both complicate and enhance athlete mental health. Media and campus expressions of approval or excitement for exemplary athletic performance certainly reinforce athletes' feelings of self-worth. But the exposure of academic fraud and athlete exploitation or campus outrage over lavish athletic facilities or special treatment for athletes can produce the opposite effect. Cultural acceptance is important, and marginalization of athlete subgroups, as expressed by unequal treatment, unequal resources, socioeconomic inequities, and discrimination based on race, gender stereotyping, gender identity or expression, or sexual orientation, creates stressors that influence the mental health of these populations. To make matters worse, evidence indicates that Black college athletes are more difficult to reach because (a) mental health services have been stigmatized in the African American community; (b) these students feel that they do not have the time to access such services due to athletic, academic, and social obligations; (c) especially among Black males, talking about emotions is considered a sign of weakness; and (d) the combined stigmas associated with being Black and a student-athlete often affect the "way they respond to and interact with other students, teachers and professors."[17]

Concerning prevention, the problems are that (a) the NCAA has failed to promulgate rules requiring institutions to address those factors that exacerbate athletes' mental health issues; (b) the rules, if passed, do not extend to all member institutions; or (c) such rules are simply inadequate. For example, in 2019, Divisions I and II adopted rules requiring that mental health services be available to athletes and that educational materials about access to such services and other mental health resources be provided to athletes, coaches, and athletic personnel. But Division III has not adopted that rule.[18] The NCAA does not require certification of sport coaches or strength and conditioning coaches, nor does it have an enforceable "code of conduct" that prohibits coaches from engaging in psychological, physical, or sexual abuse; body shaming; or team weigh-ins. Individual NCAA member institutions cannot control powerful, winning coaches, and the void created by the absence of NCAA rules leaves athletes unprotected from coach violence. The NCAA has failed to control athlete time demands, and the result is often athlete sleep deprivation. The NCAA has adopted rules related to concussion protocols and has reduced two-a-day practices but has not limited the number of full-pad or contact practices in football during the championship and nontraditional seasons, despite knowledge that such limits would reduce injuries in general and concussions in particular. Although the NCAA has published "best practices" with regard to year-round football practice contact, only a few of these "recommendations" have been adopted by the NCAA as mandated football practice limitations.[19] It is simply insufficient to require the provision of athlete mental health services without also addressing the factors that create the need for such services. We know what the controllable factors are, but the NCAA has not adopted rules to mandate "best practices" or to prohibit practices that endanger the mental health of athletes.

Awareness of Mental Health Services

Effective in 2019–20, Divisions I and II are required to provide mental health services to athletes. Notably, the rule is not applicable to Division III.

> 16.4.2. Mental Health Services and Resources. An institution shall make mental health services and resources available to its student-athletes. Such services and resources may be provided by the department of athletics and/or the institution's health services or counseling services department. Provision of services and resources should be consistent with the Interassociation Consensus: Mental Health Best Practices. In addition, an institution must distribute mental health educational materials and resources to student-athletes, including those transitioning out of their sport, coaches, athletics administrators and other athletics personnel throughout the year. Such educational materials and resources must include a guide to the mental health services and resources available at the institution and information regarding how to access them.[20]

Most colleges and universities have a student health center that provides health and counseling services, but such centers have varying resources and staff expertise. The purpose of the newly issued NCAA publication *Interassociation Consensus Document: Mental Health Best Practices* is to "provide athletics and sports medicine departments—regardless of size and resources—with recommendations for supporting and promoting student-athlete mental health."[21] The NCAA Sports Science Institute (SSI) website contains numerous resources that institutions may choose to use to fulfill this obligation to distribute educational materials.[22] Indeed, the provision of educational resources is a valuable function of the NCAA's Sports Science Institute. However, this mental health initiative includes no athlete-protection "teeth." For example, the NCAA could require every coach to be "mental health" certified by completing a NCAA Sports Science Institute online training program or by complying with an NCAA coaches "code of conduct" that prohibits psychological, physical, or sexual abuse and includes a similar training/certification requirement. The NCAA has long required coaches to be certified via a standardized NCAA-developed national test on recruiting regulations before being allowed to recruit.[23] Certainly, a required test on coaches' understanding of mental health best practices would be a reasonable expectation.

Treatment

The NCAA's *Interassociation Consensus Document: Mental Health Best Practices* specifies that treatment providers be licensed clinical mental health care professionals whose work would be coordinated by the athletic trainer and team physician.[24] The NCAA should be commended for recommending that the athlete be allowed to self-refer to a list of licensed practitioners provided by the athletics medical teams, thereby promising patient confidentiality that may be critical. The NCAA also properly cautions the institution to carefully examine the circumstance in which it hires an individual to work with athletes who is trained in performance enhancement but is not licensed to provide mental health services. The medical team must carefully consider whether an athlete's performance deficiency has an underlying mental health disorder. Ideally, if the institution is going to hire a sports performance specialist and successfully avoid the possibility of that position attempting to provide mental health services without a license, the individual should be qualified to do work across the spectrum of the most common issues presented by college athletes. Such an individual would have a PhD or PsyD in counseling or clinical psychology or be a licensed independent clinical social worker with a certification in sport social work (Alliance of Social Workers in Sports) and also be an AASP Certified Consultant (Association for Applied Sport Psychology).

Institutional Policy and Oversight Systems

If one looks up "risk" in any collegiate athletics department policy handbook, one is likely to find that any requirements will be limited to facilities and equipment. One is more likely to see a policy demanding that all college athletes exhibit sportsmanship than a policy prohibiting coaches from using exercise as punishment or engaging in other behaviors that pose health risks to the college athlete. The institutional failures to protect athlete health and well-being are grounded in eight factors: (a) acknowledged impotence in controlling the practices of powerful winning coaches, (b) lack of institutional / athletics department policy and oversight protections, (c) inadequate insurance protection, (d) the absence of national or conference rules that force institutions to install such protections, (e) denial of any institutional fault that damages its or the athletics department's brand or increases vulnerability to legal liability or lack of athlete recruiting success, (f) athletes' fear of retaliation that silences the possibility of their complaints, (g) an anachronistic athletic culture that celebrates "tough" coaches and coaching practices as builders of character and winning teams, and (h) the absence of whistle-blower protection or mandatory reporting of sport personnel behaviors that endanger athletes.

Impotence in Controlling Powerful Coaches

College presidents have clearly indicated that they have limited power to produce change on their own campuses. Among Football Bowl Subdivision college presidents, 80 percent believe that they are unable to control their commercialized athletics programs.[25] Too many presidents have lost their jobs challenging major donors, trustees, and legislators who want to win football and basketball contests. Coaches' salaries are out of control, and college presidents know that they are at risk when the winning football coach can easily go somewhere else if salary demands are not met. If the coach leaves, the president is blamed. In such an environment, challenging a powerful and winning coach about the efficacy of his or her potentially harmful coaching practices is considered by many presidents to be tantamount to voluntary termination. Even when policies exist regarding the primacy of medical-team decision-making, the job of the athletic trainer or physician may be at risk if the trainer or physician challenges a coach.[26] In a 2019 National Athletic Trainers Association survey of its membership, 19 percent of college athletic trainers reported that a coach played an athlete who had not been cleared to participate, 36 percent of respondents reported that a coach influenced the hiring and firing of sports medicine staff, and 58 percent reported the being pressured by a coach or administrator to make a decision was "not in the best interest of the student-athlete's health."[27]

Lack of Policy and Oversight Protections

If the college president is powerless to control winning coaches, who will? College athlete deaths and near deaths due to rhabdomyolysis and heat-related illness have focused the spotlight on the athletics medical team—the doctors and certified athletic trainers with credentials that cannot be ignored by the public or powerful stakeholders. Although the *Inter-association Recommendations: Preventing Catastrophic Injury and Death in Collegiate Athletes* calls for coaches and strength and conditioning specialists to "have a reporting line into the sports medicine or sport performance lines of the institution," the NCAA rulebook does not require that arrangement, and neither do the recommendations. In response to the question of whether institutions must implement the recommended reporting line by August 1, 2019, the implementation date of the recommendations, it is clear from the following NCAA response that the document is merely recommending an institutional standard of care: "August 1, 2019 is the starting line—not the finishing line—for school adoption of the recommendations in this document. Member schools should have begun the process of aligning with the document by August 1, 2019, utilizing the Checklist as a guide. This includes beginning the process of determining alignment strategies with strength and conditioning professionals."[28]

Assuming that institutions adopt the recommended "medical model," the public should know that doctors are not going to be on-campus attending team practices. Few institutions have sports medicine MDs within school health centers, and even if they do, a physician would not be used to cover practice sessions. Most institutions do not have a sports medicine physician on campus. It is more typical for the athletics department or the campus health center to enter into an agreement with an external sports medicine specialty group, usually one with a focus on orthopedic issues. Many schools are simply too small to have any MD on staff. Thus, the only licensed medical professionals in almost every athletics department are the NATA-certified athletic trainers who, like registered school nurses, operate under "doctors' orders." The NCAA does have a rule that addresses the authority of athletic trainers and sports medicine staff:

> 13.11.3.8.2. Strength and Conditioning Coach First Aid / CPR Certification and Authority of Sports Medicine Staff—Sports Other Than Football. A strength and conditioning coach who conducts voluntary weight-training or conditioning activities is required to maintain certification in first aid and cardiopulmonary resuscitation. If a member of the institution's sports medicine staff (e.g., athletic trainer, physician) is present during voluntary conditioning activities conducted by a strength and conditioning coach, the sports medicine staff member must be empowered with the unchallengeable authority to cancel or modify the workout for health and safety reasons, as he or she deems appropriate.[29]

Only football is required to have a certified athletic trainer in attendance at "voluntary" conditioning activities.[30] The policy contains a big "if" regarding the presence of a medical-team member for such activities in all other sports. Although the policy confers authority on medical staff, one must question whether an athletic trainer believes it is in the best interest of his or her continued employment to confront a powerful coach if the trainer observes a drill or conditioning activity that appears harmful to athlete safety. The policy is also limited to "voluntary conditioning sessions," when no coaches are present, rather than applying to all team practices and required conditioning sessions.

Few schools can afford large athletic training staffs. Many have one to three full-time trainers supplemented by student assistants, and still others contract for such services with third parties. Dependence on athletic trainer oversight, considering the current workloads of these positions, is problematic, especially if the trainers are expected to cover every practice session and every competition and to attend separate strength and conditioning sessions. Further, at many institutions, medical-care assignments are based on whether a sport is a revenue sport or a nonrevenue sport, as opposed to providing equitable care for all sports or being based on whether a sport has a high injury risk. Trainers will rightfully argue that multiple solutions are required: (a) increased funding to permit the hiring of more certified athletic trainers, (b) the imposition of stronger credentialing and state licensure requirements for strength and conditioning coaches, (c) more stringent credentials for athletic coaches and training programs for supervisors of sport programs, and (d) approval by the medical team of all conditioning programs created by sport coaches or strength and conditioning coaches.

Oversight over sport programs in larger and better resourced athletics programs is relegated to one or more assistant athletic directors with multiple sports in their assignment portfolio. Few of these sports managers, however, are trained to identify inappropriate strength or conditioning demands. Sports management degrees do not require courses in biomechanics or exercise physiology. Similarly, athletic directors are not always trained to promulgate coach conduct and pedagogy policies that identify impermissible practices.

Thus, although lines of authority exist on paper to identify appropriate personnel with knowledge to address potentially harmful practices, considerable policy and personnel gaps still prevent adequate athlete protection. No magic model exists in which a powerful and autonomous student health center independent of the athletics department hires and supervises a sufficient number of personnel trained in sports medicine.

Inadequate and Selective Insurance Protection

The NCAA, its member conferences, and its member institutions derive billions of dollars from television media rights for regular-season games and postseason championship events. The NCAA provides a type of catastrophic-injury insurance for all 430,000 NCAA athletes. Its member institutions must certify that all of their athletes are covered by athletic-injury insurance as a condition of participation. The minimum amount of such coverage must be equal to or greater than the deductible of the NCAA Catastrophic Injury Insurance Program. The member institution may provide medical and related expenses and services to a student-athlete, including paying for athletic-injury insurance. The operative word, though, is "may." Neither the NCAA nor its member institutions are "required" to provide primary athletic-injury insurance for athletes. Most college athletics programs require parents and student-athletes to carry their own insurance as a condition of permitting athletic participation, and most require athletes or their parents to pay for deductibles specified by those policies. College athletics departments usually carry secondary policies, and some cover the cost of deductibles. A limit of two years of benefits from the date of the injury is an insurance-industry norm. Thus, most college athletes pay for their own primary insurance and deductibles, and if medical expenses occur after the two-year coverage period, the athlete must absorb that expense.

The NCAA allows some athletes from some institutions to be better protected from medical expenses than others. Although the NCAA has 1,098 members, only 6 percent, the richest 65 member institutions of the

Power Five FBS conferences, have the autonomy to provide additional benefits to their athletes that other members may not offer or to require the funding of specified medical services. For example, the following rule, adopted in 2018, only applies to these 65 institutions and results in athletes from these institutions being totally insulated from incurring any athletic injury expense:

> 16.4.1. Medical Coverage. An institution shall provide medical care to a student-athlete for an athletically related injury incurred during his or her involvement in intercollegiate athletics for the institution. The period of care for such an injury shall extend at least two years following either graduation or separation from the institution, or until the student-athlete qualifies for coverage under the NCAA Catastrophic Injury Insurance Program, whichever occurs first. Each institution has the discretion to determine the method by which it will provide medical care, the method by which it determines whether an injury is athletically related and any policy deemed necessary for implementing the medical care.[31]

These special medical-expense benefits will probably be provided via the athletics department's purchase of insurance.

Some athletes receive disability/loss-of-value insurance coverage. Each year the NCAA distributes monies referred to as the Student Assistance Fund (SAF) to conferences for distribution to their respective member institutions. The purpose of this fund is to "assist student-athletes in meeting financial needs that arise in conjunction with participation in intercollegiate athletics, enrollment in academic curriculum or to recognize academic achievement."[32] Typically, the fund has been used to finance athletes' travel to return home upon the death of a family member or similar extraordinary circumstances. Recently, a number of institutions have used these funds to provide disability/loss-of-value insurance to star players.[33] This insurance, often costing in the $30,000 to $50,000 range per policy, provides payouts that could be in the millions of dollars if an injured player is unable to play again. Most athletes who are predicted to be selected high in the professional draft take out loans to purchase such coverage and pay off the policy when they sign professional contracts.[34] If they are not drafted, though, they must pay off the policy. Thus, institutions that pay for these policies with NCAA-furnished SAF funds are providing selected athletes with a significant benefit. Questions have been raised about whether provision of such a benefit is proper and whether the remaining amount in the SAF is sufficient to meet the needs of athletes dealing with emergencies.[35] Most observers acknowledge that such selective use of the SAF is a way of persuading an athlete to return to school for another season of collegiate eligibility instead of entering the professional draft, not a reflection of concern for athlete health and wellness.

Absence of National or Conference Rules Mandates

A subsequent section of this essay addresses the responsibility of national and conference governance organizations for athlete safety, health, and wellness. No governance-association rules mandate institutional members' compliance with best practices, and none include an enforcement system. No entity is policing the athlete-protection system. Thus, it is unrealistic to expect individual institutions to self-regulate, always acting in the best interest of the athlete. Coaches decide to play athletes before they are medically cleared, to engage in extraordinary sport drill or conditioning demands, or to require that more time be spent practicing and preparing for games because of the pressure to win. Winning enables the institution to reap brand recognition and media attention, gate receipts, and donor contributions. This commercial pressure also explains why expenditures on coaches' salaries and benefits, sport-related personnel, recruiting, marketing, promotions, and the building of lavish facilities take precedence over a sufficient number of athletic trainers and provision of adequate athletic-injury insurance with long-term coverage. It also explains why requiring better coaching credentials or funding better professional development of coaches and strength and conditioning specialists is a similarly low priority. No governance entity tells the institutions that athlete health protection must be a priority.

Protection of Brand and Fear of Legal Liability / Recruiting Failure

When significant harm to athletes occurs, institutions often go to extraordinary lengths to hide details from public view. They fear that information transparency will result in lawsuits and bad press that will, in turn, adversely affect athletic recruiting, general institutional admissions, alumni contributions, and athletic ticket sales. Higher education is an educational-product industry, and athletics is an entertainment-product industry. The brands of colleges and universities, like their for-profit counterparts, have become sacred—more important than honesty, academic integrity, and the health and protection of students. When an athlete dies or media reports or lawsuits reveal the existence of misconduct, the response of most institutions is seldom the admission of error and system change. Rather, whistle-blowers are fired or lower-level employees are thrown under the bus to protect powerful coaches or administrators. The institution's deep pockets and well-funded insurance policies frequently fuel an army of attorneys who try to outlast often underresourced complainants. If it appears that the institution will lose in court, multimillion-dollar settlements with confidentiality agreements are offered to stop the reputational bleeding. So-called independent investigations arranged by the institution in the case of athlete deaths or significant episodes of rhabdomyolysis give the public the illusion of a responsible university response but are often conducted by law firms that are "friendly" to the institution. These investigations frequently find no wrongdoing. No governance organization requires an independent, unbiased, and expert investigation, and no transparency of findings exists to foster public trust.

Athlete Fear of Retaliation

College athlete victims have the most at stake and are the least likely to report coach or other abuse. Every athlete knows that the coach holds the keys to the kingdom: decisions about the renewal of athletic scholarships, whether the athlete will be in the starting lineup, and how much time, attention, and instruction the athlete receives. Every athlete also knows that the coach can administer physical and psychological punishment, the latter in artful ways. Athletes know about the power differential between athletes and coaches, and athletics administrators do little to calm these fears. Seldom does an athletic director begin an academic year by reviewing department policy about unacceptable coach pedagogy or behavior with coaches and athletes in the same room, instructing athletes how to report such transgressions and assuring them of no retaliation. It just does not happen.

Anachronistic Athletic Culture of "Toughness"

Historically, the culture of athletics has embraced hazing and other team initiation rituals and has accepted "tough coach" practices, such as harsh communication, physical handling of students, and physical punishment in response to errors. Even though school environments generally are now intolerant of bullying, hazing, and verbal, physical, and mental abuse, the athletics culture has not caught up. Further, the focus of athletics on the physical body elevates the probability of questionable coaching practices related to inappropriate congratulatory and skill-instruction touching, frequently without athletes' permission. Such behavior is particularly risky as our society becomes more focused on sexual harassment. Add the lack of adequate credentials for coaches and strength and conditioning specialists, and the result does not bode well for the health and well-being of athletes.[36] Although the Drake Group believes that most coaches act responsibly and in the best interests of their players, unacceptable pedagogy still poses a health risk to college athletes. The coaching profession is without clear and consistent standards, and absent such guidelines, too many coaches, albeit a minority, are crossing the line that separates good practice from harm to athletes.

Absence of Whistle-Blower Protection and Mandatory Reporting

In open amateur, nonschool sport in the United States, a federal law (2018 Safe Sport Act) requires criminal background checks; coach, staff, and volunteer adult education delivered by an independent external agency (United States Center for Safe Sport, or USCSS); and that all adults working in the sport environment report the emotional, physical, or sexual abuse of athletes. This law also establishes mechanisms for athletes and others to submit reports to the USCSS with an ethical firewall established for the USCSS to receive and investigate complaints. Although Title IX, the federal law that prohibits sexual harassment and other forms of discrimination on the basis of sex, applies to educational institutions that receive federal funds, it does not have the scope of protection custom-tailored for the sport environment or any comparable independent agency like the USCSS. Institutions and their athletics departments can promulgate their own policies that offer whistle-blower protection and impose mandatory reporting. But these whistle-blower protections and reporting regimes generally do not exist, and no collegiate athletics governing organizations mandate them.

National and Conference Athletics Governance Organizations Policy and Oversight Systems

Refusal to Govern in the Area of Athlete Health and Wellness Protection Unless Threatened by Litigation

The meaning of "governance" is significant. A governance organization makes rules that require member institutions to act in certain ways, or it controls the actions of its members by prohibiting certain practices so as to achieve the purposes of the organization. The NCAA was founded in 1906 because the president of the United States threatened to ban college football, due to football player deaths, if colleges did not organize to protect students from dangerous athletics practices.[37] Despite this, the

NCAA has claimed in court documents that it is not legally responsible for protecting student-athletes.[38] It cites Article 2.2.3 of the NCAA Constitution, which states, "It is the responsibility of each member institution to protect the health of, and provide a safe environment for, each of its participating student-athletes," to support a contention that the institution, not the NCAA, is responsible for athletes' health and well-being. Despite this court claim, the NCAA recently acknowledged its responsibility in its settlement of multiple consolidated concussion cases (hereafter referred to as the Arrington Settlement).[39] In that settlement, the NCAA committed to requiring every NCAA member institution to

- conduct preseason baseline concussion testing prior to allowing an athlete to participate in any sport;[40]
- prohibit any athlete diagnosed with a concussion from returning to play or participating in any practice or competition on the same day the concussion occurred;
- prohibit return to practice or competition following a concussion until cleared by a physician;
- require the presence of medical personnel trained in the diagnosis, treatment, and management of concussion at all Division I, II, or III practices and competitions in contact sports;
- require annual certification that the member school has a concussion-management plan in place;
- require all member schools to report concussion incidents and their resolutions to the NCAA; and
- provide NCAA-approved concussion education and training to student-athletes, coaches, and athletic trainers prior to every sport season.

In addition, the Arrington Settlement mandates that the NCAA must

- establish a reporting process in which athletes, their parents, or other third parties can report concussion-management concerns; and

- provide, at the beginning of each academic year, educational materials for faculty regarding educational accommodations for athletes who have sustained a concussion.[41]

Clearly, the NCAA had the knowledge, authority, and jurisdiction to take these actions without being required to do so under the terms of a court-approved settlement. But, focused on avoiding legal risk, it failed to do so. Only in response to legal action did the NCAA make such an acknowledgment.

Why National Governing Bodies Must Exercise Rule-Making Authority to Protect Athletes

The Drake Group contends that the high-risk competitive environment of intercollegiate athletics requires the NCAA to mandate responsible actions by its members to protect the health and well-being of college athletes. This national governance organization responsibility is in addition to the responsibilities of the institutional member and athletics department employees. Each entity has different but complementary authorities to prevent harm. All three must combat the pressures of commercialized athletics programs to produce winning teams, usually without certified coaches and other personnel who are trained to recognize and mitigate health risks. The college athletics environment threatens to sacrifice the well-being of athletes on the altar of victory. It will take the proverbial village to protect athletes in this reality.

The NCAA controls the rules of play in every sport, thereby influencing any health risk associated with such rules. Yet the NCAA has been relatively passive in this regard because member institutions and coaches resist change. The reasons for the resistance range from nostalgia to maintaining the "entertainment value" of sport, even though we know we can take a great deal of contact out of football, ice hockey, lacrosse, soccer, and rugby with fairly simple rules changes. We also know we can impose rules on the conduct of practices, such as reducing the number of days in which teams are allowed to conduct contact drills, prohibiting tackling to the ground, and reducing full-field scrimmages. Many of these possible changes are recommended via consensus sport-science statements, or we know that they will work because they are the result of experimentation and research, with much of this experimentation being performed by the Ivy League. It is fair to say that an aggressive pursuit of such changes outside the Ivy League does not exist.

In addition, the NCAA has full knowledge of the causes of and the ways to prevent physical and mental harm because it obtains information from sport-science authorities, collects and analyzes injury and other information from member institutions, commissions research studies, and employs a chief medical officer. The NCAA monitors both risk and best practices recommended by medical authorities and appoints committees of experts and stakeholders (Committee on Competitive Safeguards and Medical Aspects of Sport) to address the need for governance action. The NCAA also requires its members to report fatalities, near fatalities, and catastrophic injuries on an annual basis and to participate in an annual college athlete health and safety survey. But it does not even require its members to participate in the NCAA Injury Surveillance Program, the preeminent data-collection mechanism used to produce peer-reviewed research on college athlete injuries.[42] Similarly, the NCAA regularly convenes experts to produce consensus statements defining "best practices," but it does not require members to follow these "best practices," even though it could. In the case of athlete health and safety, the NCAA consistently shirks governance responsibility.

How Should the NCAA Carry Out Its Responsibility for Athletes' Health, Safety, and Well-Being?

We know national organizations are unable to directly supervise athletics programs at the institutional level. Rather, the national organization exercises its duty of care through the adoption and enforcement of rules that require (a) compliance with certain conditions of initial and continuing institutional or conference membership, (b) the adoption of specific policies and procedures by all member institutions, and (c) adherence by all athletics department employees to behavioral or professional preparation or certification standards. It is simply not enough for the NCAA to state a constitutional "principle" without adopting an enforceable rule that defines specific "do's and don'ts" in these three areas. It must govern.

Athlete Health-Protection Rules Should Not Be Subject to Membership Vote or Based on Litigation Risk or Brand Reputation

The Drake Group maintains that athlete-protection policies should not be subject to approval via membership vote. Membership votes may subordinate athlete health and wellness to considerations such as cost, the desire of powerful coaches not to be limited in the conduct of their programs, and whether the rules give some members a competitive advantage. Neither should athlete-protection mandates be selectively applied to one class of members (i.e., Division I, II, or III) and not others. The rules should protect all athletes under the jurisdiction of a national governance association.

Further, such rules should be promulgated solely to protect athlete safety, not an organization's brand. Nor should such rules result from a fear of litigation. Yet avoiding legal and reputational risks to the NCAA is the association's stated policy behind athlete protection, as adopted by the NCAA Board of Governors:

> 2. What is the origin of the Uniform Standard of Care policy?
>
> In December 2016, the NCAA Division I Board of Directors requested CSMAS [NCAA Committee on Competitive Safeguards and Medical Aspects of Sports] assistance to develop language to capture "unified standards of care" for student-athlete health and safety matters. This request was in support of its report to the NCAA Board of Governors Ad Hoc Committee on Structure and Composition, and specifically addressed the roles and responsibilities of the Board of Governors "to monitor and provide direction in student-athlete health and safety

> matters that require a unified standard of care and/or pose legal risk to the Association."
>
> In March 2017, CSMAS satisfied this request by recommending a policy framework that would facilitate association-wide action when, on occasion, an issue of significance arises that not only poses a substantial challenge to the principle of student-athlete well-being, but also requires a uniform, Association-wide response to address that challenge. The policy calls for CSMAS to evaluate such an issue against four criteria, and then to determine if referral to the Board of Governors is indicated. The four criteria are:
>
> a. The issue involves new scientific evidence with anticipated Association-wide importance.
> b. The issue will impact a core Association-wide value.
> c. The issue poses a legal risk to the Association.
> d. The issue poses a reputational risk to the Association.
>
> The Board of Governors approved the CSMAS framework at its April 2017 meeting.[43]

In addition, this FAQ reveals that the so-called catastrophic-injury and death "policy" to which this FAQ refers is really a recommendation rather than a rule that all members must follow:

> 8. Are these recommendations or requirements? What is the difference? What is the penalty for not following these recommendations?
>
> In both name and in structure, the document is presented as recommendations, rather than legislation. The membership's embracing these recommendations stems from the emerging standard of care they collectively illuminate.
>
> The value of the endorsement of external scientific and medical organizations is that their endorsements validate the existence of a standard of care. Consequently, the recommendations are serving the membership by helping it to understand and respond to the existing landscape of expectations.

> The Board of Governors' endorsement of the recommendations under the Uniform Standard of Care policy does not transform them into legislation. Instead, the Board of Governors' endorsement:
>
> a. Establishes the recommendations as Association-wide policy and priority.
> b. Simultaneously creates a pathway to uniformity and consistency in guidance provided to the Association as a whole.
>
> Institutions are advised to review all the recommendations with campus general counsel and medical personnel to determine necessary and appropriate changes to protect and enhance the safety of student-athletes.[44]

The presentation of this "industry standard" as a "recommendation" is a rejection of the governance association's responsibility and creates confusion as to whether such a health, safety, and protection standard is mandated with regard to individual coach or member institution compliance. National governance association rules normally conform with "industry standards" because, in a lawsuit, this is the standard usually used to establish negligence or failure to perform under a contract. The Drake Group contends that the NCAA should be using its unique national governance position to require and enforce rather than "recommend" all consensus policies advanced by medical authorities that could prevent athlete harm, injury, or death.

Needed Rule-Making and Enforcement Mechanisms

Mandating that all member institutions adopt and enforce athlete-protection policies would not be difficult. In the past, the NCAA has required institutions to regularly undergo peer-review evaluation. Currently, the NCAA requires compliance reviews conducted by external authorities in other rules areas. These reviews enable the NCAA to ensure that such policies are in place. Another mechanism could be to require a review of institutional practices in the case of an athlete's catastrophic injury or death. Although member institutions must report such events to the NCAA, currently the institution is left to determine its own response, including whether to conduct its own internal investigation or commission a third party to do so. As noted earlier, internal investigations are seldom transparent, and the conflict of interest is obvious when so-called independent investigations find no fault. Rather than not-so-independent institutional investigations, such circumstances demand the hiring by the NCAA of a blue-ribbon medical team that is above reproach to conduct a proper investigation. The NCAA should mandate such inquiries in the case of every death or catastrophic injury. The institution would continue, as it is now, to be held liable for any shortfall in its duty of care, while appointment of the medical team by the NCAA would fulfill its duty of care.

The NCAA must also address the power differential between head coaches and athletes and, at many institutions, between coaches and athletic trainers, medical teams, and others. The NCAA can do so by (a) adopting an enforceable coach and employee "code of ethics" that can be used to police coach misconduct, (b) imposing rules that provide athlete and employee whistle-blower protection, (c) establishing a mechanism that permits confidential athlete complaints to a noninstitutional entity, and (d) requiring an investigation and adjudication process independent of the member institution. The open amateur, nonschool Olympic and Paralympic sports governance structure in the United States was faced with these identical athlete-protection challenges. In 2017, Congress undertook an agonizing examination of the inability of US national sports governing bodies to protect their athletes from abusive coaches and employees and the failure of the United States Olympic Committee to fulfill its governance responsibilities to protect athletes from sexual abuse. The result was a 2018 federal law that created the United States Center for Safe Sport (USCSS) as an independent agency.[45] The first act of the USCSS was to publish a comprehensive SafeSport Code, designed to clearly define sexual misconduct, bullying, hazing, emotional and physical misconduct, and the obligations of coaches, volunteers, and employees to report such conduct.[46] The USCSS also developed and implemented policies and procedures that specified the obligations of mandatory reporters and required certification of coaches and education of athletes about direct and confidential reporting of complaints. No such system protects collegiate athletes. The NCAA can replicate the USCSS model.

The NCAA must also address the fact that college coaches regularly move from institution to institution when they are let go by their previous employer. The Olympic/Paralympic system has recognized that to protect athletes' health and well-being, it must ban abusive coaches from continued employment in its programs. In the Olympic/Paralympic system, it was too easy for sex offenders, especially if they were exceptional coaches, to move from club to club, thereby avoiding discipline. The current NCAA system only suspends coaches who commit serious rules violations regarding impermissible benefits, recruiting, and so on. The NCAA has no investigatory and adjudication mechanism to ban coaches who endanger the health and well-being of their athletes. No centralized system exists among NCAA member institutions to prohibit such coaches or employees from moving from institution to institution, continuing to endanger athletes. Although Title IX, a federal law that requires gender equity in higher education, prohibits sexual abuse and harassment, it is institution specific and is limited to sex discrimination. Moreover, the federal government lacks the capacity for oversight of athlete health and well-being issues at thousands of colleges and universities and over twenty-five thousand secondary schools in the United States. Oversight is a role best played by national, state, and conference athletics governance organizations consisting of smaller numbers of institutions.

Finally, the NCAA must address the issue of college athlete violence and sexual misconduct against other athletes and nonathletes. The Drake Group has already issued an extensive position paper on this topic.[47] For example, in 2017, a Michigan State University (MSU) football player was kicked off the team after allegations surfaced that he raped a teammate's girlfriend.[48] In December 2018, he was sentenced to ten years in prison after pleading to a lesser charge. The MSU head football coach had ignored warnings that this recruit had a troubling history of sexual misconduct. The recruit was kicked off his high school team and barred from the high school campus during his senior year while facing similar allegations. MSU hired a local law firm, which cleared the three MSU coaches who ignored these warnings and sought MSU special admissions status for this recruit. The NCAA has no rules to deal with such issues.

Recommendations

The Drake Group believes that acceptance by the NCAA of its duty of care and its leadership are the keys to protecting the health and well-being of college athletes. Accordingly, we present the following recommendations.

Recommendation 1: NCAA Acceptance of Duty of Care

As a national collegiate athletics governance organization, the NCAA should protect collegiate athletes from physical and mental harm related to their participation in athletics. Specifically, the NCAA should exercise this responsibility through the following:

a. The adoption and enforcement of rules applicable to all member institutions intended to (1) prevent or reduce the occurrence of athletic injury, (2) prohibit physical, sexual, verbal, or emotional abuse of athletes by coaches, other athletes, and others, (3) permit athletes to have adequate time to sleep, recover from training, and complete academic responsibilities, and (4) require athletics personnel to meet education, certification, licensure, or other qualification standards.
b. The adoption of all such athlete health and protection rules by the Board of Governors upon recommendation of the Chief Medical Officer and the Committee on Competitive Safeguards and Medical Aspects of Sports, rather than by vote of any membership, divisional council, or competitive subdivision. These rules should apply to all athletes in all membership divisions.

c. The inclusion in such athlete health and protection rules of standards of conduct for athletics department employees that are at least as stringent as the US Center for SafeSport "SafeSport Code" regarding mandatory reporter provisions, whistle-blower protection, required criminal background checks, and completion of code of conduct training by all employees who interact regularly with athletes. The rules should also include (1) a mechanism for NCAA receipt of direct athlete complaints related to violations of the code of conduct and (2) investigatory, adjudicatory, and disciplinary powers required to process those complaints.

d. The adoption and enforcement of rules prohibiting member institutions from recruiting any high school students or two- or four-year college transfer students to participate in athletics who have been convicted of a sexually violent or other physically violent act or have been suspended from any educational institution for such an act. High school athletes declared ineligible under such a provision should have an avenue of appeal to an independent panel comprising both youth development and law enforcement experts.

e. The adoption and enforcement of rules (1) prohibiting athletics department employees from involvement in campus or external athlete sexual harassment or assault investigations and adjudication processes and requiring that athletes be treated like all other students with regard to such processes and (2) requiring the immediate suspension of the athletic participation of any athlete accused of sexual or other violence until the conclusion of any preliminary hearing, investigation, or adjudication process, and if such misconduct is found, the athletes responsible should be permanently ineligible for participation in practice, competition, and receipt of athletics financial aid at that or any other member institution of a national collegiate athletics governance institution.

f. The required participation by all member institutions in the NCAA Injury Surveillance Program.

g. Approval by the Chief Medical Officer and the Committee on Competitive Safeguards and Medical Aspects of Sports before consideration of any change in rules of play or any sport-related legislation that may affect athletes' health and protection, including athletes' time commitment to a sport.

Recommendation 2: Enforcement of Athlete-Protection Rules

The NCAA should establish the following mechanisms for the enforcement of such athlete health and protection rules:

a. A periodic external peer review of member institutions' athlete-protection policies and procedures, Injury Surveillance Program records, code of conduct violations, athlete and employee physical and mental health education programs, and employee qualifications.
b. An independent NCAA investigation requirement in the case of catastrophic injury or death at any member institution A three-person panel of experts not affiliated with the involved institution should be appointed by the College Athletic Trainers Society and the American College of Sports Medicine, at least two members of which should be medical doctors, to investigate and produce a public expert report and recommendations for the institution.
c. The requirement that all administrators responsible for the supervision of sports programs undergo an NCAA Sports Science Institute training program on the identification of dangerous or abusive pedagogy practices in the coaching of sport programs and in the conduct of strength and conditioning programs.

Recommendation 3: Adequate Insurance Protection and Provision of Uncovered Medical Expenses

The NCAA should mandate adequate injury insurance for athletes and institutional payment of athletic-injury medical expenses not covered by insurance. Specifically,

a. NCAA Bylaw 16.4.1 specifies that only autonomy institutions must provide full medical care to college athletes for athletically related injuries extending at least two years following either graduation or separation from the institution or until the athlete qualifies for NCAA Catastrophic Injury Insurance Program coverage. This provision should be extended to athletes in all NCAA divisions, and the NCAA should establish an insurance program and/or special fund for that purpose.

b. The NCAA should develop gender- and sport-neutral criteria for the institutional provision of disability / loss-of-value insurance that does not deplete institutional Student Assistance Fund allocations.

Recommendation 4: Consolidation of Athlete Health and Protection Best Practices and Rules Obligations

The NCAA's Sports Science Institute should compile and distribute annually to all member institutions all athlete health and protection "best practices" adopted by the Board of Governors. It should also compile and distribute annually, by sport, all mandated NCAA athlete health and protection rules.

Recommendation 5: More Aggressive Pursuit of Game and Practice Rules That Reduce Injury Risk

The NCAA Board of Governors should direct the Chief Medical Officer and the Committee on Competitive Safeguards and Medical Aspects of Sports to identify possible competition and practice rule changes designed to reduce athlete injury risk in all sports. The Board should also direct these entities to test the impact of such changes in every NCAA championship sport. Final decisions about the adoption of rules changes should be data driven.

NOTES

1. Traumatic injury or death is defined as caused by an external force of violence and is easier to identify because of an observable physical circumstance; nontraumatic injury or death is not produced by mechanical stress, and examples might include drug overdoses, infections, stroke, and hypertrophic cardiomyopathy.

2. For additional discussion on "moral injury," see Jeremy Jinkerson, "Defining and Assessing Moral Injury: A Syndrome Perspective," *Traumatology* 22, no. 2 (May 2016), https://www.researchgate.net/publication/301937607_Defining_and_Assessing_Moral_Injury_A_Syndrome_Perspective; William Nash, "Moral Injury: The War Inside," Volunteers of America, 2019, https://www.voa.org/moral-injury.

3. For the National Federation of State High School Associations (NFHS) listing of requirements by state, see "NFHSLearn for Coaches," https://nfhslearn.com/home/coaches. The most commonly required online coaching-fundamentals course is offered by the NFHS learning institute.

4. United States Center for SafeSport, "SafeSport Code for the U.S. Olympic and Paralympic Movements," April 14, 2019, https://uscenterforsafesport.org/wp-content/uploads/2019/05/2019-SafeSport-Code-04.15.19-Hyperlinked.pdf.

5. NCAA, *2019–20 NCAA Division I Manual*, Section 11.1.5, July 2019, 50.

6. NCAA, *Interassociation Recommendations: Preventing Catastrophic Injury and Death in Collegiate Athletics*, July 2019, 10.

7. Ibid., 11.

8. Ibid., 10.

9. NCAA, "Interassociation Recommendations: Preventing Catastrophic Injury and Death in Collegiate Athletics, July 19 2019: Frequently Asked Questions," 6, https://ncaaorg.s3.amazonaws.com/ssi/injury_prev/SSI_CatastrophicInjuryPreventionFAQs.pdf.

10. NCAA, *Interassociation Recommendations*, 11.

11. Kristen L. Kucera, David Klossner Bob Colgate, and Robert C. Cantu, *Annual Survey of Football Injury Research: 1931–2017* (Chapel Hill: National Center for Catastrophic Sport Injury Research at the University of North Carolina at Chapel Hill for the American Football Coaches Association, National Collegiate Athletic Association, and National Federal of State High School Associations, February 16, 2018).

12. James Crepea, "Former Oregon Ducks Football Player Doug Brenner Suing UO, Willie Taggart, NCAA for $11.5 Million," *Oregonian*, January 9, 2019, https://www.oregonlive.com/ducks/2019/01/former-oregon-ducks-football-player-doug-brenner-suing-uo-willie-taggart-ncaa-for-115-million.html.

13. Steve Strunsky, "College Where N.J. Football Player Died after Practice Announces Reforms. His Mom Is Skeptical," *NJ.com*, May 4, 2019, https://www.nj.com/education/2019/05/college-where-nj-football-player-died-after-practice-announces-reforms-his-mom-is-skeptical.html.

14. Brittany Britto, "UH Launches Investigation into Rhabdo Cases as New Details Emerge Related to Life-Threatening Condition," *Houston Chronicle*, June 13, 2019, https://www.houstonchronicle.com/news/education/article/UH-launches-investigation-into-rhabdo-cases-as-13992419.php.

15. Heather Dinich, "Sources: Maryland OL Jordan McNair Showed Signs of Extreme Exhaustion," ESPN, August 11, 2018, https://www.espn.com/college-football/story/_/id/24343021/jordan-mcnair-maryland-terrapins-died-heatstroke-team-workout.

16. Claudia L. Reardon et al., "Mental Health in Elite Athletes: International Olympic Committee Consensus Statement," *British Journal of Sports Medicine* 53, no. 11 (2019): 667–99, https://bjsm.bmj.com/content/53/11/667.

17. Ike Evans, "Mental Health and the Black Student-Athlete," Hogg Foundation for Mental Health, February 1, 2017, http://hogg.utexas.edu/black-student-athlete-mental-health.

18. Ibid. NCAA, *2019–20 NCAA Division I Manual*, Section 16.4.2, 232–33; NCAA, *2019–20 NCAA Division II Manual*, Section 16.4.1, 172.

19. NCAA Sports Science Institute, "Year-Round Football Practice Contact Recommendations," accessed August 20, 2019, http://www.ncaa.org/sport-science-institute/year-round-football-practice-contact-recommendations.

20. NCAA, *2019–20 NCAA Division I Manual*, Section 16.4.2, 232–33; NCAA, *2019–20 NCAA Division II Manual*, Section 16.4.1, 172.

21. NCAA, *Interassociation Consensus Document: Mental Health Best Practices*, 2019, http://www.ncaa.org/sites/default/files/SSI_MentalHealthBestPractices_Web_20170921.pdf, 2.

22. NCAA Sports Science Institute, "Mental Health Educational Resources," accessed August 20, 2019, http://www.ncaa.org/sport-science-institute/mental-health-educational-resources.

23. See NCAA, *2019–20 NCAA Division I Manual*, Section 11.5, 53.

24. NCAA, *Interassociation Consensus Document.*

25. Knight Commission on Intercollegiate Athletics, *Quantitative and Qualitative Research with Football Bowl Subdivision University Presidents on the Costs and Financing of Intercollegiate Athletics Report of Findings and Implications*, 2009, http://www.knightcommissionmedia.org/images/President_Survey_FINAL.pdf.

26. Emily Kroshus, Christine M. Baugh, Daniel H. Daneshvar, Julie M. Stamm, R. Mark Laursen, and S. Bryn Austin, "Pressure on Sports Medicine Clinicians to Prematurely Return Collegiate Athletes to Play after Concussion," *Journal of Athletic Training* 50, no. 9 (September 2015): 944–51, https://www.ncbi.nlm.nih.gov/pmc/articles/PMC4639885/; ESPN News Services / Associated Press, "Franklin Denies Ex-Penn State Doctor's Allegations," ESPN, August 26, 2019, https://www.espn.com/college-football/story/_/id/27470287/ex-psu-doctor-alleges-pressure-clear-players?platform=amp (the Penn State team doctor and director of sports medicine maintains that he was terminated after reporting pressure on multiple occasions from the head football coach to return athletes to play).

27. Paula Lavigne, "Survey: NCAA Coaches' Clout Concerns Athletic Trainers," ESPN, June 25, 2019, https://www.espn.com/espn/otl/story/_/id/27048906/survey-ncaa-coaches-clout-concerns-trainers.

28. NCAA, "Interassociation Recommendations: Frequently Asked Questions."

29. NCAA, *2019–20 NCAA Division I Manual*, 142.

30. Ibid. The same rule exists for football, but attendance by a member of the institution's sports medicine staff is required (13.11.3.7.4).

31. NCAA, *2019–20 NCAA Division I Manual*, 230.

32. NCAA, "2019 Division I Revenue Distribution Plan," accessed September 12, 2019, https://www.google.com/search?client=firefox-b-1-d&q=NCAA+Student+Assistance+Fund.

33. John Infante, "No Compliance Issue with Winston Insurance Purchase," *AthleticScholarships.net*, August 6, 2014, https://www.athleticscholarships.net/2014/08/06/no-compliance-issue-with-winston-insurance-purchase.htm; Kristi Dosh, "Assistance Funds Pay Tab to Insure Stars," *Sports Business Journal*, January 12, 2015, https://www.sportsbusinessdaily.com/Journal/Issues/2015/01/12/Colleges/Student-Assistance-Fund.aspx.

34. NCAA, "Loss-of-Value Insurance FAQs," accessed September 7, 2019, http://www.ncaa.org/about/resources/insurance/loss-value-insurance-faqs.

35. For example, see Dosh, "Assistance Funds Pay Tab to Insure Stars"; Frank Darras, "The Challenges of Funding Elite College Athlete Disability Insurance," *The Legal Blitz*, March 28, 2016, http://thelegalblitz.com/blog/2016/03/28/the-challenges-of-funding-elite-college-athlete-disability-insurance/.

36. For a more extensive discussion of coaching misconduct, see Donna Lopiano, Gerald Gurney, Fritz Polite, Brian Porto, David B. Ridpath, Allen Sack, and Andrew Zimbalist, "Athletic Governance Organization and Institutional Responsibilities Related to Professional Coaching Conduct," Drake Group (position statement), December 2016, https://www.thedrakegroup.org/wp-content/uploads/2019/06/professional-conduct-of-coaches-final-dec-3.pdf.

37. Gerald Gurney, Donna Lopiano, and Andrew Zimbalist, *Unwinding Madness: What Went Wrong with College Sports and How to Fix It* (Washington, DC: Brookings Institution Press, 2016).

38. Nathan Fenno, "In Court Filing, NCAA Denies Legal Duty to Protect Athletes," *Washington Times*, December 18, 2013, http://www.washingtontimes.com/news/2013/dec/18/court-filing-ncaa-denies-legal-duty-protect-athlet/.

39. United States District Court for the Northern District of Illinois Eastern Division, Class Action Settlement Agreement and Release, National Collegiate Athletic Association Student-Athlete Concussion Injury Litigation, MDL No. 2492, Master Docket No. 1;13-ev-09116, https://www.documentcloud.org/documents/4478836-NCAA-Student-Athlete-Concussion-Injury.html (hereafter cited as Arrington Settlement).

40. Baseline concussion testing is a preseason exam of an athlete's balance and brain function, learning and memory skills, ability to pay attention or concentrate, speed of thinking and problem-solving, and whether concussion symptoms are present at the time of testing.

41. Arrington Settlement, 32–34.

42. NCAA, "NCAA Injury Surveillance Program," accessed August 28, 2019, http://www.ncaa.org/sport-science-institute/ncaa-injury-surveillance-program.

43. This FAQ refers to the NCAA's newly released policy: NCAA, "Interassociation Recommendations: Frequently Asked Questions," 1–2.

44. Ibid., 4.

45. US Congress, "S. 534—Protecting Young Victims from Sexual Abuse and Safe Sport Authorization Act of 2017," https://www.congress.gov/bill/115th-congress/senate-bill/534/text.

46. United States Center for Safe Sport, "SafeSport Code for the U.S. Olympic and Paralympic Movements," April 15, 2019, https://uscenterforsafesport.org/wp-content/uploads/2019/05/2019-SafeSport-Code-04.15.19-Hyperlinked.pdf.

47. Donna Lopiano, Gerald Gurney, Brian Porto, David Ridpath, Allen Sack, Mary Willingham, and Andrew Zimbalist, "Institutional Integrity Issues Related to Athlete Sexual Assault and Other Forms of Serious Misconduct," Drake Group (position statement), August 2016, https://www.thedrakegroup.org/2016/09/11/institutional-integrity-issues-related-to-college-athlete-sexual-assault-and-other-forms-of-serious-violence/.

48. Paul Steinbach, "Suit: MSU's Dantonio Ignored Warnings about Recruit," *Athletic Business*, September 2019, https://www.athleticbusiness.com/civil-actions/suit-msu-s-dantonio-ignored-warnings-about-recruit.html?bid=2525489&eid=306480847.

CHAPTER 9

Compensation of College Athletes Including Revenues Earned from Commercial Use of Their Names, Images, and Likenesses and Outside Employment

Brian Porto, Gerald Gurney, Donna Lopiano, David Ridpath, Allen Sack, Julie Sommer, Mary Willingham, and Andrew Zimbalist

The Drake Group's original position statement on the compensation of college athletes for commercial use of their names, images, and likenesses (NILs) was issued in 2015 and updated in 2016, 2017, 2019, and 2020. Throughout 2019 and continuing into 2020, state and federal legislative bills were filed regarding the rights of college athletes to commercially exploit their own names, images, and likenesses.[1] These bills have different provisions, but all of the bills conflicted with National Collegiate Athletic Association (NCAA) amateur-status rules. During this period, the NCAA also appointed a special committee to reexamine its rules regarding this issue. Additionally, the media reported strongly expressed opinions of various NCAA, conference, and institutional athletics administrators, who maintained that allowing athletes to exploit their own NILs could

The Drake Group (March 24, 2015, revised February 12, 2016, December 2, 2017, December 27, 2017, September 27, 2019, October 14, 2019, November 4, 2019, and February 26, 2020).

not be accommodated without causing profound negative changes to college sports. The Drake Group disagrees with these contentions; our core position has not changed from our initial 2015 publication. We believe that national collegiate athletics governance organization control of athletes' outside employment is overly restrictive. University commercial exploitation of athletes' NILs in conjunction with college athletic events can and should coexist with athletes' rights to independently commercially exploit their own NILs prior to and during their period of eligibility for college athletics participation without disqualifying them from college competition. This updated position statement offers recommendations on the administrative rules and procedures that should be implemented to realize this compromise.

The Drake Group notes that the updated recommendations contained herein reflect a level of procedural detail not usually included in Drake position statements. This level of detail is intended to demonstrate that these or other similarly structured national intercollegiate sports governance association policies and administrative procedures can produce results that (1) protect the rights and contractual obligations of both the institution and the participating college athlete with regard to use of athlete and institutional NILs and (2) remove unfair restrictions on commercial revenues that may be derived from college athlete employment outside the educational institution. The Drake Group also believes that opening up these outside athlete employment and NIL opportunities will diffuse the current public pressure calling for institutions to pay and treat athletes like professional athletes, which would run counter to allowable practices of tax-exempt educational institutions and recent court decisions. Drake argues that higher-education institutions should direct their resources to providing education and health and injury protections that create a safe educational environment for extracurricular athletics programs. At the same time, college athletes should not be unduly prohibited from maximizing their revenue potential unrelated to their higher-education and college athletics participation obligations.

We emphasize that all existing NCAA or other collegiate athletics governance organization rules prohibiting boosters, alumni, and other representatives of athletics interests from paying athletes, promising to pay them as recruiting inducements, or providing extra benefits to athletes once they enroll remain in place in our proposal. We also note that the use of the term "recruiting" applies to recruiting of high school prospects and any two-year or four-year college transfer athletes with collegiate athletics eligibility remaining.

Finally, this position paper addresses new rules that should govern previously impermissible outside employment and NIL licensing. With respect to NILs, we propose that an independent NIL Commission be responsible for setting standards and overseeing a national NIL Eligibility Center. The Center would implement the standards.[2] We recommend that all non–de minimis outside employment agreements and agreements regarding NIL payments to athletes be reported to the athlete's institution and to the NIL Eligibility Center. We recommend that athletes be permitted to employ agents to negotiate arrangements for employment and NIL licensing. More particularly, all non–de minimis NIL agreements must be registered with the NIL Eligibility Center and the athletes' respective institutions and be consistent with the standards set by the independent national NIL Commission. The NIL Eligibility Center would also be responsible for maintaining a publicly accessible and searchable database of such agreements (with appropriate information redacted). Moreover, the institution or its representatives of athletics interests cannot directly or indirectly initiate such arrangements, as currently specified by NCAA rules. We recognize that prohibiting the institution, sponsors, alumni, and boosters from initiating such arrangements represents a compliance challenge. For example, it would be permissible for college athletes or their agents to initiate and solicit endorsement or licensing agreements from current institutional sponsors and alumnus/booster business owners as long as these entities did not directly or indirectly initiate such opportunities. However, we believe that the systems proposed—reporting and transparency requirements coupled with requirements that compensation be for services actually rendered at the going rate and other standards—are sufficient controls, in contrast with current prohibitions on athlete employment. These prohibitions precipitate under-the-table transactions that are rules violations. Reporting requirements would reveal the improper or suspicious employment practices of individual alumni or boosters. Ultimately, rules violations are always possible, but we believe that these fears do not justify the current one-sided revenue advantages of the institution.

Review of Basic Principles Guiding College Athlete Compensation

The Drake Group believes that all institutions of higher education should operate athletics programs according to financial, ethical, and other principles appropriate for tax-exempt educational organizations. Regarding college students, institutions of higher education should seek to (1) promulgate policies regarding the conduct of students or programs that maximize students' pursuit of educational goals in an environment that protects their health, safety, and general welfare; (2) protect the rights of students to accept and retain education-related inducements to enroll or maintain enrollment, such as athletic or other forms of scholarships or grants-in-aid; (3) recognize students' legal rights to the use of their own names, images, and likenesses by themselves, their educational institutions, or other third parties or groups; and (4) allow students to engage independently in employment or endorsement/licensing activities outside the institution.

Intercollegiate athletics programs must operate within this context, adopting policies and rules that balance the rights and interests of students who participate in athletics with the rights and interests of institutions that offer these extracurricular opportunities. The Drake Group has already issued a separate paper on college athlete compensation that fully explains the following summary of predicates for determining a fair balance of interests.

Primacy of Academic and Athlete Health and Protection Policies

In light of public pressure to produce winning teams, educational institutions and their national sports governance organizations have the highest obligations to promulgate policies that permit students to fully engage in and complete the academic requirements for an undergraduate degree and to protect them from physical and psychological harm. The Drake Group believes that national sports governing organizations and their member institutions lack policies that protect college athletes from educational fraud, ensure the integrity of the educational degrees they are awarded, and insulate athletes from the professional misconduct of coaches and other personnel. Similarly, athlete-protection policies related to the provision of sufficient athletic-injury-related insurance, payment of athletics-related medical expenses, and assurance of qualified medical oversight are insufficient or nonexistent. These issues are not the subject of this document, which focuses instead on athlete employment *outside* the higher-education institution. However, we strongly believe that these issues and others deserve the attention of Congress once it resolves the current NIL crisis. We therefore urge consideration of the bipartisan Congressional Advisory Commission on Intercollegiate Athletics Act of 2019 (HR 5528) as an initial mechanism to comprehensively examine the relationship between higher education and intercollegiate athletics.

Provision of Compensation from the Institution to Students Participating in Curricular and Extracurricular Offerings

The institution should not pay students for participating in curricular or extracurricular activities, except for providing scholarships in which all compensation and benefits are tethered to educational expenses. Athletics scholarships should be continued through graduation, conditioned only on (1) academic performance, (2) compliance with rules of conduct applicable to all students, and (3) enrollment in the academic subject or participation in the activity for which the scholarship was awarded. Renewal should not be conditioned on (1) sport performance, which practice should be considered athletics employment, (2) nonparticipation resulting from an injury, or (3) noncompliance with rules of conduct that do not apply to all students or that violate freedom of speech. With regard to athletics, notably, only 25 of the 1,114 athletics programs sponsored by NCAA member institutions in 2018–19 generated sufficient revenues to fully defray program expenses on an operating basis (i.e., without considering most capital costs and certain indirect expenses).[3] At the vast majority of institutions, mandatory student athletics fees, institutional general funds (e.g.., tuition), and outside donations to athletics, which sometimes come at the expense of donations to the general fund, heavily subsidize athletics programs. It is nonsensical to suggest that a tax-exempt higher-education institution be permitted to operate a professional sports business and that all students attending those institutions, many of whom are leaving college burdened with extraordinary student-loan debt, should pay professional athlete laborers salaries and bonuses, in part, via student fees and tuition dollars. Similarly, suggesting that contributions to athletics never compete with donations to support academically related programs is dubious.

Use of Revenues Generated by Extracurricular Activities

Extracurricular activities generally, and intercollegiate athletics programs particularly, are important contributors to student development. If revenues are directly generated from the staging of such activities, the revenues should be used to support that extracurricular activity, including educational scholarships[4] and the provision of adequate athletic-injury insurance, medical expenses, and other health and safety protections. Institutions should use any other excess revenues over expenditures to support themselves generally, consistent with their tax-exempt missions.

Ineligibility of Professional Athletes for College Sport

It is reasonable for college athletes to be prohibited from professional athletic employment while enrolled in college. Time demands and physical demands of college sports participation, professional sports participation, and full-time student status and degree requirements would challenge the primacy of education. College athletes now train year-round, and many attend classes in the summer to keep on track with academic requirements. Besides, the additional training, competition, and time demands of professional sports would probably heighten the college athlete's risk for overuse injuries, injuries that result from fatigue, and injuries that result from increased exposure to physical contact (e.g., repetitive hits to the head, contact with playing surfaces or boundaries).

Prohibition of "Professional Athletes" to Replace Antiquated Concept of "Amateur Status"

Why Amateur Status Rules Do Not Work

Historically, athletics governance organizations have used "amateur status" rules as a requirement for collegiate sport eligibility. These rules classify business activities with any relationship to athletic ability or fame as the equivalent of playing professional sports, declaring that any athlete who participates in such activities is ineligible for college athletics. The rules are based on the belief that almost any effort to monetize an individual's athletic skill or fame should be considered employment as a professional athlete. These rules prohibit, for example, retaining a sports agent to negotiate a professional contract even if the athlete decides not to execute the contract. They also prohibit athletes from starting their own summer sports camps for youth and advertising their status as college athletes, even without identifying their respective higher-education institutions. And the rules prohibit athletes from using their fame or athletics ability to endorse sports or other products. Some of these amateur-status rules have changed over time or have been waived in response to public objection or institutional desires to be able to recruit athletes who have been compensated for their athletic performances. Such recruits include Olympic athletes who have received bonus monies from their countries for winning medals and tennis players who have accepted prize money. Thus, amateur status has been subject to a moving definition. These amateur-status rules were discarded long ago in Olympic and open amateur sports programs with no harm to the commercial operation of the United States Olympic Committee or to our national sports governing bodies.

Use a Narrow Definition of "Professional Athlete" as the Disqualifier for Collegiate Athletics Eligibility

A simple, clear definition of "professional athlete" is offered as the standard to preclude college athletics eligibility. Thus, the Drake Group believes that any law that gives college athletes the right to pursue employment or monetize their own NILs from third parties outside the institution should also prohibit the institution from disqualifying them for doing so. Institutions should not be able to disqualify athletes from collegiate athletics because the athletes have earned compensation based on their athletic skill or fame, unless the compensation was earned for professional athletics participation.

NCAA rules restrict students to four years of collegiate eligibility within five years of enrollment. The enrollment period starts during the year following the graduation date of the athlete's high school class, and the rule charges the student with one year of used eligibility for any year of participation in organized sports competition. Accordingly, the Drake Group believes that the professional-athlete disqualification standard should only apply during collegiate enrollment for the educational, time, and health considerations discussed earlier. Allowing an athlete to test professional-sports aspirations in that five-year period after high school graduation and to decide that an education combined with collegiate athletics participation is a preferred route may produce a more educationally committed student and athletics programs less prone to academic fraud.

Definition of "Professional Athlete"

The Drake Group maintains that any one of the following policies and practices during collegiate enrollment should be used to designate a student as a professional athlete employee who is ineligible for collegiate sport:

1. Receives compensation to play a sport that exceeds actual and necessary expenses to participate in practice or competition
2. Receives, directly or indirectly, a salary, reimbursement of expenses, or any other form of financial assistance from a professional sports organization as payment for sport participation
3. Competes on any professional athletics team
4. Competes in an athletics competition or exhibition for pay or receives remuneration in excess of actual and necessary expenses to participate in such activity
5. Receives a college athletics grant-in-aid guarantee (1) for a period less than five years or until graduation, whichever occurs first, (2) which, although conditioned on continued participation in athletics, can be withdrawn for reasons of physical injury, unsatisfactory athletic performance, or improper pressure to withdraw from the team, and (3) which includes compensation untethered to educational expenses, such compensation that exceeds the institution's financial aid office's calculation of "cost of attendance."

With regard to point 5, The Drake Group contends that one-year scholarship agreements should be considered tantamount to employee-at-will agreements. We note that NCAA athletic scholarships were initiated as four-year commitments but were reduced in the 1970s to increase coach control of team composition. The significance of mandating scholarship awards for "five years or until graduation, whichever comes first," cannot be understated. First, this policy ties athlete compensation to the institution's commitment to provide the athlete with a chance to earn an undergraduate degree. Second, it would reduce the power imbalance that currently deters athletes from reporting coach misconduct or gender-equity concerns by minimizing fears associated with loss of scholarship support as a form of retaliation.

Under the preceding definition, a college athlete could participate in a professional draft combine or enter into a professional draft at any time and not lose eligibility for participation or athletics-related financial aid. To remain eligible, the athlete would have to forgo signing a professional sport employment contract and receiving remuneration for such employment in excess of reimbursement for actual expenses.[5] Further, a college athlete, like a nonathlete student, could pay for the services of a qualified lawyer or sports agent at any time to obtain professional advice or negotiate a professional contract and would retain collegiate eligibility as long as the athlete did not execute the agreement and become a professional athlete.

College Athlete Rights Related to Use of Name, Image, and Likeness (NIL)

The Drake Group believes that the following policies protect the rights of college athletes to engage in outside employment (including monetizing their own names, images, and likenesses related to their recognized athletic skills and notoriety) while imposing reasonable rules designed to ensure the primacy of academic responsibilities and prevent violation of athletics recruiting rules or rules prohibiting the provision of extra benefits.

College Athlete Employment **Unrelated** *to Athletic Ability, Reputation, or NIL*

College athletes should be treated like other students with regard to their independent efforts to engage in nonschool employment unrelated to athletic ability or reputation in their sport and not involving the employer's use of the athlete's NIL. Current NCAA rules (12.4.1) that require compensation received to be "only for work actually performed" and "at a rate commensurate with the going rate" for similar services. The institution should be permitted to require that the athlete report such employment when receiving above–de minimis remuneration[6] and attest in a statement that neither the institution nor an institutional representative was involved in obtaining such employment and that compensation is commensurate with services actually rendered and the going rate.

College Athlete Employment Related *to Athletic Ability, Reputation, or NIL*

College athletes should be permitted to obtain employment and accept remuneration for the commercial use of their own NILs in advertisements, appearances, or speaking engagements and for endorsement of commercial products at any time during the years. Such employment rights should be limited by the following policies:

1. Generally, compensation shall be for work actually performed and at rates commensurate with the going rate or fair market value, except for employment as a professional athlete. An athlete's NIL work may rely on the athlete's sport fame (e.g., for services as a coach, a fee-for-lesson sport instructor, a sport camp counselor in any sport, or a model, such as for athletics apparel or equipment in any sport). An athlete's NIL work could also pertain to endorsements, product licensing, personal appearances, books, movies, television or radio shows, autographs, and the like, as well as endorsement of commercial products or services or ownership of a sports business and so on. Restrictions such as rates commensurate with the going rate or fair market value should apply at the local level but may be inappropriate for NIL deals that are national in scope, where the free market may be a more appropriate standard.
2. Employment or work based on the use of the athlete's NIL shall not include implied endorsement, mention, or acknowledgment of affiliation with the institution of higher education or the institution's athletics or team marks, colors, brands, taglines, intellectual property, or other mechanisms of association with the institution where the

student participates as a college athlete or of that team's athletic conference or national governing organization.[7]

3. College athletes, like nonathlete students, should be permitted to pay for the services of a lawyer or certified sports agent at any time to market the athlete for employment, prospective employment as a professional athlete, or endorsement agreements at any time. Agreements with regard to professional athlete employment must not be executed while the athlete is eligible for college sports. Such agents should not be allowed to represent the athlete or otherwise participate in college athletics recruiting or scholarship processes because these activities do not constitute employment. An agent should not be permitted to promote, advance, or negotiate any NIL agreement related to a college athlete's attendance at a particular institution, including compensation for the direct or indirect use of the institution's name, brand, or marks.
4. The athlete and his or her agent shall independently obtain such employment. Such employment shall not be arranged, directly or indirectly, by the institution's employees, donors, athletics program sponsors, advertisers, or other representatives of its athletics interests. This restriction shall not preclude a college athlete or the athlete's agent from independently soliciting work from any company that also supports the institution or any company owned by alumni, donors, boosters, and so on or from applying for positions advertised by those entities.
5. Current NCAA recruiting rules that prohibit the institution or its representatives of athletics interest from offering employment incentives or any extra benefit beyond an athletic scholarship shall remain in force.
6. Employment obligations shall not result in the athlete missing classes, final examinations, or other required academic commitments.
7. Athletes' employment by any third party outside the institution shall not inhibit athletes' assignment of their own NIL rights to the institution during the championship season.

8. Third-party employers, endorsements, employment activities, and advertising and promotional activities must meet certain character and integrity standards (e.g., no association with gambling, alcohol, tobacco, performance-enhancing drugs, etc.) as established by the NIL Commission, provided such standards are also followed by the institution.
9. Athletes not meeting athletics academic eligibility requirements (i.e., good academic standing, normal progress toward the degree, full-time enrollment, etc.) shall not be permitted to renew or enter into any new outside employment agreement until they become eligible again.
10. Athlete group-licensing agreements (multiple athletes and not involving the institution) shall conform to these policies. No rules shall prevent athletes from entering into group-licensing agreements with other athletes.
11. College athletes should not be denied access to any employment market by virtue of any unreasonable college-transfer regulation. College athletes, like nonathlete students, should be permitted to transfer to another institution without the permission of their current institution and without penalty (i.e., one year of residency required prior to eligibility to compete at the new institution).[8] However, on the occasion of a second or subsequent transfer, the Drake Group does not support any rule requiring the permission of the releasing institution but does support a one-year residency requirement as a condition for athletics eligibility. The bases for this view are that transfer students (1) require a longer time to graduate than other students, (2) have a lower probability of earning a degree, and (3) when they are athletes, are more likely to transfer for athletics reasons than for academic reasons.[9]

Institutional Rights Related to Use of Name, Image, and Likeness (NIL) of College Athletes

The Drake Group believes that the following policies would properly balance the rights of the institution to commercially exploit intercollegiate athletic events, including use of college athlete NILs, with the rights of college athletes to commercially exploit their own names, images, and likenesses and be employed by third parties outside the institution.

Legal Limits on the Institution's Right to Use Athlete NILs

The higher-education institution conducting an athletics program does not require the permission of athletes for certain limited use of their NIL related to such participation. State laws dictate whether an institution conducting an athletics program must obtain the permission of or payment for the use of its athletes' NILs. There is no federal uniform law regarding rights of publicity. And there is no Supreme Court decision governing privacy, publicity, or copyright protections of college athletes. Many states have legislation providing institutions the right to broadcast live games without obtaining athletes' permission to use their NILs. Even absent state law, courts may consider live broadcasts to be noncommercial events that involve a matter of public interest. On the other hand, generally, commercial speech or events, like video games, require permission from or payment to athletes for the use of their NILs.[10]

Reasonable Policies Regarding Institutional Use of College Athlete NILs

The limited use of athlete NILs by the institution should include the following policies:

1. The institution may use athlete NILs for audio or videocast or otherwise recorded for live or delayed electronic distribution or photographed for print or digital publication during the championship

season (from the beginning of practice through the end of the championship)[11] for athletic events in which the athlete participates.

2. The institution may use athlete NILs for advertising or promoting championship-season athletic events in which the athlete participates.[12]
3. The institution may use athlete NILs for publication and sale of event programs sold in conjunction with or during the course of championship-season athletic events in which the athlete participates.
4. The institution may use athlete NILs for perpetual print and electronic publication rights for the athlete's historical performance and participation statistics and photographs of prior champions or championship teams. The institution may not commercially exploit such rights in settings other than athletic-event programs. However, such historical licenses should not extend to commercial documentary products that exist separate from the current athletic event. The inclusion of such data on the institution's official athletics internet site, which may be supported by sponsorship revenues, shall not be considered prohibited commercial exploitation.
5. The institution is prohibited from commercial exploitation of current student NILs for nonextracurricular program activities such as entering into licensing agreements using current student NILs for video games, licensed apparel, licensed products, and so on.[13]
6. The institution may engage in commercial exploitation of the exclusive right to provide official team athletics apparel or equipment to its athletics teams and to put the name of the athlete on official team uniforms. However, if the institution licenses its own NIL to a third party to sell its institutionally branded products, it cannot grant the use of the athlete's NIL to such third parties. The athlete must wear official team apparel, as specified by the institution, but retains the right to utilize his or her own "personal performance gear" (not apparel) in practice and competition. In that case, the athlete must cover the brand of any conflicting institutional sponsor during participation in

such championship-season athletic events.[14] The athlete's obligation to wear official team apparel shall extend throughout the academic year for official team practices, exhibitions, non-championship season contests, and appearances at official university events in which all attending players must wear such apparel.

7. The national collegiate athletic governance organizations and their member institutions and conferences may jointly agree to license their championship-season collective intellectual property (including college athlete NIL and national governing organization/institution/conference name, marks, logos, etc.) to third parties conditioned on such agreements excluding royalty or other payments to athletes.
8. The institution (conference or national governing organization) may not enter into a group licensing agreement with the individual college athlete during the athlete's enrollment. Neither may the institution pay proceeds from any sponsorship agreement to college athletes other than using athletics income to support athletic scholarships tethered to educational expenses. All proceeds from the institution's permissible commercial exploitation of athlete NILs related to the athletes' participation shall be used to support the athletics program or the other academic or extracurricular programs of the institution consistent with its tax-exempt status.
9. Following an athlete's completion of collegiate athletics eligibility, the institution may negotiate group licensing agreements related to sale of products subject to the provisions of the federal Unrelated Business Income Tax (UBIT). Any effort to commercially exploit *former* students' NILs requires the institution (or third party) to obtain consent from each former student for each specific use, which may include payment of licensing fees or royalties to the former students or a charitable donation of such income back to the institution or other nonprofit entity.

An Independent Commission and Administrative Center to Set Standards and Adjudicate Conflicts and Complaints

During the college athlete's enrollment, coordination will be necessary to prevent conflicts between institutional and college athlete NIL agreements with third parties. The Drake Group proposes the establishment of an independent NIL Commission to oversee the operation of a NIL Eligibility Center for this purpose because of the following:

- The rights of college athletes to outside employment are not within the purview of a collegiate athletics governance organization.
- Such national athletics governing organizations consist of higher-education institution members that have a conflict of interest with regard to resolution of competing institution/athlete interests.
- College athletes are not employees, and no labor union exists to represent their interests.
- Even though a college athlete organization exists, the organization would have a conflict of interest concerning resolution of competing institution/athlete issues.

National College Athlete NIL Commission and NIL Eligibility Center

Congress should establish a federally chartered independent 501(c)(3) organization,[15] the College Athlete NIL Commission (NIL Commission), which shall also house the NIL Eligibility Center. The Center shall be limited to performing administrative functions. The NIL Commission and NIL Eligibility Center should be financially self-supporting.

Functions of the NIL Commission

Congress should grant the NIL Commission a limited antitrust exemption and enforcement powers to perform the following functions:

1. *Set standards and adjudicate challenges.* The Commission shall set standards and resolve challenges to such standards. It shall ensure that institutional sponsorship and other third-party agreements related to use of college athlete NILs and outside employment during an athlete's period of enrollment meet established policies, as detailed earlier.
2. *Caps on employment / NIL compensation.* The Commission shall not impose caps on athlete compensation related to national agreements with third-party employers, including internet / social media sponsorship agreements, sale of NIL items on the internet, or college athletes' sport-related self-employment (local or otherwise) without third-party investors (e.g., camps, clinics, lessons). Because college athletes may be signing multiyear local endorsement or employment agreements and because large-market institutions may enjoy recruiting advantages over small-market institutions (not yet proven), the Commission shall initially establish caps on total annual local employment earnings from third-party employers. These caps shall apply to appearance-related services (autograph signing, lessons, speaking engagements, etc.). They shall also apply to advertising/endorsement local employment by businesses within a specified radius from the university or where the target market for the employer's product is within a specified radius of the athlete's institution.[16] The Commission shall reevaluate the local cap system following a review of actual agreements and compensation during the initial eighteen months of implementation.[17]
3. *Complaints related to the conduct of agents and third-party employers.* The Commission shall receive, monitor, and adjudicate complaints concerning agents, attorneys, and third-party employers related to compliance with Commission standards under the terms of previously approved employment or NIL agreements during a college athlete's enrollment. The desired end will be to report violations to the national college sports governing organization enforcement authority and/or to withhold approval of an agent or third-party employer for future

college athlete agreements. Adjudication shall be based on consideration of formal written records in an administrative proceeding.

4. *National college sports governing organization rules related to athlete outside employment and commercialization of college athlete NILs.* The Commission shall approve revisions to national college sports governing organization legislation related to college athlete outside employment and commercialization of NILs. Further, any entity (conferences, NCAA) should also receive a limited antitrust exemption for the express purpose of restricting eligibility for athletic participation consistent with the federal law and findings and conclusions of the NIL Commission.
5. *Registration of sports agents.* The Commission shall establish standards for the registration and approval of sports agents to represent college athletes who seek employment or NIL endorsement opportunities.
6. *Agent and attorney compensation.* The Commission shall set standards for college athlete agreements with agents and lawyers that specify acceptable ranges for hourly rates or percentage commissions.
7. *Appeal of NIL agreement disapprovals.* The Commission shall resolve any college athlete's or institution's appeal of a NIL Eligibility Commission decision not to approve an athlete's or institution's NIL agreement because of failure to meet established standards.
8. *Educational and instructional materials.* The Commission shall develop educational and instructional materials related to applicable standards, procedures for receiving approval for athlete outside employment / NIL agreements, and institutional agreements that include use of athlete NILs. Forms for submission of the proposed agreements to the NIL Eligibility Center for review and approval shall contain a section that requires both parties (the athlete and the institution) to attest that neither one knows that such employment has been arranged, directly or indirectly, by the institution's employees, donors, athletics program sponsors or advertisers, or other representatives of its athletics interests.

9. *Oversight of NIL Eligibility Center.* Develop all policies and procedures for and oversee the operation of the NIL Eligibility Center.

Composition of NIL Commission

The NIL Commission shall consist of nine members, each of whom shall serve a five-year term. Three members shall be economists with experience and expertise in setting prices based on marketplace benchmarks and shall be appointed by the American Economics Association. Initially, one shall be appointed for a term of five years, one for a term of four years, and one for a term of three years. Three members shall have experience and expertise in employment and sports law; at least two of them shall also have been college athletes and shall be appointed by the national Sports Lawyers Association. Initially, one shall be appointed for a term of five years, one for a term of four years, and one for a term of three years. Three other members shall have experience and expertise in intercollegiate athletics management or higher-education administration, and at least two of them shall have also been college athletes. The American Council on Education shall appoint these members. Initially, one shall be appointed for a term of five years, one for a term of four years, and one for a term of three years. The term "independent" shall mean at least two years removed from employment by any member institution of a national college sports governing organization member institution, the national college sports governing organization, the organization itself, one of its member athletic conferences, or the appointing organization and a promise not to be employed by such entities for five years following service on the Commission.

NIL Eligibility Center

Operating as the administrative arm of the NIL Commission, the NIL Eligibility Center shall be established to review and approve all non–de minimis athlete endorsement and NIL agreements for compliance with the policies and standards set by the Commission. The NIL Eligibility Center shall perform all Commission-assigned administrative functions including maintenance of a publicly available, searchable database containing approved agreements with proprietary content redacted according to policies established by the NIL Commission.

Funding of NIL Commission and NIL Eligibility Center Operations

The operating budgets of the Commission and the NIL Eligibility Center shall be funded from a small percentage charge against media-rights revenues of national collegiate championships, national collegiate sports governance organization fees, and a small percentage charge on the value of each endorsement or NIL agreement, or similar assessments. The percentage shall be established by the NIL Commission, with each year's operating assessment based on projected service volume and annually adjusted based on an independent audit of the cost of actual services rendered. Annual compensation of NIL Commission members should be established by Congress on the basis of compensation consistent with that provided for federal commission members.

NOTES

1. As of November 20, 2020, five states have passed legislation that prohibits universities in their states from not allowing their student athletes to benefit from commercializing their publicity rights or names, images, and likenesses. The first such bill was California's SB 206, which was signed into law (passing its Assembly by a 73–0 vote and its Senate by a 39–0). Bills have been filed in 2020 legislative sessions in some thirty-four additional states.

2. The NIL Eligibility Center would be the administrative arm of the NIL Commission, similar to the currently existing NCAA Academic Eligibility Center, which determines whether prospective athletes' high school academic transcripts meet NCAA freshmen eligibility standards. Like the NCAA Academic Eligibility Center, the NIL Eligibility Center would be self-supporting based on application fees that represent a de minimis percentage of the institutional and athlete agreements being reviewed.

3. NCAA Research, *14-Year Trends in Division I Athletics Finances*, 2019, http://www.ncaa.org/sites/default/files/2019RES_D1-RevExp_Report_Final_20191107.pdf.

4. The Drake Group supports priority use of intercollegiate athletics revenues for athletic scholarships that provide educational opportunities; academic support programs conducted by academic authorities, which are available to all students; and the establishment of academic trust funds to provide financial support for the completion of undergraduate or graduate degree programs. The Drake Group does not support the concept of "lifetime scholarships" to currently eligible college athletes, which

send the inappropriate message that these athletes do not have to be diligent students now because they can always return to college on full scholarship later to complete the degree. The Drake Group does support the establishment of trust funds to which any former athlete may apply and receive a completion-of-degree grant based on need or deserving circumstances.

5. The Drake Group believes it would be a simple matter and a fair rule to require any college athlete who participates in a professional draft to declares his or her intent to remain eligible for collegiate athletics within thirty days or other reasonable deadline following the completion of the professional draft. This arrangement would allow the institution to exercise its scholarship-renewal obligations or recruit to replace a departing athlete.

6. For example, the proposed NIL Commission might establish a definition of de minimis remuneration as $1,000 per year.

7. The Drake Group believes that the proposed NIL Commission should address an appropriate manner in which college athletes would be permitted to identify their status as a student at their respective university without the context of such identification implying commercial use of the institution's marks.

8. "39% of all undergraduates who initially enroll in a four-year institution transfer at least once." National Student Clearinghouse Research Center, *Signature Report: Transfer & Mobility—2018*, 2018, https://www.ncaa.org/about/resources/research-student-athlete-transfers#:~:text=A%202018%20study%20from%20the,transfer%20schools%20at%20least%20once.

9. See NCAA, "Research on Student-Athlete Transfers," accessed on October 5, 2020, http://www.ncaa.org/about/resources/research-student-athlete-transfers. Regarding the impact of transfer on time of graduation and attrition, note that issues related to nontransferable credits increase as the student advances to upper-level courses within specialized degree programs and that most institutions require transfers to meet a "minimum credits in residence" requirement as a condition for graduation. Data from a 2017 US Government Accountability Office report show that students lost an estimated 43 percent of college credits when they transferred, or an estimated thirteen credits, on average. The average credits lost during transfer are equivalent to about four courses, which is almost one semester of full-time enrollment. US Government Accountability Office, "Higher Education: Students Need More Information to Help Reduce Challenges in Transferring College Credits," *GAO@100*, August 14, 2017, https://www.gao.gov/products/gao-17-574.

10. See e.g., Keller v. Electronic Arts, 724 F.3d. 1268, 1271 (9th Circuit 2013). While the law in this area, especially with respect to live broadcasts, is somewhat unsettled, we support the proposition that institutions do not need to receive permission from athletes to use their NILs in live, in-game broadcasts (or support thereof) but must with respect to all nongame events like video games.

11. At all times other than the championship season, the athlete's interest in monetizing NILs takes precedence over institutional agreements. We envision the athlete being able to exploit any sponsorship category in which the institution does not have an agreement during the championship season. We also recognize several issues that the proposed NIL Commission will need to address. For instance, assume the institution has a Nike exclusive shoe agreement and an athlete on that team, recognizing no conflict with the shoe agreement, enters into an outside agreement with Nike, thereby being able to earn compensation during the championship season. What about other athletes on the team who are Adidas athletes, whose agreements would be in conflict and who could not exploit the shoe category in the championship season? Would this arrangement give the school any type of recruiting advantage or allow Nike-signed

players unfair advantage? Another area might be athletes monetizing their Facebook pages that are filled with photographs of the athlete in institution-branded gear. Questions related to fair use and desired use would need to be addressed.

12. Institutions must be cognizant of their Title IX obligation to promote men's and women's events equally. Failure to do so will have a significant effect on female athletes' visibility and ability to monetize their NILs.

13. The proposed NIL Commission should provide clear guidance regarding the propriety of third-party-negotiated institution/conference/athlete group licensing agreements for currently enrolled and no-longer-enrolled athletes. Commission guidance should prohibit higher-education institutions from entering into a business relationship with their students or former students for products or services not related to their tax-exempt purpose. For example, an institution enters into an agreement with a video-game company to use its marks; the video-game company enters into a separate agreement with current athletes, thereby allowing athletes to appear in a video game wearing the institution's uniform. This type of group licensing agreement would circumvent (a) the prohibition of athletes being allowed to use the NILs of their institutions for outside compensation and (b) the prohibition of institutions paying college athletes for use of their NILs other than the provision of athletic scholarships tethered to educational expenses. The Commission would also have to consider the Title IX implications of the institution knowingly entering into an agreement with a third party that would benefit the members of a male team without affording corresponding benefits to an equal proportion of female athletes. The Drake Group opposes higher-education institutions entering a business relationship with the athlete when the business is subject to UBIT or sharing institutional revenues derived from athletics in any manner other than an athletic scholarship supporting the institution's purpose of students earning accredited degrees.

14. This policy example is intended to be consistent with Olympic policies that recognize the importance of the athlete being able to control his or her own sports-performance-related equipment and other gear. This is another area in which the NIL Commission would develop policy.

15. Congress successfully established the United States Olympic Committee, a federally chartered independent 501(c)(3) self-supporting organization in 1978, via passage of the Ted Stevens Olympic and Amateur Sports Act to oversee the US Olympic, Paralympic, and open amateur sport system.

16. For example, the amount of the annual cap could be tied to the average of the median income in all markets of NCAA member institutions or all markets with the institution's competitive division. Instead of allowing athletic conferences to set their own compensation caps or limit median income computations to the markets of their members, the Drake Group believes an "honest broker," such as the proposed NIL Commission, should set national standards to prevent any conflicts of interest.

17. Following such review, if such local caps are continued to be imposed on college athletes, similar caps on outside local compensation should be imposed on college coaches. Both coaches and athletes are in high recruiting demand by institutions of higher education. One can argue that the size of the institution's market as it affects outside third-party employment opportunities might influence a coach's employment decisions just as it might influence a college athlete's attendance decision. The Drake Group believes that athletes, already experiencing more limits to outside employment created by prohibitions of nonconflict with institutional sponsorship agreements and scholarships tethered to educational expenses, should not be the lone victims of a double standard regarding any adverse effects of a cap on local third-party earnings.

PART III

Op-Eds

CHAPTER 10

Unionizing Is Proof That College Athletics Need to Be Reformed

Andrew Zimbalist

College athletics is in desperate need of reform for many reasons. One of them is the extravagant and economically irrational pay packages going to head coaches who may earn anywhere between $2 million and $9 million per year—roughly what NFL and NBA coaches are paid. The reason they are remunerated so handsomely is because the pay of the players they recruit is artificially suppressed.

Another is that college football and basketball players are promised an education in exchange for playing on the team. It's an unfair bargain for the vast majority of the students because they do not get an education. Indeed, many of them cannot read beyond a primary-school level. They are pushed through a phony curriculum of "gut" and "no-show" courses in order to keep the team's graduation rate above 50 percent.

These "student athletes" are being compensated in the form of their scholarship. While participating on their team may provide benefits in the form of character development, this is not college education any more than it is educational for a player on an NFL or NBA team.

So, yes, these athletes are primarily employees, and they should be allowed to unionize. The more complex question is, Will unionization best

---

New York Times, March 27, 2014.

promote the outcome that we want for college sports? I don't believe that it will.

Although unionization will help reduce the hypocrisy and exploitation in college sports, it will move intercollegiate athletics away from its professed purpose, which is as a secondary activity to foster balance between the more sedentary, cerebral life of a college student and the need for physical and emotional development.

Unionization still faces many hurdles: the appeal to the National Labor Relations Board, a likely appeal to the Seventh Circuit Court of Appeals, and then another to the Supreme Court. In the end, it will affect fewer than two dozen private schools in the Football Bowl Subdivision.

So, the movement for reform has to look beyond unionization. The good news in yesterday's ruling is that, together with the Ed O'Bannon publicity rights case, the Jeffrey Kessler antitrust case,[1] and the financial and organizational mess of college sports, it stimulates awareness and debate on the issue.

NOTES

1. This sentence refers to the ruling of the regional NLRB in Chicago that Northwestern football players are employees and should be allowed to unionize. This decision was invalidated when the national NLRB refused to confirm it the next year.

CHAPTER 11

College Coaches' Salaries and Higher Education

Andrew Zimbalist

One day after Jim Harbaugh was fired by the NFL's San Francisco 49ers, he signed a seven-year contract to coach at the University of Michigan. According to the Michigan athletic director, Harbaugh will be paid a guaranteed annual salary of $5 million, plus healthy bonuses for team success, a $2 million signing bonus, and an unspecified amount of deferred salary. The AD said Harbaugh's compensation package is similar to what he got from the 49ers.

How can it be that the head coach of the University of Michigan Wolverines is paid the same as the head coach of the San Francisco 49ers? The 49ers, after all, have yearly revenue in excess of $300 million. The Wolverines' revenue in 2013 is closer to $90 million. Can the coach's incremental value really be similar in the two cases? No.

Here's what's happening. Eighty-five of the athletes on the Michigan football team receive a full-ride scholarship, on average worth around $40,000 a year. (There are another thirty or so "walk-on" athletes who receive no scholarship.) According to various estimates, the top players on the best college teams have a market value well over a million dollars.

Since the athletes can't be paid, they are recruited without explicit financial incentives. Rather, the coach or his assistants makes a pitch to most promising high school footballers based on the college's reputation, its facilities, its national exposure, and its likely performance. A significant

Huffington Post, December 31, 2014.ç

part of its exposure and its performance is expected to be related to the coach's renown.

Thus, the Jim Harbaughs, the Nick Sabans, or the Urban Meyers of the college football world have an advantage in recruiting the best high school players. The coach's reputation is a part of the currency (in lieu of dollars) that is used to build a leading college football team. And, hence, the coach's salary reflects the value of the athletes he brings to the school (who are not allowed to be paid). The salary is then further boosted by two other artificial, extra-market factors: university and state subsidies to intercollegiate sports (the median operating deficit of FBS athletics programs is over $11 million)[1] and a variety of federal tax preferences.

The solution is not to pay the athletes (though they deserve better benefits and fewer arbitrary restrictions). The solution is a narrow antitrust exemption that would allow the NCAA, or another governing body, to set a limit on coaches' compensation. There is no reason for college coaches to be paid for value produced by the players.

What would happen to the quality of college football if there were a salary limit that stipulated coaches could not be paid more than, say, three times the national average salary of full professors? Absolutely nothing. The reason is that the best alternative employment for the top college coaches, in almost all cases, would pay less than $450,000. A few might go to the NFL, but they would replace NFL coaches who would then become available at the college level.

So the talent pool of college coaches would be unaffected by such a salary limit. Colleges would save a few million dollars on the head coach, but there would be more savings from downward pressure on the compensation of the assistant coaches (who together cost $2 to $5 million annually at the top fifty programs), of the athletic directors, and of the conference commissioners.

More money for athletics means less for academic excellence. Between 2005 and 2012, the average salary of head football coaches at the top twenty-five football schools increased over 60 percent, while the average college spending on academics per student dropped by 2 percent. If we are serious about maintaining the historical excellence of higher education in the United States, and the competitive economic benefits it yields, then we must take a careful look at the illogical, inefficient, and harmful resource diversion engendered by college sports.

NOTES

1. The median annual deficit of athletics programs in FBS has since climbed to $18.8 million in 2018–19.

CHAPTER 12

Time for a Presidential Panel to Investigate College Sports

Andrew Zimbalist

The recently retired Congressman Jim Moran introduced a bill last month with bipartisan support that calls for the formation of a presidential commission to study the future of college sports. Reintroduction and passage of such a bill would be a small but significant step in reining in athletics excesses.[1]

College sports is swimming in money, and most of it comes from football. The median revenue of athletics programs within the Football Bowl Subdivision (FBS) of Division I grew to $61.9 million in 2012–13 from 28.2 million in 2003–4—an inflation-adjusted increase of 76 percent. And it continues to grow. College football's new playoff system, which held its national championship game last night, yielded a twelve-year contract with ESPN worth $7.3 billion.

Despite all the new revenue—most of which flows to the colleges in the Big Five conferences in the FBS of Division I—all is not well in the world of college football. Even within those conferences—the Atlantic Coast, Big Ten, Big 12, Pacific 12, and Southeastern—it is really only a couple of dozen universities that are pulling in the big bucks. According to the NCAA's most recent figures, out of 128 schools in FBS, only 20 athletics programs have an operating surplus.

Overall, the median operating deficit in FBS athletics departments is approximately $12 million. When all capital costs (e.g., building new sta-

Chronicle of Higher Education, January 13, 2015.

diums and training facilities) are added in, the number of programs in the black shrinks to a mere handful, and the size of the median deficit increases by an additional $10 million or more.

So, what's going on—how can losses be piling up as revenues soar? First, costs are growing faster than revenues. There are no stockholders in Division I athletics. That is, athletics departments do not have to answer to a board of directors or company owners who are looking for profits to go up each quarter so the company's stock price will rise or dividends can be paid.

Athletics departments are not profit maximizers. They are win maximizers. The coaches and the athletic directors, occasional lofty rhetoric to the contrary, get fatter and longer contracts when they win. Above all, that's what they are all about, even when it means trampling academic integrity and excellence.

Without pressure to maximize profits, when revenues rise, the athletic directors find ways to spend it in pursuit of winning. That means hiring big-name coaches for big-tag salaries comparable to those earned by NFL and NBA coaches, building new or renovating old stadiums and arenas, improving training facilities, lavishing abundant resources on recruiting star high school athletes, and so on.

Second, college sports have come under increasing legal challenge, rooted in the cartel-like behavior of the NCAA and the limbo status of intercollegiate athletics in between amateur and professional sport. The most frequently cited offense is that, according to NCAA rules, athletes cannot be paid; they can only get a full-ride scholarship, which, depending on the college and the athlete's residence, is valued at between $25,000 and $50,000. Yet, according to various estimates, the top athletes at FBS schools produce a value well in excess of $1 million. The surplus produced by these players goes in part to the coaches who recruit them and in part to support the "nonrevenue" sports at the school.

As a result of the NCAA's policies, it has been the subject of several recent high-profile lawsuits, including one filed by former UCLA basketball star Ed O'Bannon, who wants athletes to have rights to their public image; one by the Northwestern football players, who are seeking to unionize in order to compel the university to provide better benefits and scholarships that cover the full cost of attendance; and a blanket antitrust suit by the renowned antitrust and sports lawyer Jeffrey Kessler challenging the association's right to limit athlete pay in any form.

The initial response by the NCAA to these suits, other than fighting them in court, has been to loosen some of its restrictions. The NCAA now allows colleges to provide four-year scholarships to players, to increase the value of a full-ride scholarship by several thousand dollars to cover the full cost of attendance, and to provide better benefits. These higher costs not only will affect the eighty-five male athletes on football scholarships and the thirteen on basketball scholarships but, because of Title IX, will probably mean that ninety-eight female athletes will also receive these richer scholarships.

However, with only a handful of colleges earning a true surplus, these additional costs of $1 million-plus will (a) make it more difficult for the vast majority of colleges—unable to afford the financial burden—to compete effectively on the playing field, (b) force these colleges into larger athletic deficits, robbing funds from the academic budget, or (c) impel some colleges to follow the lead of the University of Alabama at Birmingham and end their football program.

Thus, despite the streams of new money, college sports is faced with increased inequality and greater insolvency. Every extra dollar going to intercollegiate athletics is a dollar lost to academic programming. At the top twenty-four spenders in college sports between 2005 and 2012, football coaches' salaries calculated on a per-player basis rose more than 60 percent (several now exceed $5 million, and in forty-one of fifty states, a head coach is the highest paid public official in the state), while academic spending per student dropped 2 percent.

Meanwhile, the various litigations are pushing college sports toward greater uncertainty, if not chaos. A financially sound and organizationally stable intercollegiate athletics system is in the interests not only of the fans of college sports but also of our country's system of higher education.

The NCAA functions as a trade association of the athletic directors, conference commissioners, and coaches, especially those from the Power Five conferences, and has proven time after time that it is incapable of constructively reforming itself. (The College Football Playoff, with its multibillion-dollar television contract, is controlled by the college presidents and conference commissioners of the Power Five conferences and is outside the purview of the NCAA.)

Congress can stand idly by, as it is wont to do, and refuse to get involved in the business of college sports. Or it can recognize that it is already involved in that business—via an elaborate network of tax preferences, grants, and subsidies—and that the system needs help. In a step toward constructive bipartisan leadership, Congress should pass a bill calling for a presidential commission on college athletics and move it to Barack Obama's desk.

NOTES

1. Note that in 2019 Donna Shalala introduced House Bill 5528, which sought to establish a congressional commission to study and propose reforms for the governance of college sports. Under Title IV of the Higher Education Act of 1965 (20 U.S.C. § 1070 et seq.), in fiscal year 2019 approximately $130.4 billion of federal student support was available for higher education, including over $29 billion in federal Pell Grants. Section 2.a.(2) H.R. 5528, 116th Congress, Congressional Advisory Commission on Intercollegiate Athletics Act of 2019, https://www.congress.gov/bill/116th-congress/house-bill/5528/text?r=4&s=1.

CHAPTER 13

Paying College Athletes

TAKE TWO

Andrew Zimbalist

Last week an article ran in the *Huffington Post* that cited several economists, all affirming that big-time football and basketball colleges had more than enough money in their athletics departments to pay student-athletes. Mistakenly, I was lumped in with that group. I write this piece in an attempt to clarify what I believe is a complicated, yet important, issue.

First, college athletes have been paid since the nineteenth century. Some are paid cash under the table, some are paid in goods and services, and the vast majority in Division I football and men's basketball are paid in scholarships. When the NCAA was formed in December 1905, the clear policy was that the student-athletes were to be amateurs—that meant "any inducements" to attend a school on the basis of their athletic skills were prohibited. There was no ambiguity that this policy did not allow scholarships based on athletic prowess. (Of course, the NCAA also had a policy of home rule, which meant that there was no enforcement of this principle.) The issue at hand, then, is not whether college athletes should be paid but whether they should be paid a salary.

Second, let's get the numbers straight. Not all 350 athletics departments in Division I make money. In fact, only 20 do, and that's before considering millions of dollars a year in capital expenses. When capital expenses are included, there are fewer than 10 athletics departments a year that generate

---

Huffington Post, March 28, 2015 (revised May 28, 2015).

a true surplus. (Of course, it is true, as David Berri says, that if there were less waste and extravagance, more schools would have a surplus, but this is unavailing. A potential surplus does not pay any bills.)

It is also true that a little more than half of the 128 football teams in FBS and that a little less than half of the FBS men's basketball teams run an operating surplus (again, before capital and some indirect administrative expenses and potential partial siphoning of donations are reckoned). It is further true that these operating surpluses, where they exist, eventually are transferred to support nonrevenue sports in the department, to bloat artificially inflated salaries for coaches and administrators, and to finance extravagant expenditures on stadiums, arenas, training facilities, recruiting, and team travel.

The mechanism of this transfer is manifest. Schools do not compete for players by offering higher salaries; rather, with salaries proscribed, they attempt to attract the desired recruits by having the most famous coaches, the best performance records, the fanciest facilities, the most lenient course requirements, and so on. In short, the coaches end up being paid for the economic value of the athletes they help to recruit.

So, the idea that there's plenty of money to pay the athletes a salary largely comes from the existing system of surrogate pay and superfluous expenditure that currently exists. If the athletes get salaries, then the coaches no longer get the proxy pay—and one cost offsets the other. This is logical at first blush, but there are problems.

First, many coaches are on multimillion-dollar long-term contracts that go as long as eight years. Even when these contracts end, there will be expectations and momentum that will prevent an immediate adjustment to much-lower compensation levels. Hence, we can expect a transition period of a decade or longer during which the schools will be paying both high coaches' salaries and salaries to the student-athletes. Along with athlete salaries comes the obligation to pay into Social Security and workers' compensation. This transition period will further bleed academic budgets and/or put additional pressure on escalating student fees.

Second, many of the largest expenditures to attract students in lieu of offering market salaries to athletes entail major capital projects, such as new stadiums and arenas. The funds for these projects are already encumbered, as they come from long-term bonds and must be paid off over decades. Paying athletes a salary will again constitute a doubling of the financial burden and lead to large deficits over a long transition period.

There are other reasons why we should be cautious before paying athletes a salary besides the financial drain involved. It would be disruptive to academic culture. We don't use the market system to allocate resources within the university. I don't auction the right to be in my sports economics class to the students willing to pay the highest fee. The first violinist in the school orchestra does not get paid even though tickets are sold to the concert; nor do leading thespians or dancers get paid for their public performances.[1]

A labor market for high school football and basketball players would be both chaotic and emotionally difficult for seventeen-year-olds. Once they are in college, the existence of disparate pay, where one player received $3 million and another $10,000, would be disheartening to team spirit.

Finally, nonrevenue and women's sports would take a significant hit. College sports, in addition to providing entertainment and excitement for the college community, offer important developmental experiences for the participating athlete. Those positive experiences should be made equally available to men and women.

So, absent paying football and basketball players a salary, what is to be done? The leading athletes on these teams are being exploited in economic terms. Worse still, a majority of them come from low-income, minority families. These players help generate the revenues that then subsidize the nonrevenue sports, such as tennis, volleyball, golf, and swimming, whose athletes are predominantly from white, middle-class families. There is a reverse–Robin Hood racial injustice here.

If we want to preserve the educational model of intercollegiate athletics, here's a more attractive option: take the definition of amateurism away from its current arbitrary, hypocritical, and morphing state imposed by the NCAA and follow the lead of the AAU and other amateur organizations. The working definition should be simple: an amateur athlete is one who is not paid a salary for playing his or her sport.

So, a college athlete could continue to receive the considerable benefit of a tax-free athletic scholarship and, in addition, earn outside income from use of his or her publicity rights (perhaps via a trust fund and/or group licensing). A college athlete could sign with a lawyer or an agent and enter a professional sport draft and not become ineligible to play college sports until he or she signs his or her first professional contract.

Further, in addition to offering athletes a cost-of-attendance stipend (approved at the 2015 NCAA Convention) as part of an athletic scholarship, institutions should be mandated to provide a "benefits package" consisting of (a) year-round health insurance; (b) lifetime health insurance for injuries related to playing their sport (including concussions, which might not show obvious symptoms when the athlete stops playing in college); (c) disability insurance that covers lost income, including for athletes with a professional career trajectory; and (d) due process rights for accused violations.

Naturally, to extend these benefits will cost money. As discussed earlier, there are many sources of waste in our current system—some of which can be controlled by Congress granting the NCAA or another organizing body a limited antitrust exemption, which would be conditioned on capping coaches' and athletic directors' (ADs') salaries and providing the "benefits package." It may also be necessary to cut back on the athletic scholarships issued to middle-class athletes in nonrevenue sports.

Lastly, the NCAA controls the postseason tournaments in all of its sports except the football playoff championship for the Power Five conferences in FBS. The NCAA should take control of that competition and use the funds (annually over $500 million in 2015 and anticipated to rise to $1 billion) to support the reform program just outlined. Congress could mandate such control and use of funds as a condition for the limited antitrust exemption or Higher Education Act funding.

The bottom line is that while the current system could be converted into a college football and basketball minor league existing outside the nonprofit educational institution, there is a more attractive educational reform option available.

NOTES

1. There are some exceptions to this practice, but the amount of pay is very modest and normally at a work-study level.

CHAPTER 14

Antitrust Exemption May Aid College Sports' Untenable Situation

Andrew Zimbalist

The finances and the legal framework of college sports are both on shaky ground. The status quo, even with some tweaking, will not provide a stable foundation going forward.

The NCAA just released its latest *Revenues and Expenses Report* for Division I athletics programs. The picture is not pretty. At the FBS level, the median deficit of the 128 athletics programs was $12.9 million in 2014–15. At the FCS level, it was $12.0 million; and at Division I without football, $11.8 million. The largest financial loss on an operating basis in FBS was $44.6 million, and 52 programs had operating losses of more than $16.6 million.

Overall, only 24 of the 128 programs (18.75 percent) experienced a net operating surplus (generated revenue exceeded operating costs).

As troublesome as these operating deficits are, the actual financial situation of FBS athletics programs is still worse. First, most capital costs, particularly facilities financed by debt outside the athletics department, are not included in these operating figures. An NCAA study in 2005 estimated that the average FBS program had capital costs exceeding $20 million annually. Second, many indirect expenses, such as a pro rata share of the university president's and top staff's compensation, along with their

Sports Business Journal, November 28, 2016.

office rent and operating costs, are not included. Third, donations to the athletics program are considered part of generated revenue, yet some of these funds may come at the expense of donations to the general fund. (Some of these additional expenses are offset by overcounting tuition costs related to athletic scholarships.)

When a full and proper accounting is done, there are typically only half a dozen or so FBS programs in any given year that experience a true financial surplus.

How can typical FBS athletics programs be throwing off tens of millions of dollars of deficits every year when television, postseason bowl, and sponsorship revenue has been growing so robustly and athletes' compensation is suppressed?

To be a competitively successful program, with salary payments to athletes prohibited, the most effective way to recruit the best athletes is by providing successful coaches, lavish facilities, higher cost-of-attendance allowances, and effective support systems.

Unlike a typical commercial enterprise, college sports programs do not have stockholders who demand a profit at the end of each quarter so that the price of the company's stock will rise or that dividends may be paid out. Rather, college sports programs have stakeholders (e.g., boosters, season-ticket buyers, alumni, administrators, students, and state legislators) who, above all else, want winning teams. The primary pressure placed on athletic directors is to find a way to win, not a way to make profits.

What this means is that when the typical AD at a Power Five conference school sees additional revenue entering the program, the first and dominant thought is, "How can I put that revenue to use to build a more successful program?" In the hypercompetitive world of big-time college sports and the arms race it engenders, there is always some additional enhancement that an AD is yearning to make.

In short, the current situation is not financially sustainable.

The legal standing of college sports is also on thin ice. In recent years, there have been numerous antitrust challenges to NCAA rules through cases involving pay and benefits to college athletes, the number and duration of athletic scholarships, athletes' ability to receive advice or representation from an agent or lawyer, length of the playing season and selection of teams for postseason championships, and payment of assistant coaches. The nation's antitrust laws are not easily applied to college sports.

The Sherman Act of 1890 prohibits all contracts, combinations, or conspiracies in restraint of trade that are unreasonable. It was intended to govern commercial activities. Colleges and universities enter into contracts and combinations in order jointly to compete in sports. In antitrust cases involving intercollegiate sports, the first question is whether the challenged rule is fundamentally commercial in nature. If answered affirmatively, the next question is whether the rule is unreasonable because it causes significant anticompetitive effects.

If the rule causes anticompetitive effects, then these effects must be balanced against any procompetitive effects it engenders. There are, however, no clear rules, no clean-cut balancing tests with objective criteria, and few other mechanisms to make these judgments unambiguously. The outcomes of court cases, then, depend heavily on the subjective evaluation of evidence by judges in different jurisdictions at the trial, appeals, and Supreme Court levels. Unfortunately, last month the US Supreme Court denied certiorari in the *O'Bannon* case, leaving substantial confusion about the interpretation of amateurism and its impact on the popularity of intercollegiate athletics.

Litigations based on labor law against the NCAA also have been brought, and at least one case remains under appeal.

These litigations not only end in nebulous and shifting guidelines for the rules of college sports but also require gargantuan resources to prosecute. The *O'Bannon* case was first filed in 2009. After the trial-court decision, the *O'Bannon* plaintiffs were awarded costs of more than $40 million to be paid by the NCAA. The NCAA had to pay its own legal expenses on top of that. The costs rose further as the case was prosecuted twice at the appeals-court and Supreme Court levels.

One solution, as suggested by Gerry Gurney, Donna Lopiano, and myself in *Unwinding Madness: What Went Wrong with College Sports and How to Fix It*, is to provide college sports with a limited and conditional antitrust exemption. It would permit the NCAA and its member schools to impose certain rules such as prohibiting payment for play (e.g., salaries) to athletes without fear of violating the antitrust laws, while allowing certain types of payments and benefits (e.g., payments for third-party endorsements) to athletes. These exceptions would be provided if cost-control measures are implemented (e.g., capping coaches' salaries and facilities spending) and player-centric measures are implemented (e.g., protecting the health, safety, and well-being of college athletes and requiring the primacy of academics in intercollegiate athletics). Thus, the proposed limited and conditional antitrust exemption would promote socially and educationally desirable policies while simultaneously promoting greater cost savings in intercollegiate athletics.

It is time for Congress to set public policy regarding college sports.

CHAPTER 15

The NCAA's Women Problem

Andrew Zimbalist

As the University of Connecticut Huskies enter the third round of the NCAA basketball tournament this weekend, they have won seventy-one consecutive games. Seventy-one! And they won national championships in 1995, 2000, 2002, 2003, 2004, 2009, 2010, 2013, 2014, and 2015—that's ten times in the last twenty-one years and nine times in the last fifteen. Now, that's major news. Only it isn't . . . because this is the UConn *women's* team.

Even if this year's Huskies win the tournament, the NCAA will pretty much ignore them, too. Certainly it will neglect them financially. Over at the men's tournament, the NCAA pays for success: each game a team plays (not including the championship) earns the team's conference roughly $260,000 this year plus $260,000 each of the five following years. So the total value of a victory in the men's tournament is approximately $1.56 million. By contrast, a win in the women's tournament brings a reward of exactly zero dollars. That's right, zero dollars.

That sends a strong signal that the women's tournament is less significant and less worthy than the men's, and it's a policy that perpetuates a historical pattern of discrimination against women in institutions of higher education. The NCAA needs to start rewarding women for their victories.[1]

The federal law Title IX requires equal opportunity for each gender in activities (including athletics) sponsored by institutions of higher education that receive federal funding. But the NCAA, a nonprofit that makes its money from selling television rights, tickets, and corporate sponsorships,

New York Times, March 25, 2016.

does not get federal funding and is not considered by the courts to be a state actor. It does not have to follow the rules of Title IX.

And it doesn't. The NCAA used to seriously encourage the compliance of member schools with Title IX and other regulations through a certification process every ten years—a collaborative effort that involved faculty, students, and administrators. But in 2011, an NCAA board put a moratorium on that certification process. Though the NCAA has devised a superficial substitute, there are now no adequate gender-equity compliance reviews in college sports.

The NCAA also doesn't protest when its member schools engage in the counting chicanery—unfortunately permissible under federal guidelines—that overstates their numbers of female athletes. Male basketball players who practice with a women's team can be counted as female athletes. Women who run track can be counted as members of three teams: indoor track, outdoor track, and cross-country. Female rowing teams sometimes list as many as 100 members, a preposterously high number that is obviously arranged as a Title IX "offset" to the average squad size of 120 men on FBS football teams.

The Office for Civil Rights at the Department of Education is charged with enforcing Title IX, but it doesn't have enough resources to fully address all the complaints that come in about specific programs, let alone undertake its own compliance reviews of university athletics departments. Without either the NCAA or the Office for Civil Rights applying adequate pressure, gender equity has lagged in intercollegiate athletics. Last year 57 percent of all college students were female, yet only slightly more than 40 percent of college athletes were women. Over the past decade, the number of male athletes in college has increased by 53,317, while the number of female athletes increased by only 44,474.

The NCAA's policy of providing no financial reward for victories in the women's basketball tournament is emblematic of another problem: athletic administrators and overseers treat college sports like a commercial venture. If men bring in the money, the thinking goes, then men should get the money. (Well, some men—the coaches, conference commissioners, and athletic directors but certainly not the players themselves.)

This reasoning is faulty on two levels. First, the men's tournament may have higher ratings and sell more expensive tickets, but the women's tournament is also a moneymaker: it is broadcast by ESPN and sells out many games. Even by conventional commercial standards, the men shouldn't get $1.56 million per victory while the women get nothing.

Second, college sports are not supposed to be treated as purely commercial activities. The NCAA constitution considers college sport an amateur activity with redeeming physical, social, and educational value. There is no clause in Title IX that says "except if one gender generates more revenue than the other."

College sports benefits from preferential fiscal treatment in a variety of forms: no taxes on revenues generated by men's basketball and football, deductibility for individual donations that are required to buy good seats,[2] exemption on interest payments for bonds to pay for stadiums and arenas, no requirement for player payroll taxes or unemployment insurance, and so on. College sports programs also receive billions of dollars of subsidies from state governments annually.

If intercollegiate athletics, under the auspices of the NCAA, wants to continue to receive such preferential treatment, it has to adhere to the educational goals that it purports to represent. This means equal treatment of men and women in all aspects of the educational experience—including granting financial rewards for their March Madness victories. Go UConn!

NOTES

1. As I review this op-ed in March 2021, the NCAA tournament payout policy still has not changed.
2. As explained in the essay in chapter 1, the deductibility provision was ended by the tax reform of 2018.

CHAPTER 16

Big-Time College Basketball in the Crosshairs

Andrew Zimbalist

The FBI has been investigating a subterranean recruiting scandal in college basketball for the past two years. The most successful teams in the country are in the agency's crosshairs, and Mark Emmert, president of the National Collegiate Athletic Association, is shocked that there is gambling in his establishment.

Mr. Emmert says that if the claims of underground recruiting networks and impermissible benefits to athletes are true, he will initiate systemic change. The NCAA is, he says, wedded to the principle of amateurism. Say what?

More than any other organization, the NCAA has confused and obfuscated the meaning of amateurism. In its early years, the NCAA, which was founded in 1906, averred that amateurism in college sports meant athletes could get no remuneration or material benefit from playing.

According to the NCAA's early constitution, violations included "the offering of inducements to players to enter colleges or universities because of their athletic abilities or maintaining players while students on account of their athletic abilities, either by athletic organizations, individual alumni, or otherwise directly or indirectly." That is, athletic scholarships violated amateurism rules.

In 1948 the NCAA passed what is referred to as the Sanity Code. This legislation allowed—for the first time ever—colleges to award athletically

---

Chronicle of Higher Education, March 22, 2018.

related financial aid as long as it was limited to tuition and incidental expenses and the athlete qualified for need. Aid exceeding tuition could be granted only if based on superior academic scholarship. The Sanity Code, which stipulated that aid could not be withdrawn if a student ceased playing, was abandoned in 1950, when the NCAA membership voted not to expel colleges that had violated the rule.

Six years after the demise of the Sanity Code, the NCAA allowed athletic scholarships to cover commonly accepted educational expenses. In 1957 an "official Interpretation" defined expenses as room, board, tuition, books, fees, and $15 for laundry. Few people who attended the NCAA's first convention, in 1906, could have conceived that by 1957 NCAA rules would allow a university to use those types of financial inducements to recruit high school athletes.

In 1967 the NCAA moved even further from its original conception of amateurism when members began to complain that athletes were accepting four-year scholarships but deciding not to participate in their sport. One athletic director opined that this was "morally wrong." He then added that "regardless of what anyone says, this is a contract, and it is a two-way street."

To address that problem, the NCAA passed rules that allow the immediate cancellation of a scholarship for an athlete who voluntarily withdraws from sports or does not follow a coach's directives.

The NCAA made a total break from the traditional model of amateurism in 1973 by requiring that athletic scholarships be considered for renewal on an annual basis. That rule allows a coach to cancel an athlete's scholarship at the end of one year for just about any reason, including injury, contribution to team success, the need to make room for a more talented recruit, or failing to fit into a coach's style of play.

The contractual nature of this relationship and the control it gives to the coaches over the players' behavior exhibit many of the trappings of an employment contract.

In 2012 the NCAA approved legislation that gives Division I colleges the option to award multiyear scholarships. In 2015, pursuant to various antitrust lawsuits, the NCAA extended the scope of athletic scholarships by a few thousand dollars to include the "cost of attendance."

The NCAA has also allowed approved gifts to go to athletes. For instance, it permits players in football bowl games and the March basketball tournament to receive gifts well in excess of a thousand dollars.

An article in the *Sports Business Journal* in March 2012 provides some details: "For example, a senior on a team that runs the table and wins championships for the regular season, postseason conference tournament, and NCAA tournament could secure gifts valued at up to $3,780. Up to 25 gift packages can be provided to a team by its school and by its conference for participating in this month's conference tournaments, according to NCAA bylaws." All this in the name of amateurism.

The NCAA's double talk notwithstanding, the concept of amateurism is straightforward. An amateur is one who is not paid to perform an activity. If we apply that idea to intercollegiate athletics, it implies that athletes should not receive a salary for playing their sport. It allows, however, for athletes to receive medical insurance and payment by third parties for use of their publicity rights. It implies, too, that the athletes, as amateurs, are students first and deserve a first-rate education. Many educational reforms follow from that concept.

The real locus of control in the NCAA is with the coaches and athletic directors, who profit the most from "amateurism." It is, after all, the head coaches and their assistants who get paid for the value of the players they recruit, because the players cannot be paid. So if we want to reform the morass of corruption that is big-time college basketball, we had better look beyond the NCAA.

The good news is that, while long dormant, the US Congress has begun to note that college sports have lost their way. Rep. Charlie Dent, Republican of Pennsylvania, introduced a bill in the last Congress to create a presidential commission to study intercollegiate athletics and make recommendations for its reform. Taking up the cudgel, Sen. Chris Murphy,

Democrat of Connecticut, and his staff plan to issue a series of reports on the challenges of intercollegiate athletics.

So enjoy March Madness while you can. The FBI and Congress are coming.

CHAPTER 17

In the End, Commission's Reform Suggestions Only Provide a Smokescreen of Legitimacy for the NCAA

Andrew Zimbalist

The FBI and the Justice Department have been investigating corruption and fraud in Division I college basketball over the past two years. In September, the US Attorney's Office for the Southern District of New York arrested ten people in relation to this ongoing investigation. The FBI charged that these individuals were involved in a scheme with sneaker companies, agents, summer basketball camps, and college coaches to arrange to pay players and their families, to direct high school athletes to certain college programs, and to provide remuneration to cooperating coaches.

Although this scheme had apparently been around for over three decades and has been widely written about and publicly discussed since the 1990s, the dramatic action by the FBI prompted a Captain Louis Renault response from NCAA president Mark Emmert: Mr. Emmert was "shocked, shocked" that there was fraud and corruption going on in his establishment. Accordingly, Emmert appointed friends of the establishment to a commission to look into what went wrong and how to fix it. Condoleezza Rice headed this commission, and after six months of inter-

Forbes, May 10, 2018.

views and discussions with other friends of the establishment, the commission released its sixty-page report at the end of April.

The report recommended several changes. Some of these make eminent sense; none of them are novel. Others constitute an appeal to third parties, such as the NBA and the National Basketball Players Association (NBPA), to take action. Together, the commission's package of reforms falls woefully short of addressing the root causes of fraud, corruption, exploitation, excess, and inequity that afflict college basketball and top-level intercollegiate athletics.

One-and-Done

Let us turn to consider the report's most salient recommendations. First, it calls for an end to "one-and-done," which refers to an NBA rule from the league's 2006 collective bargaining agreement that allows college athletes to enter the league draft after one year in college basketball. In recent years, between nine and eighteen players annually have entered the draft after completing only one year in college.

One-and-done players go to college because they are not allowed to go directly from high school to the NBA and because playing for a team like the University of Kentucky is the best way to promote their professional career. They do not go to college to study and earn a degree. The commission urges the NBA and the NBPA to change this rule and allow players to enter the draft at any age.

The recommendation is sensible and has been made numerous times in the past. In fact, the NBPA has never been in favor of it. Since Spencer Haywood brought a successful antitrust suit against the NBA in the 1970s to allow him to enter the draft out of high school, up until 2006, there were no restrictions. Then, during the 2005–6 collective bargaining negotiations, the NBA insisted on a restriction.

Lewis Katz, former owner of the New Jersey (now Brooklyn) Nets, gave an impassioned speech at the negotiating table—I was there representing the players—lauding the value of a college education. The NBPA knew well what the owners really cared about, and it was not college education. They wanted to

1. give their players an additional year of being socialized and exposed to the pressures of the national media;
2. give their players a year of comparable competition during which they could improve their skills and reveal their true talents against worthy opponents; and
3. reduce the number of years in which players would be eligible for free agency before retirement.

To be sure, the owners wanted a two- or three-year restriction on entering the draft. Eventually, the NBPA yielded on the one-year restriction in exchange for concessions from the owners on other elements of the agreement.

Suggestions

Will the NBA owners comply with the commission recommendation? Perhaps. It depends on how they evaluate the alternative, which might entail harming the existing system of college basketball—a system that serves as a free minor league and marketing tool for the NBA.

The irony of the commission's recommendation is that it puts the onus on the NBA, not the NCAA. While the NBA should be targeted, it is also true that the NCAA has some options that could alleviate the problem; to wit, the NCAA could

1. reinstate the old rule of first-year student ineligibility;
2. decide that teams could not recover the scholarship slot vacated by a one-year player; and
3. impose the loss of an additional scholarship slot when players leave before their senior year.

Second, the commission also seeks to protect athletes by allowing them to

1. return to play college basketball if they enter the NBA draft and do not get selected;
2. get professional advice on their prospects prior to the draft;
3. receive funding to complete their college degree later in their lives; and
4. benefit from the NCAA certifying and carefully regulating agents and summer camps.

These measures, too, would all constitute incrementally positive steps that would alleviate some sources of athlete exploitation, and they have all been previously proposed.

The commission also proposes the NCAA make the promise of college education real. While the commission includes some ideas to promote a "real" education, none of them are compelling or sufficient to alter the present dynamic.

Indeed, the commission states, "Keep focused on the prize here—a college degree." Actually, the intended "prize" is not the degree itself; it is an experience in learning and loving to learn, developing critical thinking, improving writing and speaking acumen, socialization, and building a community of friends. The degree symbolizes the completion of this process.

The commission's report repeatedly states that a college degree raises lifetime earnings by an expected $1 million. Perhaps some of this enhanced earning capacity emanates from the degree credential itself, but surely some of it comes from new skills acquired in college. Getting a hollow degree from enrollment in empty courses or in courses where others perform the work is hardly conducive to skill acquisition. It is training in hypocrisy and living a lie.

Trouble

The commission recommends that the NCAA put some additional resources and teeth behind its enforcement program. The NCAA devotes such a diminutive share of its budget to enforcement that it is no longer making this line-item expenditure public information. The commission calls for an enforcement committee with independent members, stricter penalties for violators, and required cooperation with investigators. The commission also wants to see independent members on the NCAA and divisional executive committees.

These reforms are reasonable, but the devil is in the details and in their implementation. Who, for instance, will appoint the "independent" members?

The commission completely avoids the elephant in the room: athlete compensation or, more specifically, athlete payment for their names, images, and likenesses (NIL) rights. The report states that because this matter is still being adjudicated in the courts (the Ninth Circuit in the *Jenkins/Alston* case), it would not be appropriate for it to comment. Really? The issue has been in the courts over the past decade in the *White*, *Keller*, and *O'Bannon* cases and is likely to remain there for years, if not decades, to come, unless the NCAA changes its position or Congress takes a stand.

Whatever happens in district court in *Jenkins/Alston* is likely to be appealed, at least once, and the ultimate ruling will apply in only one of twelve circuits. Is it really prudent to wait for the courts to rule?

NIL Issues

In the ruling in *O'Bannon*, the Court of Appeals for the Ninth Circuit nixed deferred payments of NIL rights on the grounds that such payments would not be tethered to the cost of receiving a college education (as, for instance, are athletic scholarships). As such, the court ruled that allowing athletes to receive NIL payments would be a quantum leap away from amateurism. Perhaps, but there's another way to look at NIL income.

The NCAA's definition of amateurism has morphed repeatedly over the years. Between 1906 and 1956, NCAA amateurism meant that athletes could not receive any benefits, including athletic scholarships. That definition proved both inconvenient and impractical, so it changed. Today, college athletes can receive Olympic prize money, gifts potentially worth thousands of dollars for success in the College Football Playoff or in March Madness, Pell Grants, and cost-of-attendance stipends, inter alia.

Even if one agrees with the NCAA that it is important to maintain amateurism in the name of the primacy of education over athletics—and it is a stretch to believe that the NCAA ever treated this priority seriously—there is little reason to accept the NCAA's definition du jour.

There is a commonly held understanding of an amateur: it is one who engages in an activity for the love of the experience and not for an extrinsic reward. Applying this understanding, it is perfectly reasonable for athletes to receive NIL income. It is not receiving payment for playing their sport. It is receiving payment for allowing a company to use their name, image, or likeness. Of course, the nature of NIL income, as well as its extent, would have to be regulated.

More importantly, until the issue of NIL payments is resolved, it will be very difficult to eliminate the underground market that has evolved for college athletes. The commission simply sidestepped this conundrum. It also sidestepped the issues of

- exorbitant salaries for coaches, ADs, and conference commissioners;
- special admission standards for athletes;
- phony curricula;
- inadequate medical coverage for athletes;
- the abomination that the NCAA pays men's teams $265,000 per win per year for six years in March Madness and the women's teams zilch; and
- the potential role of public policy.

In the final analysis, all the reasonable recommendations of the commission have been made before multiple times. The commission's real role for Mark Emmert has not been to provide ideas for serious reform. It has been to tinker and provide a smokescreen of legitimacy for the NCAA's professed concern about academic integrity.

CHAPTER 18

One-and-Done

TAKE TWO

Andrew Zimbalist

Last week the NBA announced a new policy regarding the drafting of elite high school basketball players: it would now select a few such players to join its G League (essentially a minor league for the NBA) and pay them a $125,000 salary.

This policy is in response to an ascending chorus of criticism, which became more audible last April when the commission headed by Condoleezza Rice called for various reforms for college basketball. Rice's commission appealed to the NBA to end the "one-and-done" system and to allow star high school players to go directly into the league's draft. The new policy is presumably aimed at heading off more radical reforms at the pass when the current collective bargaining agreement expires after the 2020–21 season.

"One-and-done" refers to an NBA rule, from its 2006 collective bargaining agreement, that allows college athletes to enter the league draft after one year in college basketball. In recent years, between nine and eighteen players annually have entered the draft after completing only one year in college. One-and-done players go to college because they are not allowed to go directly from high school to the NBA and because playing for a team like Kentucky is the best way to promote their professional career. They do not go to college to study and earn a degree.

Wall Street Journal, October 25, 2018.

In 1971, Spencer Haywood brought a successful antitrust suit against the NBA to allow him to enter the draft out of high school. Up until 2006, there were no age limits on when a player could enter the league. Then, during the 2005–6 collective bargaining negotiations, the NBA insisted on a restriction. Former owner of the New Jersey (now Brooklyn) Nets Lewis Katz gave an impassioned speech at the negotiating table (I was there representing the players) lauding the value of a college education. The NBPA knew well what the owners really cared about, and it was not college education. Rather, they wanted their players to (a) have an additional year of being socialized and exposed to the pressures of the national media, (b) have a year of comparable competition during which they could improve their skills and reveal their true talents against worthy opponents, and (c) benefit from the public relations exposure and notoriety afforded by Division I college basketball. To be sure, the team owners wanted a two- or three-year restriction. Eventually, the NBPA yielded on the one-year restriction in exchange for concessions from the owners on other elements of the agreement.

The new NBA policy appears to be a step in the right direction. It serves no legitimate interest to force a scholastically underprepared or uninterested high school basketball star to adopt a false identity as a college student. The problem with the new policy is not that it makes this option available; it is that the NBA has not stipulated how many positions will be open at $125,000. Will it be three, five, ten? Whatever the number, it will be small relative to the number of high school students who would benefit by a direct route to pro basketball in the United States. Moreover, the existing policy already provides the option of being selected for the G League, but at a $35,000 salary. Hence, although the new approach will provide a more robust income for a few players, it doesn't do a lot to alter the landscape.

Two broader points should be made. First, the NBA has 30 teams, and the G League has 27 teams. Major League Baseball has 30 teams and over 160 minor league teams.[1] The 30 Major League Baseball teams pay the salaries of all the minor league players in their system. The average baseball team spends over $20 million yearly in player development. Both the NBA and the NFL have exploited US universities by having them do player development for them, basically free of charge. The NBA can and should do more.

Second, the NCAA too can do more. To reduce the number of one-and-done players, the NCAA could (a) reinstate the old rule of first-year student ineligibility, (b) decide that teams could not recover the scholarship slot vacated by a one-year player, or (c) impose the loss of an additional scholarship slot when players leave before their senior year.

Public pressure is the road to reform. Let us not be diverted by the NBA's latest gesture.

NOTES

1. In 2020, MLB announced its intention to reduce the number of affiliated minor leagues to 120.

CHAPTER 19

How Financial Pressures Can Lead to Athletic Scandals

Andrew Zimbalist

There is no shortage of bad news coming out of intercollegiate athletics these days. Among the most exasperating and depressing stories has been the June death of offensive lineman Jordan McNair on the University of Maryland football team. Nineteen-year-old McNair showed signs of extreme exhaustion, had trouble standing upright while running 110-yard sprints, and had convulsions and a seizure on the field. An hour later he was taken to a local hospital, where he died of heatstroke suffered during the workout. Two weeks earlier he had collapsed during a workout.

Although McNair's death was the most tragic and reprehensible incident, it was hardly an isolated example of gross mistreatment of Maryland team members. A report to the university identified graphic videos depicting animal cruelty being shown to players during meals, physical abuse of players by coaches, verbal assaults including homophobic slurs, and punitive exercise requirements, inter alia. The previous year, the school's athletic director was dismissed because, without approval, he used university funds to pay lawyers who were hired to defend two football players accused by a fellow student of sexual misconduct.

Now, there's a debate at Maryland about whether the football culture was toxic, whether the coach should have been fired against the wishes of

Chronicle of Higher Education, November 9, 2018.

the Board of Regents, and whether the college president should have been pushed to resign. There are better questions to debate: Why did the Board of Regents defend the coach, and how did the football culture at Maryland develop in the first place?

Consider first that the Maryland athletics department ran annual operating deficits of between $13.7 million and $18.1 million every year during FY 2009–FY 2014. In FY 2015, Maryland moved from the Atlantic Coast Conference to the more lucrative Big Ten Conference, and the school's revenue jumped $19 million. However, expenses increased by a similar amount, and the operating deficit was $14.5 million in FY 2015. If this figure were adjusted for an $11.6 million loan that the school received from the Big Ten (treated as conference revenue in the accounts), the deficit would be $26.1 million. The department's deficit averaged $15 million in FY 2016 and FY 2017.

Even though Maryland looks forward to receiving a full share of Big Ten television revenue by FY 2022, the outlook is not bright. While it is true that Big Ten schools receive far more television revenue than ACC schools do (about $20 million per year per school more), playing football in the Big Ten is more competitive and more demanding. Thus, Maryland's football record since 2015 is a mediocre twenty-five wins and thirty-four losses. With such an unalluring performance, Maryland's attendance is lagging: its ticket sales in FY 2017 were just $15.3 million, compared to the Big Ten average of $27.9 million. Its recently fired coach, D. J. Durkin, was earning $2.5 million annually, before potential bonuses and perquisites, and is owed $5 million in buyout pay.

As pricey as it is, Durkin's salary ranked just fifty-third among the sixty-five programs in the Power Five conferences. Maryland athletics received $12.3 million in donations in FY 2017, less than half of the Big Ten average of $25.1 million. Meanwhile, Maryland's stadium has a capacity of 52,000, while it competes against schools like Michigan with stadium capacity of 108,000.

So, how is Maryland supposed to be able to compete? Obviously, the program needs more money, but it is already at least $15 million in the red each year. One answer appears to be to squeeze as much as possible out of the existing resources—or more than is possible, hence the brutality and fear at football practices and the genuflecting Board of Regents at the altar of the football coach.

And Maryland's situation is likely to grow worse before it grows better. The 2018 tax changes actually hit college sports programs quite hard: donations made in order to purchase good seats at football or basketball games are no longer deductible, and salaries over $1 million are now subject to a 21 percent excise tax. Antitrust suits and Fair Labor Practice Standards challenges threaten to spike labor costs. On top of these new financial drains, Maryland still has Title IX work to do before gender equity is achieved (47 percent of its student body, yet only 43.7 percent of its athletes, is female.) And structural changes along with audience fragmentation are likely to deflate the Big Ten television bonanza in coming years.

While Maryland's case might be the most egregious this year, the financial pressures it faces are commonplace in big-time college sports. In the FBS, the most commercialized NCAA subdivision with 130 schools, only about 20 programs annually show an operating surplus—a surplus that usually disappears when full capital costs and other indirect costs are counted. Unlike private-sector companies, college athletics departments have stakeholders who want wins, not stockholders who want profits. Accordingly, rather than falling to the bottom line, new revenues are put at the service of attracting top high school players via hiring fancy coaches with exorbitant compensation packages, building elaborate stadiums and training facilities, engaging in lavish recruiting practices, and maintaining accommodating tutoring programs.

So the transgressions at Maryland and at other recently upgraded programs are perhaps more extreme, but the general pattern of mismanagement, abuse, and waste is widespread in intercollegiate athletics. The NCAA has proven itself incapable of meaningful self-reform, and judicial challenges are slow, costly, and erratic and ultimately rest with an unreliable Supreme Court. The path to true reform lies either in Congress or in an awakening at the Association of Governing Boards and the American Council on Education.

CHAPTER 20

Female Athletes Are Undervalued, in Both Money and Media Terms

Carrie N. Baker, Emma Seymour, and Andrew Zimbalist

This year's Equal Pay Day was April 2—the day that symbolizes how far into a second year that women must work, on average, to earn what men earned in the previous year. But that's the economy-wide average. For women in professional sports, it would take years to catch up with their male peers.

Professional women's soccer players, for example, work harder and perform better than the men yet earn much less. The US women's soccer team has won four Olympic gold medals; the men, none. The women have won three World Cups; the men, none. The women's team is ranked number one in the world, yet they are paid at a rate of just over one-third of what the men get.

The pay gap in basketball is much worse. WNBA players make $71,635 on average, while the average NBA salary is $6.4 million. Last year's number-one WNBA draft pick, A'ja Wilson, is earning just $52,564. And bonuses amplify this discrepancy.

In the March Madness basketball tournaments, the NCAA gives the men's teams' conferences over $1.6 million for each win, while the women's teams get absolutely nothing for their wins. Yet thousands of people attend the women's tournament, millions watch their games on television, and

---

Forbes, April 10, 2019.

the NCAA receives millions of dollars from advertisers. How does the NCAA come to the conclusion that the women's games have no value?

The NBA justifies these differences by pointing to revenues: the men have larger audiences and more lucrative broadcast-rights deals. But the pay rates on revenue differ as well: NBA players receive 50 percent of league revenue, while WNBA players receive an estimated 25 percent of their league's revenue.

Even when women earn more revenue than men, they are paid less. According to a pay-equity lawsuit filed last month, the US women's soccer team played more games and brought in more revenue in 2017 than the men, yet US Soccer still paid the women significantly less than the underperforming men.

This undervaluing is nowhere more evident than in the media coverage of women's sports. According to one study of sports television coverage in Southern California, women and girls account for over 40 percent of athletes, yet they receive less than 4 percent of the coverage on news shows. The study's authors—Cheryl Cooky, Michael A. Messner, and Michela Musto—found a "stark contrast between the exciting, amplified delivery of stories about men's sports and the often dull, matter-of-fact delivery of women's sports stories."

Print-media coverage is also dismal. We did our own count of stories in the sports section of *USA Today* from March 22 to April 2 during March Madness. Over this twelve-day period, there were ninety-two stories—eighty-two about men and ten about women. Of the eighty-nine photographs of athletes, only four were of women. On the front page, there was only one photograph of a woman over the entire twelve-day period, while there were thirty-seven photographs of men. There was only one front-page story about a female athlete, while there were thirty-one stories about male athletes. On March 25, two full pages were dedicated to the bracket for the men's tournament, with only a quarter page for the women's tournament. On March 28, there was no mention of women's sports at all, including the women's basketball tournament.

This neglect of women's sports also shows up in the social media presence of the organizations that are supposed to be promoting women's sports. On March 25, the NCAA tweeted, "When you find out there are no #MarchMadness games until Thursday," with a clip of the *Parks and Recreation* character Ron Swanson throwing his computer in a dumpster. Seattle Storm forward Breanna Stewart responded, "Sounds about right, coming from a page that has posted nothing about the women's tournament. How can we get others to respect us when the NCAA doesn't?! There were eight women's games on the 25th."

This disrespect of female athletes—whether by the NCAA, *USA Today*, US Soccer, or the NBA—is an important reason for the vast pay gap between men's and women's sports. Whether in a paycheck, on television, in print media, or on social media, we need to do better to recognize the value and power of women in sport.

CHAPTER 21

The Collegiate Sports Model Is Broken

IT NEEDS HELP

Andrew Zimbalist

California Fair Pay to Play Act (SB 206) woke up politicians across the nation. The act, signed by Governor Gavin Newsom on September 30, makes it illegal for Californian colleges to prevent students from receiving income for use of their NILs (names, images, and likenesses). Twenty-eight other states have introduced or are planning to introduce similar bills, and related legislation has been presented in the US Congress.[1] SB 206 is a good step, but it is not sufficient and should not lead us to taking our eye off the ball.

The Football Bowl Subdivision (FBS) of NCAA's Division I represents the 130 most commercialized athletics programs in the country. According to the most recent NCAA report, these schools' athletics departments experienced a median deficit of $16. 3 million during 2017–18, and this figure fails to account for most capital spending and many indirect costs.[2] Meanwhile, to help cover these financial shortfalls, school tuition and mandatory student fees rise.

These deficits have grown steadily over time, despite tax preferences due to the presumed educational function of commercialized intercollegiate sports, Pell Grant subsidies from the federal government worth over $30 billion a year, lavish state-government support for new facilities, and

---

Forbes, December 20, 2019.

the absence of unions and collective bargaining to promote the interests of the athletes themselves.

What's going on? College athletics departments do not have shareholders who demand profits for dividend payouts or stock appreciation; rather, they have stakeholders (boosters, alums, students) who demand victories. This means that when extra revenues pour in (by the tens of millions), the athletic director (AD) invariably finds a use that will help the teams compete. The career trajectories of the ADs and coaches are a direct function of the competitive success of their teams.

Further, the players are considered to be students (not employees) and are not paid. Since there is no players market where schools offer higher compensation to attract high school athletes, schools attempt to attract athletes by building ever-fancier facilities, hiring well-known coaches at astronomical salaries, and spending freely on recruiting. In 2019, there were 176 college football and men's basketball coaches who received salaries exceeding $1 million, 71 coaches' salaries exceeded $3 million, and 38 exceeded $4 million. The highest paid coach was Dabo Swinney at Clemson, with a guaranteed salary of $9.3 million plus bonuses of $1.1 million and a potential buyout clause worth $50 million. Swinney's assistant coaches pulled in a total pay of $6.8 million, raising the total for all football coaches to $17.2 million, without considering their handsome perquisites and possible outside income.

Into this scenario comes the issue of athlete NIL rights. Nonathlete students have NIL rights, so too should the athletes. Granting such rights (with some needed controls to prevent the creation of a surrogate players market, for example, via trumped-up endorsement deals) can be accomplished and still retain the amateur model. Although the NCAA has presented an ever-changing concept of amateurism over the years, the common meaning of amateurism is clear. An amateur is one who engages in an activity for fun or intrinsic reward, not for money or extrinsic reward. By this reckoning, college athletes should not be paid for playing their sports; they can, however, be paid by third parties for endorsing products, allowing use of their avatars, or social media activity based on their notoriety.

One issue with the introduction of NIL payments is that today's corporate sponsors of college teams will begin to divide their promotional budgets between the schools and the athletes. Depending on how this division is made, it will have more or less of an impact on the athletics departments' revenues. But, other things equal, school revenues will dip, and deficits will grow.

Of course, on top of these financial problems, there are many other areas for concern. First, a large share of athletes at the big-time programs are being cheated out of an education. Second, particularly in football, athletes are subjecting themselves to possible brain damage and other life-altering ailments. Third, unless prohibited by future national legislation, legalized gambling is coming to college sports, and college athletes, without remuneration, will be vulnerable to the wiles of gambling rings.

The NCAA justifies itself on the grounds that it fosters the educational experience of the university. Perhaps this claim holds in Divisions II and III and some of Division I. It does not hold, however, for dozens of Division I colleges. The NCAA restructured itself in 1996 to yield control over its policies to precisely these most heavily commercialized athletics programs. The NCAA has had plenty of time to reform itself and to conform to its vision of intercollegiate athletics as an extracurricular program. It has failed utterly.

Thus, Congress has a role to play. National policy already intervenes in college sports through tax preferences and massive subsidies. It is time for a more constructive intervention and for the appointment of a congressional commission to consider public policy options moving forward.

NOTES

1. As of March 2021, there are thirty-nine states that have introduced legislation legalizing college athletes receiving income for their NILs. Six states have already passed such legislation, with Florida's NIL law set to take effect before the 2021–22 season.
2. In October 2020, the NCAA released its financial report for 2018–19. The median FBS reported financial deficit rose to $18.8 million.

CHAPTER 22

Sports Being on Hiatus Gives the NCAA an Opportunity to Rethink the Structure of College Sports

Andrew Zimbalist, Gerry Gurney, and Donna Lopiano

Tragedy begets opportunity, calling to mind the old admonition to "never waste a good crisis." Educators and college athletics administrators should heed those words during the current hiatus from competition and develop a plan to redirect college athletics toward academic integrity, financial sanity, and athletes' well-being. We suggest that such a plan should contain the following elements.

Governance

Return the National Collegiate Athletic Association (NCAA) to a one-member, one-vote structure, with all 1,100 member institutions promptly voting on the five-year reform program proposed here. Three principles should guide the vote: first, the NCAA should promote the economic interests of all its members, not just the athletically powerful; second, it should emphasize the health and well-being of the athletes; and third, it should protect the economic interests of all enrolled students whose tuition and mandatory athletics fees are subsidizing athletics programs.

Forbes, April 25, 2020.

Athletes' Well-Being

Replace the current College Football Playoff, which awards 75 percent of its proceeds to the Power Five conferences (65 schools) and 13 percent to the Group of Five conferences (65 schools), with a sixteen-team NCAA Football Bowl Subdivision (FBS) national championship structured like the existing NCAA Football Championship Subdivision (FCS) national championship. The new structure would dedicate 100 percent of its media-rights proceeds to providing basic athletic-injury insurance, long-term disability insurance, and coverage for uninsured medical expenses to the 480,000 NCAA athletes of all 1,100 member institutions.

Acknowledge the irreplaceable nature of the human brain and heed the lessons learned from concussion research. Change the rules in contact sports and sports in which athletes are susceptible to head trauma by requiring minimum-contact practices and ending, for example, "checking" in ice hockey and "headers" in soccer.

Allow college athletes to earn income from the use of their names, images, and likenesses and to engage in outside employment, like any other student. Deter abuses by enforcing academic restraints such as prohibiting employment activities that result in missed classes, exams, or other class-related activities; prohibiting the use of institutional assets in an athlete's commercial venture; and establishing other guardrails.

Require future head coaches to have at least a master's degree in physical education or a related discipline (e.g., exercise physiology) and to have teaching experience in school settings. After all, if we want athletes to be students, shouldn't we require coaches to be teachers?

Athletics Facilities

Prohibit the construction of new facilities open to varsity athletes only. Dollars from students' tuition and fee payments help to build these facilities, so they should be available to everyone.

Athletics Staff Salaries

Ask Congress to enact a limited, conditional antitrust exemption so the NCAA can cap the salaries of coaches, athletics staff, and administrators. Their salaries should not exceed that of the tenth-highest-paid faculty member or the college president, whichever is lower, and Congress should condition federal higher-education funding on compliance with this requirement. The responsibilities of running a university far exceed those of coaching; the relative salaries of presidents and coaches should reflect that reality.

Other Financial Reforms

Prohibit off-campus, in-person recruiting by athletics personnel. Restrict communication with prospective college athletes to recorded electronic video/audio platforms. When campuses reopen, allow the institution to pay for one on-campus visit and scholarship audition per prospect and strictly limit the cost of on-campus meals and entertainment during that visit.

Prohibit mandatory student fees that exceed the percentage of varsity athletes in the undergraduate student body; if varsity athletes are 5 percent of the student body, the percentage of the student activity fee allocated to athletics should not exceed 5 percent. And the amount of the subsidy to athletics should be specified on a student's bill.

Prohibit the scheduling of nonconference away competitions in locations beyond the states that are contiguous to the state in which a member institution is located.

Gradually phase in a requirement that 25 percent of any cash donation to a member institution's athletics program or of any revenues derived from television-rights fees be designated to support the institution's academic enterprise.

The NCAA Board of Governors should seize the opportunity of the current shelter-in-place crisis to suspend normal operating rules and conduct a mail vote of the presidents of its member institutions on the plan presented here or an equivalent. The Board has a historic chance to demonstrate courage by promoting the health and well-being of 480,000 college athletes and the financial best interests of all 1,100 members, instead of the narrow enrichment of the 130 members of the FBS.

If the NCAA fails to act, Congress could require adoption of the plan presented here as a condition of institutions receiving Higher Education Act funding. Alternatively, it could enact HR 5528, which would establish a bipartisan Congressional Advisory Commission to examine these issues. Inaction by both the NCAA and Congress would squander a unique opportunity for urgently needed reform.

CHAPTER 23

Has Higher Education Lost Its Mind?

Donna Lopiano and Andrew Zimbalist

On June 12, the University of Houston suspended all athlete workouts when six players tested positive for COVID, less than two weeks after June 1, when college fall-sports teams were allowed to return campus for supposedly voluntary summer workouts. Why the rush? As one freshman athlete stated, "So when the University of Texas tells you that you've gotta bring your ass back to campus, guess what you've gotta do? Bring your ass back to campus, because that's your job. They're paying for your education. At the end of the day, it is what it is."

Throughout the country, college athletes hopped on airplanes to return, while Americans were being discouraged from high-risk air travel, or drove across state lines using gas-station restrooms that were not likely to be bastions of sanitization. Who gave coaches permission to expose college athletes to these risks when the best public health experts in the world have implored us to heed their warnings not to do this? College presidents? Boards of Trustees? The silence is deafening. Has higher education lost its mind?

Each day the media reports on athletic directors' plans to cope with COVID. They boast about required testing, quarantines upon arrival, and regular retesting. Power-lifting racks in the weight room will be spaced ten feet apart, we are told. Yet there are no reports of rules requiring face masks or limiting grunts and forceful exhales during maximum lifts. Some

Forbes, June 13, 2020.

volleyball teams have said they will rotate six game balls instead of three, maybe giving them more time to rub them down with hand sanitizer? But no mention is made of concerns for opposing blockers face-to-face at the net or smothering an attacking hitter. How do you practice social distancing when soccer players set up their wall to defend a penalty kick or gang up in front of the net to field a corner kick or players position themselves nose-to-nose across the football line of scrimmage? And what happens if, forty-eight hours prior to the game, any member of the team tests positive? Even more disconcerting are athletic directors' plans to have crowds in football stadiums. Nebraska's athletic director, Bill Moos, is not worried about someone limiting attendance to forty thousand, contending that if forty thousand are allowed and forty thousand attend, Nebraska will preserve its home-game sellout streak. Whatever happened to six-foot social distancing? He's also not worried about fans getting the virus: "They're adults. If they are worried about the prospect of getting this virus, that can be a personal decision." Jeez, that's caring about your neighbors! Ohio State AD Gene Smith is ready with social-distancing models for twenty thousand to fifty thousand fans. What? Fifty thousand fans in a one-hundred-thousand-seat stadium is social distancing? Oregon State will mandate social distancing in restrooms. Perhaps the lines going in can loop around the concourses. Will the local hotels and bars be open and ready as the population of smaller college towns doubles on a football Saturday? Are these administrators really assuring us that they have it all figured out and they can stop this virus? And we thought it required a vaccine.

More than a few folks are wondering what the athletics department is going to do with these players for the next six months. When no students return to campus following Thanksgiving, will athletes remain and be further exposed to the normal flu season? Do we really think coaches are going to control the social activities of eighteen- to twenty-two-year-old students in a college town? Will the other students on campus be tested as frequently, or do the athletes get special protection because they are the athletics department's meal ticket? Why this "Hail Mary"?

Could it possibly be that all of the foregoing reveals the ultimate contradiction of college sports? Could the "tail be wagging the dog"? Does the financial exigency of athletics trump athletes' health? Do college presidents believe their jobs are at stake if they reject the wishes of their football and basketball coaches? Are they convinced that alumni will stop giving if the university doesn't have football? Do higher-education leaders believe that students will not attend their colleges and deliver tuition dollars if they don't have football for entertainment? When did athletic entertainment become the overarching purpose of higher education?

CHAPTER 24

Theater of the Absurd and the Immoral

COLLEGE FOOTBALL 2020

Donna Lopiano and Andrew Zimbalist

College coaches, faced with justifying why they were bringing fall-sports athletes back to campus for voluntary on-campus workouts in June, when the pandemic in the United States was not close to being under control, came up with some pretty compelling story lines. They argued and are still arguing, "The kids are safer here than at home" or "These are poor kids. They need the scholarship money we can give them when they return to train, even though our campus is closed and athletes are not attending summer school." Athletic directors added more story lines. There was the denial of doing it for money: "Oh, this isn't about football and money. We're bringing back our fall sports like soccer and women's volleyball too." Right.

And then there are the lines about football games lifting the students' spirit out of their pandemic depression or helping community businesses that are dependent on game days to recover economically. And there are detailed stories boasting about all of the special arrangements made to keep athletes safe from COVID-19: "We are going to test them when they arrive and quarantine them before they start practice and then retest and sanitize the weight-training facilities, take their temperatures every day, and retest once or twice a week and provide single rooms and retest two days before games."

Forbes, June 28, 2020.

Athletics departments purposely created the public impression, "We've thought of it all. We can deal with this." Why? Fear of millions of dollars in lost TV revenues if college football teams did not take the field? Fear that closing down athletics would endanger seven- and eight-figure head-coach salaries and bonuses and the lucrative compensation of athletic directors? Fear that corporate sponsors would find other billboards to display their logos? Fear that alumni and fans would not continue their generous athletics and institutional giving without football fueling campus affinity? Answer: All of the above.

Well, the athletes returned, and what happened? Predictably, the story lines crumbled. Every day we read reports of the numbers of quarantined, tested, sanitized, young and strong athletes who have tested positive for COVID-19. As of June 27, at least 150 college athletes had contracted the virus, despite the fact that 66 out of 130 FBS schools refuse to report the number of new cases. But the show must go on. Football practice must go on. Football games must happen this fall no matter what the cost. However, new story lines were needed because the "we have it all figured out" and "athletes are safer here" stories turned out to be fake news.

Now we are truly in the world of "Believe It or Not." Would you believe that coaches and athletic directors are scheming to use sick kids as a strategic ploy to win games by invoking health privacy rules to justify not reporting the identity of infected players to the media (something they could not do if their unavailability was the result of athletic injury)? One athletic director ruminated that the football team could play its second-string *running* quarterback instead of the sick-but-we-won't-tell-anyone great passing quarterback to thwart their opponents' defensive game plan. The storytellers are even suggesting a new ethics lesson—that teams are not morally compelled to tell the other team who is sick; they are only morally bound not to put a sick player in the game. Are teams ethically bound to tell opposing schools and players that they are about to compete against a team on which a player or players tested positive several days earlier—to give them the opportunity to refuse to play? Or is playing a shell game to win, maybe hiding the asymptomatic great player, okay? Hey, it's like the flea-flicker pass—just a little gamesmanship, right?

But wait, the schemes get even more nefarious. Some people wonder whether the sixty-six schools that refuse to report infection numbers have a different plan—get everyone on the team infected (herd immunity!) before the season starts so that they can play all their games at full strength. So what if an athlete or two die in the process? So what if the team infects all other teams it plays against and anyone else in the community? So what if a few older or more vulnerable community folks die? So what if infected players develop microcardia or other long-term infirmities? Could such a thought, so stunning in its immorality, be on the mind of any seven- or eight-figure-salaried football coach?

The silence of college presidents and trustees in the face of such insane behavior is just as deafening as it was during public consumption of the first round of unsuccessful stories. Thus, we no longer think higher education simply has lost its mind, as we wrote two weeks ago on these pages ("Has Higher Education Lost Its Mind?"). We take it back. It's worse: higher education has lost its mind *and* its morality. Why? Because the monetary fruits of commercialized college sports have trumped the integrity of higher education, its obligation to provide a safe educational environment, and its duty to demonstrate respect for human life.

But it is even more than that; we are morally injured because of those students whom colleges and universities choose to place at risk. They didn't pick the school's National Merit Scholars or seniors about to graduate or graduate students conducting important research to be the guinea pigs to test campus openings. Whom did they choose? Who are these poor kids who were going to be financially better off or safer on campus than at their homes (a trope for not in the suburbs)? When are we going to tell Mr. and Mrs. Public that at the top sixty-five Division I football schools, football teams that are 46 percent Black are now practicing and risking COVID so they can be prepared to entertain a student body that is 61 percent white and no more than 5 percent Black—and that these decisions are being made by athletic directors and football coaches who are 75 percent and 80 percent white, respectively. This is why this latest offense is not just about choosing money over the lives of students. It is a continuation of a long-standing and sordid history of college revenue sports exploiting athletically talented Black athletes. We join in the refrain of Black Lives Matter, lamenting that college sports belongs in the same conversation as US policing, voter suppression, and Confederate monuments.

Compounding the problem, universities are also forcing their student-athletes to sign health waivers and behavioral pledges before they are allowed to engage in supposedly "voluntary" summer workouts and pre-season practices. Yes, you read that correctly. Public health officials have warned that it is not safe for college athletes to be playing again, and Dr. Anthony Fauci stated, "Unless players are essentially in a bubble insulated from the community and they are tested every day, it would be very hard to see how football is able to be played this fall." These waivers and pledges require the athletes to acknowledge the COVID-19 risk, and in at least one school, Southern Methodist University, the waiver requires the athlete to absolve the school and its employees from any legal claims related to the virus. Athletes who refuse to sign these waivers and pledges risk losing their scholarships. These waivers are coercive, of questionable legality, and morally repugnant. Thankfully, this week Senators Richard Blumenthal and Cory Booker will introduce the "College Athlete Pandemic Safety Act," which would outlaw such waivers.

It is well past time for our government to step in to address more than COVID-19-related exploitation issues. The NCAA continues to be AWOL, ignoring its governance responsibilities and paying lip service to its so-called commitment to athletes' health and safety and education, while acting as a trade association to maximize the revenues of its member institutions.

College athletes who are students rather than employees are without the collective bargaining agreements that protect professional athletes. No entity is left to protect them except Congress. They would be well served to have Congress engage in a comprehensive investigation into the need for collegiate athletics reform such as that proposed by Representatives Donna Shalala (FL-D) and Ross Spano (FL-R). HR 5528, supported by a slate of bipartisan cosponsors, would establish a Congressional Advisory Commission to execute a two-year investigation and propose remedies. It's time to right the wrongs done to our college athletes and set intercollegiate sports onto a healthy, pro-education course.

CHAPTER 25

Rutgers' Athletics Deficit Reveals the Hidden Caste in the College Sports Hierarchy

Andrew Zimbalist

The Rutgers athletics department should be required to hang a sign outside its front office: DANGER, KEEP OUT. It has been running growing financial deficits since 2003; piled up hundreds of millions of dollars in debt; been upgraded to the Big Ten, where its football team is accumulating a dismal competitive record; and experienced multiple coaching and AD scandals.

Most observers are well aware of the extant hierarchies in the NCAA: Division I (DI) generates much more revenue than Division II (DII), which produces much more revenue than Division III (DIII). Within DI, FBS is the commercial leader over FCS and the schools without football. Within FBS, the Power Five conferences (with median generated revenue of $106.3 million in fiscal year 2018, according to the NCAA's revenues and expenses report) dominate the Group of Five conferences (with median generated revenue of $13.9 million).

It turns out there is also a sharp distinction between the top half and the bottom half among the sixty-four Power Five schools. Whereas the top thirty-two athletics programs have median generated revenues of $144.5

Forbes, August 16, 2020.

million and report a median operating surplus of $3.2 million in fiscal year 2018, the bottom thirty-two programs have median generated revenues of $98.1 million and a median operating deficit of $10.6 million.

Most athletics directors in DI and DII are looking to move their programs to higher levels in the hierarchy. There is little evidence, however, that upgrades pay off. More often, they lead to a school making major investments in facilities, coaches, and recruiting. In exchange, they get the right to play superior competition, garner a depressing record, and experience decreases in attendance.

Rutgers is a case in point. After six years in the Big Ten, its football team's playing and financial performance remain abysmal. The athletics program ran a reported deficit of $45.2 million in fiscal year 2019. In the fiscal year 2020 budget, from before the coronavirus took hold, the projected revenues were $82.5 million, and the projected expenses were $102.8 million, yielding an apparent projected operating deficit of $20.3 million. But there's more. On the revenue side, there's an $8.3 million subsidy from the university and a $2.9 million subsidy from the state. Without these subsidies, the projected revenues fall to $71.3 million, and the projected deficit rises to $31.5 million. There were also contributions and gifts to athletics of $4.5 million. To the extent that some of these gifts may have substituted for donations to the university's general fund, the deficit would be still larger. Another $12.5 million came from student fees—a different form of subsidy at the students' expense.

But it gets worse. As part of the price for being admitted to the Big Ten, Rutgers had to renovate its stadium at a cost of around $160 million. And from the athletics program's annual operating losses since 2003, it has also accumulated a debt of $444.5 million. Hence, total borrowing for athletics is over $600 million, yet the athletics department's budget reports spending only $10.9 million on interest and principal! Thus, there seems to be another $20 million to $30 million in unreported debt-service costs. The athletics department budget does acknowledge a capital and maintenance expense of $16.5 million, but it puts it below the line. Add all this up, and the actual deficit in fiscal year 2020 begins to push $70 million—all before the landing of COVID-19.

Are such expenses possibly justifiable? One line of defense is that Rutgers' membership in the Big Ten is about to pay off. While it is true that 2020–21 will be the first year that Rutgers will get a full share of the conference's TV booty, it is also true that the Rutgers athletics department borrowed $48 million from the conference (over and above the debt referenced earlier) at 0 percent interest over the past several years. Repayment of that loan will commence during 2020–21 and continue through 2027, lowering the net conference revenues. These revenues will probably be further lowered because of the current and prospective weak condition of the economy and the growing availability of competitive video entertainment options, leading to lower subscriptions to the Big Ten Network, among others.

Then there's the new economics of big-time college sports that is about to take hold. First, name, image, and likeness payments to athletes should be a reality in the next year or two. It is hard to imagine that this won't divert corporate promotion funds away from athletics departments to the athletes. Second, the Ninth Circuit recently ruled that athletic scholarships can include unlimited benefits above the cost of attendance as long as these benefits are educationally tethered—think laptops, internet, streaming subscriptions, cars for traveling to school, study abroad, graduate school later in life, maybe a Steinway piano for music majors, and so on. As schools in recruiting wars begin to compete over the offering of these benefits, athletics department deficits will grow deeper and deeper. How will Rutgers and the rest of the bottom half of the Power Five do in the increasingly competitive recruitment game?

COVID-19 will add tens of millions of dollars to already-yawning financial shortfalls. It has turned a precarious situation into an unstable and untenable one. A shake-up is coming.

Index

Academic Enhancement Fund (AEF), 99
academic fraud, 17, 74, 221–222, 307; protection from, 285; year-round training and, 251–252
Academic Oversight Committee, 222–223
Academic Progress Rate (APR), 17, 74, 212–221; coaches', 196; creation of, 196; Graduation Success Rate and, 212–216, 225; learning disabilities and, 213–214, 216; penalties of, 212–213, 217–219; summer school and, 213
academic standards, 195–225
Ackerman, Val, 123
Adidas, 142n85, 303n11
ADs. *See* athletic directors (ADs)
agents, 287, 290; for NIL compensation, 68, 129–130, 283; registration of, 299; right to, 75, 122, 130
Agnew v. NCAA (2012), 48, 52
Alexander, Donald L., 164
Allensworth, Rebecca Haw, 83n35
Alliance of Social Workers in Sports, 256
Alston v. NCAA (2015), 11, 46, 58–59, 86n88, 111–114, 145n125
Alzheimer's disease, 10
Amateur Athletic Union (AAU), 17, 21n17, 74
amateurism, 74, 110, 287–288, 318–319; cash prizes in, 98; definitions of, 17, 21n17, 95, 100, 111–112, 349; eligibility rule for, 47, 54, 56, 287; history of, 95–99; litigation over, 105–119; NCAA's bylaws on, 99–100, 124, 135n6, 139n52, 328–330; professional athletes versus, 287–290; proper role of, 100–105; scholarship rules for, 53; Thomas on, 67
Amateur Sports Act (1978), 76, 77, 133, 303n15
Amato, Louis, 158
American Athletic Conference, 86n88
American College of Sports Medicine, 276
American Council on Education, 300
American Economics Association, 300
American Football League (AFL), 77, 132–133
Anderson, Michael L., 165–167
antitrust exemption of college sports, 12–19, 39–79, 310; MLB and, 77, 133; Power Five conferences and, 191–194; precedents for, 76–78; proposed reforms of, 67–76, 131–133, 321–324
arbitration, right to, 194, 233, 237–238
Areeda, Phillip, 82n34
Arrington Settlement, 266–267
Association for Applied Sport Psychology, 256
athlete advocates, 238
athletic culture, 246; moral injury and, 242–243; of "toughness," 248, 256, 264
athletic directors (ADs), 41, 101, 156, 315; oversight by, 246; salaries of, 319
Auburn University, 222
automatic qualifying (AQ), 43, 187n37. *See also* Bowl Championship Series (BCS)
Autonomous Conferences. *See* Power Five conferences

Baade, Robert A., 163
Banks v. NCAA (1992), 84n52, 84n57

baseball, 8, 30, 340n1; antitrust exemption for, 77, 133; recruitment rule in, 150n186
basketball, 15, 21n13, 30, 89n119, 328–331; academic standards and, 195–225; generated revenue of, 43, 44; Graduation Success Rate in, 206; revenue-sharing plan for, 21n12, 192; Rice Commission on, 154; women's, 58, 99, 111, 325–327, 345–347
Behagen v. Amateur Basketball Association of the U.S. (1989), 92n154
Belichick, Bill, 34
Berger v. NCAA (2016), 59, 86n93, 88n118
Berri, David, 317
Big Five conferences. *See* Power Five conferences
Big Ten Conference, 86n87, 154, 312, 341–342; *Alston* lawsuit and, 145n125; commissioner's salary in, 34; NIL compensation and, 121–122; Rutgers University and, 363–365; threat to leave NCAA by, 191
Big 12 Conference, 86n87, 145n125, 154, 312; commissioner's salary in, 33; eligibility compliance at, 214; threat to leave NCAA by, 191
"Bill of Rights" for college athletes, 20n12
Bimper, Albert, Jr., 209
Black Coaches Association, 22n30, 91n139
Blade, Janet, 239–277
Blumenthal, Richard, 20n12, 361
Board of Regents case. See *NCAA v. Board of Regents of University of Oklahoma*
Booker, Cory, 20n12, 361
Bowl Championship Series (BCS), 43, 187n37
Bowlsby, Bob, 33
Bradford, Steven, 142n79
Brand, Myles, 25, 27
branding issues, 10, 156; legal liability and, 263; value of, 169
Brooker, George W., 162
Bryant, Paul "Bear," 15, 16, 34
Bybee, Jay, 12, 56–57, 85n77, 110
Byers, Walter, 136n25

California Fair Pay to Play Act (2019), 93–94, 104, 113, 133, 142n79, 301n1, 348
Calipari, John, 16, 22n23, 90n130, 161
capital expenses, 40; accounting methods for, 80n3, 155, 316–317; tax-exempt bonds for, 26–27
Carnegie Foundation on intercollegiate athletics, 96
Castle, Joshua, 185n16
Catastrophic Injury Insurance Program, 260–261, 277. *See also* health insurance
Centenary College (Shreveport, LA), 15, 34
certification standards: for coaches, 243–245, 253, 352; for performance specialists, 247–248, 253, 258
Championship Football Playoff (CFP) system, 75
"championship season," 291–296, 302n11
chronic traumatic encephalopathy (CTE), 10, 239, 266, 319, 352
Clemson University, 73, 140n62; coaches' salaries at, 14, 102, 349
Clotfelter, Charles, 21n18
COA. *See* cost-of-attendance (COA) stipends
coaches, 72; assistant, 53, 71–73, 102, 310, 349; certification standards for, 243–245, 253, 352; misconduct by, 239–240, 244–246, 341–342; oversight of, 256–260, 265–267; "restricted-earnings," 53; strength and conditioning, 247–253, 258–259
Coaches' Academic Progress Rate (APR), 196, 220–221, 224
coaches' salaries, 14–15, 21n18, 33–34, 41, 309–311; adjustments to, 90n130; athlete salaries and, 317; effect of paying athletes on, 101–102; *Law v. NCAA* on, 53; limits on, 71–73, 102–103; perquisites to, 72, 102, 349
collective bargaining agreements, 68, 84n54, 118. *See also* unionization
College Athletes Players Association (CAPA), 60–61, 118, 131, 238
College Athletic Trainers Society, 276
College Football Playoff, 192, 193
Collegiate Licensing Company, 64, 115
Commission on Opportunity in Athletics, 92n161
community colleges, 201–202
complaint-reporting system, 245–246
concussions, 10, 239, 266, 319, 352

Conference USA, 86n88
Cooky, Cheryl, 346
copyright laws, 105, 114–116, 147n156; fair use standards of, 116, 120, 127, 148n161, 149n182, 303n11. *See also* NIL (names, images, likenesses) compensation
cost-of-attendance (COA) stipends, 7, 12, 45, 137n34; calculation of, 20n7, 85n71; guidelines for, 97–98, 144n115, 194; *O'Bannon* case on, 55, 109–110
COVID-19 pandemic, 5–6, 355–361, 365
CTE. *See* chronic traumatic encephalopathy (CTE)
Curt Flood Act (1988), 77, 133

Dawson v. NCAA (2019), 117
debt service cost, 80n3
Degree Completion Program (DCP), 215
Delaney, Jim, 34
dementia, 10
Dent, Charlie, 330
Dittmore, Stephen W., 186n28
Dodd-Frank Wall Street Reform and Consumer Protection Act (2010), 76
donations to athletics departments, 4, 80n4, 256–257, 322, 353; by alumni, 162–163; Anderson on, 165–166; tax deduction for, 6, 20n11, 37n1, 325–327
Drake Group, 18–19, 91n142, 191–194; on academic standards, 195–225; athlete advocates of, 238; on health protection, 240, 264–277; mission of, 22n32; on NCAA enforcement system, 230–238, 271–274; on NIL compensation, 281–301
Duke University basketball, 99, 169
Durkin, D. J., 342
duty of care, 241, 274–276

economic rent, 35, 73
Electronic Arts, 64, 114–115
eligibility standards, 17–18, 74, 129–130, 225; athletes' appeals of, 233; continuing, 203; for four-year college transfers, 202–203; for high school students, 197–200; learning disabilities and, 213–214, 216; for two-year college transfers, 201–202
Emmert, Mark, 328, 332
employment rights, 291–293
Equal Pay Day, 345
Equity in Athletics Data Act (EADA) reports, 81n9
Ericson, Jon, 221
Exceptional Student-Athlete Disability Insurance Program, 89n120

Faculty Athletic Representatives Association, 131
Fair Labor Standards Act, 106
Fair Pay to Play Act. *See* California Fair Pay to Play Act (2019)
fair use standards, 116, 120, 127, 148n161, 149n182, 303n11
FBS. *See* Football Bowl Subdivision (FBS)
FCS. *See* Football Championship Subdivision (FCS)
Federal Education Rights Protection Act (FERPA), 221
Federal Graduation Rate (FGR), 204–211, 215–220, 223
Federal Labor Standards Act (FLSA), 59
Final Four Basketball Championship: graduation rate in, 206–209
First Amendment, 120; rights-of-publicity claims and, 114–116
501(c)(3) status, 26–33
Florida NIL legislation, 94
Florida State University, 250
Football Bowl Subdivision (FBS), 2, 164; generated revenues of, 3–5, 43, 44, 312, 363; Graduation Success Rate in, 206; median deficit of, 321; operating deficits in, 40, 312–313; revenue distributions by, 192, 194; tax exemptions for, 31–32; team size in, 16, 22n24, 73
Football Championship Playoff (FCP), 40, 43, 44
Football Championship Subdivision (FCS), 16, 164, 352; coaches of, 73; generated revenues of, 3, 363; median deficit of, 321; scholarships of, 80n4; tax exemptions for, 31–32
four-year transfer loophole, 203
Franklin, Missy, 142n83

gambling, 10, 21n15, 293, 328
gender, 318; culture of "toughness" and, 248, 256, 264; salary inequality and, 345; sexual abuse/harassment and, 239, 242–245, 252–253, 272–274; women

gender (*continued*)
athletes and, 58, 99, 111, 325–327, 345–347. *See also* Title IX
GIA. *See* grant-in-aid (GIA) scholarships
GitHub.com, 167
Goff, Brian, 186n25
golf, 16, 19n2, 73, 318
Gould, Roland, 113
governor salaries, 72, 102
grade point average (GPA), 74, 198–200; for good academic standing, 204; standardized tests and, 199
Graduation Success Rate (GSR), 196, 204–211; Academic Progress Rate and, 212–216, 225; Federal Graduation Rate and, 216–220
grant-in-aid (GIA) scholarships, 85n71, 119, 144n115; *Jenkins/Alston* cases on, 111–114; *O'Bannon* case on, 53, 55–56, 109–110
Grimes, Paul W., 162–163
Group of Five conferences, 4, 154, 352
Gurney, Gerald, 191–194, 324, 351–354; on academic standards, 195–225; on athlete health protection, 239–277; on NCAA enforcement system, 228–238; on NIL compensation, 281–301
gymnastics programs, 16, 73

Hampton University, 214
Harbaugh, Jim, 89n126, 309–310
Harper, Shaun R., 209–210
Hart v. Electronic Arts (2013), 114–115
Haywood, Spencer, 339
health insurance, 75, 193, 260–262, 276–277; coverage of, 6–7, 10, 18; for lost income, 99, 103, 277
health protection, 239–277; coach misconduct and, 244–246; duty of care and, 241; moral injury and, 242–243
heat-related illness, 239–240, 243, 249–250, 257, 341
Hemphill, Scott, 65–66
Higher Education Act (HEA), 193, 204, 230, 319
historically Black colleges and universities (HBCUs), 210–211, 213, 214. *See also* students of color
hockey, 21n12
Hovenkamp, Herbert, 83n36
Hudson, Sheila, 239–277
Humphreys, Brad R., 163–164
Hutchins, Robert, 1–2

Improving America's Schools Act (1994), 77–78, 133
income-replacement insurance, 68–69, 89n120, 103
Infractions Appeals Committee, 229–230, 235–236
injured players, 22n24; health insurance for, 75, 193, 260–262, 276–277; income-replacement insurance for, 68–69, 89n120, 103; risk-reduction practices and, 247, 267–268, 277
Injury Surveillance System Summary reports, 90n133
Integrated Postsecondary Education Data System (IPEDS) surveys, 167
intercollegiate athletics, 312–315; Carnegie Foundation on, 96; economic system of, 2; as extracurricular activity, 70; guiding principles for, 126–127; taxation of, 25–36
Intercollegiate Athletics Act (2019), 285
International Olympic Committee (IOC), 89n122

Jenkins v. NCAA (2014), 11, 46, 58–59, 86n90, 111–114, 145n125
Johnson, Trey, 148n167
Jones, Willis A., 164
junior college transfers, 201–202

Katz, Lewis, 333–334, 339
Keller v. Electronic Arts (2013), 114–115
Kern, William, 164
Kessler, Jeffrey, 86n90, 308, 314
Knight Commission, 19n4
Koo, Gi-Yong, 186n28
Kostelnik, Robert, 185n16
Krzyzewski, Mike, 35

Law v. NCAA (1998), 53, 82n27, 140n69
learning disabilities, 213–214, 216
Ledecky, Katie, 142n83
Lee Committee, 229–230
Left Eligibles (LEs), 205–206
legislative appropriations, 163–164
less restrictive alternative (LRA), 48–50, 106; in *Board of Regents* case, 51;

Hemphill on, 65–66; in *O'Bannon* case, 55, 56, 109–110
LGBTQ+ issues, 253
Litan, Robert E., 159
Lopiano, Donna, 18–19, 191–194, 324, 351–362; on academic standards, 195–225; on athlete health protection, 239–277; on NCAA enforcement system, 228–238; on NIL compensation, 281–301

Major League Baseball (MLB), 77, 133, 150n186, 340n1
Marshall v. ESPN (2016), 116, 120
McCormack v. NCAA (1988), 84n57
McCormick, Robert E., 157–158
McMillen, Tom, 91n148
McNair, Jordan, 239, 250, 341
McNeely, Kathleen, 87n104
medical exceptions, 214–216
Medical Resident Matching Program Exemption, 78, 133
mental health issues, 252–256
Meyer, Jayma, 39–79, 195–225
Meyer, Urban, 310
Michigan State University, 242, 273–274
Mid-American Conference, 86n88
missed term exception, 214–215
Mississippi State University, 162–163
Mississippi Valley State University, 214
Mixon, Franklin G., Jr., 158, 185n7
Mondello, Michael, 163
Moos, Bill, 356
moral injury, 242–243
Moran, Jim, 312
Mountain West Conference, 86n88
Mueller Pasta Company, 28
Murphy, Chris, 94, 330–331
Murphy, Robert G., 158

names, images, likenesses. *See* NIL (names, images, likenesses) compensation
Napier, Shabazz, 137n32
Nassar, Larry, 242
National Association for Athletics Compliance, 131
National Association of Collegiate Directors of Athletics, 131
National Athletic Trainers Association, 257
National Basketball Association (NBA), 15, 21n13, 30, 89n119
National Basketball Players Association, 333–334
National Center for Education Statistics, 167
National Collegiate Athletic Association (NCAA), 1–3, 21n13; Academic Eligibility Center of, 301n2; bylaws of, 99–100, 124, 135n6, 139n52; Committee on Competitive Safeguards and Medical Aspects of Sports, 268, 269, 274, 276, 277; founding of, 1, 265–266; Injury Surveillance System Summary reports of, 90n133; legitimacy of, 332–337; lobbying expenses of, 87n104; NIL recommendations of, 93–94, 104, 123–126, 133; *Revenues and Expenses* reports of, 81n9; "Sanity Code" of, 96; Sports Science Institute of, 254–255, 276, 277
National Commission for Certifying Agencies, 248
National Football League (NFL), 22n24, 30; AFL merger with, 77, 132–133; college players drafted by, 21n13; player salaries in, 89n119; team revenues of, 15
National Labor Relations Board (NLRB), 60–62, 67, 106, 118–119
NCAA Athletic Grant-in-Aid Cap Antitrust Litigation (2019), 119, 124
NCAA enforcement system, 228–238, 335–336; for athlete health protection, 268–274, 276; cost estimates for, 234–238; due process rules for, 231–234, 238; Lee Committee on, 229–230
NCAA Injury Surveillance Program, 22n24, 268, 275, 276
NCAA v. Board of Regents of University of Oklahoma (1984), 11, 42, 50–52, 57, 87n109, 107–108
NCAA v. Miller (1992), 135n5
need-based aid, 136n22
Nevada, 135n5
Newsom, Gavin, 93, 133, 142n79, 348
New York NIL bill, 94
Nike, 147n158, 302n11
NIL Commission (proposed), 130–131, 283, 297–301
NIL Committee, 123–126

NIL (names, images, likenesses) compensation, 127–128, 281–301, 336–337, 348; agents for, 68, 129–130, 283; amateur status and, 100; athletes' use of, 129–130; California law on, 93–94, 104, 133, 142n79, 301n1, 348; clearinghouse for, 151n206; copyright laws and, 105, 120, 147n156, 303n11; deferred payment of, 12–13, 55–57, 119–120; disadvantages of, 6–9; guardrails for, 17; institutional rights and, 294–296; NCAA's recommendations for, 123–126; *O'Bannon* case on, 53, 64; potential scope of, 119–122; proposed federal implementation of, 126–133; standards for, 130–131; Title IX and, 103–105, 120–121, 303n12; for women athletes, 104–105
NIL Eligibility Center (proposed), 283, 297, 300–301
Non-Autonomous conferences, 4, 154, 352
"nonrevenue" sports, 16, 31–32, 80n6, 156, 259, 318–319
Northwestern University, 46, 60–62, 67, 117–119, 191, 314

Obama, Barack, 315
O'Bannon, Edward, 108, 308, 314
O'Bannon v. NCAA (2016), 12, 46, 53–59, 88n110, 108–111; impact of, 191, 193, 194, 323; resources spent on, 62–64; rights-of-publicity claims and, 114–116
Ogunbowale, Arike, 142n86
Ohashi, Katelyn, 104–105
Ohr, Peter Sung, 60–61
Olympic athletes, 2, 16, 69, 288; cash prizes for, 98, 138n39, 141n71; popularity of, 103; SafeSport program for, 244–246, 272–273, 275
"one-and-done" rule, 333–334, 338–340
operating surplus, 79n1, 80n6
Operation Gold, 98
Orszag, Peter R., 32, 37n11, 159
oversight systems, 256–260, 265–267
overuse injuries, 244, 252, 287

Pac-12 Conference, 86n87, 154, 312; commissioner's salary in, 33–34; *Dawson* lawsuit and, 117; threat to leave NCAA by, 191; University of Utah and, 188n41
Paralympic athletes, 244–246, 272–273, 275
Parkinson's disease, 10
pay for play, 8, 67–69, 284–285; California's law on, 93–94, 104, 113, 133, 142n79; cost to schools of, 69; NCAA bylaws on, 99–100, 139n52; Olympic athletes and, 69; state laws on, 93–94
Pell Grants, 10, 98, 137n36, 337
Penn State University, 232, 279n26
Pitino, Rick, 90n130
player development costs, 30
Pope, Devin G., 159–160
Porto, Brian, 191–194; on academic standards, 195–225; on athlete health protection, 239–277; on NCAA enforcement system, 228–238; on NIL compensation, 281–301
Power Five conferences, 4, 154, 315; donations to, 6; members of, 86n87; revenue distribution to, 75–76, 352; threat to leave NCAA by, 191–194
private inurement, 32–35
professors' salaries, 21n18, 310, 353
punishment workouts, 239–240, 244–245, 248

"quick look" rule of reason, 82n26
Quist, Gordon, 12, 56–57

race. *See* students of color
regional sports network (RSN), 6, 43
Reid, Andy, 34
remediation programs, 200
Renault, Louis, 332
research assistants, 87n102, 149n174
reservation wage, 35
"restricted-earnings coaches," 53
revenue-sharing plan, 21n12, 192
reverse causality, 187n34
rhabdomyolysis, 239–240, 249–250, 257
Rhoads, Thomas A., 163
Rice, Condoleezza, 105, 142n86, 154, 332–333, 338
Ridpath, David, 191–194; on academic standards, 195–225; on athlete health protection, 239–277; on NCAA enforcement system, 228–238; on NIL compensation, 281–301
rights-of-publicity claims, 114–116

risk-reduction practices, 247, 267–268, 277
Rivers, Glenn Anton "Doc," 35
Rock v. NCAA (2013), 84n53
Romney, Mitt, 94
Roosevelt, Theodore, 1
Rubio, Marco, 94
rule of reason analysis, 48–52, 67, 106; in *Board of Regents* case, 107; in *Jenkins/Alston* cases, 112; in *O'Bannon* case, 54, 55; "quick look," 82n26
Rutgers University, 363–365

Saban, Nick, 16, 22n23, 71, 310
Sack, Allen, 191–194; on academic standards, 195–225; on athlete health protection, 239–277; on NCAA enforcement system, 228–238; on NIL compensation, 281–301
Sackos/Anderson v. NCAA (2014), 86n93
SafeSport Code, 244–246, 265, 272–273, 275, 278n4
Salzwedel, Matthew, 221
Sandusky, Jerry, 232
"Sanity Code," 328–329
Sankey, Greg, 33
Sarbanes-Oxley Act (2002), 91n140
SAT scores, 157–159
Scalia, Antonin, 83n40
scholarships, 285–286, 309; financial aid versus, 95, 99; "lifetime," 301n4; multi-year, 97; number of, 52; *O'Bannon* case on, 53, 55–56; opportunity cost of, 155; team size and, 16, 73; Title IX and, 314. *See also* grant-in-aid (GIA) scholarships
Scott, Larry, 33–34
seat purchases, tax deduction for, 6, 20n11, 37n1, 325–327
sexual abuse/harassment, 239, 242–245, 252–253, 272–274
Shalala, Donna, 315n1, 362
Sherman, Mike, 21n19, 90n127, 140n65
Sherman Antitrust Act (1890), 12–13, 47, 106, 323; *Board of Regents* case, 51, 52; reforms of, 66–67; unionization and, 60
Sigelman, Lee, 162
Skiles, Scott, 35
Skinner, Nancy, 104, 142n79
slavery, 13
Smith, D. Randall, 159
Smith, Gene, 123, 356
Smith, Milan, 113
soccer, 16, 73, 240, 250, 345–346, 358
Sommer, Julie, 281–301
South Carolina, 94
Spano, Ross, 362
Spielman, Chris, 147n158
sports betting, 10, 21n15, 293, 328
Sports Broadcasting Act (1961), 76–77, 91n149, 132, 153n222
Sports Lawyers Association, 131, 300
Sports-Reference.com, 167, 170
Sports Science Institute (SSI), 254–255, 276, 277
standardized tests, 74, 198–200; GPA and, 199; for students of color, 22nn30–31, 91n139, 198
Stewart, Breanna, 347
Stinson, Jeffrey L., 163
strength and conditioning coaches, 246–253, 258–259
Student Assistance Fund (SAF), 99, 261–262
student loans, 10, 98, 137n36, 337
students of color, 318; graduation rates of, 209–210; historically Black colleges and universities and, 210–211, 213, 214; mental health services and, 253; standardized testing of, 22nn30–31, 91n139, 198; in traditional white sports, 19n2
summer-school financial aid, 213
Sun Belt Conference, 86n88
Swafford, John, 33
Swinney, William Christopher "Dabo," 14, 102, 349

Tarkanian v. NCAA (1984), 229
tax-exempt bonds for facility construction, 26–27
teaching assistants, 87n102, 149n174
Ted Stevens Olympic and Amateur Sports Act (1978), 76, 77, 133, 303n15
television broadcasts, 42–43, 127; fees for, 6, 312; as restraint of trade, 11; rights-of-publicity claims and, 116; taxing of, 29
Tennessee right-of-publicity law, 116, 120
tennis programs, 16, 19n2, 73, 98, 288, 318
Thomas, Bill, 25

Thomas, Sidney, 12, 56–57, 110, 113; on *Keller* case, 115; on *O'Bannon* case, 85n79, 120; on pay for play, 67
Title IX, 8, 325–327, 343; compliance with, 18, 75, 101; legal liability from, 6; NCAA antitrust exemption and, 92n161, 325–326; NIL compensation and, 103–105, 120–121, 303n12; quasi-enforcement of, 2; revenue-sharing plan and, 21n12; scholarships and, 314; US Center for Safe Sport and, 265. *See also* gender
Toma, J. Douglas, 158–159
transfer regulations, 205–206, 293, 302nn8–9
trust-fund stipends, 12–13, 55–57, 119–120, 194
Tucker, Irvin B., 158, 159
Turner, Sarah E., 163

Under Armour, 81n23
Uniform Standard of Care, 269–271
unionization, 60–62, 106, 122, 307–308; collective bargaining agreements and, 68, 84n54, 118; of Northwestern football players, 46, 60–62, 67, 117–119, 191, 314; *O'Bannon* impact on, 193, 194
United States Center for Safe Sport, 244–246, 265, 272–273, 275, 278n4
United States v. Brown University (1993), 81n21
United States v. Trans-Missouri Freight Association (1897), 88n117, 144n120
University of Alabama, 188n48, 214, 314
University of Arkansas–Pine Bluff, 214
University of Connecticut, 161, 325
University of Houston, 240, 250, 355
University of Kentucky, 333
University of Maryland, 239, 250, 341
University of Massachusetts, 161
University of Michigan, 309
University of North Carolina, 222
University of Oklahoma, 11, 42, 50–52, 57, 107–108, 214
University of Oregon, 250
University of South Carolina, 140n62
University of Southern California, 214
University of Texas, 214
University of Utah, 188n41
university presidents, 14–15, 21n18, 256–257, 353
Unrelated Business Income Tax (UBIT), 19n3, 26, 69; athlete salaries and, 119; avoidance of, 28–30; licensing agreements and, 296

video games, 94, 294; copyright of, 105, 114–116, 120; *O'Bannon* lawsuit on, 53, 64, 108
volleyball, 8, 318, 355–356, 358
Voluntary Support of Education (VSE) surveys, 167
"voluntary" workouts, 251–252, 355, 358

Walker, Adam G., 186n28
Walker, Mark, 94
Waxman, Seth, 113
Weis, Charlie, 33
wellness protection programs, 239–277
Western Athletic Conference, 86n88
whistle-blower protection, 18, 75, 233–234, 256, 263–265
White v. NCAA (2008), 84n57
Wilken, Claudia, 12, 53–56, 58–59, 64, 108–109; on First Amendment rights, 116; on *Jenkins/Alston* cases, 111–113; on less restrictive alternatives, 109–110; on revising antitrust law, 66–67; on rule of reason analysis, 67, 112
Williamson, Zion, 99
Willingham, Mary, 191–194; on academic standards, 195–225; on NCAA enforcement system, 228–238; on NIL compensation, 281–301
Wilson, A'ja, 345
women athletes, 58, 99, 111, 325–327, 345–347
Women Leaders in College Sports, 131
Women's National Basketball Association (WNBA), 345
Women's Sports Foundation, 92n161, 141n73
work-study stipends, 21n14, 60

Zimbalist, Andrew, 1–19, 328–331, 351–362; on academic standards, 195–225; on antitrust exemption, 39–79, 321–324; on athlete health protection, 239–277; on athletic scandals, 341–344; on athletic success measures, 159; on Big Five power grab,

191–194; on coaches' salaries, 309–311; on collegiate sports model, 348–350; on future of college sports, 312–315; on gender inequality, 325–327; on NCAA enforcement system, 228–238; on NCAA's legitimacy, 332–337; on NIL compensation, 281–301; on "one-and-done" rule, 338–340; on paying student-athletes, 316–320; on Rutgers' athletics deficit, 363–365; on taxation of college sports, 25–36; on unionization, 307–308

About the Author

Andrew Zimbalist is the Robert A. Woods Professor of Economics at Smith College in Northampton, Massachusetts, where he served as the Smith College faculty athletic representative to the NCAA for over ten years. He has consulted widely in the sports industry for groups including players' associations, teams, leagues, law firms, universities, and members of Congress and is a frequent media commentator. He has published twenty-seven books, including *No Boston Olympics: How and Why Cities Are Passing on the Torch* and *Unwinding Madness: What Went Wrong with College Sports and How to Fix It*, and over one hundred articles. Zimbalist lives with his family in Northampton, Massachusetts.